V. Stein - My Antique   7/07   12.50

A FUTURE FOR

ARCHAEOLOGY

Peter Ucko in his office.

A FUTURE FOR ARCHAEOLOGY

The Past in the Present

Edited by Robert Layton, Stephen Shennan and Peter Stone

UCL PRESS

First published by UCL Press in 2006

UCL Press is an imprint of Cavendish Publishing Limited

The name of University College London (UCL) is a registered trade mark used by UCL Press with the consent of the owner

Cavendish Publishing Limited, The Glass House,
Wharton Street, London WC1X 9PX, United Kingdom
Email: info@cavendishpublishing.com
Website: www.cavendishpublishing.com

Published in the United States by Cavendish Publishing
c/o International Specialized Book Services,
5824 NE Hassalo Street, Portland,
Oregon 97213-3644, USA

Published in Australia by Cavendish Publishing (Australia) Pty Ltd
45 Beach Street, Coogee, NSW 2034, Australia

British Library Cataloguing in Publication Data
A future for archaeology
1. Archaeology – Social Aspects. 2. Archaeology.
I. Ucko, Peter J. II. Layton, Robert, 1944–. III. Shennan, Stephen. IV. Stone, Peter G., 1957– .
930. 1'01

Library of Congress Cataloging in Publication Data
Data available

Hardback ISBN 10: 1–84472–126–4
Hardback ISBN 13: 978–1–84472–126–9

1 3 5 7 9 10 8 6 4 2
Typeset by Newgen Imaging Systems, Chennai, India
Printed and bound in Great Britain

This book is dedicated to Peter Ucko and the humanistic archaeology he has pioneered, in acknowledgement of his vision, his achievements and the inspiration he has provided.

CONTENTS

LIST OF FIGURES

LIST OF MAPS

Map 12.1: Map of Easter Ross and the Black Isle, northeast Scotland, showing key sites mentioned in the text (drawn by A. Mackintosh).

Map 13.1: The location of the Melrose and Coincoin plantations within the Cane River region, and within the USA.

Map 13.2: Composite of the 1813–1814 survey maps showing triangulation to 'the House of Louis Metoyer [ca.1813–14]' versus the location of Yucca House.

Map 13.3: Schematic reproduction of the 1877 Hertzog map, with an inset (oriented magnetic north) of the current layout of the historic core of the property.

NOTES ON CONTRIBUTORS

Dr George Okello Abungu is the Proprietor and Chief Executive of Okello Abungu Heritage Consultants, working as an independent consultant and advisor for various organisations and heritage training programmes in Africa, Europe and the USA. From 1999 to 2002 he was the Director General of the National Museums of Kenya and Director for Regional Museums, Sites & Monuments from 1996 to 1999. Earlier, he was Head of the Department of Coastal Archaeology/Head of Coastal Museums Programme based in Mombasa. He was the founding Chairman of Africa 2009 and the Programme for Museum Development in Africa, and is currently the Chairman of the International Standing Committee on the Traffic in Illicit Antiquities. He is on the Executive Council of the International Council of Museums (ICOM), and has recently been elected the Kenyan government delegate for the UNESCO World Heritage Committee.

Neal Ascherson is a journalist and writer. He was formerly a foreign correspondent of the *Observer* and Associate Editor of *The Independent*. Recent books include *Black Sea* (Cape 1995) and *Stone Voices* (Granta 2002). He is Editor of the journal *Public Archaeology* and an Honorary Lecturer at the Institute of Archaeology, UCL.

Peter F. Biehl is currently a Lecturer in Archaeological Theory and the Prehistory of Europe in the Department of Archaeology at the University of Cambridge. His interests include archaeological theory, cognitive archaeology and the social meaning of visual imagery and representation, and the use of multimedia in archaeology. His focus is primarily on the European Neolithic. He currently directs the excavation of the Neolithic circular enclosure in Goseck, Germany (http://www.praehist.uni-halle.de/goseck/index1.htm) and has published widely on the meaning and functions of Neolithic and Copper Age figurines.

Beverley Butler is Lecturer in Cultural Heritage and Museum Studies at the Institute of Archaeology, UCL. She is co-author (with K. Littlewood) of *Of Ships and Stars: A History of the National Maritime Museum, Greenwich* (Athlone Press 1999). She has a specialist focus upon North Africa and the Eastern Mediterranean and upon Alexandrian/ Egyptian and Palestinian cultural heritage and cultural politics. Her interests include the theorisation and conceptualisation of cultural heritage studies, as well as museum historiography and museological theory.

Henry Cleere was Director of the Council for British Archaeology from 1974 to 1991. Between 1992 and 2002 he worked in Paris as World Heritage Coordinator for ICOMOS (International Council on Monuments and Sites), the advisor on cultural heritage to the UNESCO World Heritage Committee. Since 1998. he has been an Honorary Professor at the Institute of Archaeology, UCL.

Michael Day is an Emeritus Professor of London University who occupied the Chair of Anatomy at St Thomas's Hospital School for 17 years. He is best known for his work on fossil man from East Africa including hominids from Olduvai Gorge and Laetoli in Tanzania, as well as East Rudolf in Kenya that were recovered by Louis, Mary and Richard Leakey. His contributions are documented in many scientific papers and books including his text *Guide to Fossil Man*.

He was asked by Peter Ucko to Chair the Board of Directors of the company that had been formed to run the World Archaeological Congress (WAC) when the British National Committee of the IUSPP collapsed in disarray due to a dispute over the attendance of South African delegates. He later chaired the Steering Committee that established the WAC as a world-wide international organisation in the field of archaeology.

Cressida Fforde works as a Museum and Heritage Consultant, specialising in repatriation issues. She is co-editor of *The Dead and Their Possessions: Repatriation in Principle, Policy and Practice* (Routledge 2002) and author of *Collecting the Dead: Archaeology and the Reburial Issue* (Duckworth 2004).

Jack Golson retired in 1991 after 30 years in a department of the Australian National University with archaeological programmes in Australia and the southwest Pacific. His own work came to concentrate on Papua New Guinea and he continues to publish on this as a Visiting Fellow of the University.

Fiona J.L. Handley completed her PhD at the Institute of Archaeology, UCL in 2004 on the presentation of the history of Transatlantic slavery to the public at plantations and historic homes in southern USA. Her research interests include the history and arhaeology of the Cane River, Louisiana, the archaeology of Transatlantic slavery and its interpretation to the public, and Egyptian archaeological textiles. She is currently working in the private sector on a variety of heritage and cultural projects, and is an Honorary Research Assistant at the Institute of Archaeology, UCL.

David Harris is Emeritus Professor of Human Environment at the Institute of Archaeology, UCL, and was formerly the Institute's Director. His interests include the ecology and evolution of agricultural and other subsistence systems, plant and animal domestication and the origins and spread of agriculture. He is editor of *The Origins and Spread of Agriculture and Pastoralism in Eurasia* (London, UCL Press and Washington, Smithsonian Institute Press 1996).

Fekri A. Hassan is Petrie Professor of Archaeology at the Institute of Archaeology, UCL. He is a member of many international committees. His interests include cultural heritage management, water and civilisation, archaeological perspectives on ethics, the relevance of archaeology to contemporary human issues and the origins of civilisation and state-societies. His regional interests lie in North Africa and the Middle East and he has conducted fieldwork in Egypt, Algeria, Lebanon and Jordan. He is the editor of *Droughts, Food and Culture: Ecological Change and Food Security in Africa's Later Prehistory*, (Kluwer Academic/Plenum Publishers, New York, 2002).

Jane Hubert is a social Anthropologist and Senior Research Fellow at St George's, University of London. Recent edited books: *Madness, Disability and Social Exclusion: The Archaeology and Anthropology of 'Difference'* (Routledge 2000) and (with Cressida Fforde and Paul Turnbull) *The Dead and Their Possessions: Repatriation in Principle, Policy and Practice* (Routledge 2002).

Siân Jones is Senior Lecturer in Archaeology at the University of Manchester. Her research focuses on the archaeology of identity, particularly ethnicity, and the politics, meanings and values surrounding archaeological heritage in contemporary societies. Siân's publications include *The Archaeology of Ethnicity* (Routledge) and *Early Medieval Sculpture and the Production of Meaning, Value and Place* (Historic Scotland).

Jacquie Lambert, OAM, is Executive Officer at the Australian Institute of Aboriginal and Torres Strait Islander Studies (AIATSIS) where she has worked for the past 33 years. She has a BA in History from the Australian National University, where she is currently undertaking a higher degree on the history of AIATSIS.

Aubra L. Lee is Vice-President and Senior Project Manager of Earth Search, Inc. of New Orleans, Louisiana. His archaeological research over the past 25 years includes prehistoric societies in southern USA as well as colonial and plantation archaeology. More recently, his research has focused on the history and development of sugar cane plantations and their labour systems in southern Louisiana.

Kevin C. MacDonald is Senior Lecturer in African Archaeology at the Institute of Archaeology, UCL. His research interests cover West African complex societies, the African Diaspora, pottery analysis, archaeozoology, prehistory of African pastoralism and historical archaeology in the New World. His books include. *The Origins and Development of African Livestock: Archaeology, Linguistics and Ethnography*. (London: UCL Press, 2000) co-authored with R. Blench.

Arkadiusz Marciniak is Associate Professor of Prehistoric Archaeology at the University of Poznan. He has published widely on archaeological theory, history of archaeological thought, Neolithic archaeology, and zooarchaeology. He was a Junior Representative for Eastern Europe in the World Archaeological Congress in the years 1990–1999. His recent book *Placing animals in the Neolithic: Social Zooarchaeology of Neolithic Farming Communities* was published in 2005 by UCL Press. He is currently working at Catalhouyk as a co-director of the Polish team.

David W. Morgan is Archaeology and Collections Program Manager at the United States National Center for Preservation Technology and Training [NCPTT]. Before joining the NCPTT, Morgan served as an Assistant Professor in the School of Social Sciences at Northwestern State University of Louisiana where he was also the Assistant Director of the Cultural Resource Office. His research focuses on prehistoric and historic North America, especially southeastern USA, with fieldwork in Alabama, Mississippi, and Louisiana. Morgan holds a PhD in Anthropology from Tulane University, an MA in Anthropology from the University of Alabama, and a BA in English from Millsaps College.

Emma Morley completed her MA at the Institute of Archaeology, University College, London in 2004 on Chronological Implications of Construction Materials: when was Yucca House built?

Nicolas Peterson is a Professor of Anthropology at the Australian National University. He has carried out fieldwork in northeast Arnhem Land with Yolngu speakers on ecological issues and in central Australia with Warlpiri speakers on religious life and territorial organisation. He has a long standing interest in land and sea tenure and has worked on twelve major native title and land claims, including the test case for native title in the sea. He has compiled and introduced *Donald Thomson in Arnhem Land* (2003, MUP) and co-edited *Photography's Other Histories* (2003, Duke) with Chris Pinney and *Citizenship and Indigenous Australians* (1998, Cambridge) with Will Saunders.

Gustavo G. Politis is a Researcher at the Consejo Nacional de Investigaciones Científicas y Técnicas (CONICET) and Director of the Doctorate Program at Universidad Nacional del Centro del la Pcia de Buenos Aires, Argentina. He is Professor at this University and at the Universidad Nacional de La Plata. He teaches Argentine archaeology, archaeology and ethnography of hunter-gathers and current issues in theoretical archaeology. His previous books include *Nukak* (Instituto Sinchi, 1996), *Archaeology in Latin America* (Co-edited with B. Alberti, Routledge 1999) and *Teoría Arqueológica en América del Sur* (co-edited with R. Peretti, INCUAPA 2004). His current interests include the archaeology of the Pampean region, the peopling of the Americas, the ethnoarchaeology of South American tropical hunter-gatherers and issues in theoretical archaeology.

Michael Rowlands is Professor in Material Culture at UCL. Present research interests lie in the fields of cultural heritage and material culture. His most recent book is *Social Transformations in Archaeology* (with K. Kristiansen) and he is an Editor of *Critique of Anthropology* and *Journal of Material Culture*.

Tim Schadla-Hall is Reader in Public Archaeology at the Institute of Archaeology UCL. He teaches Public Archaeolgy and Museum management. He was previously Director of Leicestershire Museums. Apart from publishing on various aspects of Public Archaeology he continues to work on the early Mesolithic and post-medieval houses and landscapes.

Colin Tatz is currently Honorary Visiting Fellow at the Australian Institute of Aboriginal and Torres Strait Islanders, Adjunct Professor of Politics at Macquarie University and Visiting Professor of Political Science at the Australian National University. His recent books include *With Intent to Destroy: Reflecting on Genocide*, Verso (2003), and *Aboriginal Suicide is Different*, second edition, Aboriginal Studies Press (2005). His current research is on South African Jewish migration to Australia and New Zealand.

David Wengrow is a lecturer at the Institute of Archaeology, UCL. His research and teaching interests focus upon the comparative archaeology of the Middle East and Eastern Mediterranean. His first book, *The Archaeology of Early Egypt: Social Transformations in North East Africa, 10,000–2650 BC*, will appear in 2006.

FOREWORD

Peter Ucko is a remarkable man. I am tempted to use the word 'unique', but that is rather meaningless because in the marvellous mixing of genes and environments in human beings every individual is unique. However, it is true for me of Peter that I have never met anyone in the least like him. He has exceptional qualities developed to a remarkable degree.

One of the first things I feel inclined to say about Peter – which many people will recognise – is that he is a wonderful 'hater'. It is not just that he does not suffer fools gladly – many of us do that, although in Peter's case the fool concerned is liable to catch the whiplash of an expressively caustic tongue or of a sabre-like silence. No, the reason Peter is such a good hater is the motivation which powers the hate – a deeply-felt anger at unfairness and injustice.

I first became aware of this in connection with the congress of the Union International des Sciences Pre-et Protohistoriques (UISPP) planned to be held at the University of Southampton where Peter was Professor and Head of the Department of Archaeology. I had previously been a member of the Permanent Council of the UISPP and Peter was the Organising Secretary of the proposed Southampton Congress. Then came the United Nations ban against the invitation of anyone from apartheid South Africa to any cultural occasion with which the UN or UNESCO was associated. The suggestion of excluding South African scholars evoked the cry in academia of 'assault on Academic Freedom'. The academic world began to be divided between those prizing the ideal of academic freedom and those who felt that the discrimination against blacks and coloureds in South Africa by the white minority was an evil of racism to fight against which overruled any other consideration. The denial of humanity to some millions of human beings was involved.

There was never any doubt where Peter's sympathies lay, and his implacable hostility to apartheid brought out the best of his hating qualities, however mindful he was at the same time of the ideal of academic freedom. The story of that fight has been told elsewhere, so it is pointless for me to repeat it – except to stress my admiration at the time for Peter's incredibly tireless energy and devoted endurance in a conflict painful and exhausting. The net result, as everyone now knows, is that the UN ban was upheld, to the fury of a number of academics, and the congress became The World Archaeological Congress (WAC). This title also betrays Peter's hand as its architect, since he had already planned that the Southampton Congress should break the excessive Eurocentrism of the UISPP and that it should be genuinely representative of archaeologists from all over the world – not least from those younger nations just emerging from colonial domination. Another part of Peter's architecture for WAC-1 was the breaking away from the dominant UISPP tradition of swapping the latest findings in the cultural histories of different areas to a theme-based structure which handled topics of importance to archaeology throughout the world and to profitable comparative study of the results.

In spite of the enormous and unexpected success of WAC-1, it was not immediately apparent how this success was to be followed up. There was no permanent secretariat, no established source of funding. How did it survive, and over the years go on from success to success, even if with some hiccups on the way? The answer, once again, is Peter's drive and energy.

Another of Peter's convictions lay in the archaeologist's old adage 'Excavation is destruction'. A site, or part of a site, once excavated, can never be excavated again.

Therefore it is incumbent on the excavator not only to keep detailed records with the utmost meticulousness, but also to publish these. Many archaeologists have been sinners in this respect, inasmuch as they have gone to their graves without publishing all the details of all their fieldwork. Peter was fiercely insistent on the importance of publishing the results of the WACs and worked unceasingly to edit and publish the *One World Archaeology* series – in which once again his drive and energy produced important results in spite of many difficulties. Archaeology has always had political and social overtones and undertones. Peter has been responsible for enlarging these dimensions in the archaeological agenda by asking the question 'To whom does archaeology belong?' – yet another of his innovative contributions.

There is absolutely no doubt that by his resolute stand against apartheid in 1986, by his creation of the WAC and by his editing and production of the *One World Archaeology* series, Peter has made a seminal and lasting contribution to archaeology world wide.

Thurstan Shaw

Cambridge

December 2005

CHAPTER 1

INTRODUCTION

Robert Layton, Stephen Shennan and Peter Stone

Archaeology is my interest and my life. I believe and teach that the study of the past is important for all, from primary school children to adults. I believe that to be able to identify with a past, and to be proud of it, helps people to have respect for themselves and for the group of people from whom they have derived.

(Peter Ucko, *Academic Freedom and Apartheid*, p. 5)

The wide and diverse spread of authors, subjects and geographical areas represented in this book reflect the extraordinary range of interests, and breadth of vision, that Peter Ucko has brought to archaeology (and, we hope and expect, will continue to bring for many years to come). In this short introduction we trace the early years of Peter's career, before the momentous events that are charted by other contributors. We also try to emphasize some of the key threads to Peter's life and work. We do this not as a reflection on a career ended but as a comment on a career that is changing focus, a career that has influenced his chosen discipline perhaps more than any other scholar of his generation.

Archaeology became the dominant interest in Peter's life long before he became a student in the late 1950s. As a young child he saved all his pocket money to buy small Egyptian artefacts that he found in unlikely places such as Portobello Road market – a collections policy that would be utterly frowned upon today by most archaeologists but one that led him directly to undertake his undergraduate studies in the Anthropology Department at University College London (UCL), next door to the College's Egyptology collection.

After graduating with a degree in Anthropology from UCL, Peter undertook a PhD at the nearby Institute of Archaeology on the study of prehistoric figurines (see Biehl, Chapter 18, in this book). He then returned to the Anthropology Department at UCL in 1962 to organise the teaching of material culture in the undergraduate degree.

Peter owed his first teaching appointment to the broad vision of anthropology held by Professor Daryll Forde, who had been head of department since 1945 (Smith 1969: xv). After completing his own doctorate, Daryll Forde had been awarded a Commonwealth Fellowship in Anthropology for the years 1928–1930 to study at the University of California Berkeley. Here Forde was taught by Robert Lowie and Alfred Kroeber, developing a commitment to the four-field approach characteristic of US anthropology.

By 1960 the undergraduate degree at UCL thus already embraced both social and biological anthropology, and students were registered for a BA or a BSc according to their A-level qualifications. Peter's appointment made courses on material culture central to the syllabus (previously, lectures on the topic had been delivered in a more ad hoc fashion by various staff and guest lecturers). When Mike Rowlands and Robert Layton began their undergraduate studies in 1963, their degree not only included compulsory courses in archaeology across the road at the Institute of Archaeology but they were also encouraged to attend linguistics lectures at the University's School of Oriental and African Studies. Here they were introduced to the structural linguistics of Saussure and the Sapir–Whorf hypothesis concerning the relationship between language and thought (Whorf 1956, Saussure 1959).

Throughout Peter's lectures to first year students runs a sense of respect for non-Western cultures, a willingness to consider other cultures on their own terms, which was later to be translated into political action during Peter's years in Canberra and Southampton. Robert Layton's notes on Peter Ucko's first lecture in his introductory course on *Primitive Technology* begin:

> '*Primitive*' doesn't imply 'inferior,' nor necessarily 'non-literate'. It means Pre-industrial, that is *predominantly for home use.*
>
> The terms hunting and gathering, and farming, are *exclusive* terms, hence *inaccurate.* Agriculturalists nearly always fish as well, also some tribes may revert from farming to hunting.

Later in the lecture Peter contrasted the theory of 'the survival of the fittest' with Tylor's progressive theory of evolution according to which 'we find everywhere the relics of stages through which society has passed'. Daryll Forde's influence is clear in Peter's observation that the environment imposes problems and provides material for their solution, but it offers a choice to the culture, not compulsory laws; this effect can be seen in variations between cultures inhabiting similar environments.

Peter's course was memorable for the detailed hand-outs he prepared, illustrated with lucid diagrams, which provided the structure for his lectures that were comprised of discovery and invention, environment and culture, diffusion, cultural parallels and independent invention, skeuomorphs and so on. Peter emphasised the importance of not confusing contemporary variation in artefact form with supposed evolutionary sequences for which there was no material evidence. On the topic of diffusion versus independent invention Layton has noted: 'If diffusion is assumed, you must also assume diffusion between places that are impossible to link ... Arguments for diffusion based on similarities of two cultures are less convincing in detail, e.g. when similar needs of two cultures are considered.' However, Peter then moved on to well-documented cases of diffusion, such as the spread of tobacco smoking from South America to Europe and then Asia.

'What is an improvement?' Peter asks in one lecture, giving the answer: a technique improves if there is less waste. To a people who don't mind labour, a labour-saving device is not an improvement. England's (then) refusal to adopt the decimal system was cited as an example of conservatism.

Robert Layton found it particularly interesting to rediscover in his notes a record of Peter's detailed presentation of Time and Motion Studies as a new way of illuminating the relationship between technology and social organisation. The diffusion of new artefacts or techniques could alter the division of labour. When the US government introduced the wagon to the Papago of Southern Arizona and metal containers replaced pottery, the women had more spare time. Men undertook additional labour to construct the roads for the wagons, but improved transport meant fewer people were required to make a trading journey to exchange grass baskets for grain. The course also looked at Lauriston Sharp's famous case of the introduction of steel axes to the Australian Yir-yiront (both these examples are from Spicer 1952). Here, no doubt, is the inspiration for the research Layton undertook as part of his PhD on social change in rural France, on the spread of new agricultural techniques, and time and motion studies on their relative effectiveness (eventually published in Layton 2000). At the time, however, the message does not seem to have been absorbed. Peter's response to Layton's first essay on material culture exemplifies his unflinching critical standards. The essay, submitted in December 1963, was titled: 'In what ways can a study of material culture illumine the study of social institutions?' Layton's approach is decidedly evolutionist: group size increases as the food supply becomes more secure and society becomes more hierarchical. In the margin of the first page, Peter has scribbled in his inimitable handwriting, 'What is this all about? The connection with material culture is unclear.' His final comment is

Most of this is irrelevant. Much of it is factually wrong. Almost all of it is obscurely written. This question was aimed at a consideration of the value of studies isolating individual techniques and material objects (such as Yir-yiront axes) which, combined with time and motion studies, may aid our understanding of social institutions.

Peter Ucko's equally influential course on 'Primitive Art' was introduced as a third year option within the UCL Anthropology degree in 1967. Nine of the students taking the course persuaded Peter to lead members of the student anthropology society on a 10-day expedition to the Palaeolithic caves of the Dordogne in April that year. The total cost per student was 18 pounds, including six pounds in French francs to pay for food and cave entrance fees. Equipped, as instructed, with plenty of old, warm clothing, sleeping bags and tents, and a torch with new batteries, 13 undergraduates and postgraduates set off in a minibus embarrassingly emblazoned 'Adventure Unlimited' along the side, while Peter took a parallel course in his car.

Ucko and Rosenfeld's book *Palaeolithic Cave Art* (1967) had just been published and Peter took several copies to present to French researchers who had helped with its production. When it appeared, Ucko and Rosenfeld's study was most notable for its challenge to the structuralist interpretations of Leroi-Gourhan (1958, 1964). As the expedition travelled from cave to cave, however, another interesting research question emerged. Comparing the drawings by the famous French archaeologist Breuil that were reproduced in *Palaeolithic Cave Art* to the originals showed some startling discrepancies between incomplete and ambiguous figures on the cave wall and Breuil's confident reconstructions. Out of this realisation grew the Hornos de la Peña rock art project, based in a little-visited cave near the more famous Spanish sites of Castillo and Pasiega, and carried out under Peter's direction between 1971–1973 (Ucko 1987b, Layton 1991).

The frustration of not knowing anything about the cultural context of Upper Palaeolithic rock art increased Peter's interest in promoting the study of recent hunter–gatherer rock art, particularly in Australia. He had already been in correspondence with Percy Trezise, a freelance rock art researcher (Trezise 1969), and Fred McCarthy, who was at that time the Principal of the Australian Institute of Aboriginal Studies (Ucko and Rosenfeld 1967: 228–231). In 1972 Peter moved from UCL to succeed McCarthy as Principal of the Australian Institute of Aboriginal Studies in Canberra. It is probably not too extreme to say that this appointment not only changed Peter but also that it changed the way archaeologists and anthropologists studied Aboriginal society. Peter announced his arrival in Australia with a paper declaring that Aboriginal people would have more to tell researchers about their cultures's rock art than Australian researchers had recognised (Edwards and Ucko 1973; contrast Wright 1973, Maynard 1979). At that time the Institute was a totally white, semi-governmental research organisation whose task was to record, using the time-honoured methods of academic 'objectivity', the languages and customs of Aboriginal Australians whose culture was assumed to be dying out. Such an approach failed to take into account the views and concerns of what Peter found to be still-existing Aboriginal communities who had, unsurprisingly, strong views on the value, need and ethics of such research. It is at this point in the story that we hand over to some of the other contributors to pick up particular periods and events in Peter's later career (Tatz and

Lambert, and Golson for Australia; Day and Stone for WAC). However, although the chapters that follow emphasise Peter's enormous influence, they do not paint a complete picture of his seminal contribution to the study of the past, nor of his personal qualities.

Despite what many might think and say, Peter is actually a rather shy individual. One of us, Peter Stone, well remembers it becoming rather an 'in-joke' amongst the taught postgraduate students at Southampton (of which he was one) that the newly appointed Professor of Archaeology was definitely going to meet with his MA students at this or that seminar. Days and then weeks went by and more and more apologies were received as to why he could not make a succession of promised rendezvous. Eventually, after another failed attempt to get Peter to a seminar, it was arranged that he would meet us in the pub. His then Secretary, Sue Stevenson, brought him in, introduced everyone and then left. An obviously extremely nervous Peter retreated into his own territory and individual interrogations began: Who are you? Why are you doing postgraduate work? Why are you doing *this* MA? What are you going to do afterwards? And then the most telling question – How can I help you? The interrogations revealed two sides to Peter's character that only appear by implication in the following chapters: He is genuinely interested in people and their education; he wants to ensure everyone gets the most from education by supporting them as much as possible but also by devising and offering an education that is stimulating and challenging.

This interest in education has been a common thread throughout Peter's career. After he had developed the new courses at UCL mentioned earlier, he ensured that education was a central element of his work in Australia and, on his return to the UK, he completely revised and modified the curricula at both Southampton and the Institute of Archaeology. At Southampton he revolutionised a rather traditional curriculum by introducing large elements of anthropology to the undergraduate degree and encouraging the staff to confront the wider implications of archaeology by taking sabbaticals in, for example, Cameroon (Stephen Shennan), the USA (Tim Champion) and Australia (Clive Gamble). At the Institute of Archaeology, against some resistance, he not only introduced anthropology, theory and public archaeology into the undergraduate curriculum but also took Museum Studies and Conservation beyond a concern with method and technique to a consideration of their social role and the implications that they have for different groups in different societies, as well as starting a whole series of new Masters programmes exploring many different aspects of the relationship between the past and the present. Peter's ability to encourage and provoke colleagues into developing their own particular specialisms as well as his own contributions to a number of these areas is reflected in the contributions of Peterson, Cleere, Fforde and Hubert, Butler and Rowlands, Jones, MacDonald *et al.*, Biehl, Hassan, and Harris. The range and scope of these contributions and the huge changes in approach or understanding they reflect is a powerful reminder of Peter's influence over so many varied aspects of our discipline.

In fact, Peter's interest in how and what aspects of archaeology should be taught at university was immediately provoked on his return to the UK in the early 1980s, when, as head of department at Southampton, he automatically became a member of the British Universities Archaeology Committee (BUAC). The university sector was under enormous pressure from Mrs Thatcher's Conservative Government, embodied in swingeing cuts imposed by the national University Grants Committee. While Peter did not succeed in carrying through what he thought at the time was a necessary rationalisation of the university discipline at a national level, he did start a debate about the nature of university courses in archaeology that led to the development of the discipline's teaching, with the acceptance of a common core for courses not necessarily of period and area content but of theory and methodology.

In his work with BUAC Peter argued that it was difficult to see why students should opt to study archaeology at university when the subject was hardly taught in schools. With characteristic zeal, he therefore set about trying to remedy this failing by working with the Joint Matriculation Board to develop an A-Level in Archaeology and also by finding the funding to create the 'Archaeology and Education Project' at Southampton. This team, a mixture of archaeologists, teachers and the long-term unemployed, worked with local schools showing how they could use the physical remains of the past that were all around them to enhance their teaching. The team was an enormous success and its work only stopped when government funding was re-targeted. However, its legacy remained as, with customary attention to spreading good practice, Peter had insisted that as much of the team's work as possible be published – resulting in ten teachers's handbooks being produced.

If education has been a life-long interest then so equally has been Peter's insistence that archaeology be seen as a global discipline that actually affects how we live and interact today. This was one of the background assumptions behind the development of the World Archaeological Congress (WAC) at Southampton and has been explicit in, for example, his re-structuring of the curricula in Southampton and London, in the content of the A-Level he developed, in the development of WAC as an organization and in countless initiatives taken since his return to the UK, such as the links brokered between the UK and the Soviet Union and China. This belief in global and comparative archaeology drove Peter to conceptualise, edit and produce the *One World Archaeology* (*OWA*) series that has been hailed all over the world as changing the way archaeology is perceived as a discipline. Such an accolade would be enough for many people but it must be remembered that the *OWA* series is but one of many of Peter's achievements. A number of contributors reflect Peter's belief in comparative global archaeology (e.g. Abungu, Marciniak, Politis, Wengrow and Harris) and show how he and WAC have been influential in such developments.

Perhaps the last thread that has woven Peter's life is his belief that a voice should be given to those affected by the practice of archaeology. This has been epitomised by his insistence that indigenous people with no obvious (i.e. Western) qualification as 'expert' be accorded the opportunity to have their voice, their opinion, heard and respected. This insistence has led to numerous confrontations and heated debates, both between archaeologists and indigenous peoples *and* between factions within archaeology. However, it has also led to a far deeper and more wide-ranging understanding between two groups that tended to be categorised as enemies. Both sides have won and lost various battles in this war of differing interpretations of, and control over, the past. Peter's contribution has been to emphatically show that Western science is not only far poorer if it attempts to ignore indigenous perceptions, beliefs and rights but that in the twenty-first century Western science *cannot* ignore the contribution of all with a legitimate interest in the past, and in the use of the past in the present. As with all of his career, Peter lived this academic belief and resigned from his role as Principal of the Australian Institute of Aboriginal Studies at a time many thought he should have stayed to continue his work in helping to give Aboriginal communities a voice in how, if and by whom they were to be studied. He had, however, come to the conclusion that he had done all that he could and that by staying on he would be blocking further developments. One of his final acts was to ensure that he handed over to the first Aborigine to hold the post of Principal.

It will be apparent from many of the chapters that follow that Peter Ucko is, among many other things, a brilliant 'facilitator', a creator of space and the environment for others to shine and develop, both as individuals and as contributors to their field, but he is also an endless, and tireless (but to others tiring), innovator and thinker. We do not exaggerate in our claim that no other colleague would have dared to think of the idea of WAC and certainly no one known to us would have continued to fight for it for so long. Nor would many (any?) have been able to walk away at a time that most others saw as the deserved pinnacle of achievement (Stone, Chapter 7, in this book). Peter is not personally ambitious but is immensely ambitious for his view of the importance of the past as personified in the quote at the top of this Introduction. The past matters to Peter Ucko because the past influences the present and shapes the future. As yet, we do not know how he will spend his retirement. Various projects and roles have been discussed. What is certain is that he will not withdraw meekly to his beloved cottage, no longer to play a role. We look forward with anticipation and a little trepidation to a refreshed Peter Ucko, no longer diverted by university administration, continuing to cajole, provoke and contribute to the study of the past, and to making it relevant to the future.

REFERENCES

Edwards, R. and P. Ucko (1973) 'Rock art in Australia', *Nature*, 246: 274–277.

Layton, R. (1991) 'Figure, motif and symbol in the hunter–gatherer rock art of Europe and Australia', in *Rock Art and Prehistory,* P. Bahn and A. Rosenfeld (eds), Oxford: Oxbow, pp. 28–38.

Layton, R. (2000) *Anthropology and History in Franche Comté*, Oxford: Oxford University Press.

Leroi-Gourhan, A. (1958) 'La fonction des signes dans les sanctuaires Paléolithiques', *Bulletin de la Société Préhistorique Française*, 55: 307–321.

Leroi-Gourhan, A. (1964) *Les Religions de la Préhistoire*, Paris: Presses Universitaires de France.

Maynard, L. (1979) 'The archaeology of Australian Aboriginal art', in *Exploring the Visual Art of Oceania*. S. Mead (ed), Honolulu: University of Hawaii Press, pp. 83–110.

Saussure, F. de (1959) *Course in General Linguistics* (trans.), C. Bally and A. Sechehaye, London: Owen.

Smith, M.G. (1969) 'Foreword', in *Man in Africa*, M. Douglas and P. Kaberry (eds), London: Tavistock, pp. xv–xxvi.

Spicer, E.H. (1952) *Human Problems in Technological Change: A Casebook*, New York: Wiley.

Trezise, P. (1969) *Quinkan country*, Sydney: Reed.

Ucko, P. and A. Rosenfeld (1967) *Palaeolithic Cave Art*, London: Weidenfeld and Nicolson.

Ucko, P. (1987a) *Academic Freedom and Apartheid*, London: Duckworth.

Ucko, P. (1987b) 'Débuts illusoires dans l'étude de la tradition artistique', *Bulletin de la Société Préhistorique Ariege-Pyrenées*, 42: 15–81.

Whorf, B. (1956) *Language, Thought and Reality: Selected Writings of Benjamin Whorf*, New York: Wiley.

Wright, B.J. (1973) 'The art of the rock engravers', in *The Australian Aboriginal Heritage*, R.M. Berndt and E.S. Phillips (eds), Sydney: Ure Smith, pp. 128–154.

CHAPTER 2

PETER UCKO'S 'HUMANE ARCHAEOLOGY'

Jack Golson

Peter Ucko was Principal of the Australian Institute of Aboriginal Studies (AIAS), as it was then called, from the beginning of November 1972 to the end of October 1980, appointed from and returning to England. In appreciation of his life and work, I want to talk about his influence on the Australian scene in those years, but also about Australia's influence on him and how this was important in the context of his subsequent career. The issue that I use in illustration of these points is the national site recording programme, for which the Institute accepted responsibility and government funding in 1973.

ENGLAND

As an undergraduate Peter read Anthropology at University College London (UCL), with Egyptology and Prehistoric Archaeology as special options. After graduation in 1959, he enrolled as a PhD student in the Department of Prehistoric European Archaeology at the Institute of Archaeology, studying anthropomorphic figurines of the eastern Mediterranean. Awarded his PhD in 1962, he returned as Lecturer in Anthropology to UCL.

His PhD research at the Institute (Ucko 1968) was his entry into the archaeology and anthropology of art. He developed this with his joint work with Andrée Rosenfeld (1967) on Palaeolithic cave art, which he credits with stimulating an interest in Australia (Ucko 1987: 2). The book was part of a series being developed for Weidenfeld and Nicolson by Colin Haycraft, who became a friend and for whom Peter edited many volumes in a series called Art and Society. At some stage Haycraft moved to Duckworth, but not only did the association continue, it flourished.

The Annual Report of the Institute for Peter's last year there, 1961–1962, records a proposal for the establishment of a Research Seminar in Archaeology and Related Subjects to draw together research workers and others interested in the discussion of archaeological and anthropological studies. The proposal received widespread support from people across a wide range and the Seminar was successfully established, thanks to 'the energies of Mr P.J. Ucko, a student of the Institute and University College jointly' in its formative stages (BIA 1964: 298).

Before Peter left for Australia two research seminars, in 1968 and 1970, had been planned as respectively two-day and three-day conferences at the Institute, each of them organised round an important theme that required an interdisciplinary and international approach to its consideration. Papers were precirculated to allow more time for discussion at the conference itself and were revised in the light of this extended discussion before publication. The seminars and the books they produced (Ucko and Dimbleby 1969; Ucko *et al.* 1972) had so strong an impact that the series continued after Peter's departure. Colin Renfrew organised the third Seminar over three days at the University of Sheffield in late 1971 to the Ucko formula (Renfrew 1973: ix–x) and there were three others within the next 10 years. All but the last were published by Colin Haycraft at Duckworth.

AUSTRALIA

The 1974 conference

Peter reorganised the twice-yearly Newsletter of the Australian Institute of Aboriginal Studies so that in the first number of any year he as Principal presented an extended account of activities over the previous year. The new series was launched at the beginning of 1974 and in the first issue Peter covered activities for 1973, substantially the period since he took over (Ucko 1974). It shows the extraordinary expansion in people and activities that had already taken place. It is true that none of this could have happened without a substantial increase in the Institute's budget provided by the highly sympathetic Whitlam Labor government, which came to power in late 1972. At the same time there can be little doubt that the new Principal was the moving force, with the members of the Institute's Council, Executive and other bodies responding to the excitement of his vision. This is 'only a beginning', he wrote (Ucko 1974: 14). 'The Institute will have failed if, over the next year, it does not manage to place Aboriginal studies in its [sic] rightful position within the world context of the study of human societies.'

This seems to be an oblique reference to the conference noted later in the same Newsletter as planned for the occasion of the Institute's Biennial General Meeting of 1974 (AIAS Newsletter 1974; cf. Ucko 1977). Indeed, it is highly likely that Peter had broached the question of such a conference with the expanded Executive Committee of the Institute that interviewed him for the Principal's position in Canberra in late 1971. Eight symposia were planned by the academic Advisory Committees of the Institute: one each by Human Biology, Psychology and Prehistory, one jointly by Material Culture and Prehistory and two each by Linguistics and Social Anthropology. The structure of the conference was ideally to be in the Ucko mode, though in the event not all symposia conformed (e.g. Berndt 1977): there was to be international participation; papers were to be precirculated, with the bulk of the available time spent in discussion and the Institute would undertake publication of the papers and results of the deliberations about them. The Council recommended that symposia did not overlap, so that the conference was scheduled from 16 May to 2 June, with the Institute's Biennial General Meeting to be held in the course of it.

The conference stimulated a series of openly critical reactions from Aboriginal activists. There was a five-page open letter of late March in the name of Eaglehawk and Crow (Widders et al. 1974; Tatz and Lambert, Chapter 3, in this book). This was signed by five young people, one of them non-Aboriginal, another someone who had helped to set up the Aboriginal Tent Embassy on the lawn in front of (then) Parliament House on 27 January 1972 (Attwood and Markus 1999: plate 29). The letter began by asking why the conference was being held, suggesting that it would make no positive contribution to the position of Aborigines in the total Australian society and went on to question the aims and philosophy of the Institute as a whole. On 24 April Jim Stanley, President of the National Aboriginal Consultative Committee (NACC) recently formed to advise the federal government on Aboriginal issues, sent a telegram on behalf of his organisation (rendered as NAC – there was politicking over the name) expressing its opposition on the same grounds. On 22 May Charles Perkins, who had been prominent on the Freedom Ride of early 1965 through outback northern New South Wales and was now chief departmental adviser to the Minister of Aboriginal Affairs in the setting up of NACC (Horton 1994: 861), telegraphed Prime Minister Whitlam accusing AIAS of being racist, anti-Aboriginal and exploitative, partly because there were no Aborigines participating in the conference (Rowse 2002: 301). In fact, there were two indigenous people who presented papers at the conference, one of whom was a Torres Strait Islander. Only one other Aborigine is known to have attended, a representative of the Aboriginal Arts Board, though a number of invitations were sent out (Jacquie Lambert personal communication 2005; cf. Tatz and Lambert, Chapter 3, in this book).

Summing up in his Principal's report for 1974, Peter was able to say that '[t]he academic nature of the conference was clearly envisaged even prior to [his] taking up the position of Principal' (perhaps because it had been discussed and agreed on at the time of the interview), with funds being made available for the purpose (Ucko 1975: 12). He continued:

> I consider that the meeting of experts from all over Australia with leading authorities from other countries to discuss particular problems, particular groups of data or specific themes of theoretical interest is one of the hallmarks of a healthy academic and research situation. I am convinced that one of the most important duties of this Institute is to foster and represent such a situation.

The 1974 General Meeting

To deal with the issues raised by Eaglehawk and Crow, Council agreed to set aside part of its General Meeting and to invite (and pay the expenses of) signatories to the letter as well as representatives of NACC. The meeting took place on the afternoon of 25 May, following the Institute's General Meeting for members in the morning. On the agenda of the morning's meeting was a proposal to move the Institute from its current cramped accommodation to two floors of a headquarters building being erected for the Australian Mining Industry Council. Given the recent fraught relation between miners and Aborigines (e.g. Broome 2002: 145–146), Charles Perkins expressed his outrage at the proposal in his telegram to Whitlam of 22 May (see earlier) and Tatz and Lambert (Chapter 3, in this book) mention a similar telegraphed protest on behalf of the Victorian Aborigines Advancement League. Members of the Institute at their General Meeting recommended Council not sign a lease for the premises.

The day before this vote was taken Barrie Dexter of the Council for Aboriginal Affairs, the federal government's advisory body, reported to the Minister his opinion that the mining premises were suitable in space and rent and taking up residence there would be advantageous to both parties. This was because over the two previous years AIAS had developed close contact with the Mining Industry Council through its work on the record and protection of Aboriginal sacred sites throughout Australia, including on mining land (Rowse 2002: 301). What Dexter was referring to was the Institute's assumption of responsibility for a national site register in 1973.

Sites in the landscape

The first Principal of the Institute, F.D. McCarthy, had kept a register of archaeological sites and been an advocate for legislation to protect them during his many years of previous service as Ethnologist at the Australian Museum, Sydney (Attenbrow and Khan 1994: 9). On moving to Canberra in 1964 McCarthy announced plans for the Institute to record Aboriginal 'relics' all over Australia, cataloguing items like quarries, ceremonial grounds, cave paintings, rock engravings and stone arrangements. The card catalogue that he initiated incorporated State listings of sites (Moser 1994: 25).

On the occasion of a Biennial General Meeting of 1968, the Institute convened a conference bringing together archaeologists and associates from universities and museums, as well as government representatives and others, to discuss the conservation and legal protection of Aboriginal antiquities in Australia. Selected papers from the conference were published by the Institute (McCarthy 1970).

Legislation to register and protect sites was being passed from time to time and in various forms by individual States, but funds were inadequate and trained staff unavailable, so that destruction continued (AIAS Newsletter 1973b: 13). As a result another conference was convened in 1972, again on the occasion of an Institute General Meeting (Edwards 1975). This was a two-day National Seminar on Aboriginal Antiquities opened by the Minister for the Environment, Aborigines and the Arts, Peter Howson. It was attended by members and 'invited representatives of all interests concerned with the study, exploitation or protection of these antiquities – State and Commonwealth departments, State museums and other authorities administering legislation, tourist, management and mining organisations, anthropologists and conservationists' (AIAS Newsletter 1972: 24), though no Aborigines.

At the beginning of the conference Minister Howson stressed the need for the location, mapping and protection of sacred sites all over Australia (AIAS Newsletter 1972: 24). He suggested that 'a measurable period, say, of five years' might see the completion of the job, 'at least within the areas of greatest need and risk', the job being 'to delineate and protect areas of land both inside and outside reserves' (Dix 1978–1979: 4). He asked the seminar to consider how the Commonwealth might 'assist the State authorities in the development and administration of their own legislation on Aboriginal antiquities' (Dix 1978–1979: 4).

Strangely, the Institute refused to administer the funds that the government offered for site recording (Dix 1978–1979: 6; cf. Moser 1995: 160), but the decision was reversed by Peter. This must have been very shortly after he became Principal, since Robert Edwards was appointed Deputy Principal of the Institute on 1 February 1973 (AIAS Newsletter 1973a) and took the chair of the committee that the Institute set up to meet the responsibility that it had now accepted from government for the recording of all sites of traditional or historic importance to Aborigines (AIAS Newsletter 1973b: 13; cf. Moser 1995: 160). Peter briefly refers to the Institute taking over responsibility for the programme of site recording from the Department of Aboriginal Affairs, but mistakenly dates it to 1974 (Ucko 1983: 15).

The Sites of Significance Committee, as it was originally called, was responsible for formulating a coordinated site recording programme and there was a sum of $500,000 at the disposal of the Principal to use according to the Committee's recommendations (Steering Committee 1975: 21). Representatives from the responsible body for site protection in each State and the Northern Territory sat on the Committee and in 1974 (Ucko 1975: 7) it was said to include at least one traditionally oriented Aboriginal and at least one Aboriginal nominated by the National Aboriginal Congress, as NACC now called itself (Jacquie Lambert pers. comm. 2005). By 1 August 1975 when the Steering Committee set up at the 1974 General Meeting delivered the report on its review of the Institute's operations (see Tatz and Lambert, Chapter 3, this book), it gave details of 22 appointments that had been made by the Sites of Significance Committee in development of its recording work and five appointments in its programme of Aboriginal training and employment (Steering Committee 1975: 21, 84–85). The 22 appointments to the recording programme were mainly of site recording officers and covered all States and the Northern Territory, but two positions for archaeological salvage appear in the listing, one as yet unfilled, as well as a sites record officer, a rock art conservationist and a site registrar at headquarters at the Institute.

Looking back over the roughly five years that Minister Howson had envisaged for the recording programme, Warwick Dix pronounced it as having been 'dramatically successful' as regards two major aspects of which Howson had spoken: the delineation and protection of areas of land both inside and outside reserves and assistance to State authorities. Previously small and struggling, State agencies with responsibility for sites and relics had become soundly established and able to absorb many of their Institute-funded appointments into their own State-funded systems (Dix 1978–1979: 6). Similarly in the Aboriginal training area, Institute funding had provided for 12 positions, several of which had become permanent within the State systems (Dix 1978–1979: 6).

Moser (1995: 161–163) gives an assessment of the Sites of Significance Recording Programme in wider context. She thinks the important point to make about the Programme is that archaeologists were brought face to face with the strength and complexity of Aboriginal associations with the landscape. Sites were no longer just dots on maps, but could represent nodes of interconnection in a peopled landscape for Aborigines. Moser (1995: 162) quotes Peter Ucko on the manoeuvring there was from AIAS to get site recorders to focus on sites of significance to *living* Aborigines and the inter-relationships of such sites. What Peter concluded was that association with Aborigines over the recent period had 'transformed the academic discipline of archaeology from an aseptic one of purely scientific enquiry into a humane investigation of the past development of cultures whose practitioners still live in the country of their origin' (Ucko 1983: 22).

By the time he made this statement he was already back in England and embarking on what would prove to be the farthest-reaching undertaking of his career.

THE WORLD

Before the South African ban

In May 1981 Peter was appointed Professor of Archaeology at the University of Southampton. A few months later he was approached to become National Secretary of the XI Congress of the International Union of Prehistoric and Protohistoric Sciences (IUPPS), for which there was to be a bid for it to be hosted by Britain in 1986. There can be no doubt that he received this invitation because of the success of the Research Seminars in Archaeology and Related Subjects of the late 1960s, of which he was 'the founder and guiding force' (Renfrew 1973: ix) and which continued after he went to Australia.

There were also concerns about the future of IUPPS Congresses. Some of the trouble lay with their growing size and the difficulties this posed for their organisation and running. Peter takes the example of the large IX Congress held in Nice, which S.J. de Laet described as 'chaos' and after which Glyn Daniel wondered whether there would be a X Congress (Ucko 1987: 218, 220). In addition there were grave doubts about the International Union and its Congresses in any way serving the interests of world archaeology and archaeologists worldwide as they were expected to.

In a report on the VIII Congress of 1971 in Belgrade, which Peter quotes at length (Ucko 1987: 218–219), the British archaeologist John Alexander said that it would be better to 'consider it a European event … It is the world role of the congress which seems most in jeopardy … To fulfil this role it will have to change its present form considerably' Reporting on the X Congress of 1981 in Mexico City (cited in Ucko 1987: 220–221),

Alexander expressed regret that the hopes raised by the first holding of a Congress outside Europe went 'largely unfulfilled and the development of a genuine World Congress still rests in the future'. He listed four main reasons for this failure: the presence of only a few North and South American archaeologists at the Congress, with only a small number from Mexico itself; the 'overwhelming predominance' of Europeans working in Western Europe; the failure to choose topics that could be discussed as 'international problems'; and the interpretation of the Protohistoric of the Congress title in such a way as largely to exclude discussion of the development of the urbanised states of the Americas. Alexander went on to say that the Congress 'still remains what it has been for the past fifty years of its existence, a European regional conference to which small groups from the other continents come to hold lively but largely separate sessions'.

Before he agreed to become National Secretary, Peter required certain assurances about the British Congress, which were readily given (Ucko 1987: 3, 10). Prominent among them was that the Congress would be fully committed to the genuine participation of the Third World and the indigenous peoples of the Fourth World; that on this basis the themes chosen for discussion at the Congress would allow not only archaeologists, but anyone with an interest in the past, from anywhere in the world, to participate as equal members and that the primary aim was real academic discussion, which implied precirculation of papers and post-Congress publications. By the time of the First Announcement of the Congress early in 1983, several major themes of universal interest had been proposed to accommodate the worldwide participation not only of archaeologists but also of people of relevant expertise and experience beyond the profession. The Congress, by now called the World Archaeological Congress (WAC), was officially launched through its Second Announcement on 27 September 1984 (Ucko 1987: 47–48).

At this stage it was going to be a 'somewhat unusual meeting' (Ucko 1987: x) by comparison with the IUPPS Congresses that had preceded it and in ways to which his Australian experience had contributed. It was about to become radically more so as a result of imminent events (for a summary of these see Ucko 1987: 253–256).

After the South African ban

In September 1985 WAC announced a ban on South African participation on the grounds that 'its apartheid regime placed it outside all normal principles and regulations' and Namibia as a dependent territory was included in the ban in October. In January 1986 the International Executive Committee of the International Union threatened to expel WAC should its South African/Namibian ban not be removed by 15 February. Despite resignations and withdrawals WAC announced that its Congress would proceed, which it did from 1 to 5 September, with a Plenary Session on 6 September.

The Plenary Session set up a Steering Committee, to serve for a year, to discuss areas of disagreement between WAC and the International Union and to consider the formation of a new world archaeological association should the joint discussions lead nowhere. Michael Day, President of WAC and Chairman of the Steering Committee, wrote in the Committee's final report that there had been no success with the first part of the remit, so attention was concentrated on the second (Day 1988: 5–6).

The task was the transformation of the experience of a single conference into the structure and operation of a continuing institution. In addressing it, the Steering Committee produced a document in six sections (Day 1988: 6–11), covering aims, organisation, institutional and individual membership, planned activities, Executive and Council. Of most relevance in the present context is WAC's acceptance of 'a social as well as an academic responsibility' in the interests of a 'humane archaeology' that 'recognises the importance of archaeological evidence about the past to the rights and aspirations of those directly affected' by the discipline (Day 1988: 7–8).

Because the nature of the traditional ownership of the land by indigenous peoples is seen as forging a link with archaeology, representatives of such groups are given a role on WAC's Executive and Council (Day 1988: 8). Similarly, among the themes identified (Day 1988: 7) for attention at future meetings are some touching on the interests and concerns of Third and Fourth World peoples: the effects of archaeology on host communities; the ethics of archaeological enquiry; the ownership, conservation and exploitation of the archaeological heritage and the treatment and disposition of human remains. Day indeed was already able to report (1988: 9) on the organisation, in association with two American Indian organisations, of an Inter-Congress on Archaeological Ethics and the Treatment of Human Remains to be held at the University of South Dakota in August 1989 (the subsequent subject of reports in WAC 1989).

FINAL WORD

Peter says that in looking back at the period of the South African ban he sees the parallels with his Australian experience (Ucko 1987: 4). That experience he thinks made him slowly aware that his initial reluctance about supporting a ban on grounds of academic freedom was wrong and the ban on South Africa morally correct (Plenary Session 1986: 6). I see the corresponding episode in his Australian experience as his radicalisation by Aboriginal reactions to the events of 1974 involving the Institute that he came from England to head and stayed to transform (Ucko 1987: 2). These two episodes, in Australia and on the wider stage of WAC, became seedbeds for understanding and compassion.

ACKNOWLEDGEMENTS

For Peter's years in London in the 1960s I have been able to draw on the memory and the papers of Mary-Jane Mountain and Andrée Rosenfeld, who were around the Institute of Archaeology at the time.

For Peter's early years in Canberra I have been able to talk with people who were associates of his in the affairs of the Australian Institute of Aboriginal Studies, like Les Hiatt, John Mulvaney and Colin Tatz. Later-comers to the Institute like Geoff Gray and Graeme Ward have been helpful with information and literature and the former saved me from a signal error of historical fact. I was helped by being able to talk with Gordon Briscoe at the Australian National University about Aboriginal politics of the 1960s and 1970s.

I owe a great debt to Jacquie Lambert, who has been at the centre of Institute affairs for over 30 years. She has set me firmly in the time and place of which I am writing and cast a sharp eye over the final text.

REFERENCES

AIAS Newsletter (1972) 'AIAS Biennial General Meeting 1972', *AIAS Newsletter*, 3(5): 24–25.

AIAS Newsletter (1973a) 'Appointment of Deputy Principal', *AIAS Newsletter*, 3(6): 3.

AIAS Newsletter (1973b) 'National Register of Aboriginal Sites', *AIAS Newsletter*, 3(6): 13–16.

AIAS Newsletter (1974) '6th Biennial General Meeting and Conference', *AIAS Newsletter* new series 1: 24–25.

BIA (1964) '19th Annual Report of the Institute 1961–62', *Bulletin of the Institute of Archaeology*, 4: 291–310.

Attenbrow, V. and Khan, K. (1994) 'F.D. McCarthy: his work and legacy at the Australian Museum' in *Archaeology in the North: Proceedings of the 1993 Australian Archaeological Association Conference*, M. Sullivan, S. Brockwell and A. Webb (eds), Darwin: North Australia Research Unit, Australian National University, pp. 5–16.

Attwood, B. and A. Markus (1999) *The Struggle for Aboriginal Rights: A Documentary History*, St Leonards, Sydney: Allen and Unwin.

Berndt, R.M. (1977) 'Preface', in *Aborigines and Change: Australia in the '70s,* R.M. Berndt (ed.), Canberra: Australian Institute of Aboriginal Studies, pp. vii–xiii.

Broome, R. (2002) *Aboriginal Australians: Black Responses to White Domination*, 3rd edn, Crows Nest, Sydney: Allen and Unwin.

Day, M. (1988) 'Final report of the Steering Committee of the World Archaeological Congress', *World Archaeological Bulletin*, 2: 4–11.

Dix, W. (1978–1979) Review of achievement of the Sites of Significance Programme, *Site Recorders' Newsletter for 1978–1979*, 1(4): 4–7.

Edwards, R. (1975) *The Preservation of Australian Aboriginal Heritage*, Canberra: Australian Institute of Aboriginal Studies.

Horton, D. (1994) *The Encyclopaedia of Aboriginal Australia*, vol. 2, Canberra: Aboriginal Studies Press.

McCarthy, F.D. (1970) *Aboriginal Antiquities in Australia: Their Nature and Preservation*, Canberra: Australian Institute of Aboriginal Studies.

Moser, S. (1994) 'Building the discipline of Australian archaeology: Fred McCarthy at the Australian Institute of Aboriginal Studies', in *Archaeology in the North: Proceedings of the 1993 Australian Archaeological Association Conference* M. Sullivan, S. Brockwell and A. Webb (eds), Darwin: North Australia Research Unit, Australian National University, pp. 17–29.

Moser, S. (1995) 'The "Aboriginalization" of Australian archaeology: the contribution of the Australian Institute of Aboriginal Studies to the indigenous transformation of the discipline', in *Theory in Archaeology: A World Perspective*, P.J. Ucko (ed.), London and New York: Routledge, pp. 150–177.

Plenary Session (1986) *Edited Version of the Plenary Session of the World Archaeological Congress Held in the Guildhall, Southampton, England on 6 September 1986*, Southampton: World Archaeological Congress, Department of Archaeology, University of Southampton.

Renfrew, C. (1973) 'Preface' in *The Explanation of Culture Change: Models in Prehistory*, C. Renfrew (ed.), London: Duckworth, pp. ix–x.

Rowse, T. (2002) *Nugget Coombs: A Reforming Life*, Cambridge: Cambridge University Press.

Steering Committee (1975) *The Institute's Philosophy and Function*, Canberra: Steering Committee Report, Australian Institute of Aboriginal Studies.

Ucko, P.J. (1968) *Anthropomorphic Figurines of Predynastic Egypt and Neolithic Crete with Comparative Material from the Prehistoric Near East and Mainland Greece*, London: Andrew Szmidla.

Ucko, P.J. (1974) 'Review of AIAS Activities 1973', *AIAS Newsletter* new series 1: 5–15.

Ucko, P.J. (1975) 'Review of AIAS Activities 1974', *AIAS Newsletter* new series 3: 6–17.

Ucko, P.J. (1977) 'Preface' in *Form in Indigenous Art: Schematisation in the Art of Aboriginal Australia and Prehistoric Europe*, P.J. Ucko (ed.) Canberra: Australian Institute of Aboriginal Studies, pp. 1–4.

Ucko, P.J. (1983) 'Australian academic archaeology: Aboriginal transformation of its aims and practices, *Australian Archaeology,* 16: 11–26.

Ucko, P.J. (1987) *Academic Freedom and Apartheid: The Story of the World Archaeological Congress*, London: Duckworth.

Ucko, P.J. and G.W. Dimbleby (eds) (1969) *The Domestication and Exploitation of Plants and Animals*, London: Duckworth.

Ucko, P.J. and A. Rosenfeld (1967) *Palaeolithic Cave Art*, World University Library, London: Weidenfeld and Nicolson.

Ucko, P.J., R. Tringham and G.W. Dimbleby (eds) (1972) *Man, Settlement and Urbanism*, London: Duckworth.

WAC (1989) 'WAC First Inter-Congress', *World Archaeological Bulletin*, 4: 14–28.

Widders, T., P. Thompson, G. Williams, L. Thompson, B. Bellear and L. Watson (1974) 'Open letter concerning the Australian Institute of Aboriginal Studies to the Institute Members, Associate Members and other interested people'. Brickfield Hill, Sydney: Eaglehawk and Crow.

CHAPTER 3

EAGLEHAWK AND CROW

Colin Tatz and Jacquie Lambert

We live in an ahistorical age. L.P. Hartley opened a novel with his now familiar sentence: 'The past is a foreign country; they do things differently there' (Hartley 1953). For us, the Institute[1] is very much home country: between us, our aggregated association with that organisation is now a weighty 77 years. We have what is quaintly called 'baggage', which doesn't mean bias or ideology but rather involvement and memory. Jacquie – formerly administrative officer and executive officer since a decade ago – is the longest-serving staff member; Colin, who was present at the inaugural meeting of the embryonic Institute in 1961, is still a member and currently an honorary visiting fellow. That accumulated experience is valuable as we review aspects of past Institute history and as we experience some of its present-day fruits. In so many ways, the past is still present and so, assuredly, is the echo of Ucko.

THE 'DISAPPEARING ASPECTS'

In May 1961, Dr W.E.H. (Bill) Stanner convened a meeting in University House, Australian National University, to establish the need for, and the basis of, an institute of Aboriginal Studies. The doctorhood of elders assembled, namely, A.A. Abbie, Catherine and Ronald Berndt, Arthur Capell, J.B. Cleland, A.P. Elkin, F.D. McCarthy, N.W.G. Macintosh, C.P. Mountford, Marie Reay, Donald Thomson, Norman Tindale, A.D. Trendall, W.C. Wentworth, Helen and Stephen Wurm, and others (Sheils 1963: 484–488). Three juniors attended as Australian National University doctoral research scholars: Lester Hiatt, Diane Barwick and Don Laycock. Colin was allowed an 'unofficial' presence, on condition he made no mention of his intended doctoral work on the administration of Aboriginal affairs in north Australia. The Stanner message then, and for a longish period thereafter, was plain enough: the past was 'in', the contemporary 'out'. Stanner wasn't alone in believing that any 'intrusion' into the contemporary world could, or would, cruel the pitch for future anthropology students, or for the established academics who had carved out their domains. Anthropologist Donald Thomson's excursions into newspaper articles critical of Presbyterian mission policies and practices in Cape York in the 1930s had led to some bureaucratic paranoia about fieldwork 'intruders'. That state of mind infected some academics, even 30 years after Thomson.[2] In 1964, the 'disappearing-aspects-of-Aboriginal-life-before-it-is-too-late' research philosophy was cemented with the passing of the new Institute's enabling statute. Senator John Gorton's second reading speech specifically excluded contemporary 'welfare' issues: 'The permanent institute will not be concerned with current problems as they affect the Australian aborigine. Its work will be scientific and anthropological … Its programme will be designed to ensure that important material now available is not lost forever' (Hansard 1964). 'Anthropology' and science were now officially conjoined as bedfellows, and all other 'current problems' were not to be countenanced – at least not within the Institute.

When Colin joined Monash University in April 1964 he persuaded the University council to establish the Centre for Research into Aboriginal Affairs (CRAA). Monash agreed, provided the agendas of this Centre and the Institute didn't overlap. He was dispatched to address the Institute on the new Centre, with its applied and action research agenda on Aboriginal health, housing, involvement with the criminal law, education and participation in the economy (Monash University 1966). He was given a crystal-clear nod that there would be no overlap or conflict; with some anger and a little immaturity he even proffered that if ever the Institute changed its 'conservation–preservation' track he would seek the disestablishment of the Centre.[3]

Soon after, CRAA approached the Institute for a grant to study aspects of Aboriginal health – specifically, the establishment of a model to measure the health levels of Aboriginal communities in Gippsland. The Institute's administrative assistant, on behalf of Principal Fred McCarthy, advised that such an application was possible, provided that the time frame for investigation was before the year 1910! Anything later would be seen as breaking the bounds of the Institute's mandate. CRAA and the Australian Institute for Aboriginal Studies (AIAS) went their clearly separated ways.

In early 1974, Colin, then at the University of New England in Armidale, attended a cocktail party at an Institute function at the Lakeside Hotel in Canberra. Jacquie asked him why he avoided, even disavowed, the Institute. He said he was willing to bet a year's salary that if he again applied for a research grant on serious contemporary health issues he would be knocked back. A voice piped in: 'you'd lose!' It was the voice of Ucko, this London whirlwind, hell bent on taking this conservative Institute into the present, willing to wager that his energy, his breadth and his imagination could and would take on employment, health, education, police and legal issues, even the mining ventures under way or being mooted.

THE POLITICAL CONTEXT

As always in this kind of historical (and personal) memoir, context is essential. In the late 1960s, a number of Aboriginal intellectuals and leaders were taken to task by a handful of American and Papua New Guinean activists for their conservatism and for their subservience to white authority, even in Aboriginal welfare leagues and progress associations. The radical and revolutionary Rap Brown (later Jamil Abdullah Al-Amin) and Albert Maori Kiki (later Sir Albert) influenced the Aboriginal members of the Aborigines Advancement League (AAL) in Victoria; they, in turn, influenced thinking in the smallish world of the Federal Council for Aboriginal (and later, Torres Strait Islander) Advancement (FCAATSI). Both were dominated by white executives, albeit by men and women whom we now see as radical, even heroic, figures.

In 1969 Maori Kiki visited Melbourne and attended the AAL annual ball in Northcote Town Hall. He was so appalled at what he saw as comic Aboriginal imitation of white middle-class 19th-century manners and values that he left in a huff. If such was their assimilationist goal, he shouted, then he had nothing to contribute. Less than a week later, Stuart Murray, son-in-law of Pastor Doug Nicholls, announced that he and his fellow Aborigines were taking over the executive of the AAL. All of these organisations had preached that when Aborigines were 'ready' they would be 'allowed' to take over their operation. They were, indeed, ready, and the Maori Kiki blast was their trigger for action. White dominance of welfare leagues was about to end across the country.

The AAL and FCAATSI had been the two primary pressure groups in black-white politics. These two organisations had done all the politicking on the removal of people from Mapoon, flogging of girls at Hopevale mission, protection of the people at Maralinga, Albert Namatjira and his convictions for supplying alcohol to his sons, equal pay for equal work, federal voting rights and on the campaign for the 1967 referendum. By 1977, FCAATSI was so imbued with a spirit of revolt against white domination that it changed its name, not altogether surprisingly, to the National Aboriginal and Islander Liberation Movement (NAILM) – an echo of both African and Middle Eastern political movements. NAILM's basic aims were cultural revival and survival, guarantees of customs and culture, self-governing programmes, land rights, abolition of discriminatory laws, activism as a political party and 'liberation education' for Aborigines.

Just prior to the 1972 federal election, nine Aboriginal men and women visited China as part of a lobbying exercise to enlist Chinese support for the Aboriginal advancement movement, just as that country had supported minority peoples in Africa. By now, Aboriginal intellectuals – like Chicka Dixon, Lilla Watson, Gerry Bostock, Lyn Thompson, Cheryl Buchanan, Ken Winder, Ruby Hammond, Phillip Long and Terry Widders – were looking for support internationally. When the Labor Party came to federal power in December 1972, Prime Minister Gough Whitlam and his ardently pro-Aboriginal Minister for Aboriginal Affairs, Gordon Bryant, promised much for an Aboriginal future. Bryant had always been an avid supporter and member of the AAL and FCAATSI. So pervasive was the feeling that all would now be well with men like Bryant at the helm, that FCAATSI/NAILM went into a decline. There was more than a glimmer to hand that Aborigines could and would speak on their own behalf *within* government rather than against it.

In February 1973, Bryant announced the creation of a National Aboriginal Consultative Committee (NACC), a body to be elected as 'a structure of authority within Aboriginal groups' to negotiate with government. Bryant was soon replaced by Senator Cavanagh – whereupon he made it very plain indeed that the NACC was merely an advisory body, 'a *forum* for the expression of Aboriginal people'. Whitlam, as Prime Minister, confused the issue by talking about Aboriginal 'power to make their own decisions about their own way of life' (Tatz 1979: 41–48). Accordingly, in February 1974 the NACC voted to change its name to the National Aboriginal Congress, with all the implications that the word Congress had in colonialist politics in South Africa and elsewhere. Wrangling continued, until finally the word became National Aboriginal Conference (NAC), a more apt term for what was, after all, the reality. 'Consultation' was to become the buzz word, meaning that Aborigines would be 'allowed' to discuss decisions that had already been taken.

The then Department of Aboriginal Affairs expressed its views to the Hiatt Committee on the NACC in 1976: it opposed a nationally *elected* body such as the NACC. What they needed was an advisory body: 'advisory bodies are likely to be effective in influencing Government when they devote themselves unostentatiously to giving advice and avoid making public criticism of Government actions'. That was almost 30 years ago. Given the present Government's attitudes to elected bodies like the (recently abolished) Aboriginal and Torres Strait Islander Commission (ATSIC) and its preference for 'unostentatious' advice, the past is not a foreign country but a domain with which we are very familiar.

The initially-elected NACC comprised 39 men and two women, most of them of an older generation than the China group. David Anderson and Bruce McGuinness, both of Victoria, at the centre of the moves towards some kind of real political autonomy in this new structure, were among the first of a small group of Aboriginal graduates. At that time, there were less than a dozen Aboriginal men and women at university (Dunn and Tatz 1969: 60).

In 1972, a compulsory course on Aboriginal Studies was introduced into the syllabus for final year teacher trainees at what was then Armidale Teachers College (ATC). Emerging Aboriginal spokespeople lectured some 120 students each year, presented Aboriginal viewpoints and, one hoped, helped debunk the many myths about Aboriginality. There were contributions from, *inter alia*, Mum Shirl, Kevin Gilbert, Charlie Perkins, Chicka Dixon, Pat (Miller) O'Shane, Paul Coe, Gordon Briscoe, Rex Marshall, Ted Fields, Harry Jagamara Nelson, Ken Colbung, Michael Anderson and local Armidale activist, Vera Lovelock (Tatz 1975). No one focused specifically on the Institute and its essentially non-Aboriginal governing Council, but the general tenor was clear: Aborigines insisted on speaking for themselves. Black Power, political advancement and development, self-determination, potential violence and criticism of white values were very much the themes of these often angry speakers.

One young resident of Armidale at that time was Terry Widders. Another regular visitor and participant in the ATC Aboriginal Studies programme was Gary Williams. Both joined Lyn Thompson, Peter Thompson, Bob Bellear and Len Watson as signatories to the Eaglehawk and Crow[4] letter to the Institute in March 1974.

In sum, there was ferment in Aboriginal affairs, especially from the younger and emerging group of intellectuals. They attacked the 'sovereignty' of all that was done for or about them by government and by welfare leagues. Not surprisingly, they also attacked the 'sovereignty' of the all-too noticeable white academy which had, till then, dictated most of what was researched, written and taught about Aboriginality.

THE EAGLEHAWK AND CROW LETTER

The AIAS May 1974 sixth biennial general meeting was the forum for discussion of a five-page open letter, dated 29 March 1974, to Institute members, associate members and other interested people. The Eaglehawk and Crow letter was an attack on the Institute on a range of fronts – in particular, its forthcoming 16-day, AU$100,000, international conference on Aboriginal Studies. All signatories except Peter Thompson were Aboriginal people. The event came to be seen as a major catalyst in making the Institute seriously reassess its relations with Aboriginal and Torres Strait Islander people.

The letter was a stinging attack on the Institute, on the Principal, Peter Ucko, and on what he had been trying to achieve since taking office some 16 months earlier. The condemnation was intensified by Eaglehawk and Crow's decision to circulate replies it had received to its open letter. Among some eminent scholars who replied, T.G.H. Strehlow endorsed the sentiments expressed by Eaglehawk and Crow, and congratulated the group for having 'made out an excellent case against the Institute'.[5] While many of the respondents had sent copies of their responses to the Principal, others had not, including some of those who not only heartily endorsed the concerns of Eaglehawk and Crow but who took the opportunity to put a heavy boot into the Institute.

The Eaglehawk and Crow letter, which had also been published on 6 May 1974 in the Australian Union of Students newsletter, the *National U*, argued that the Institute's forthcoming (and expensive) conference would have no significance for Aborigines and their position in the world. As Eaglehawk and Crow saw it:

> For the Institute, and especially its Principal, Peter Ucko, the conference is a major weapon for gaining international prestige and a modern relevant image. This, we know, is to impress the government enough to make it think the Institute, as it is now constituted and under the guise of its current 'relevant' programs, is worth more money and worth listening to for advice on Aboriginal matters. This will have the effect of extending the power academics exercise over the lives of the people they study. (Eaglehawk and Crow 1974)

The conference cost was attacked; so was the lack of any meaningful response by the Institute to an earlier suggestion from one of the signatories that three members of their group should be approached about giving papers, specifically at the seminar on social and cultural change. The Institute was rebuked for its past and present policies, focusing on a range of related issues. Eaglehawk and Crow deplored the partial breakdown of the Aboriginal oral intellectual tradition *vis-à-vis* the power and the value given by society generally to the written intellectual tradition employed by anthropologists. There was lack of respect for and consideration by the Institute about the lives and interests of those being studied. The Institute was not involved in land rights, it focused on 'tribal' Aborigines to the detriment of other Aboriginal people and it had no involvement in education and translation-literacy programmes.

The letter showed an intimate knowledge of the Institute. Reference was made to the 1970 subcommittee on membership, the banning in 1971 of anthropologist Richard Gould by the Western Desert people (for what was considered a gross breach of trust in publishing secret-sacred material) and to a subsequent meeting organised by the Institute on 'Access to the Field'. Eaglehawk and Crow expressed their hopes for the future. They deplored tokenism. Anthropologists should cease collecting and interpreting esoteric information but should act 'to help all people ... understand the general and complex features of Australia's situation (unresolved colonialism, capitalism and privilege and authority/ power) and so work to change it in a more humanising, liberating direction'. Aboriginal communities should commission research and control funding, which – together with a satisfactory land base with full land rights – was the only way of ultimately altering what was said to be the unsatisfactory relationship between anthropologists and Aborigines (Eaglehawk and Crow 1974).

Less than a month later, on 24 April 1974, the Institute received another blast, this time in a telegram from Jim Stanley, the President of the NAC. He strongly opposed the biennial conference – to which NAC members had been invited by Peter Ucko on 3 April 1974 as participants, paper-givers or discussants. The conference, he declared, would do nothing for Aboriginal people and he demanded to know whether the conference cost would be coming from the global Aboriginal affairs budget. In likening the relationship between academia and Aborigines as 'synonymous to a truck racing down a mountain road without brakes', the telegram concluded: 'We ... trust that our opposition will curtail this useless exercise in academia' (Stanley 1974). This broadside was followed by another from an NAC(C) meeting of 24–31 May 1974, asking that a clear majority of the Institute's Council be appropriately qualified individuals of Aboriginal descent (Department of Aboriginal Affairs 1975).

Eaglehawk and Crow was considered at Council's meeting on 20–21 April 1974. The Principal was given freedom to initiate some kind of meeting with Eaglehawk and Crow, and Council set aside a formal period at the 25 May General Meeting to discuss the letter. In response to one of the Eaglehawk and Crow criticisms, namely, the lack of any meaningful reply by the Institute to the suggestion that three of the signatories should be approached about giving papers at the social and cultural change symposium, it was agreed that Aboriginal people should attend that session to discuss their views, but no additional papers would be accepted. The signatories' conference attendance would be paid for and, at the Principal's discretion and in consultation with the Secretary of the Department of Aboriginal Affairs, Barrie Dexter, the attendance of a few NAC members would be funded (AIAS Council 1974a).

No one present at the biennial general meeting in the Coombs Theatre at the Australian National University on 25 May 1974 has forgotten the rage and passion engendered by the discussions, the strutting and posturing of some of the academic participants or the vigorous challenges to the status quo. The morning session centred on a decision taken by Council, in the context of a more than four-fold increase in staff numbers since Peter Ucko's arrival, to move from its current cramped premises in NRMA House in Lonsdale Street, Braddon, to Mining Industry House, a prestigious newly constructed building on Northbourne Avenue in the heart of Canberra.

The proposed move came at a time when relations between the mining industry and Aboriginal people were at an all-time low, as evidenced by a terse telegram to the AIAS Chairman from Stewart Murray on behalf of the Victorian AAL, strongly objecting to Council's decision to move into the Mining Council's property, Mineral House (sic) (Murray 1974). Acrimony reigned, resulting in a Council resolution not to sign a lease for Mining Industry House, but for the Institute to remain where it was or move to non-contentious accommodation (later, the premises at Acton House) (AIAS General Meeting 1974).

The ambience was set. There were no representatives present from the NAC but two of the Eaglehawk and Crow signatories, Peter Thompson and Terry Widders, attended the afternoon session. At their request, the session was chaired by Ken Colbung, who had been elected that morning as one of the 13 new Aboriginal or Torres Strait Islander members, from a total of 15 newly elected members. (In that era, membership was seen as a special badge of honour, with the statute fixing the total membership at 100, with provision for an additional 20 members to be appointed by the AIAS Council.) Following Colbung's departure mid-afternoon, Colin was asked to take the chair. *Sturm*, drama, much fire and a fair dose of brimstone arose from Eaglehawk and Crow. The politeness that had generally pervaded Institute gatherings was now out the doors and windows.

The NAC proposal that the Institute Council should be reconstituted to consist only of Aboriginal people was defeated (3 : 53, with 15 abstentions). A subsequent motion, 'that this meeting believes research and information is a co-operative venture between people conducting research and those with whom they are working and that because of this the Council of the Institute should reflect this co-operation in its membership', was carried (67 : 0, with six abstentions). This resolution was conveyed by telegram to the NAC; they were advised that 13 Aboriginal people had been elected as members earlier in the meeting and that elections to Council had been delayed for up to six months to enable them to stand for the election.

The debates earlier in the day opened up discussion about the possible restructuring of the Institute, leading to a resolution from the biennial meeting:

That a small committee (with the powers to co-opt) of the total membership (both Members and Associate Members) of this Institute, not necessarily comprising all Council members or a majority of Council members, should be formed to re-examine the nature, scope, function, academic jurisdiction, role, composition and membership of the Australian Institute of Aboriginal Studies and report back to the membership.

A postal ballot of all members and associate members to elect the membership of the small committee was suggested, a recommendation subsequently endorsed by Council in October 1974. There were 24 contenders, and Colin Tatz (chairman), Bob Edwards, Jack Golson, Dick Roughsey (the only Aboriginal member) and Bill Wentworth were elected to what had become, by then, the steering committee on 'The Institute's Philosophy and Function'.

That committee finalised its report in August 1975 and presented its findings to the AIAS general meeting on 18 May 1976. In the 16 months between Eaglehawk and Crow and that date, much had changed. Peter Ucko led what could almost be called a charge, and in this he was strongly supported by members like Lester Hiatt, Jack Golson, John Mulvaney and Ronald Berndt. Peter was both advised and supported by three Aboriginal members: the sociologist maverick, Michael Mace, the ever-present and innovative Ken Colbung and the traditional elder Daymbalipu Mununggurr. There were now 12 advisory committees as opposed to the initial seven. The 'newcomer' committees included research and membership, Aboriginal advisory, publications, ecology, sites of significance and education. The latter showed how far the Institute had come from the earlier mandate. The education committee's work included responding to Aboriginal requests for materials, innovating and supporting 'action' programmes that could improve the quality of people's thinking about Aborigines and their societies, publishing kit materials and bibliographies for secondary and tertiary teachers and disseminating work on race relations education carried out in the UK, the USA, Canada and South Africa.

The steering committee's work was made easy by the rapidity of these changes. In just over ten years, the Institute had moved a considerable distance from its initial mandate. This inquiry was able to conclude, with solid evidence, that 'the Institute is not in need of major revision of its nature, scope, charter, function, role or academic jurisdictions'. For Colin to preside over such a finding was an indicator of enormous change in Institute theory and in practice, given his earlier hostility to the 'disappearing-aspects-only' charter of a decade earlier.

Much of Eaglehawk and Crow was, on the face of it, justifiable criticism of the Institute. The sentiments expressed were fair and in some ways even mild. The repercussions were anything but mild, with the correspondence producing much *angst* and soul-searching, to say nothing of endless phone calls and discussions well into the night. The May 1974 biennial conference was very expensive (although the eventual cost was closer to AU$75,000 than AU$100,000) and there was virtually no Aboriginal or Torres Strait Islander participation.[6] It was, however, an academic conference and – notwithstanding Peter's invitation to the NAC – it was the academic emphasis, not racial identity, that determined participation. Academically, the conference was a monumental success, resulting in much acclaim at the time and the publication of eight separate volumes.

In 1974, in announcing the establishment of a new 'contact' bibliography in the Library, Peter Ucko said: 'If we are to keep pace with the changing political and social situations of the Aborigines, the Institute can no longer afford to deal only with traditional Aboriginal life' (Ucko 1974). Initially, Institute involvement with contemporary issues lay only in areas with which it had traditionally been concerned, like the disposal of Truganini's skeletal remains. Council's involvement came about following an approach from the Tasmanian Museum in 1974 seeking Institute support for a mausoleum to be built to house her remains; this would allow the possibility of later study for research purposes.

Following an address to Council by Aboriginal activist, Harry Penrith (later known as Burnum Burnum), who was then involved with the Tasmanian Aboriginal community, Council totally rejected the mausoleum proposal, declaring that the remains of Truganini should be disposed of in accordance with her own wishes or those of her descendants which, in the event, they were. As Peter subsequently wrote, 'it was felt that the case of Truganini, a known historical person, (was) an exceptional one and that the moral issue involved overrule(d) any other considerations' (Ucko 1975). A few years earlier the Tasmanian Museum would have been confident of Institute support over such an issue (AIAS Council 1974b).

In the next six years the Institute was involved in many initiatives, including more overt political issues, as it attempted to keep pace with the changing political and social situations of Aboriginal and Torres Strait Islander people. While Peter was intent at that time on making the Institute more relevant, it was not, as claimed by Eaglehawk and Crow, to serve the desires and interests of the government, although in some areas the Institute attempted to influence government policy (Eaglehawk and Crow 1974). In the heady 1970s, the increasing involvement of the Institute in contemporary political issues, including those issues highlighted by Eaglehawk and Crow meant, at times, traversing difficult terrain as Council struggled to maintain its academic integrity and distance itself from party politics (AIAS Council 1979).

Although it was not in the pipeline in 1974, Eaglehawk and Crow's concern about the Institute's non-involvement in land rights would soon be addressed. In 1975, the Northern Land Council (NLC) sought Institute assistance in the compilation of claims for Crown Land, which had to be submitted by the end of that year. Institute involvement with both the NLC and, to a lesser extent, the Central Land Council (CLC), took the form of library research as well as contacting fieldworkers, primarily anthropologists, and co-ordinating their assistance, particularly to the NLC (Ucko 1976). Subsequently, the NLC Chairman, Silas Roberts, wrote, 'the Institute is regarded as a vital part of the Aboriginal affairs scene and no doubt history will acknowledge this' (Roberts 1978).

As well as providing assistance to the NLC and CLC, Council involved itself – albeit peripherally – in the 1978 Aurukun and Mornington Island debates. A major clash emerged between the Commonwealth and Queensland governments over Queensland's determination to gain control over the Uniting Church-run communities at Aurukun and Mornington Island. Following a Council meeting on 12 May 1978, the Institute unanimously and publicly affirmed its support of Aboriginal people conducting their own affairs. It also called on all state governments to legislate for Aboriginal land and other rights (AIAS Council 1978). [In the end, Queensland steamrolled the Commonwealth by a series of technical tricks, thereby frustrating Commonwealth attempts to provide better economic futures for these two communities (Tatz 1979: 66–81).]

One way or another during Peter's principalship, the Institute became involved with many of the other Eaglehawk and Crow issues. In the early 1970s, it led the way in support of bilingual education in the Northern Territory and was central in fostering initiatives in the area of oral history recording as well as in supporting self-determination in the context of the outstation movement. A 'Topical Issues' paper was published on the matter. Other initiatives included, as mentioned earlier, the establishment in October 1974 of an education advisory committee and, in 1975, the appointment of two education research fellows to the staff; payment of a percentage of author royalties from Institute publications to Aboriginal and Torres Strait Islanders, their families or groups who had contributed – other than as authors – to the publications; the establishment of Aboriginal and Torres Strait Islander training programmes; a lecture series for Aboriginal prisoners at Goulburn Gaol, New South Wales and the monitoring of the social impact of uranium mining in the Northern Territory (discussed later).

There was much activity in governance. Early in Peter's principalship, the Institute facilitated the membership and Council membership of Aboriginal people and their increased participation. In March 1974, there were only two Aboriginal members of Council from a total membership of 22, namely, Dick Roughsey and Senator Neville Bonner. In October 1974 there were six Aboriginal Council members. Although a long way from the NAC's call for the Council to be fully Aboriginalised, it was an advance for Aboriginal aspirations. Within four years, at the Council meeting of 12 May 1978, Ken Colbung was elected unopposed as the first Aboriginal deputy chairman of Council. He was elected, unopposed as the first Aboriginal chairman in May 1984. (All chairs since that time have been held by Aboriginal people.) In 2002, and under the Institute's amended constitution, eight of the nine Council members of what was by then the Australian Institute of Aboriginal and Torres Strait Islander Studies (AIATSIS) were Aboriginal or Torres Strait Islander people. Most of these Council members hold tertiary qualifications in Aboriginal Studies.

In October 1974, the six Aboriginal members of Council – Burramarra, Ken Colbung, Dennis Daniels, Eric Deeral, Dick Roughsey and Lazarus Lamilami – were appointed as the core members of a new Aboriginal advisory committee. As well as meeting to conduct its own business, by 1976 – with an expanded membership – committee members were assigned, with full voting rights, to each of the other Institute advisory committees. The Aboriginal Advisory Committee, which in 1978 was renamed as the Aboriginal and Torres Strait Islander Advisory Committee, was to become a major force during Peter's principalship. By 1976, all advisory committees also included within their membership Aboriginal or Torres Strait Islander social issues advisers.

In 1974, Peter was already addressing the Eaglehawk and Crow call for Aboriginal people themselves to commission research and control funding as the only way of ultimately altering the 'unsatisfactory relationship' between anthropologists and Aborigines. At that time, the budget included a special allocation for urgent research and training requested by Aboriginal groups, to be carried out by 'hired' researchers or by members of the groups themselves, with the Principal having executive discretion over such funding (AIAS Executive 1974). In practice, funding was allocated at the discretion of the Aboriginal and Torres Strait Islander Advisory Committee or, between meetings, by the Principal with the chairman of that committee, and one other committee member selected by the chairman. Before 1974, a small number of Aboriginal people had received grants of equipment and tapes to record their culture.[7] Under Peter, from October 1974 research grants were increasingly awarded to Aboriginal and Torres Strait Islander people, including the payment of salaries, field expenses and equipment. In September 1975, for example, 19 grants were awarded to Aboriginal and Torres Strait Islander people in areas as diverse as language studies, ethnobotany, recording of sites, recording of traditional law, and urban studies training in Chicago, USA (AIAS Newsletter 1976).

By the financial year 1979–1980, c. AU$300,500 was allocated to Aboriginal research and training from a total of c. AU$827,000 available generally for research grants (AIAS 1979–1980). With the increasing number of Aboriginal and Torres Strait Islander people gaining tertiary qualifications, however, the policy of earmarking funds for their research began to be seen as inappropriate. It was abandoned in 1981, when it was evident that their research projects were of a standard comparable with those from non-Aboriginal people, and that the concept of special funding carried with it overtones of patronage (AIAS Executive 1981). By 2004, Peter's initiative to fund Aboriginal and Torres Strait Islander people to carry out their own research had grown to the point where over half the applicants awarded research grants were either Aboriginal or Torres Strait Islander scholars working independently or in collaboration with non-indigenous researchers.

THE URANIUM ISSUE

In 1982, Colin wrote that 'if one had to think up a set of irreconcilables one could hardly do better than Aborigines, a national tourist park and uranium mining' (Tatz 1982, especially 118–122). The second Fox Report of May 1977 – which the federal government readily accepted – did not pussyfoot about its choices:

> There can be no compromise with the Aboriginal position [to oppose mining]; either it is treated as conclusive, or it is set aside … In the end, we form the conclusion that their opposition should not be allowed to prevail. (Ranger Inquiry 1977)

The commissioners – Justice Fox, G.G. Kelleher and Professor Charles Kerr – were nevertheless concerned about the social repercussions. They revealed anxiety about the influx of white miners and families and the mining impacts on Aboriginal employment, morale ('then at a low ebb'), educational and training opportunities, health and venereal diseases especially, alcohol devastation, racial tensions and conflicts. There would have to be environmental controls, they wrote, but they made no recommendation on measuring these foreseeable impacts on Aborigines.

The NLC, a child of the *Aboriginal Land Rights (Northern Territory) Act* 1976, was concerned about impacts and joined with the Department of Aboriginal Affairs in urging monitoring. The appointed Supervising Scientist, recommended by Fox, showed no inclination to look at anything apart from what he considered to be the physical environment, and so the Minister for Aboriginal Affairs, Ian Viner, wrote to the Institute in March 1978 asking AIAS to take on the human aspect of monitoring, initially for five years.

Peter Ucko negotiated a special allocation of AU$126,000 annually, rising later to AU$180,000 – then a considerable sum – and a Uranium Project Steering Committee was established, responsible to Council. Council in turn was responsible to the Minister and the Minister to Cabinet. Colin told Peter that he wanted the task, although it was Council, not the Principal, who made such appointments. Council appointed the core uranium committee in October 1978: Dr H.C. (Nugget) Coombs; Isaiah Burrunali, Jacob Nayinggul and Nathaneal Maralngurr, three traditional owners in the uranium province; three ex-officio members – Ken Colbung, then deputy chairman of the Institute, Lester Hiatt, chairman of AIAS and Peter Ucko as Principal and three Council members – Ronald Berndt, W.C. (Bill) Wentworth and Colin Tatz (as chairman). Eric Willmot replaced Peter as Principal in 1981 and John Mulvaney became chairman of AIAS after Hiatt. Max Kamien, Diane Smith, Len Smith, Carmel Schrire and Leslie Hunter were key consultants.

Peter could be, and often was, outrageously imaginative about some things, and stubborn, perhaps truculent and difficult about others. This steering committee was as broad as could be at the time, but Peter, a month before the committee's establishment, effectively appointed the core staff who would undertake the practical field monitoring. Lines of command and loyalty became murkier than was necessary or effective.

The committee reported six-monthly to the Minister, from October 1978 through to early 1984, and presented its consolidated report, entitled *Aborigines and Uranium*, to the then

Labor Minister for Aboriginal Affairs, Clyde Holding, on 30 June 1984. Throughout this exercise, Peter was the essence of support, ideas and conflict resolution. For reasons still not clear, there was a general belief that this AIAS Committee could, if it so chose, close down or in some way diminish the two mining operations, at Narbalek and Ranger. At a Hunter-Gatherer conference in Quebec City in 1980, Colin was asked how powerful his committee was. He replied that he didn't know – to which the noted anthropologist Milton Freeman responded: 'Don't be naïve, you are as powerful as you are perceived as being.'

Whatever the perceptions while the committee was operating – and there were many instances of perceived power and positive reactions to it – there is no doubt about the final political outcome: not zero but something close. Clyde Holding, a sometime friend and colleague of Colin's from Aborigines Welfare Board and Victorian Labor Party days in Melbourne, tabled the consolidated report in October 1984, in the dying minutes of the parliamentary year. There was no debate, no discussion, and no reaction, at least in political circles. The exercise was, nevertheless, valuable in a number of ways: among others, it established a template of how to monitor social impacts; it spread some of its ideas and findings to Canada and the USA; it helped in training Aboriginal fieldworkers in data collection and in becoming partners in the research enterprise; it assisted the Gagudju Association in finding ways of handling its royalty payments and it helped stall the development of the Koongarra mining project. [As we write, the formal moratorium on Koongarra is about to end and it may well be that a new mine is opened.] One of its essential conclusions was achieved, in part through AIAS efforts: a moratorium on further mining for at least ten years. Aborigines, the conclusions stated, needed respite and a breathing space. One other recommendation didn't alter what was seen as an ever-present danger:

> Uranium is a hazardous substance. There must, therefore, be immediate Government intervention in the form of serious and substantial education for Aborigines about what it is, why we need it, what we do with it, and how dangerous it can be to their natural diet, their environment, and their physical lives. The [monitoring] Project would be remiss if it did not express its concern about radiation safeguards and their enforcement for all residents in the Region. (AIAS 1984: 304).

That was written when there had been two major spillages of water in the tailings ponds that are meant to safeguard the dispersal of the toxic sludge and slurry of uranium milling. Two decades later, at least 120 such leaks and spillages have been reported. Given the Navajo uranium mining experience, of uranium's 'trail of tears' due to kidney injury, toxic neuropathy, leukaemias and lung cancers, and given the chromosomal abnormalities which have presented following Hungarian, East German and Czechoslovakian uranium mining, it would be an amazing finding that uranium has not in some way been a health hazard to Aborigines in the Alligator Rivers region of the Territory.

In reflecting on the past and Ucko's place in it, it is fitting to end with reference to the Walsh Review. In 1981, the federal government recommended an external review of the Institute. Professor R.J. (Bob) Walsh, an eminent medical dean and geneticist, began his task early in 1982 and reported in September that year. The Walsh Review caused consternation among Institute members and staff: no one knew what lay behind a review of this kind and many were fearful of major changes towards the conservative. Walsh, though seriously ill at the time, produced a warm report consonant with the Institute's 'Philosophy and Function' review (Walsh 1982). There was an important recommendation that 'the Institute should support research on contemporary Aboriginal situations and problems, as well as research into the traditional culture of Aboriginals'. There were also some odd and contradictory views, notably, a strong recommendation that the Institute should not in any way be involved in anything to do with land rights. However, Walsh was very much in favour of the uranium impact monitoring project, then under way.

From an AIAS perspective, the uranium exercise brought the Institute fully into the realm of 'current problems'. Ucko was an integral part of the radical transformation from the 'disappearing-aspects' era of the early 1960s. By mid-1970, the turn was not quite 180 degrees, but somewhat greater than a left angle. The increasingly robust Aboriginal political climate; the Gough Whitlam era and its promises; land rights legislation in the Northern Territory under Malcolm Fraser's prime ministership and the birth of the powerful NCL and CLC; the growth of incorporations generally across Aboriginal Australia; the Aboriginal decision to fight uranium and then, having lost, the decision to go with it and to want more of it; the new place and space for anthropologists in land rights issues and the willingness of some older Institute members, such as R.M. Berndt and W.C. Wentworth, to widen their perspectives all made for the right context for the right man in the right place. His name was Ucko.

NOTES

1. The Australian Institute of Aboriginal Studies (AIAS) was established in 1964. It became the Australian Institute of Aboriginal and Torres Strait Islander Studies (AIATSIS) in 1989.
2. In the late 1960s, Thomson told Colin he needed the money, hence the journalism; but he always had a genuine and humane concern for the people incarcerated in what were clearly draconian institutions.
3. CRAA became the Aboriginal Research Centre, then the Koorie Research Centre and is now known as the Centre for Australian Indigenous Studies (CAIS). Its directors have been, in order, Colin Tatz, Elizabeth Eggleston, Colin Bourke, Eve Fesl, Lachlan Chipman, Sharon Firebrace, Helen Curzon-Siggers, Eleanor Bourke and Lynette Russell. While the Centre offers courses for degree programmes, after Colin Tatz left – and after the early death of Elizabeth Egglestone, it became essentially an information resource about Aboriginal culture, and a companionship and support group for Aboriginal students at Monash.
4. Terry Widders (personal communication with Colin Tatz 5 April 2005) confirmed that the unanimous decision of the group to write under the name Eaglehawk and Crow had its basis in Aboriginal mythology, where Eaglehawk and Crow symbolises a complex relationship of contrast: antagonism mixed with friendship. Eaglehawk and Crow were struggling to achieve a meaningful place for Aboriginal people and Aboriginal aspirations within AIAS and to redress the balance in the relationship, which they saw as favouring the aspirations of white academics.
5. Replies were also received and circulated by Eaglehawk and Crow from Dianne Fulcher, Fay Gale, Fred McCarthy (the previous AIAS Principal), Richard A. Gould, R.G. Hausfeld, Derek Freeman, W.J. Gray, John Wilson, Arnold R. Pilling, Elizabeth Eggleston, Peter White, J.W. Warburton, Isobel M. White, Alan Thompson, Del Thompson (two letters), Martin Tuck (convenor of the Quaker Race Relations Committee, who enclosed a response he had received from the Minister for Aboriginal Affairs, J.L. Cavanagh), Jack Golson and the AIAS Principal, Peter Ucko.
6. From over 300 papers presented, there was a joint paper by an Aboriginal and non-Aboriginal author, Margaret Valadian and Diane Barwick on Aboriginal identity; and a joint paper by a Torres Strait Islander and non-Aboriginal author, Ephraim Bani and T. Klokeid on Kala Lagau Langgus, and Ephraim Bani presented a paper on his own account on the language situation in Western Torres Strait, AIAS conference programme, 1974 biennial conference, AIATSIS.
7. AIAS 1969–1970. Equipment grants were made to a number of Aboriginal people, including Jimmy Barker, Peter Coffin, Ken Colbung, Constance Bush and Lazarus Lamilami.

REFERENCES

AIAS (1969–1970) *AIAS Annual Report* 1969–1970, p. 21.

AIAS (1979–1980) *AIAS, Annual Report* 1979–1980, p. 20.

AIAS (1984) Aborigines and Uranium: Consolidated Report on the Social Impact of Uranium Mining on the Aborigines of the Northern Territory, Canberra, AGPS.

AIAS Council (1974a) AIAS Council Minutes, April 1974, (74/47), AIATSIS.

AIAS Council (1974b) 1 AIAS Council Minutes, October 1974, (76/69(a)) AIATSIS.

AIAS Council (1978) AIAS Council Minutes, May 1978 (78/22b), AIATSIS.

AIAS Council (1979) AIAS Council Minutes, March 1979, 79/7, AIATSIS.

AIAS Executive (1974) AIAS Executive Committee Minutes, November 1974 (74/24), AIATSIS.

AIAS Executive (1981) AIAS Executive Committee Minutes, July 1981 (81/27), AIATSIS.

AIAS General Meeting (1974) AIAS General Meeting Minutes, May 1974 (3(b)), AIATSIS.

AIAS Newsletter (1976) *AIAS Newsletter*, New Series No. 5, January, p. 22.

Department of Aboriginal Affairs (1975) Letter from Principal Executive Officer, Department of Aboriginal Affairs to Principal dated 25 June 1975 conveying NACC resolution from meeting 24–31 May 1974, File 74/30, part 3, central filing system, AIATSIS.

Dunn, S.S. and C.M. Tatz (eds) (1969) *Aborigines and Education*, Sun Books.

Eaglehawk and Crow (1974) Letter from Eaglehawk and Crow dated 29 March 1974, File 73/119, central filing system, AIATSIS.

Hansard (1964) Hansard, 7 May: 1027–1028.

Hartley, L.P. (1953) *The Go-Between*, London: Hamish Hamilton.

Monash University (1966) *Monash University Gazette*, 3, 1, September 7–8.

Murray, S. (1974) Telegram dated 24 May 1974 to Professor N.W.G. Macintosh from Stewart Murray, Aborigines Advancement League, File 73/119, central filing system, AIATSIS.

Ranger Inquiry (1977) *Ranger Uranium Environmental Inquiry Second Report*, AGPS, Canberra, p. 79.

Roberts, S. (1978) Silas Roberts, Chairman of the Northern Land Council letter to Principal, in Peter J. Ucko, 'Review of AIAS activities 1977', *AIAS Newsletter*, New Series No. 9, January 1978, p. 19.

Sheils, H. (ed.) (1963) *Australian Aboriginal Studies: A Symposium of Papers Presented at the 1961 Research Conference*, Oxford: Oxford University Press.

Stanley, J. (1974) Telegram dated 24 April 1974 from J. Stanley, President, NAC to the Australian Institute of Aboriginal Studies, File 74/30, part 3, central filing system, AIATSIS.

Tatz, C. (ed.) (1975) *Black Viewpoints*, Sydney: ANZ Book Company.

Tatz, C. (1979) *Race Politics in Australia*, Armidale: University of New England.

Tatz, C. (1982) *Aborigines and Uranium and Other Essays*, London: Heinemann.

Ucko, P.J. (1974) 'Review of AIAS activities 1973', *AIAS Newsletter*, New Series No. 1, January 1974, p. 8.

Ucko P.J. (1975) 'Review of AIAS Activities 1974', *AIAS Newsletter*, New Series No. 3, January 1975, p. 7.

Ucko, P.J. (1976) 'Review of AIAS Activities 1975', *AIAS Newsletter*, New Series No. 5, January 1976, p. 8.

Walsh, R.J. (1982) *'Report of the Review of the Australian Institute of Aboriginal Studies'*, September.

CHAPTER 4

REPOSITIONING ANTHROPOLOGY, 1972–1980

Nicolas Peterson

On leaving the Principalship of the Australian Institute of Aboriginal Studies (AIAS) in 1980, Peter wrote two articles, one on archaeology (Ucko 1983) and the other on social anthropology (Ucko 1985) setting out his perspective on the impact of the Institute in these two fields during his incumbency.[1] The article on social anthropology is largely a critique of the Institute's 'Social Anthropology Advisory Committee' whose members were, initially, all academics. Collectively they fare poorly, coming across as conservative, overly academic and lacking innovation (Ucko 1985: 71). Individually, they often supported policies and projects initiated elsewhere in the Institute. According to Peter, anthropologists who imagined themselves to be best able to represent Aboriginal expectations (Ucko 1985: 71) often could not and did not achieve this in the context of the Committee.[2]

The specific charges are that of four major undertakings of the Institute, none was directly initiated by the Social Anthropology Advisory Committee, although, in Peter's view, this might have been expected. The Committee did not initiate the drive for training Aboriginal people and allocating funds to a new all Aboriginal Advisory Committee; it did not initiate the push for a new committee to look at matters relevant to social and public policies affecting Aboriginal people – this did not actually come about but led to the attachment of Aboriginal Social Issues Advisors to each advisory committee; it did not initiate the Institute's drive to support the outstation movement and it did not initiate the idea of the Institute becoming involved in the preparation of Northern Territory land claim reports (Ucko 1985: 67–68). His claim is that by the end of his incumbency the Committee was involved in all these areas and that the Institute had played a key role in the repositioning of anthropology in its relations with Aboriginal people, in revamping the anthropological research agenda and in making it of more practical relevance.

In this contribution I want to briefly look at this claim, focussing on the land claims issue, for it was this more than anything else that led to the emergence of a well-established stream of applied anthropology in Australia.[3]

THE SEA CHANGE IN AUSTRALIA

Peter Ucko arrived in Australia to take up the Principalship of the AIAS in 1972 at the beginning of a sea change in Australian society, whose effects were to extend even to anthropology. After 23 years of conservative governments that had vigorously opposed the recognition of land rights, and were committed to assimilation until their dying days, a Federal Labor government was elected that moved Aboriginal affairs to centre stage. The newly elected Prime Minister declared that Australia would be judged on how it treated its indigenous people and proceeded to immediately set up a commission overseeing Aboriginal land rights to implement the election promise that they would be recognised. A great deal of money was injected into Aboriginal affairs and as Les Hiatt said in his farewell speech for Peter, he displayed 'a phenomenal talent in obtaining whatever was humanly possible to squeeze out of a reluctant Treasury. He was not only one of the last great spenders but one of the last great procurers' (Hiatt 1980). Under Peter's eight-year leadership the Institute expanded from 13 to 57 staff and the budget increased five-fold.

When he arrived in 1972 the Institute was entirely the preserve of white academics and only slowly inching away from the perceived constraints of its charter, to confine research to the traditional. Grants for the investigation of social change and of the relations between whites and Aboriginal people were being recommended for support by the Social Anthropology Advisory Committee, although they were only a small proportion of the supported projects. This was because the Prime Minister, Sir Robert Menzies, had only assented to the establishment of the Institute on the understanding that its brief would not interfere with the responsibilities of the government in the administration of Aboriginal affairs and policy.

Peter's arrival was a breath of fresh air. He brought with him huge energy and new ideas. His proposal that the members of advisory committees should meet face to face in Canberra was a masterstroke in making the Institute central to Aboriginal studies across the continent and in invigorating academic networks. But, as the events of 1974 were to show, he had not yet quite got his finger on the pulse of indigenous affairs, although he was quick to respond when he found it. His plans to move the Institute into new premises on the ground floor of Mining Industry House brought to a head simmering discontents among urban Aboriginal activists and their supporters and unwittingly he provided them with the ideal platform for their protest.[4]

Peter turned the sixth biennial general meeting of Institute members into a mammoth international conference that ran from 16 May until 2 June 1974. The business meeting of Institute members was held in the Coombs lecture theatre at the Australian National University on 25 May. There was an enormous air of anticipation, making this the best ever attended such meeting, because members had received an open letter addressed to them, attacking the Institute, and Peter had invited the signatories to the meeting.[5] The Eaglehawk and Crow letter[6] (see also Tatz and Lambert, Chapter 3, in this book), as it became known, had been sent on March 29, criticising the holding of the conference, accusing the Institute of only being interested in increasing its own power by ingratiating itself with government, of failing to act on a 1970 sub-committee recommendation that Aboriginal people be welcomed into the associate membership and that all Aboriginal committees be set up to recommend lines of research. Further, the writers argued, while the subject matter of research was getting increasingly relevant to Aboriginal people, the relationships between anthropologists and Aboriginal people were not. At least 20 members had replied to the letter in advance of the meeting, including Peter, who commented that, 'I find that your letter raises many important points which are concerning myself very greatly at the moment, and several which the Institute has already considered for some time' and went on to invite them to Canberra to discuss the matter further (29 April 1974). The business meeting was the most tumultuous ever held, and the events of that day are engraved on the minds of all who were present. The practical outcome of the meeting was the setting up of a committee to review the philosophy and functions of the Institute.

Peter grasped the challenges and opportunities offered by these events effectively and swiftly. He suspended certain rules to delay elections for the Council until new members had been chosen. As a result two Aboriginal people were elected to Council, Ken Colbung and Dick Roughsey, and four more appointed by the Governor General, and these six people were made the core members of the new Aboriginal Advisory Committee by the Council. Undoubtedly the Social Anthropology Advisory Committee was not leading the push for rapid and radical change: this had come from outside the Institute. Within the Institute it was Peter himself who was providing the leadership. It is also quite true that the Social Anthropology Advisory Committee unquestioningly worked within its established brief and was slow to take up the opportunities that Peter had introduced in 1973, which encouraged the committees, now that they met face to face, to become policy-recommending bodies. However, during the course of the first two such face to face meetings in 1973, the Committee recommended the establishment of a professorial or sub-professorial university position in Aboriginal urban or rural studies and two three-year social anthropological research positions at the Institute, recognising as the Newsletter says, 'its responsibility for the analysis of rural and urban "contact" studies as well as more traditional anthropological investigations … [and] that future policies must be based on adequate and relevant research and analysis' (Newsletter 1974: 5–7). At that time the Committee membership was J. Beckett (Chair), D. Barwick, R. Berndt, M. Calley, R. Edwards, F. Gale, L. Hiatt, K. Maddock, C. Rowley, W. Stanner, Peter Ucko and myself. In the same year the Material Culture Advisory Committee, advising in an area in which Peter was particularly interested, and regarded as his own, was recommending a two-year fellowship for a study of boomerangs (Newsletter 1974: 6).

As far as land rights were concerned, it is significant that the Institute did not make an official submission to the Aboriginal Land Rights Commission which reported in April 1974 and that the only person who gave the Institute as their affiliation was Noel Wallace, a charming, if idiosyncratic, independent researcher from time to time supported by the Institute.

THE INSTITUTE'S INITIAL INVOLVEMENT
IN LAND RIGHTS ISSUES

In 1979, Les Hiatt, then President of the Institute and the Chair of its Council, stated that the beginnings of the Institute's involvement lay in a conversation I had with him in Darwin on 15 August 1975, in which I mentioned that the Northern Land Council (NLC) was having difficulty in coping with its commitments because it had neither the funds nor the personnel to carry out the preparation of land claims, nor to make recommendations for the division of royalties (1982: 47). My concern arose from having been the Research Officer to the Aboriginal Land Rights Commission whose report led to the drafting of the the *Aboriginal Land Rights (Northern Territory) Bill* (Cth) (ALR(NT)Act) and from my continuing interest in the work of the land councils.[7] By September 1 Hiatt was consulting with both the NLC and the CLC (Central Land Council) about the problems facing the two councils in respect of matters anthropological, and later that month, the Council of the Institute formally endorsed 'the continuing involvement of the Institute [in]contacting fieldworkers to assist them to be of assistance to the NLC and CLC and any other similar bodies wherever land rights are involved' (Hiatt 1982: 48).

My concerns were borne out during the conduct of the Ranger Uranium Environmental Inquiry under Mr Justice Fox into the mining of uranium in the Kakadu area of western Arnhem Land (see Fox 1977). This Commission was appointed on 16 July 1975 to inquire into the environmental aspects of the mining of uranium. Because many of the submissions sought a recommendation against uranium mining, a first report was issued dealing with this issue. By the time that the report was delivered to the government on 28 October 1976 it was evident that the Aboriginal Land Rights Bill was likely to be passed and that its operation needed to be taken into consideration in any recommendations made by Fox. Under Section 11.2 of the *Aboriginal Land*

Rights (Northern Territory) Act 1976, passed on 9 December 1976 but not coming into operation until 26 January 1977, Mr Justice Fox was empowered to make a finding on Aboriginal traditional ownership in the Kakadu area as if he were an appointed Aboriginal Land Commissioner.

Submissions were made to the Inquiry in mid-December 1976 by the NLC in respect of Aboriginal traditional ownership in the Kakadu area. The NLC was only a fledgling body at this stage, having been established in 1974 but without any experience in conducting land claims, its main task up until this time having been to organise Aboriginal representation to the Woodward Commission, (Woodward 1974) through the conduct of meetings. Although an excellent anthropological report had been prepared by Ian Keen and George Chaloupka, Keen was then only a postgraduate research student at the Australian National University, and Chaloupka, a Northern Territory Sites Survey Officer. It was felt that it was important to involve more senior anthropologists, although this was to prove difficult. Further and more importantly, the formal presentation of the case to the Inquiry was so palpably poor and ill prepared that Fox actually gave the NLC the opportunity to make a further presentation. Along with other parties, Ian Keen, Basil Sansom and I made a joint submission to this second hearing in relation to the matter of succession in Darwin between 22 and 25 February 1977.[8]

The concerns of parliamentarians and the mining industry about the research side of land claims were different. They were concerned about the size and length of the task of identifying traditional owners and their country, since the Act gave the traditional owners a veto over mining. The latter clearly could not be asked if they supported mining until they, and their land interests, were identified (see Ucko 1977: 1029). By May 1977, when the Institute made a formal submission to the Joint Select Committee on Aboriginal Land Rights in the Northern Territory, it was able to say that it had assisted in finding and supporting the following people to prepare land claim reports. For the NLC:

Patrick McConvell: Yarralin Community, Victoria River Downs

John Bern: Roper River and Limmen Bight

John Avery: Borroloola areas

Ian Keen and George Chaloupka: Alligator Rivers areas

Basil Sansom: Humpty Doo area

Patrick McConvell: Kidman Springs and Jasper Gorge

George Chaloupka: Cobourg Peninsula

For the CLC:

Jim O'Connell: Alyawarra areas

Nicolas Peterson, Stephen Wild and Patrick McConvell: Warlpiri and Kartangarurru-
    Kurintji areas

And it was able to provide a comprehensive list, running over four and a half pages, of anthropologists who could be approached to assist in the documenting of title in lands that were handed back under Schedule 1 of the Act, without land claims, which meant that there had been no identification of traditional owners.

THE DIVERGENCE BETWEEN THE NLC AND THE CLC

From quite early on in the life of the land councils a difference in style and political orientation emerged between the NLC and CLC. Although the senior executive officers in both organisations were initially seconded from the Department of Aboriginal Affairs (DAA), the NLC, based in Darwin, always remained much more bureaucratic than the CLC and was seen by outsiders to be dominated by ex-DAA staff and to be politically unadventurous and conservative. By contrast the CLC in Alice Springs quickly saw itself as much more closely aligned with Aboriginal people's 'real' interests and prepared to take the government on. It rejected the bureaucratic model of organisation and prided itself on being more culturally appropriate and close to the Aboriginal traditional owners.[9] While there was some truth to this, and it partly reflected the fact that the NLC was under the control of its general manager while the CLC was colonised by leftwing lawyers from the Central Australian Aboriginal Legal Service (Eames 1983), it was also the case that the NLC was under enormous political pressure over uranium mining, while the CLC had, as its main opposition, an economically marginal pastoral industry, many members of which privately wanted nothing more than Aboriginal people to purchase their properties at inflated prices.

The CLC was, therefore, much less interested in having the Institute involved in its work in any formal way. It rejected a proposal that the CLC's anthropologist should be employed by the Institute, preferring to have its own in-house person. It did, however, ask the Institute for help in finding such a person. Later, when Peter was presenting evidence to the Joint Select Committee on Aboriginal Land Rights, he suggested that the case for having the anthropologists attached to the Institute was that it had an undoubted advantage in terms of checking the quality of the reports and investigations (Ucko 1977: 1059).

When Peter visited Alice Springs in June 1976 with Athol Chase, the Chair of the Material Culture Advisory Committee, and the Institute's Research Co-ordination Officer, Graham Barker it was not in respect of land claim issues but in response to the proactive demands of the CLC that museums return sacred objects and the working out of some process for doing this. As it turned out, land claim research and the matter of the task of identifying traditional owners was not even discussed as the meeting was overtaken by the introduction of the Land Rights Bill into Federal Parliament during their visit (Ucko 1976: 1).

The relationship with the CLC and the Institute remained an 'informal working relationship', as Hiatt describes it (1982: 50), with one exception, an agreement for Robert Layton to prepare a land claim for Uluru. For the NLC, which was under much greater pressure, a formal agreement was to emerge. The pressure for a more formal arrangement was precipitated by the politics surrounding the mining veto, the pressure for mining in the uranium province of western Arnhem Land and the awareness that the Northern Territory, which had in 1978 acquired partial statehood, had announced that it was going to discontinue the freeze on the alienation of unalienated Territory land after August 1980. A consequence of this change was that it raised the possibility of the remaining unalienated land being made unclaimable. This gave an urgency to land claim research and finding people to prepare the claims. Finding people had often been problematic, mainly because for anthropologists employed by institutions it was difficult to get time off to do the field research. It was these circumstances that resulted in the agreement between the NLC and the Institute in April 1979, after protracted negotiations, for the Institute to take responsibility for finding people to research the claims. To help him in these negotiations, Peter had set up a largely internal committee to advise him on the terms of the agreement.

In May 1979 the Institute organised a Land Claims Workshop with the help of the newly appointed Research Coordinator, Myrna Tonkinson, who had taken over from Graham Barker. The workshop brought together anthropologists and lawyers with experience in claims to share their knowledge with those yet to become involved, and to talk about the expectations and the nature of the collaboration, the latter an issue that has become of ever-increasing importance.[10] A wide range of technical issues were canvassed, but much discussion centred around the Act's definition of traditional owner and whether so-called managers could be contemplated for inclusion in this category, if that were empirically valid.

In his introductory speech to the workshop, Hiatt referred to the fact that there were criticisms of the role the Institute was now playing in the land claims process. Some of these criticisms harked back to the establishment of the Institute and the explicit understanding that its charter was to deal only with Aboriginal culture, and not become involved in policy and practical issues. In his address Hiatt canvassed a number of other issues dealing with professional ethics including whether academics should hire out their services, either for fee or free;[11] whether an agreement that committed the Institute consistently to one category of litigants in a series of forthcoming cases was acceptable and why the Institute should wish to make such a commitment (1982: 51). This provoked a misdirected *ad hominem* attack on Hiatt's alleged aloofness from politics and his concern with objectivity (see Cowlishaw 1983: 51–53 and Hiatt's reply 1983: 53–54).

By this time it was clear just what kind of political minefield the Institute was working in, for in 1978 the Institute filmmakers, David and Judith MacDougall, had caught Ian Viner, then Minister for Aboriginal Affairs and responsible for the Institute, on film making promises to the people of Aurukun that he was later forced to break. In a spirited move Peter supported the showing of this material on ABC television, in relation to the political struggle between the Federal and Queensland government over land issues, embarrassing the Minister. This caused a temporary freeze in relations and a delay in the Institute receiving its budget that year (see Bryson 2002: 64,74). On the surface it seemed that the freeze did not last when, in the next year, the Institute was given special funding by the government to monitor the social impact of uranium mining on Aboriginal people in the Northern Territory, which involved it in another highly political issue, that would have been seen to be way outside its charter in the pre-1974 days. Nevertheless, it was to become clear that there were people in government who were not happy about this active engagement of the Institute in such politically controversial areas as land claims.

In 1979 the Institute took a bold step at the recommendation of the Social Anthropology Advisory Committee, when it agreed to fund an anthropologist, Kim Akerman, to work with the Kimberley Land Council for three years, mainly on recording sites so they could be protected from mining activity. There was no land claim process in Western Australia, but in doing this the Institute was seen to be supporting Aboriginal people in their opposition to mining, especially because it was the time of the conflict at Noonkanbah station, between Amax, which wanted to drill for oil there, and the local Aboriginal people, who felt the drilling was too close to sacred sites on their station. Although the specific issue was the protection of sacred sites, it was plain to the nation at large that the real issues were related to land rights.

In 1980 Marcia Langton and I organised a major conference on Aboriginal land rights for the Institute's biennial meeting. It brought together Aboriginal people, anthropologists and lawyers for the first time on this topic and resulted in the publication of two volumes (Peterson 1981; Peterson and Langton 1983). It was a lively affair with two walkouts, one by Aboriginal people and the other led by Ron Berndt, keen to protest a case taking place in the courts that day. It must have added to the concerns of those government members who felt that the Institute was becoming too politically active. The result was that in 1981 an external review of the Institute was recommended by the parliament, leading to the establishment of the 'Inquiry into the Australian Institute of Aboriginal Studies' conducted by R.J. Walsh (1982), a professor of physiology. The terms of reference were:

> To examine and report on the activities of the Australian Institute of Aboriginal Studies in relation to its statutory functions of promoting Aboriginal studies and
>
> To make recommendation about the future conduct of the Institute's activities, taking into account the inter-relationship between the Institute and the proposed Museum of Australia, and the Australian Heritage Commission.

Recommendation 1.25 on land rights reads:

> The Institute, as a statutory authority, should not in future associate with submissions of claimants or other interested parties involved in hearings or negotiations under Aboriginal land rights legislation. The Institute, however, should continue to make the Library's facilities available to interested parties.

The body of the report sheds no light on the reasons for this recommendation other than to say:

> there have been reports that members of the staff of the Institute have been concerned with the actual preparation of claims on behalf of plaintiffs. At least two members of staff have been seconded to the Northern Lands Council specifically to prepare land claims for the plaintiffs. It is thought that the Institute should not in future associate with submissions of claimants. (Walsh 1982: 36)

Peter had already left the Institute before the Walsh review was established, and it looked as if the Institute's very active involvement in Aboriginal affairs would end with his departure. But this was to reckon without a change of government. When the Institute's new President wrote to members in 1984 it was clear that the new Labor government did not endorse this recommendation of the Walsh inquiry.

CONCLUSION

Peter made a huge contribution to the role and the significance of the Institute in Australian academic and public life and to enhancing the quality and the amount of research work carried out in Aboriginal studies, in both the universities and at the Institute. Arranging for the advisory committees to meet face to face was a key driver of the energy he injected into the Institute and Aboriginal studies generally. However, without detracting from his imagination, organisational skills and academic leadership, one can also say he was in the right place at the right time. He certainly came to the Institute with a whole lot of new ideas, but he was not attuned to the specificities and complexities of Aboriginal issues at the outset, although he recognised the need for the Institute to reinvent itself from the beginning and grasped every opportunity presented to enable it to do so.

With Jeremy Beckett as Chair, and Diane Barwick, Fay Gale, Charles Rowley and Bill Stanner on the Social Anthropology Advisory Committee, it had among its members people who between them did their own pioneering research in settled Australia from the 1950s, who wrote extensively about policy, history and social change and, who, in the case of Charles Rowley, was a well-known public advocate of Aboriginal rights. Why these members did not make the Social Anthropology Advisory Committee more of a ginger group is not entirely clear, but before Peter brought the committee members together they were working separately by correspondence. Anthropologists, for the most part, have not been in the advance guard in the push for Aboriginal rights, although they have nearly always been strong supporters. The repositioning of anthropology in its relation to Aboriginal people, and to applied research through the land claim process, was not the achievement of the Institute but a product of the sea changes, that took place in Australian society with the election of the Whitlam government that created possibilities and opportunities that even a year or two earlier had seemed remote, and of external pressures. The very considerable contribution made by Peter, and the Institute, was to seize the moment and facilitate the process.

ACKNOWLEDGEMENTS

I would like to thank Les Hiatt and Jacquie Lambert for their helpful comments.

NOTES

1. A third unpublished piece on the Institute's film unit, 'The creation of European Australian oral history' was circulated privately but not published. Earlier in 1978 he had written a review of Australian Aboriginal studies in retrospect and prospect.
2. Absent from the references in this paper is Berndt (1981) although one might be forgiven for thinking that it had some influence on it.
3. Recognition should here be given to the Aboriginal Housing Panel of the Royal Institute of Architects in Australia which had as its director an anthropologist, although the people it employed were architects.
4. The mining industry was the most public face of the opposition to land rights and through its exploration programmes, the industry most likely to damage sacred sites.
5. Five of the six signatories of the letter were Aboriginal people: Terry Widders, Gary Williams, Lyn Thompson, Bob Bellear and Len Watson. The sixth signatory was Peter Thompson.
6. The name of the letter was taken from two common moiety totems found among Aboriginal groups in southeastern Australia.
7. The Northern and Central Land Councils were established in 1974, two years before the ALR(NT)Act became law, in order to facilitate representation of Aboriginal views to the Commission.
8. This submission relates to an issue that has turned out to be central to most land claims and native title applications (see Peterson, Keen and Sansom 1977).
9. In the early days this went so far as to reject any kind of centrally organised filing system, the floor of the room of the person working on an issue, being the preferred locality for files.
10. The recent decision in *Jango v Northern Territory of Australia* (No 2) [2004] FCA 1004 has underlined the complete dominance of the native title proceedings by the legal profession as a result of the 1998 amendments to the Native Title Act 1993 requiring that the normal rules of evidence apply in native title cases. This requirement has only come to be enforced rigidly with the Jango decision.

11. The first claims were done by anthropologists who saw compiling the claim as a form of reciprocity for the people they had been working with and so did not seek payment other than for field expenses. Subsequently some anthropologists felt they should be paid as consultants in the same way as the lawyers working on the claims were. This was resisted by many anthropologists but increasingly the land councils insisted on paying people in order to gain greater control over them. This then led to tensions about the rates of pay and the comparison with the lawyers working on the cases who were paid a great deal more, but were almost entirely dependent on the work done by the anthropologists.

REFERENCES

Berndt, R. (1981) 'A long view: some personal comments on land rights' *Australian Institute of Aboriginal Studies Newsletter*, 16: 5–20.

Bryson, I. (2002) *Bringing to Light: A History of Ethnographic Filmmaking at the Australian Institute of Aboriginal and Torres Strait Islander Studies*, Canberra: AIATSIS Report Series.

Cowlishaw, G. (1983) 'On "The role of the Institute in land claims research" ', *Australian Aboriginal Studies*, 1: 51–53.

Eames, G. (1983) 'The Central Land Council: the politics of change,' in *Aborigines, Land and Land Rights*, N. Peterson and M. Langton (eds), Canberra: AIAS, pp. 268–277.

Fox, R. (1977) *Ranger Uranium Environmental Inquiry: Second Report*, Canberra: Australian Government Publishing Service.

Hiatt, L. (1980) Farewell speech to Peter Ucko, Principal of AIAS on relinquishing his principalship, Manuscript in AIATSIS library, Canberra.

Hiatt, L. (1982) 'The role of the Institute in land claims research', *Australian Institute of Aboriginal Studies Newsletter*, 18: 47–53.

Hiatt, L. (1983) 'Reply to Dr Cowlishaw', *Australian Aboriginal Studies*, 1: 53–54.

Peterson, N. (1981) *Aboriginal Land Rights, A Handbook*, Canberra: AIAS.

Peterson, N. and Langton, M (eds) (1983) *Aborigines, Land and Land Rights*, Canberra: AIAS.

Peterson, N., Keen, I. and Sansom, B. (1977) 'Succession to land: primary and secondary rights to Aboriginal estates', in *Official Hansard Report of the Joint Select Committee on Aboriginal Land Rights in the Northern Territory*, 19 April: 1002–1014, Canberra: Government Printer.

Ucko, P. (1976) 'Report on the meeting of the Central Land Council', Manuscript 2328, Canberra: AIATSIS Library.

Ucko, P. (1977) 'Submission to the Joint Select Committee on Aboriginal Land Rights in the Northern Territory', in the *Transcript of Evidence of the Australian Parliamentary Joint Select Committee on Aboriginal Land Rights in the Northern Territory*, pp.1029–1064. Canberra: Government Printer.

Ucko, P. (1978) 'Australian Aboriginal studies: retrospect and prospect', *Survival International Review*, 3(3): 18–20.

Ucko, P. (1983) 'Australian academic archaeology: Aboriginal transformations of its aims and practices', *Australian Archaeology*, 16: 11–26.

Ucko, P. (1985) 'Australian Aborigines and academic social anthropology' in *The Future of Former Foragers: Australia and Southern Africa*, C. Schrire and R. Gordon (eds), Cambridge, MA: Cultural Survival Inc, pp. 63–73.

Walsh, R. (1982) *Report of the Review of the Australian Institute of Aboriginal Studies*, Canberra: Australian Government Publishing Service.

Woodward, E. (1974) *Aboriginal Land Rights Commission: Second Report*, Canberra: Australian Government Publishing Service.

CHAPTER 5

PETER UCKO AND THE WORLD ARCHAEOLOGICAL CONGRESS (WAC)

Michael Day

Today the WAC is one of the leading international organisations in archaeology. It was not always so. Indeed it came as a shock to realise that a generation of young archaeologists has grown up since the birth of WAC who may be unaware of the furore that accompanied that event in 1986 and of the pivotal role of Peter Ucko in its conception, gestation and continued success.

For many years the only truly international organisation to stage regular congresses in the field of archaeology was the International Union of Prehistoric and Protohistoric Sciences (IUPPS). This was an association with strong European representation and French was its official language. Congresses were held every five years to allow archaeologists to meet and to give papers on archaeological science. In October 1981 the X IUPPS Congress that was held in Mexico was not a success. It was poorly organised and poorly attended to such an extent that the future of the Congresses was called into question. The situation was so serious that three British members of the IUPPS Council were asked if the next Congress, slated for 1986, could be held in Britain on the grounds that Britain would do a better job.

Peter had recently returned from Australia and was newly appointed to the Chair of Archaeology in Southampton. He was approached in 1981 to organise and run the 1986 congress in London taking on the role of National Secretary. He agreed, with initial reluctance and only after laying down several conditions. These included an assurance that there would be meaningful participation by Third World and Fourth World (indigenous) peoples, express arrangements for young archaeologists and students and finally that the academic sessions would be held outside London. This was agreed. In 1982 the XI IUPPS Congress was formally offered to Britain.

The Congress that he envisaged was innovative and would set it apart from any previous international meeting in the field. He dismissed the usual format of 'preferred' papers, in which individual participants are given 10 minutes to show a few slides, in favour of sessions organised around agreed themes. Each participant was obliged to submit a pre-circulated paper that would be discussed under the chairmanship of a theme organiser. Subsequently the papers would form the chapters of a book. Advances on the books would help to pay for the participation of Third and Fourth world colleagues as well as students.

The themes that were chosen were not the usual 'stones and bones' archaeology but new developing subjects that related the past to the present. Themes such as 'Cultural Attitudes to Animals', 'Multiculturalism and Ethnicity in the Archaeological Record' and 'The Social and Economic Context of Technological Change' were chosen and session chairmen selected. In other words a revolution was planned in the way that archaeology was to be presented and discussed. It was an exciting prospect that was geared to new approaches, a younger generation and an inclusive view of archaeology.

The framework of the Congress was built, therefore, on the foundations of set and agreed themes within a broadened approach to archaeology and strong representation from the Third and Fourth Worlds. It was accepted that these people were not always 'archaeologists' in the traditional sense but people who are culturally in touch with their pasts in their daily lives, people who would previously have never dared to attend such a meeting.

The planning of the Congress proceeded throughout 1983 with the circulation of the First Announcement and many meetings of the Executive and National Committees. There were fund-raising efforts and more meetings throughout 1984. Things were progressing well under Peter's guidance and with his customary energy. This was destined not to last. It was not as though Peter and the Congress organisers were unaware that a multicultural, multiracial Congress might be affected by political considerations, but it seems that in 1984 nobody had fully realised the effects that the worsening political situation in the Republic of South Africa could have on academic life two years later.

The abhorrent and cruel policy of apartheid, or separate development, in the Republic of South Africa had led to repressive laws that sanctioned state sponsored racism. Unscientific and arbitrary racial 'classification' was applied and South African black and mixed race (coloured) people were denied rights of residence other than in defined areas and were forbidden to enter into mixed marriages. Organisations such as the African National Congress (ANC) were becoming more active and militant within South Africa at this time and unrest increased. As a result of this the Pan African Association of Prehistory and Related Studies, representing the whole of Africa, had urged its members to have no contact with South African colleagues. When this news reached the Executive Committee Peter clearly saw the storm clouds ahead.

By 1985 a State of Emergency was declared in the Republic of South Africa since rioting had led to dozens of deaths and the detention without trial of many hundreds of black and coloured people. The South African press was muzzled. The UN called for mandatory sanctions against South Africa but they were vetoed by Britain and the USA. Later voluntary sanctions were agreed while Britain and the USA abstained. The Anti-Racism Committee of Southampton University's Students' Union raised the problem locally followed by the City of Southampton and the Southampton Branch of the Association of University Teachers. Nationally, the Anti-Apartheid Movement and others began to voice their disapproval of the possibility that South African archaeologists could come to the Congress and be welcomed. It was made clear that facilities would be withdrawn and that demonstrations would take place to such an extent that the Congress would be disrupted. In addition, it became clear that many participants from the developing world would be forbidden to come by their governments or local organisations if South Africans were present, a circumstance that struck at the heart of the intentions of the organisers of the Congress. It appeared that only a ban on the participation of South African colleagues would allow the XI IUPPS Congress to take place in peace and harmony with the wide representation that Peter envisaged.

The principal argument against a ban rested on the concept of 'academic freedom' being interpreted as being above politics, and that anybody who wished to attend should be welcomed by the host nation regardless of race, creed, philosophy etc. It was believed, at first, that this was enshrined in the constitution of the IUPPS. A little research showed that this was not the case. There was only a pious statement to the effect that scholars from all countries should collaborate. Despite this a strong body of opinion felt that to deny attendance to South African scholars, both black and white, for pragmatic reasons, was morally wrong and would amount to giving in to blackmail and threats of disruption and even violence. Pressures were mounting and other organisations were beginning to face the same problems. A ban on South African participation in many international meetings, in other fields, was being considered by their organisers.

The Chairman of the WAC Executive Committee was Professor John Evans and Peter was the Secretary. Professor John Evans was also President of the IUPPS and thus a clear conflict of interest was looming. Time was running out for a decision to be taken by the Executive on whether a ban was to be imposed since the Final Announcement of the Congress was in draft. At a tense and emotional private meeting the situation was discussed. Up to this point the position of the Chairman was that he would not continue if *anyone* was banned but he did not confront the pragmatic problems of that principled stand. Meanwhile the screw tightened, in that Southampton City Council confirmed in writing that all support of the council would be withdrawn if South African participation were allowed. The Swedes, the Nigerians and the Indians indicated that they could not take part if there was no ban. The Executive Committee bowed to the pressure since cancellation would mean bankruptcy, and transfer of the Congress to another venue would only lead to the same problems. It was agreed that South African names would be omitted from the Final Announcement.

The outcome was predictable. Many senior figures in America such as the late Professor Desmond Clark, Professor Carmel Schrire and Professor Lewis Binford were outraged and campaigned against the Congress. A detailed and reasoned letter from Professor Philip Tobias asked the Executive to reconsider their decision. His reputation as a fierce and courageous opponent of the apartheid regime from within as a South African citizen demanded a detailed reply by the Executive Committee. It was forthcoming and penned by Peter Ucko. He set out the position and the alternatives and sought to assure that the decision had not been taken lightly.

The local and national press was now beginning to take an interest and *Nature, The Times Higher Education Supplement* and *The Times* newspaper carried letters and articles, many taking issue with the decision, but some such as the Association of University Teachers were supportive. A meeting of the National Committee was convened and was virtually unanimous in its support for the Executive Committee. The Chairman, Professor John Evans, was instructed, as Chairman of the IUPPS, to convene a meeting of the International IUPPS Executive Committee in London on 13 December 1985. His dilemma was due to his various roles in this whole problem. Not only was he Chairman of the IUPPS but he was also President of the Society of Antiquaries, who deplored the action of WAC in a resolution passed after he vacated the chair at a meeting but also absented himself from the discussion and the vote. Later he allowed the meeting of the IUPPS Executive Committee to be moved to Paris and postponed until January 1986, a grave disadvantage, as pointed out by Sir David Wilson, a leading member of the National Executive.

The meeting in Paris, were it not so serious, could be described in terms of farce. Every obstacle that could be found by the Secretary General Jacques Nenquin was put in the way of the WAC delegation. These included the insistence that all the proceedings should be conducted in French, raising objections (later overcome) to an official translator as well as the refusal to allow Peter to have his secretary by his side to help him find papers in his voluminous files. The Secretary General conducted the meeting. There were seven voting members present and others, like Professors Desmond Clark and Philip Tobias, representing somewhat dubious interests. The meeting lasted for a whole day with no meeting of minds. Peter brilliantly defended the position of the British National Executive decision to ban South African participation but to no avail. Late in the day the Secretary General cut the discussion short and read from a prepared statement culminating in the following sentence: 'Therefore the Executive Committee refuses to recognise the Southampton meeting as the IUPPS Congress.'

The British delegation left the room but the President stayed behind. It later transpired that the Secretary General had broken down in tears and that the President had remained seated at the table. He later resigned from the International Executive Committee. A bitter *Times* leader suggested that if WAC went ahead alone it would be 'a rump congress attended by a disreputable group of British Communists and "Third World" archaeologists', a jibe resented by archaeologists to this day.

At this point Peter could see that cancellation was looming but he was determined to try again for the sake of the Third World colleagues whom he was determined not to let down. He devised two possible strategies. One was to ask the South Africans to withdraw voluntarily and to include a full discussion of apartheid within the Congress. The second was to approach all those who opposed South African presence to withdraw their opposition on this *one* occasion so that the ban could be removed and similarly to agree to a full discussion within the meeting. Neither of the two suggestions gained the support needed despite valiant efforts and serious negotiation. Finally, on 6 February 1986 the National Anti-Apartheid Movement, on instructions from the ANC in Lusaka, said that they were not willing to make an exception and allow the Congress to accept South African scholars.

The Executive met on 8 February 1986 at 10:00 am at the British Museum under the Chairmanship of Sir David Wilson. They were informed that the compromise suggestions were not acceptable to all parties. The procedure to be followed at the National Committee was agreed. The National Committee followed immediately and was attended by 45 people. There were two options only to discuss. One was to continue with an independent Congress or to cancel. Thirty-two members spoke and the discussion was temperate and cool with opposing views in about equal numbers from both sides. The meeting closed at 12:45 pm. The Executive reconvened almost immediately.

Peter argued strongly that the Congress should not be cancelled for three reasons (1) to show support for the Third World (2) to show that we would not be a 'rump' Congress without the IUPPS title and (3) for financial reasons. The debate was anguished and continued until 4:00 pm when Peter was given one final chance to put his arguments. After he finished there was an agonising silence. This was broken when the Chairman Sir David Wilson, Colin Renfrew and Leslie Alcock resigned from the Executive Committee and from the Company that had been formed to run the Congress. The remaining members of the Executive, including Peter and Derek Hayes, a lawyer, were left to run the Congress without a vote having been taken. In a sense the rest is history. It was urgent that new Directors were found for the Board of the Company and Peter approached this task with care. He obtained acceptances from Thurstan Shaw, Tim Champion, Stephen Shennan, Ian Hodder, David Harris, Michael Rowlands, Juliet Clutton-Brock, Andrew Fleming and myself. Later Leslie Alcock joined, having changed his mind about his previous resignation. At the first meeting I was elected Chairman of the newly constituted Board of Directors. Our first task was to issue a press statement that the WAC was going ahead as planned under its own name. Later 3,000 notices went out to potential participants explaining what had happened and inviting them to Southampton in September 1986. Peter had little over six months in which to complete the programme, organise accommodation, arrange simultaneous translation, to encourage attendance, adjust budgets, distribute pre-circulated papers – the list was endless but it was done.

The day of the Congress dawned dry and sunny and they came! Over 1,000 archaeologists from almost 100 countries arrived. Many countries had never sent a representative before to a Congress and many participants had never left their own countries before. It was an emotional experience for all of those who had fought for the survival of the

Congress to see people streaming into the sessions and taking part in the discussions of the 20 volumes of pre-circulated papers from which 22 books were finally published.

The final Plenary Session discussed motions submitted by many of the 500 people from 62 countries who attended. One motion from the dais proposed that a Steering Committee be set up to discuss with the IUPPS the views of the Plenary Session and to consider the formation of a new world archaeological organisation should the joint discussion fail. This motion was accepted and eventually led to the foundation of the WAC as an international organisation that built on the success of Southampton and now thrives (see Stone, Chapter 7, in this book, for an account of how it has managed to survive). Since the first Congress in Southampton there have been full Congresses in Venezuela, India, South Africa and America as well as a number of successful single topic Inter-Congresses.

Without a shadow of doubt Peter's courage, tenacity and conviction in the face of bitter opposition was the key factor in the survival of the first WAC but he would be the first to say that he was magnificently supported by those immediately around him, Jane Hubert, Paul Crake, Caroline Jones, Peter Stone, David Bellos and many others. His capacity to inspire, to lead and to induce affection is unsurpassed.

REFERENCE

Ucko, P. (1987) *Academic Freedom and Apartheid*, London: Duckworth.

CHAPTER 6

ARCHAEOLOGICAL OVERTHROWS

The 1980s Seen Through the Rear Window

Neal Ascherson

Almost 20 years ago, the small, contented planet Archaeology was hit by three comets. Since then nothing has been the same and few familiar perspectives remain. Within a few years, which in Britain were concentrated into the 1980s, this triple impact metamorphosed the material prospects for archaeology, the profession's relationship to society and, most important of all changes, its self-understanding.

One impact was privatisation. Here, for better or worse, Mrs Thatcher's Britain led the world. Only a decade before, Martin Biddle's plan for a co-ordinated rescue archaeology had foreseen something like the opposite: a British archaeological service, with elaborate regional structures and promotion prospects – almost a 'National Past Service' in uniform (Biddle and Thomas 1975). Now, quite suddenly, both field and academic archaeologists found themselves the employees or directors of commercial companies, jostling to tender competitively for a developer's contract. The profession became much bigger as jobs multiplied. But traditional research archaeology, now starved of public funding, grew rarer.

The second impact, rather more gradual but requiring less than a decade to take its full effect, was the victorious spread of the 'Heritage' concept. In a sense – and this was one of those paradoxes about power distributed and power concentrated which were typical of the Thatcher phenomenon – Heritage licensed the state to repossess the control over the past which it was relinquishing through privatisation. In one way, this was not new: it was a hundred years since the official scheduling of ancient monuments had begun in Britain. The fresh element was the energising ideology which was adopted for the care of the past during the 1980s and 1990s; material relics of the past were now subsumed into the new 'public culture', which was being built around purposes of political and commercial exploitation. As Robert Hewison wrote, 'when the arts are captured by public policy, they become subject to its ruling concerns, which are primarily economic' (Hewison 1995: 305).

Highly authoritarian, the 'public-culture' ideology encouraged government to 'commission' Heritage. Selected relics of material culture (later, whole cultural landscapes) were gazetted as official items of the national past, and a surprised public was commanded to respect these 'heirlooms' and hand them on in good condition to successor generations. 'Some day, son, all this will be yours – whether you want it or not!' Rapidly, a heritage-management profession sprang up with a career structure twined into all levels of local government, into new museums and theme parks and into flexible commercial consultancies. Here too, jobs open to those with archaeological training began to appear in substantial numbers.

It was the third impact which most deserves the simile of an astral collision. Nobody could have foreseen that the XI Congress of the International Union of Prehistoric and Protohistoric Sciences at Southampton in 1986 would explode: a prolonged and compound blast out of whose wreckage a quite new structure, the World Archaeological Congress (WAC), would emerge. This is not the place to retell that story, passionately recorded in Peter Ucko's *'Academic Freedom and Apartheid: The Story of the World*

Archaeological Congress' (Ucko 1987; and see also Day, Chapter 5, in this book). But to re-read that book, as I did the other day, is to recall just how fierce and exhausting the struggle was. Ucko, as host and organiser, intended the Congress to inaugurate a revolutionary 'world' model of archaeology, no longer Eurocentric or narrowly positivist but open to dynamic interpretations from other continents and to indigenous understandings of a living past. The dilemma which suddenly blocked his path was painful but historic. In order to make sure that participants from the post-colonial continents could attend and that the vision of a world archaeology could be realised, it became clear that he would have to respect the contemporary cultural boycott of apartheid South Africa. Ucko chose to take this course. But when he disinvited South African scholars, a deluge of abuse fell on him as senior European and American archaeologists accused Ucko of betraying 'academic freedom'. The profession split, and many shocking, hysterical things were said by people who do not now like to remember their own words. To his eternal credit, and under appalling pressure, Ucko stuck to his guns. WAC was born.

Since then, WAC has established itself as the leading global association of archaeologists (see Stone, Chapter 7, in this book for the subsequent history of the WAC). Many of those who abandoned or condemned the Southampton Congress have quietly made their peace with the new body, and its broad philosophy has been widely accepted in Britain and in most of the post-colonial continents. But it is far too early to claim that WAC's cluster of ideas has conquered the globe. In much of Central and Eastern Europe, for example, many archaeological establishments remain defensive, suspicious of political involvement and of imaginative leaps in theory and often constrained by remnants of the old 'culture-historical' approach. (It should be noted, though, that those establishments are being slowly invaded by younger generations more open to theory and to political self-awareness. See for example Härke 2000; Halle and Schmidt 2001). In the USA, which was so fertile with radical theories in the 1960s, there is now a preoccupation with practicalities and a distinct distrust of postmodern speculation. Nevertheless, anyone sampling the contents lists of recent academic journals, or the topics of sessions and contributions at archaeological conferences, or even the information panels and display strategies of new museums, must at once register how widely the family of ideas and practices associated with 'World Archaeology' has spread through the bloodstream of the profession in the years since 1986.

What are these ideas? Some of them could be summarised in a few slogans: 'Archaeology is about now, not then. Archaeology is more about the present than the past, and more about the living than the dead. Indeed, it is primarily an activity conducted by the living among the living and even on the living.' The implication here is that, like any other social activity conducted in the present, archaeology is inescapably political. As two Greek practicants wrote a few years ago, 'Recently we have experienced the dusk of the era of political innocence in archaeology … We cannot underestimate archaeologists' significant contribution to the social construction of the past and its prominent role in the negotiation of identity roles and power relations in modern society' (Hamilakis and Yalouri 1999). I wrote at about the same time:

> An elderly Victorian science, still convinced that academic freedom guaranteed it immunity from the struggles of the rest of the human race, met its Waterloo in 1986 at the Southampton congress … archaeology was a profession bearing all the obligations and rights of any other social actor in the present. It was at least as political as banking, civil engineering or commercial publishing. Often, in fact, it was more sharply and immediately political than any of them. (Ascherson 2000)

More interesting questions arise when those three astral impacts are related to each other. What is the connection, if any, between the concerns of World Archaeology, the spread of the Heritage Industry and the introduction of market-driven contract archaeology which – in England – was defined by the policy guidance document PPG 16?

I think the connections are manifold. It would be ridiculous to say that archaeology only emerged into 'the real world' at Southampton – ridiculous, because the profession was already being evicted from the unreal world by powerful currents of political change. Almost a century of intimate involvement with the nation-state – in the course of which archaeology was instituted as a scientific profession enjoying academic immunity in return for decorating the imperial monument with trophies and improving the state's successive myths of origin – was coming rapidly to an end. Now archaeology, like many other departments of national culture, was cut off with a penny and booted out into the snow. This had three results. The first was the replacement of the state by the market as the source of funds, and the consequent changes in priorities. The second was that archaeology was offered the chance radically to rethink its purpose. No longer privileged servants of the state, both field and theoretical archaeologists were forced to form a relationship with the public 'out there', to take seriously local views about how sites and monuments should be treated and in general to acquire the habit of promoting themselves and their schemes through public contact and the media.

The third result, also a challenge to the very 'identity' of archaeology, was that the newly disinherited profession had to witness the commodification of the past by the state-sponsored Heritage industry. The Heritage authorities no longer treated historic or prehistoric sites as primarily objects of research. Instead, they were rebranded as components of a national resource, to be exploited for purposes as various as 'combatting exclusion', 'community-building' or merely promoting tourism. Aneurin Bevan[1] once observed that 'this island is almost made of coal and surrounded by fish'. By the end of the 1980s, the islanders had fished their cod and haddock to the verge of species collapse and, with the assistance of riot police, had closed down their coal mines. But now the Heritage promoters came to the rescue. They pointed out that the island was entirely covered by past: a sort of precious guano thousands of years thick which could be strip-mined, sold to visitors in briquette form or used as fuel to power social regeneration.

This raised in a new form the question: 'Who owns the past?', a question constantly put in the debates and literature generated by the Southampton Congress. The Heritage apparatus returned a thoroughly nationalist answer: We (meaning the imaginary collective formed by the nation-state and its subjects) own the past. Foreigners must not have it, but we Britons have a duty – inherited, inescapable as the Shirt of Nessus – to maintain it. Critics of Heritage suggested that 'we' in reality meant only the combination of state and quango bureaucracies, which in the 1980s acquired an administrative monopoly over 'ancient monuments' that had never existed before. It was not apparent that ordinary people, although burdened with Heritage duties, had been offered any corresponding Heritage rights over how items of this patrimony should be commissioned, decommissioned, interpreted or marketed. Whoever owned this public past, it was not the public.

Archaeologists, accordingly, have found themselves pushed in intriguing directions. Many, of course, have found work in the posts and opportunities created by Heritage. Others have recognised the degree of hypocrisy in that slogan of 'we are all the owners', and have become much more interested in what the public, national but especially local, really do think about the past and its treatment. Ideas about the authenticity of local interpretations, first developed in Australia or Africa, turn out to apply with almost equal force to 'indigenous Europeans'. It was once unthinkable that peasants looting archaeological sites in Afghanistan or Iraq could be regarded as anything but assassins of 'world heritage' (only two years ago, an American professor visiting Iraq said that the only way she could see the looting being stopped was for someone/the authorities to shoot some looters). But today it has become at least acceptable to study why looters do what they do and what they think they are doing. Even in contemporary England, the Portable Antiquities Scheme has been trying to change perception of the metal-detector clubs from the image of criminals to that of potential archaeological collaborators with a genuine interest in the past. There is enlightened self-interest in that, naturally: to enlist 'treasure seekers' as archaeological auxiliaries is to reduce the loss of the profession's raw material. But (I like to think) there is also an element of self-criticism or self-doubt here. University-trained experts, it's now acknowledged, are not the only people capable of appreciating the material culture of the past, and 'ordinary punters' may not go metal-detecting exclusively out of greed for cash.

It seems, then, as if these three impacts have been complementary, each in some ways enhancing the effect of the others. Unexpectedly enough, both privatisation and the Heritage industry have helped to emancipate archaeology from the insulated, interconnecting enclosures of state patronage and academia. 'Emancipated' archaeologists, in turn, have given parts of the Heritage landscape a distinctly subversive allure, inviting visitors to form their own interpretations in the best post-processual manner. Eviction from state patronage, moreover, has given the profession a chance at last to look back at itself and at the purposes which it has been made to serve over the preceding century or so. This reflexive view reveals some very large unanswered questions. Can archaeology still remain a 'profession' under the new suzerainty of market forces and the patronage of big private developers? Or is it now better regarded as a trade, entitled – as plumbers and estate agents are – to a code of working ethics, but not to a priestly authority over whatever the soil may conceal? Close to that question is another. In these new conditions, does the old 'unity of theory and praxis' which has made archaeology seem so attractive – the winter spent in the university teaching and breeding ideas, the summer spent in open-air fieldwork – still make sense? Or can it be that a single profession is now beginning to divide into two: the qualified itinerant field-worker moving from one rescue job to another, and the academic ideologist who digs only into the Internet?

On balance, the crisis of the 1980s did archaeology a great deal of good. Supports were knocked away but barriers were knocked down. One major consequence was that the interdisciplinary frontiers separating archaeology, anthropology, sociology and even geography fell open and permitted the free movement of people and ideas. In turn, it was this interdisciplinary ferment which brewed up the new specialism of public archaeology.

The teaching of this subject has become increasingly fashionable in recent years. And yet only a generation ago, public archaeology was a course almost 'unknown to science', which some university veterans at first suspected to be a trendy amalgam of leftish, postmodern correctness. As the editor of *Public Archaeology*, the journal which has been reporting and exploring this subject for almost five years, I can testify that it is no such thing. The concerns of public archaeology courses meet those of the students, who enter university with large and justified questions about what archaeology thinks it is doing and where it draws ethical lines. The courses also prepare students for the moral and intellectual pressures of the market-driven environment in which they are going to seek employment and undertake research. They learn how the profession arose and how it now operates, socially and politically. But they also learn that other, very different systems for doing archaeology are possible.

All the same, the fashion is not universal. A recurrent problem in my own editorial work is that the very phrase 'public archaeology' means different things in different cultures. It seems to have originated in the USA, possibly with C.R. McGimsey who wrote a book in 1972 with that title. At that time it meant – roughly – an archaeology financed by public monies which recognised its social responsibility and conducted its operations in ways which were open to local people and contained some element of wider educational purpose. A comparable phrase in the USA might be 'public broadcasting', as in the PBS networks. It remains a pretty non-controversial concept, and carries little obtrusive ideological baggage.

If that is what 'public archaeology' is still held to mean in America, it means something rather different in Britain and – increasingly – over much of northern Europe. The distinction is well caught in an exchange some years ago between Francis P. McManamon, chief archaeologist of the US National Park Service, and Cornelius Holtorf, at the time teaching in Cambridge. McManamon had written a paper on 'archaeological messages and messengers' which, in American terms, pushed boldly at the conventional envelope by insisting on the importance of public outreach and strongly urging that archaeologists take a respectful interest in local and/or indigenous views.

> It is important to recognise that many people may have views of the past and places associated with it that differ substantially from those held by archaeologists with their research-based knowledge. Using such public perceptions about heritage effectively may be crucial for site preservation and obviously must be dealt with in order to ensure accurate interpretation programmes. (McManamon 2000a)

But for Holtorf, this attitude, open and liberal as it appeared, was in fact far too prescriptive. McManamon's language, he declared, 'frightens me'. He claimed to detect an assumption that only the professionals were entitled to lay down the terms of archaeology, while the opinions of others were important only instrumentally insofar as they contributed to the achievement of the professionals's ends. Holtorf suggested that many issues – he cited 'the alleged non-renewability of archaeological resources', the supposed urgency of 'rescuing' sites from developers, the enigma of authenticity and the ethical assessment of the illicit antiquities trade as examples – were in intense dispute. They deserved proper discussion between archaeologists and others. 'To my mind, ideologically sound declarations that proclaim definitive "answers" and aim for discursive closure are not helpful' (Holtorf 2000).

McManamon defended himself stoutly, insisting that he 'was not implying or proposing to initiate a "big brother" system of archaeological oversight'. But he reiterated his point that archaeologists were duty-bound actively to resist anything which threatened 'the archaeological record', including threats from 'alternative views' – by which he meant, among others, the views of collectors or of aboriginal peoples who blocked the practice of archaeology on their territory (McManamon 2000b).

Here, in a nutshell, is the difference between the two uses of the term 'public archaeology'. The American usage – admittedly more faithful to what the two words are usually held to mean – sees public archaeology as one pragmatic branch of the discipline among others: roughly, doing the sort of archaeology which involves interacting with the public. The British version, in contrast, has become a *Stoa* in which the most fundamental theories about the past, its exploitation and the political role of archaeology are questioned and investigated. Its academic courses certainly embody the WAC perception that archaeology is about 'now' rather than about 'then', and that its activities concern the living more than the dead. With that comes inevitably a leaning towards post-processual relativism, a new subjectivism which somehow has to be reconciled with an even more powerful emphasis on political and social responsibility. Students are taught, for instance, about hyperdiffusionist archaeo-fantasy and para-science, but shown how to recognise their internal contradictions and understand the strange compulsions which keep them popular. They discuss the often bizarre slogans and representations of archaeology found in the media. But they also learn that many – perhaps most – of these distortions actually emanate from archaeologists, who in their symbiosis with journalism have almost always been the manipulators rather than the manipulated. Public archaeology (British and North European style) is in short a bundle of apparently disparate concerns, bound together by the fact that they all raise ultimately ethical questions. As a sub-discipline, it is now well rooted and seeding itself across the landscape.

Twenty years on, is it possible that the impetus of those three great impacts is dying away? It would not be surprising. American archaeology had its flowering of creative theory in the 1960s. The UK became the most intellectually exciting place to do archaeology in the 1980s and 1990s. But many of the iconoclastic ideas and practices generated then have now become familiar, assimilated as almost obvious by new cohorts entering the profession. The teaching of public archaeology has its own momentum, it seems, and will continue to expand and flourish. Elsewhere, there may be a danger of a relapse into insularity. It is here that the struggle has to be fought: to defend the perception that a mainly Eurocentric archaeology is a branch of learning whose roots are inadequate, and which is doomed to wither. The future will be made by those who interpret their own dilemmas in the museums and fieldwork communities of Iraq or Kakadu, of Nunavut or Botswana or the Amazon basin or Sichuan. If men and women from such places no longer crowd the corridors of European centres of archaeology, as they have done since the revolutions of the 1980s, then we will know that 'The Force' of innovation is no longer with us.

NOTE

1. In a speech at Blackpool, 18 May 1945.

REFERENCES

Ascherson, N. (2000) 'Editorial', *Public Archaeology*, 1(1): 1–4.

Biddle, M. and N. Thomas (1975) *Archaeology and Government: A Plan for Archaeology in Britain*, RESCUE and Council for British Archaeology.

Härke, H. (ed.) (2000) *Archaeology, Ideology and Society: The German Experience*, Frankfurt am Main: Europäische Verlag der Wissenschaften.

Halle, U. and M. Schmidt (2001) 'Central and East European Prehistoric and Early historic research in the period 1933–1945', *Public Archaeology*, 1(4): 269–281.

Hamilakis, Y. and E. Yalouri (1999) 'Sacralising the past: cults of archaeology in modern Greece' *Archaeological Dialogues*, 6: 115–135, 154–160.

Hewison, R. (1995) *Culture and Consensus: England, Art and Politics Since 1940*, London: Methuen.

Holtorf, C. (2000) 'Engaging with multiple pasts: reply to Francis MacManamon', *Public Archaeology*, 1(3): 214–215.

McGimsey, C. (1972) *Public Archaeology*, New York: McGraw Hill.

McManamon, F. (2000a) 'Archaeological messages and messengers', *Public Archaeology*, 1(1): 5–20.

McManamon, F. (2000b) 'Promoting an archaeological perspective: a response to Cornelius Holtorf', *Public Archaeology*, 1(3): 216–219.

Ucko, P. (1987) *Academic Freedom and Apartheid: The Story of the World Archaeological Congress*, London: Duckworth.

CHAPTER 7

'ALL SMOKE AND MIRRORS ...' THE WORLD ARCHAEOLOGICAL CONGRESS, 1986–2004

Peter Stone

A shorter version of this chapter was published in *Archaeologies*, 2005.

I am still not sure why I had ventured into the Archaeology Departmental office at the University of Southampton, where I was registered as a part-time PhD student with Peter Ucko, one day in the summer of 1984. Whatever the reason, I can still hear Peter's voice call out from his smoke-filled room next door: 'Is that Pete? Send him in.' I took the then customary last gulp of fresh air before going in to hear Peter ask if I would take on a small job. He claimed that it would take an hour or so a week between then and 1986 and then a week of my time in 1986 and that 'it would look good on your CV'. He wanted me to become the Student Liaison Officer for the big conference he was organising – the XI Congress of the International Union of Prehistoric and Protohistoric Sciences. I was not sure what the role of a Student Liaison Officer would actually entail, and looking back on it I'm not at all convinced Peter did either. However, it sounded interesting and I said 'yes'. Little were either of us to know that that conversation would lead to my becoming a part of the Steering Committee that created the World Archaeological Congress (WAC), a member of the voluntary WAC Secretariat and, since 1998, WAC's Chief Executive Officer. With that short conversation, he changed my life.

Since the First Congress in 1986 in Southampton, UK WAC has achieved a considerable amount. As an 'insider', knowing how WAC functions, I frequently wonder how so much has been achieved. Many others believe there is a great edifice behind the public face of WAC, a large Secretariat steadily working away to support the elected Officers. I can still see the look of astonishment and incredulity on the face of Joan Gero, the Academic Secretary for WAC-5 held in Washington DC in June 2003, when she realised that this was not so: 'You mean it is *all* smoke and mirrors.' Joan had, along with, I suspect many others, assumed that there was some physical infrastructure to WAC that existed outside the Congresses, Inter-Congresses, the *One World Archaeology* series, the *World Archaeological Bulletin*, the WAC *Newsletter* and the other things in which WAC was involved. How else could so much actually be achieved?

In some respects we have to go back to the events of the mid-1980s, and in particular September 1986, to answer that question. What became the first WAC had been planned to be the XI Congress of the International Union of Prehistoric and Protohistoric Sciences (IUPPS), the main archaeological organisation affiliated to the United Nation's Educational, Scientific, and Cultural Organisation (UNESCO). Planning for the Congress appeared to be going well until the issue of the UN's total academic and cultural boycott of South Africa was raised – initially by the Students' Union at the University of Southampton.

The story of the Southampton Congress, the banning of South African and Namibian colleagues, the removal of IUPPS support for the meeting and the Congress's eventual success has been told elsewhere (Ucko 1987, and see Day, Chapter 5, in this book). However, the South African ban was not the only issue involved here, for while the established committees of the IUPPS had initially accepted the plans for the Congress, there had been an unspoken unease amongst many key individuals regarding some of the then innovative initiatives associated with the Congress. There had long been lip-service to the idea that IUPPS meetings should include archaeologists from all over the world but little, if anything, had been done to alter the almost entirely European and North American domination of IUPPS meetings. That the organisers of the Southampton Congress were going out of their way actively to encourage the rest of the world to attend and were seeking funding to support colleagues who otherwise had no opportunity of attending was a new departure that threatened the dominance of European and North American scholars, their methodologies, theories and interpretations. This unease was exacerbated by plans to discuss world archaeology not through narrow chronological and geographical sessions but within thematic blocks that would allow – indeed force – colleagues from around the world to discuss contributions from outside their normal expertise. That one of these Themes was entitled 'Objectivity in Interpretation' increased concern that the Southampton Congress was going to question the bastion of the European 'culture history' approach based on scientific 'fact' and reason, a concern exacerbated by the stated intention of the organisers to include representation of those groups *affected* by archaeology such as indigenous communities. The Southampton Congress, from the outset, had a particularly non-IUPPS feel and it is not too outrageous to suggest that IUPPS officials saw the debate over Academic Freedom as a welcome lifeboat, a suggestion made not through the rose-tinted spectacles of hindsight but on a reading of IUPPS conference programmes from both before and after the Southampton Congress, from my own knowledge of the discussions and meetings between the Southampton organisers and IUPPS officials in the years before 1986 and from meetings with IUPPS officials since 1986.

At the Plenary Session of the Southampton Congress speaker after speaker commented on the success of the Congress in bringing those involved in the study of the past from around the world together for the first time. The late Professor Bassey Andah from Nigeria commented: 'it is clear that the World Archaeological Congress has made a breakthrough in discussing and finding solutions to the practical problems of man understanding fellow man [*sic*]' (Andah 1987: 8). The indigenous archaeologist Jo Mangi from Papua New Guinea took up the thread:

> It is a pleasure to know that the hobby of the middle upper crust of Europe – of collecting and writing about their hobbies – [that] the pastime of the middle upper class of Europe is gone. It is a pleasure to be here and to say that archaeology has finally changed, thank God. (Mangi 1987: 10)

That Plenary Session entrusted a Steering Committee of senior archaeologists, but also including representatives for indigenous peoples, women and students/young archaeologists, to negotiate with the IUPPS or to 'consider the formation of a new world archaeological organisation in the event that joint discussions should prove unsuccessful' (Hodder 1987: 24).

The Steering Committee met three times and, at its last meeting in Venezuela in 1987, agreed 'the details of the main lines of the aims, structure and organisation of the new World Archaeological Congress' (Steering Committee minutes 1987: 10). This document was reproduced in the second issue of the *World Archaeological Bulletin (WAB)* the following year (WAB-2 1987: 6–11). The document, much of which was actually based on draft material developed by Jack Golson, reflected much that had been proposed at the 1986 Plenary Session in that it was based on individual membership with regional (and not country) representation on an elected Executive Committee that included both senior

Figure 7.1   Peter attempts a traditional English dance with Jo Mangi at the party at the end of WAC-1. *Credit*: Giles Gardner.

and junior members, with 'due regard to a balance between the sexes' (WAB-2 1988: 8) and had spaces specifically identified for indigenous members. 'Having taken these decisions it only remained for the Steering Committee to set in motion the arrangements for setting up the new organisation and to arrange two Inter-Congresses ... in 1990 it is hoped to hold the second World Archaeological Congress in Venezuela' (Day 1988: 11).

That simple statement, 'it only remained' is an interesting one and returns us to Joan Gero's 'smoke and mirrors'. What the Steering Committee had, understandably, failed to do was to identify or secure any practical means by which any of its suggestions could be delivered. The actual administration of the Steering Committee and the identification of funding for its members to travel to meet the production of the *Edited Version of the Plenary Session* (of the Southampton Congress), and the production of two issues of *WAB* had all been achieved by a small group of volunteers in Southampton led by Peter Ucko in his position as Secretary to the Steering Committee, on top of his new role as series editor for the *One World Archaeology* series of books coming from the Southampton Congress. Much was done by the late Caroline Jones, the young personal assistant that Peter had appointed to help run the Congress, who was kept on in employment for a few extra months to help with Steering Committee business, as the result of the generosity of a few WAC supporters who anonymously contributed to paying her salary. Caroline actually joined us again in 1988 'for two months at a time when the elections for the Executive had stretched the voluntary team beyond its capacity' (Anonymous 1989). Paul

Crake, the other full-time member of the WAC-1 secretariat, took on the editing of the first two *WAB*s and Peter Ucko and Jane Hubert both continued to commit themselves to the idea that was WAC.

The constituency for the new organisation had been identified by the organisers of the Southampton Congress, now referred to as WAC-1, as all those with a genuine interest in the past and this was enshrined within the document drafted by the Steering Committee (WAB-2 1988: 7) and later in the WAC Statutes (Article 4) as agreed by Council in 1990 (Statutes, 1990: 134). The Steering Committee set the scope of the organisation:

> ... beyond its essential academic functions and appreciates that archaeology has a social, as well as academic, responsibility ... [WAC] also recognises the importance of archaeological evidence about the past to the rights and aspirations of those directly affected by archaeology (Steering Committee minutes 19/20 October 1987: 12), but also identified several areas 'in no particular order' that were '... neither intended to be exhaustive nor exclusive' (Steering Committee minutes 19/20 October 1987: 11–12):

1. education about the past;
2. the role and control of the past in the creation of gender and group and regional and national identity;
3. the ownership, conservation and exploitation of the archaeological heritage;
4. the treatment and disposal of human remains;
5. the funding, organisation, control and choice of archaeological research projects;
6. the effects of archaeology on host communities;
7. the ethics of archaeological enquiry.

Thus was WAC created.

It was intended to run WAC's first Inter-Congress on *The Role of Cultural Centres/Culture Houses in the Presentation and Maintenance of Tradition*, in association with the Cultural Heritage sub-theme of the Waigani Seminar to be held in Port Moresby, Papua New Guinea in September 1998, but the meeting had to be cancelled at short notice in August 1998 when promised funding from UNESCO for the Seminar failed to materialise (Golson 1989: 1).

The second WAC meeting therefore was the Inter-Congress on *Archaeological Ethics and the Treatment of the Dead* held in South Dakota in August 1989. The Inter-Congress was organised by Larry Zimmerman, who had appeared very late on the scene at WAC-1, presenting a paper 'Made radical by my own: an archaeologist learns to accept reburial' in a session arranged after the ban on South African participation, entitled 'Material Culture and the Making of the Modern United States: Views from Native America', organised by Russell Handsman and Randy McGuire. Here were a group of American colleagues apparently overtly supporting the WAC stance over Apartheid South Africa by not only arriving in person in Southampton but also equating issues of exclusion of Native American understanding and control over the past with some of the exclusion of the majority in South Africa from their own history. It had been an exceptionally well attended and immensely thought-provoking session that totally vindicated Peter's view that the conference should be thematically organised with common issues being explored in a global framework.

Reburial was (and is) an extremely controversial issue, perhaps especially in the USA at that time, as American archaeological opinion was heavily divided over its response to demands from Native American groups for control over their ancestral remains held in museums and university laboratories. The meeting was held the year *before* the Native American Grave Protection and Repatriation Act (NAGPRA) became law and, while it may not have been a major factor in the decision to pass the law, it certainly provided American politicians and archaeologists with an international view on the issue. It is probably fair to say that the Inter-Congress cemented the opinion of many North American archaeologists, who had been actively and vociferously opposed to the Southampton Congress's adherence to the UN academic boycott of South Africa, that WAC was not only an extreme, but also a potentially dangerous, organisation.

The South Dakota Inter-Congress also provided the first opportunity for the newly elected Executive to meet and discuss the draft Statues and other urgent issues. One of these issues was what should happen to the WAC Charitable Company set up to organise WAC-1. The Company had a zero bank balance but was anticipating income from royalties from the *One World Archaeology* series. After considerable discussion the Executive unanimously agreed that the Company should continue, and 'for the present' continue to be based in England. The Executive further recommended that new Directors be appointed from the 'new' WAC organisation and that these Directors should be in a majority (Executive minutes 6 August 1998 Item 2a). This preponderance of Directors coming from those involved in the 'new' WAC organisation was accepted by the existing Directors and is still the expectation although mainly because the Directors frequently meet with only original members present owing to financial difficulties of getting non-UK residents to meetings.

The voluntary Secretariat in Southampton was supplemented in the lead up to both WAC-2, in Venezuela, and WAC-3, in India, by the short-term appointment of recent archaeology graduates to salaried posts (Cressida Fforde for WAC-2 and Vanessa Balloqui

Figure 7.2   The sign we never thought we would see again! This sign greeted the Southampton secretariat as we arrived in Vermillion for WAC's first meeting after WAC-1 in 1986. *Credit*: Olivia Forge.

Figure 7.3   Peter watches with Jane and Larry Zimmerman as archaeologists dig a hole to receive remains of Native American ancestors disturbed by road construction, during the reburial ceremony at the Wounded Knee Reservation, at the end of the South Dakota Inter-Congress in 1989. Jane has been by Peter's side throughout the history of WAC (and before). Her personal, administrative and academic contribution to WAC is frequently overlooked: quite simply I am not sure WAC would exist without Jane's contribution. *Credit*: Lydia Maher.

Figure 7.4   Peter carrying some of the remains of Native American ancestors reburied on the Wounded Knee Reservation, at the end of the South Dakota Inter-Congress in 1989. *Credit*: Lydia Maher.

for WAC-3). The complexity of trying to run an international organisation with meetings away from the normal conference centres of the 'First World' was clearly demonstrated by the failure of the Papua New Guinea Inter-Congress and by the problems that arose in relation to both WAC-2 in Venezuela and WAC-3 in India. WAC-2 was moved from Venezuela to Colombia because of the collapse of the economy and then back again (to a different location) because of the Colombian drug wars. WAC-3 suffered not only because many potential participants were deterred by outbreaks of malaria and plague, but also as a result of significant and (eventually) explicit manipulation by Hindu nationalists (although see Golson 1995). WAC-3 was seen by a few who attended, and by many who did *not*, as a chaotic failure (Chippindale 1995; Colley 1995; Golson 1995). However, most of those who were present remember it as a typical WAC event, with stimulating academic debate, provoked by the presence of colleagues with hugely differing backgrounds and approaches, which produced a number of excellent *One World Archaeology* volumes – albeit set within what most would argue to have been an unacceptable level of chaotic organisation. The banning of discussion of the destruction of the mosque at Ayodhya imposed on WAC totally backfired, if its purpose was to avoid discussion of the event, as coverage of the ban and of the destruction of the mosque was front page news every day in almost every newspaper in New Delhi and India during the entire conference, ensuring a level of coverage that certainly would not have happened without the ban. The issues surrounding WAC-3 in particular serve not only to show the difficulties of organising conferences outside the 'First World' but also underline one of the founding concepts of WAC – that archaeology has a significant social role and political context.

WAC-2 in Venezuela in 1990 saw the formal adoption of the WAC Statutes as proposed by the Steering Committee. Between the final Steering Committee report in 1989 and WAC-2 in 1990 Peter had grappled not only with being series editor for *One World Archaeology* and the double-movement of the venue for WAC-2 but also, with the help of the voluntary Secretariat, with setting-up elections for Junior and Senior Representatives for the 14 Electoral Colleges and eight indigenous members of the WAC Executive, using what seemed to be an impossibly complex system known as 'Single Transferable Voting'. Organising elections is a rather thankless and time-consuming activity under the best of circumstances. These were elections to a totally new organisation, the democratic ethos of which had to be explained countless times to colleagues from all over the world who simply anticipated that the positions would be taken by 'the great and the good'. That it was *really* being suggested that junior people were to be elected to the decision-making body of an international organisation with the same voting rights as their academic seniors was a concept many found difficult to grasp. That the Executive in Venezuela had almost total democratic representation was little short of a miracle, made possible by a huge amount of work put in by Peter and the Southampton team. The Council (since 2003 known as the Assembly) of WAC is perhaps the most democratic organ of any organisation of which I am aware. It consists of the elected members of the Executive and then one elected representative of each nationality present at the particular Congress. Given that Council usually meets on the second day of a Congress its membership has to be established as early in the Congress as possible. Elections to Council have been the nightmare of Officers and Secretariat since it first met in Venezuela. However, that nightmare was chased away from all of our minds as members of Council began to arrive for its inaugural meeting at WAC-2. Here, finally, was the fruit of everything that had happened since the WAC-1 Plenary Session. For many of us it was a very emotional moment as representatives from all over the world began to gather, enthusiastically discussing the agenda and already debating issues that were to be discussed. Participants from South Africa were welcomed to this

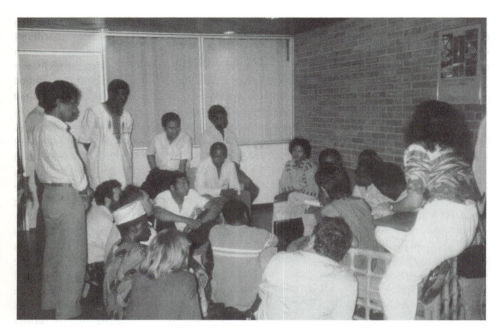

Figure 7.5   African participants at WAC-2 gather to discuss WAC's continuing stance regarding South African participation at WAC meetings. *Credit*: Olivia Forge.

Congress, provided they had the support of the ANC/UDF, but they were not granted rights to attend WAC business meetings as national representatives. One South African participant was allowed to attend the meeting of Council as an Observer.

At this meeting of Council Item 5 was the election of officers. I had already informally approached Larry Zimmerman to see if he would be willing to be nominated as Secretary. He had agreed, but noted, with an astute understanding of the time and commitment put in to get WAC to where it was, that 'I am *not* Peter Ucko'. On the agenda for the meeting that had been circulated before the conference it had been indicated that 'none of the current Officers … are standing for (re)election'. Many, probably most if not all, of those present expected that this implied that Peter would not accept nomination as Secretary but that he would stand as President.

Discussion of nominations for the post of Secretary were begun by Peter extolling the virtues of Larry Zimmerman, who had proved his commitment to WAC not only by attending WAC-1 but also by organising such a successful Inter-Congress in the face of significant professional opposition in the USA. Larry was proposed for Secretary by Hirini Matunga, the leader of the Indigenous Group of the Executive, and, after Mike Rowlands (UK) had declined a nomination by Mario Sanoja (Venezuela), nominations for Secretary were closed. Nominations were then opened for the post of President and Simiyu Wandibba immediately nominated Peter who, to the surprise of the meeting, declined the nomination. The following discussion centred around an almost unanimous view that Peter was the only person for the job and he was again nominated – this time by Mike Rowlands. He again declined. Debate became increasingly animated as members heaped increasing pressure on Peter to accept. Over the next half-an-hour Peter declined a further nine nominations. It was only after about half of these had been declined that it really dawned on those who knew him well that he really had no intention of allowing

Figure 7.6   Peter hands on the responsibility of WAC to its new President, Jack Golson, Venezuela, 1990. *Credit*: Olivia Forge.

himself to be pressurised into the post. The meeting was losing direction and then Peter delivered his *coup-de-grace* by himself nominating Jack Golson as President. Jack, who was not nearly as well known by all of those present as Peter, was an obvious choice: a senior academic in the Pacific region, a strong supporter of the stance taken over WAC-1, and a key member of the Steering Committee who had provided drafts of major parts of the WAC Statutes. And so Peter withdrew from the lead role in WAC to allow the organisation to grow away from being associated entirely with him and the 1986 ban. He did retain his role as one of the Directors of the WAC Charitable Company.

WAC is governed by elected Officers supported by a series of elected Committees as outlined in its Statutes (www.world archaeologicalcongress.org/statutes). However, the difficulty of the Secretariat having no formal standing in the organisational structure of WAC was increasingly problematic – especially given the fact that for one reason or another, WAC only functioned with one out of three effective Officers for much of the period 1990–2003. It was this lack of standing that led the then Secretary, Julian Thomas, to suggest to the Executive meeting held on Brač at the 1998 Inter-Congress that I be provided with the title 'Assistant Secretary', so that, at the most basic of levels, I had a title with which to sign letters. The central role played by the voluntary Secretariat was acknowledged by the Executive when they rejected this suggestion but rather insisted that I take the title of Honorary Chief Executive Officer, as they felt it better reflected my role in supporting elected Officers and providing the continuity that is so essential for the organisation to be allowed to grow and develop. It is instructive that it is only the good will of the University of Newcastle and my family that has allowed me to continue to serve WAC in this way. It is not clear how long this situation can go on. To try to run an international organisation effectively, one that could achieve its ambitions, without a paid Secretariat of some description – especially an organisation that aimed specifically to include colleagues from disadvantaged areas of the world who had limited access to communication and severely limited access, if any, to funding – was always seen to be ridiculous if not impossible. It still is and WAC will never be able to achieve its full potential until it has a secure financial foundation and salaried Secretariat.

So what has WAC achieved? Since 1986 WAC has held four more major international Congresses and a number of Inter-Congresses. All have included not only academic views but also the wider social aspects of the past, notably indigenous perspectives from around the world. Some, such as the Inter-Congress on the *Destruction and Conservation of Cultural Property*, held in Croatia in 1998, have addressed full-on the contemporary political context of the past. All, until WAC-4, have been precarious financially and WAC-5 is the only meeting to have produced a significant surplus.

Despite this precarious financial situation, WAC has achieved much more. The *One World Archaeology* series has been hailed by many as changing the face of archaeology and as a 'splendid series ... [which] makes great gesture in the direction of drawing the squabbling ... sciences of man back together' (Fox 1993). The high cost of the series has drawn criticism from a number of quarters and has been the topic of numerous discussions in WAC committees, but advances and royalties from the series have provided much of the finance necessary to ensure widespread participation in WAC meetings. It is only with the, albeit potentially short-term, financial security provided by the WAC-5 surplus that it has been possible to break away from our financial reliance on publication advances and to move to a publisher willing to produce cheaper books, as well as immediate paper-backing.

WAC has also produced a number of seminal protocols such as the *Vermillion Accord* on the treatment of human remains and the *Code of Ethics* regarding obligations to indigenous peoples, that have been used by numerous national organisations as the basis for their own statements and codes. WAC has organised and helped to fund training programmes in Ghana, India, Nigeria, Romania, Sri Lanka and Zimbabwe; it has paid for the travel of colleagues from less wealthy nations to lecture in Europe and has distributed *OWA* and other books and journals to libraries in the so-called developing world that, according to one librarian in receipt of such a donation, provided 'the only recently published texts' in his university library. WAC has also been pivotal in ensuring that the cultural heritage has been taken seriously by the World Commission on Dams and has made a number of important contributions to regional issues.

Another important aspect of WAC's work has been to remind colleagues who do not have access to funding that they are vitally important to the discipline and that WAC will continue to do as much as possible to secure their voice in world archaeology. Since WAC-5, international contact and debate has been facilitated and made easier for many by a significantly enhanced web-presence. Though WAC cannot rely entirely on the web, as access is still not easy or cheap for many colleagues, it does offer an effective means of communication for an increasing section of the WAC community. We can anticipate that web access will grow and continue to encourage international debate. Yet WAC still needs to do more including: ensuring that the dominance of the English language does not exclude non-English speakers; identifying more publication needs (already underway, see (www.world archaeologicalcongress.org/publications); sponsoring more training initiatives and, of course, finding additional sources of funding for these and other activities.

What is WAC's full potential? Why is WAC needed in the twenty-first century? Some argued, after WAC-4 was held in Cape Town, that the controversy begun in the mid-1980s had been resolved, that WAC had come full circle, had served its purpose and had come to the end of its natural life. This is totally wrong. The following three, heavily intertwined, examples underline that WAC is needed now more than ever.

First, the emphasis at WAC-1 on comparative archaeology has been crucial to the development of the discipline. WAC-1 participants did not simply politely listen to, and learn about, the cultural history of other parts of the world but rather compared, contrasted and learnt from differing circumstances, theories, methodologies and resulting interpretations. Such cross-cultural exchanges are vitally important for all those interested in world archaeology and play a crucial role for those working in more remote parts of the world where access to web and paper-based resources are still severely limited. It is through such exchanges that archaeology will develop into a mature discipline and contribute to the wider academic debate far more easily, effectively and influentially than if we revert to hiding in our narrow chronologically and geographically defined trenches.

Second, WAC has a major responsibility regarding education. In 1943 Grahame Clark argued that archaeology, and especially prehistory, should form the basis of school curricula around the world as such study would emphasise what we have in common rather than our differences. Clark argued, perhaps naively, that had these subjects formed the curriculum in Germany, Italy, and Japan in the early half of the twentieth century then the populations of these countries might have declined to follow their leaders into war. The 1990 review of school curricula in some 20 countries revealed that Clark's suggestion had not been taken up and that archaeology, and especially prehistory, were, along with the past as perceived by minority and/or indigenous groups, parts of an 'excluded past', rejected by curriculum planners around the world (Stone and MacKenzie 1990). More recent reviews paint a slightly improved, but still overwhelmingly exclusive, situation (Stone and Planel 1994; Malone *et al.* 2000). The past as taught in schools around the world still focuses on what differentiates us rather than what we have in common. This is an increasingly important issue as the world appears to be dividing into antagonistic camps that refuse to comprehend each other.

Finally we need to accept that archaeology is part of the wider cultural heritage – a heritage increasingly identified as fundamental to the economies of countries throughout the world. In 2002 there were 715 million 'international arrivals' in the world; the World Travel Organisation projects that this figure will rise to nearly 1.6 billion by 2020 (http://www.world-tourism.org/facts/2020/2020.htm). In 2002 tourists spent US$643 billion on travel throughout the world. We can only anticipate a huge increase in such spending by 2020. A large proportion of this travel is to see the cultural heritage of other countries. By visiting other places, by being aware of the history and culture of other places, is one way of not being afraid of other places, of other people. Such widespread tourism must support the formal educational use of archaeology and prehistory as envisaged by Clark. We need to equip existing and future generations not with a fear of 'the other' but with an acceptance of our common roots, our shared problems and our entangled future. As archaeologists we have a responsibility to engage with the wider ramifications and opportunities of our discipline. WAC has been the one international organisation to identify and accept that responsibility.

Although the world has changed considerably since WAC-1, all of the areas of interest identified by the Steering Committee are still relevant in 2005. Perhaps they are more so. As the world is faced by extreme fundamentalism from both East and West we need more than ever to sit and discuss, to listen and learn, to debate and compromise. Archaeologists will never stop wars (and see Hamilakis 2003; Stone 2005) but they can perhaps contribute to an atmosphere where war is increasingly unacceptable – just as the decision to ban South African and Namibian colleagues from WAC-1 did not, in itself, topple Apartheid but rather it made a tiny contribution that helped define and underscore the unacceptability of Apartheid and contributed an extra straw to eventually break its back.

REFERENCES

Andah, B. (1987) 'Statement on behalf of the African participants', *Edited Version of the Plenary Session of the World Archaeological Congress, 6 September 1986*: 8–9.

Anonymous. (1989) 'Obituary: Caroline Jones', *World Archaeological Bulletin*, 4: 33–35.

Chippindale, C. (1995) 'Editorial', *Antiquity*, 69: 7–8.

Clark, G. (1943) 'Education and the study of man', *Antiquity*, 27: 113–121.

Colley, S. (1995) 'What happened at WAC-3?' *Antiquity*, 69: 15–18.

Day, M. (1988) 'Final Report of the World Archaeological Congress Steering Committee', *World Archaeological Bulletin*, 2: 4–11.

Fox, R. (1993) 'Review of the *One World Archaeology*: an appraisal', *Anthropology Today* 9(5): 6–10.

Golson, J. (1995) 'What went wrong with WAC-3 and an attempt to understand why', *Australian Archaeology* 41: 48–54.

Golson, K. (1989) 'Introduction', *World Archaeological Bulletin*, 3: 1–3.

Hamilakis, Y. (2003) 'Iraq, stewardship and "the record": an ethical crisis for archaeology', *Public Archaeology*, 3: 104–111.

Hodder, I. (1987) 'Discussion of motions to the Plenary Session', *Edited Version of the Plenary Session of the World Archaeological Congress, 6 September 1986*: 21–29.

Malone, C., M. Baxter and P.G. Stone (eds) (2000) 'Special section: archaeology in education', *Antiquity*, 74: 122–218.

Mangi, J. (1987) 'Statement on behalf of independent archaeologists', *Edited Version of the Plenary Session of the World Archaeological Congress, 6 September 1986*: 10–11.

Statutes. (1990) WAC Statutes, *World Archaeological Bulletin* 51990: 133–138.

Stone, P.G. (1987) 'Statement on behalf of students and low paid workers', *Edited Version of the Plenary Session of the World Archaeological Congress, 6 September 1986*: 20.

Stone, P.G. (2005) 'The identification and protection of cultural heritage in Iraq conflict: A peculiarly English tale', *Antiquity,* 79: 933–943.

Stone, P.G. and R. MacKenzie (eds) (1990) *The Excluded Past: Archaeology and Education*, London: Unwin Hyman.

Stone, P.G. and P. Planel (eds) (1994) *The Presented Past: Heritage, Museums and Education*, London: Routledge.

Ucko, P.J. (1987) *Academic Freedom and Apartheid: The Story of the World Archaeological Congress*, London: Duckworth.

CHAPTER 8

THE WORLD HERITAGE CONVENTION
Management By and For Whom?

Henry Cleere

INTRODUCTION

Among Peter Ucko's guiding principles are an abiding belief in the fundamental equality of all humankind and an awareness of the deep spiritual significance of the past for present and coming generations. These are tempered by a healthy, and frequently justified, suspicion of the underlying motivation of politicians and administrators of all kinds and nations. In many ways, therefore, the UNESCO World Heritage Convention of 1972 may be said to epitomise for him, and for the many others who share his paradoxical combination of idealism and scepticism in equal measure, both the best and the worst of contemporary perceptions of and approaches to the tangible and intangible legacy of countless generations of ancestors. One of the most serious charges levelled against the Convention (or, rather, against those who implement it) is the way in which it is often seen to ride roughshod over the rights and aspirations of local and indigenous communities. This chapter, based on more than a decade working at the heart of the World Heritage process, is an attempt to provide a personal overview of the achievements and shortcomings of the Convention, with particular reference to the impact of inscription on the rights of those who live and work in World Heritage sites.

THE CONVENTION

The 1972 UNESCO *Convention Concerning the Protection of the World Cultural and Natural Heritage* (better known as the World Heritage Convention) is based on the premise that 'parts of the cultural or natural heritage are of outstanding interest and therefore need to be preserved as part of the world heritage of mankind as a whole.' An elaborate structure has been created for selecting, nominating, evaluating, managing and monitoring sites and monuments considered to possess this quality of 'outstanding interest'.

States Parties (i.e. those countries that have ratified the Convention) are required to submit elaborate nomination dossiers to UNESCO, consisting of statements of significance, detailed descriptions and historical accounts, administrative documentation relating to legislative protection, planning provisions, and much more, accompanied by maps, plans, graphics and supporting literature. These dossiers are then evaluated according to the requirements of the UNESCO World Heritage Committee and the criteria used to define the somewhat elusive quality of 'outstanding universal value' by one or both of the two official Advisory Bodies – the International Council on Monuments and Sites (ICOMOS) for cultural properties and the World Conservation Union (IUCN) for natural properties.

To qualify for inclusion on the World Heritage List, a cultural property must comply with at least one of the following criteria (UNESCO 2005, para 77):

    i. represent a masterpiece of human creative genius; or

    ii. exhibit an important interchange of human values, over a span of time or within a cultural area of the world, on developments in architecture or technology, monumental arts, town-planning or landscape design;

    iii. bear a unique or at least exceptional testimony to a cultural tradition or to a civilization which is living or which has disappeared;

    iv. be an outstanding example of a type of building or architectural or technological ensemble or landscape which illustrates (a) significant stage(s) in human history;

    v. be an outstanding example of a traditional human settlement, land-use, or sea-use which is representative of a culture (or cultures), or human interaction with the environment, especially when it has become vulnerable under the impact of irreversible change;

    vi. be directly or tangibly associated with events or living traditions, with ideas, or with beliefs, with artistic and literary works of outstanding universal significance (the Committee considers that this criterion should justify inclusion in the List only in exceptional circumstances and in conjunction with other criteria cultural or natural).

The reports and recommendations of the two Advisory Bodies are presented to the Committee at its annual meeting, which takes place in a different country each year, when decisions are taken regarding inscription on the World Heritage List. Currently (September 2004) there are 788 properties[1] inscribed on the World Heritage List – 611 cultural, 154 natural and 23 mixed properties (i.e. qualifying under both cultural and natural criteria) – in 134 of the 178 States Parties.

AN UNBALANCED LIST

The Committee has been agonising over the imbalances on the List almost since the first properties were inscribed in 1978 (Pressouyre 1993). The most recent analysis (ICOMOS 2004) shows that over 50 per cent of the properties on the List are located in the Europe/North America Region (which also includes Israel and Turkey) and less than 5 per cent in Africa (the UNESCO Region excludes the Arab states of North Africa), whilst the majority of the 18 per cent in the Asia/Pacific Region are located in China, India and Japan.

There is a similar imbalance in terms of categories of cultural property. 'Architectural and artistic monuments and ensembles' (non-religious structures such as castles, palaces etc.) predominate (23 per cent), followed by historic towns (18 per cent) and religious properties (cathedrals, mosques, temples, monasteries, etc.).[2] Archaeological properties are well represented (12 per cent), the majority of these being the great prehistoric sites of Egypt and the Near East, classical sites of the Mediterranean and prehispanic monuments in Latin America.

THE GLOBAL STRATEGY

In 1994 a high-level expert meeting was convened at the UNESCO Headquarters in Paris to carry out an examination in depth of all the studies made over the preceding 10 years with the intention of improving the representative character of the World Heritage List and of arriving at concepts and a common methodological procedure as a result of a detailed analysis of the different approaches that had been adopted. In their report (UNESCO 1994), the experts identified some areas as having high potential to complete gaps in representation (it was considered that such areas should be considered in their broad anthropological context through time):

1. Human coexistence with the land
    i. movement of peoples (nomadism, migration);
    ii. settlement;
    iii. modes of subsistence;
    iv. technological evolution.

2. Human beings in society
    i. human interaction;
    ii. cultural coexistence;
    iii. spirituality and creative expression.

Hitherto, the perception of what constituted a 'monument' or a 'site' adopted by the World Heritage Committee was very much derived from the traditional Western European art-historical model. However, the new dimension, influenced to a considerable extent by the anthropologist members of the expert group, was to introduce new problems in terms of the management of World Heritage sites and monuments.

THE MANAGEMENT OF WORLD HERITAGE

Among the requirements of the World Heritage Committee is that each nominated property must:

> have adequate long-term legislative, regulatory, institutional and/or traditional protection and management to ensure their safeguarding. This protection should include adequately delineated boundaries. Similarly State Parties should demonstrate adequate protection at the national, region, municipal and/or traditional level for the nominated property. (UNESCO 2005, para 97)

In the early years of the Convention this management requirement, at least so far as cultural properties were concerned, was blithely ignored by the Committee and its Advisory Body, ICOMOS. It was not until the mid-1990s that it began to be taken seriously, not only for new nominations but also for sites and monuments that were already on the List. In the latter connection, the UK set a good example, since English Heritage entered into a campaign for the formulation of management plans for all the World Heritage sites and monuments in England, working closely at the outset with the UK National Committee of ICOMOS.

Until comparatively recently this requirement was rigidly interpreted by the Committee as necessitating the formulation and application of a management *plan*, largely as a result of pressure from those concerned with the natural heritage, notably the then Director of the UNESCO World Heritage Centre, whose background was in environmental conservation. This was perhaps not surprising, in view of the fact that so many of the natural properties on the World Heritage List are National Parks, where management plans are *de rigueur*.

One of the major problems has been that of defining precisely what is intended by a management plan, and how this differs, if at all, from a master plan or a conservation plan. This is reflected in publications by experts on the subject (e.g. Pearson and Sullivan 1995; Sullivan 1997; Teutonico and Palumbo 2000; Clark 2001). It becomes apparent when reading the literature relating to heritage that the terms are being used almost interchangeably. A useful definition which embraces the main issues that concern the World Heritage Committee was recently proposed by the UNESCO World Heritage Centre (UNESCO 2003):

> A plan which, following upon the definition of cultural and/or natural values, protects them by applying legal, administrative, financial and professional conservation methods and tools, and by prescribing certain strategies and specific actions.

The standard work on the management of World Heritage cultural properties (Feilden and Jokilehto 1998) does not attempt a definition *per se*, but describes the planning process in a systematic manner, identifies the key elements to be considered and suggests a standard format for management plans.

MANAGING CULTURAL LANDSCAPES

All this is fine for historic towns or archaeological sites in European and North American countries, the managers of most of which were already familiar with the need for management planning in some form or other. However, a complication had been introduced as early as 1992, when the World Heritage Committee acknowledged the claims of a new category of property, that of *cultural landscape*, for consideration for World Heritage Listing.[3] This type of property is defined in the *Operational Guidelines* (UNESCO 2005, Annex 3) as follows:

6. Cultural landscapes are cultural properties and represent the 'combined works of nature and of man' designated in Article 1 of the Convention. They are illustrative of the evolution of human society and settlement over time, under the influence of the physical constraints and/or opportunities presented by their natural environment and of successive social, economic and cultural forces, both external and internal.

9. Cultural landscapes often reflect specific techniques of sustainable land-use, considering the characteristics and limits of the natural environment they are established in, and a specific spiritual relation to nature. Protection of cultural landscapes can contribute to modern techniques of sustainable land-use and can maintain or enhance natural values in the landscape. The continued existence of traditional forms of land-use supports biological diversity in many regions of the world. The protection of traditional cultural landscapes is therefore helpful in maintaining biological diversity.

10. Cultural landscapes fall into three main categories, namely:

   i. The most easily identifiable is the clearly defined landscape designed and created intentionally by man. This embraces garden and parkland landscapes constructed for aesthetic reasons which are often (but not always) associated with religious or other monumental buildings and ensembles.

   ii. The second category is the organically evolved landscape. This results from an initial social, economic, administrative, and/or religious imperative and has developed its present form by association with and in response to its natural environment. Such landscapes reflect that process of evolution in their form and component features. They fall into two sub-categories:

- a relict (or fossil) landscape is one in which an evolutionary process came to an end at some time in the past, either abruptly or over a period. Its significant distinguishing features are, however, still visible in material form.

- a continuing landscape is one which retains an active social role in contemporary society closely associated with the traditional way of life, and in which the evolutionary process is still in progress. At the same time it exhibits significant material evidence of its evolution over time.

iii. The final category is the associative cultural landscape. The inclusion of such landscapes on the World Heritage List is justifiable by virtue of the powerful religious, artistic or cultural associations of the natural element rather than material cultural evidence, which may be insignificant or even absent.

The first category causes no problems: it applies to designed landscapes such as the gardens of Aranjuez, Studley Royal, or Versailles in Europe or the Shalamar Gardens at Lahore, for all of which some form of management has been acknowledged to be essential (albeit rudimentary in the case of Lahore). It is the second and third categories which raise problems of management *pur sang*.

Moving forward to the third category, no major problems have so far been encountered. The first two World Heritage cultural landscapes were Tongariro (New Zealand) in 1990 and Uluru-Kata Tjuta (Australia) in 1994. Both of these are National Parks – the former the second oldest in the world – and so have management plans of different kinds. They were also already inscribed on the World Heritage List for their natural values. There are, however, some potential category iii cultural landscapes in the pipeline where problems of definition and limited cultural significance may be encountered: for example, the Montagne Sainte-Victoire in Provence, the subject of so much of the *œuvre* of Paul Cézanne, or Mount Fuji in Japan, where the management issues will be much less clear-cut.

It is the category ii cultural landscapes, and more particularly those considered to be 'continuing landscapes', which pose the most questions in management terms. The first to be inscribed on the List, in 1995 (shortly after the promulgation of the Global Strategy), was the dramatic landscape of the rice terraces of the Philippine Cordilleras in central Luzon. This ancient agricultural system is still operating exactly as it did many centuries ago. The villages and their rice terraces, with communal woodland, form socio-economic units that are coherent and viable, operating what is in effect a subsistence economy and governed by the communities themselves according to age-old custom and practice. It is, however, gravely threatened in the socio-economic context of twenty-first century Philippines. To quote Fowler (2004: 39):

This highly structured landscape remains … a working landscape … That structure contains, and must continue to contain if the structure is to be maintained, skilled, knowledgeable and sympathetic manual labour, with the emphasis on 'manual' for the fragility and topography of the terrace systems inhibit the use of machines … No wonder, therefore, that many of the young people look to a life beyond the mountains … Those who remain look to an income from tourism but perhaps even to replace their livelihood from the fields. The danger, however, is obvious, for if the fields are not worked tourists would look at 'dead' remains of a former system, a fossil archaeological landscape rather than a living landscape intimately related to the life and society of those who worked it.

Despite efforts by the regional and central governments to devise and impose a form of management planning, the steady and seemingly irreversible decline of rice cultivation has continued. The seriousness of the situation was acknowledged by the World Heritage Committee in 2002, when the Philippines rice terraces were put on the List of World Heritage in Danger.

There is an interesting parallel here with the World Heritage property of Portovenere, Cinque Terre, and the Islands (Palmaria, Tino, and Tinetto) in northern Italy, which was inscribed on the List in 1997, but where the problem of desertion of the terraces has been solved. This dramatic strip of the Ligurian coastline, its steep cliffs broken only by narrow ravines with small villages where the rivers that run down them meet the sea, was for centuries renowned for the quality of its wines, produced on terraces rising precipitously up the cliffs. Drastic social and economic changes in this region over the past century have led to the decline of viticulture and wine production and the almost total abandonment of the terraces. However, there has been a determined effort by some local administrators, assisted by the designation of the area as a National Park with its obligatory management plan, to revive the industry, which is making slow but steady progress by inviting outsiders interested in owning their own vineyards to purchase derelict holdings and employ local people to work them.

The Committee's requirements as set out in the *Operational Guidelines* (UNESCO 2005, para 97) refer to 'adequate long-term legislative, regulatory, institutional and/or traditional protection and management'. The use of the qualifier 'traditional' here is a relative recent introduction, dating from the time of the Global Strategy, and it has been used very sparingly since it was introduced. The most relevant example of its application to date is probably that of the Sukur Cultural Landscape in Nigeria, inscribed on the List in 1999.

In its evaluation, ICOMOS described this historic terraced landscape on a high plateau close to the frontier with Cameroon in north-eastern Nigeria as 'a remarkably intact physical expression of a society and its spiritual and material culture'. Its recommendation that Sukur should be inscribed on the World Heritage List under criteria iii, v, and vi was accepted by the Committee. Ownership and management of the property is vested in the Hidi-in-Council, which has been the traditional governing body of the local community for centuries. A form of remote supervision is exercised by the National Commission for Monuments and Museums (NCMM), which maintains a resident on-site archaeologist with a small support staff, since the Sukur landscape has been designated a State Monument under National Decree No. 77 (1979). This legal instrument empowers the NCMM to protect the monument and participate in its management: the use of the word 'participate' here is significant. There is a management plan drawn up by the NCMM in consultation with the local community, but priority is given to local custom and practice in day-to-day management and administration.

The recognition now being accorded to cultural landscapes, coupled with the Global Strategy and its stress on the significance of 'non-monumental' heritage, is likely to cause more problems in terms of the management requirements of the Committee. There has been considerable discussion in recent years of the eligibility of sacred groves in, for example, sub-Saharan Africa for World Heritage Listing, and also of areas still being used intensively by hunter–gatherer communities and of vast stretches of grassland used by nomadic pastoralist societies in central Asia and Siberia. So far the only area of this kind on the List is the Laponian region in northern Sweden used by reindeer herdsmen on a seasonal basis. Even though the Saami herdsmen move over vast distances, from northern Russia to Norway, it is only Sweden that has so far succeeded in reaching an agreement with the indigenous people of the region.

WHO REALLY MANAGES WORLD
HERITAGE SITES AND MONUMENTS?

Much lip-service is paid by UNESCO and its World Heritage Committee to the participation of local communities in the protection and management of those 'parts of the cultural and natural heritage [which] are of outstanding interest and therefore need to be preserved as part of the world heritage of mankind as a whole', to quote the Preamble to the Convention. The Convention takes great pains to point out that it is the countries within which these monuments and sites are located that are responsible for their management: there is no question of the international body exercising some superior level of ownership and management. Nonetheless, there are procedures in force for the regular monitoring of the quality of stewardship of these fortunate countries.

For the overwhelming majority of the 788 properties on the World Heritage List, ownership and management responsibility is clear. It is the municipal administrations, the national antiquities services, the religious communities, the national park authorities and the individual proprietors upon whom this heavy duty is laid. In what is probably no more than a slender majority of the States Parties to the Convention there is some semblance of democratic structure which gives to individual citizens a notional participation in the management of their own heritage. The ballot box enables citizens to appoint legislatures at national and regional level and to delegate this responsibility to them, to appoint specialist commissions for cultural and environmental conservation and protection. Much of this is, however, no more than formal: individual citizens are for the most part interested in little beyond the boundaries of their own communities, and they only attempt to intervene when their personal interests are threatened – the Nimby phenomenon.[4]

Nomination to the World Heritage List can sometimes provoke vigorous opposition. For example, when Taos Pueblo in New Mexico (USA) was nominated in 1992 the Taos People expressed their strong opposition. In this case, however, the motive was probably not the perception of a threat to the tribal way of life, but rather the risk of greater Federal meddling in Native American affairs. In the event, the matter was resolved by the Governor of the State of New Mexico giving an assurance on the morning of the meeting when the property was presented to the World Heritage Committee in Santa Fe that there would be no such interference (coupled with a substantial financial grant to the Taos People).

One of the most serious problems is the failure of States Parties to acknowledge the significance of the heritage of indigenous peoples living within their frontiers. One of the few examples of this being done successfully is the Laponian region in northern Sweden quoted earlier, the nomination of which was the result of protracted discussions between the government in Stockholm and the well-organised Saami community. On the other hand, no property representing the heritage of the Kurdish people has yet been nominated in Iran, Iraq or Turkey. Only recently has the People's Republic of China begun to identify properties that illustrate the non-Han heritage of its indigenous communities such as the Uiygurs of Xinjiang Autonomous Region or the Tibetans (beyond the Potala and other palaces in Lhasa).

Two examples of a lack of consultation between central governments and indigenous groups will serve to illustrate the more extreme problems resulting from a failure to involve the latter in the management of cultural properties. The significance of the Chan Chan archaeological site in Peru was recognized by World Heritage Listing in 1986. Most of this extensive site has not been excavated, and there has been occupation of large parts of the unexcavated area by Indian groups for several centuries. The Peruvian

Government, anxious to capitalise on what it saw as a major tourist asset, decided to drive the indigenous communities off the site without making provision for their rehousing. The result was violent demonstrations and clashes between local people and Government forces. At the present time this action has been suspended, but it has to be resolved. A draft Management Plan has been prepared, but it still fails to give adequate recognition to the rights of dispossessed settlers.

The removal of resident groups of whatever ethnicity from archaeological sites is, of course, not a rare occurrence. For example, at the World Heritage sites of Anuradhapura (Sri Lanka) and Petra (Jordan) small communities living inside the archaeological sites were rehoused outside the site boundaries – in the former case amicably but with some rancour still surviving at the latter. In Sri Lanka there were lengthy discussions before action was taken and the views of the people about to be displaced on the design and location of their new houses was taken into account, but at Petra the decision was taken in Amman with minimum consultation of the local Bedu.

The other example of failure to involve indigenous peoples is at Kakadu (Australia). When the first *tranche* of this National Park was put on the World Heritage List in 1981 a small enclave was exempted from the inscribed site. This was where uranium had been mined for a long period and where mining leases seemed to outweigh all other considerations in decision-making. This relatively small area is of immense religious significance to the Mirrar people, the Traditional Owners of this part of the Kakadu region. At that time there was only one mine in operation and the disruption to sacred sites of the Mirrar was minimal. However, in the late 1990s the mining company proposed to activate a long-term concession that it had to sink another mine within the enclave. Permission was granted without obtaining the consent of the Mirrar people, who protested against the desecration of their sacred sites, and their protest sparked off a lengthy and bitter dispute between the Commonwealth of Australia and the UNESCO World Heritage Committee. The world market for uranium has declined steeply over the past decade and so work on the second mine has been suspended, but it will break out again should there be an upturn in the market.

CONCLUSION

This has been no more than a sketchy overview of the objectives and operation of a complex and controversial convention. It is a well-intentioned initiative and it has laboriously achieved a substantial measure of approval despite considerable criticism and opposition. When UK ratified it in 1984 it was roundly condemned by a distinguished English archaeologist at his most orotund as 'Nothing more than an archaeological beauty contest.' This is assuredly not the case. Originally promoted in the late 1960s when it was belatedly recognised that the cultural and natural heritage of the planet was being vandalised in the name of progress, the Convention has ensured the survival of some of the most fragile evidence of the story of human achievement and has demonstrated that the material heritage of humankind manifests itself in many forms.

The Convention undeniably has its faults, the most serious of which are perhaps the non-representative character of the World Heritage List, the over-prescriptive approach to conservation and management, and the failure to recognise the significance of indigenous and minority communities and their right to be involved in management and decision-making. Nevertheless, these faults are capable of correction, and slow progress is being made in doing so. If the Convention did not exist in 2005, there can be no doubt that it would have to be invented.

NOTES

1. The neutral term 'property' is favoured by UNESCO, to avoid the ambiguities of 'site' or 'monument' when translated into other official UN languages.
2. There are currently nearly a score of Gothic cathedrals on the List in their own right, plus an equivalent number in the European historic towns.
3. This subject is discussed authoritatively in a recent book by Fowler (2004).
4. Not In My Back Yard.

REFERENCES

Clark, K. (2001) *Informed Conservation: Understanding Historic Buildings and Landscapes*, London: English Heritage.

Feilden, B.M., and J. Jokilehto (1998) *Management Guidelines for World Cultural Heritage Sites*, 2nd edn, Rome: ICCROM.

Fowler, P. (2004) *Landscapes for the World: Conserving a Global Heritage*, Macclesfield: Windgather Press.

ICOMOS (2004) *The World Heritage List: Filling the Gaps – An Action Plan for the Future*, World Heritage Committee Document WHC-04/28.COM/INF.13A, Paris: UNESCO World Heritage Centre.

Pearson, M. and S. Sullivan (1995) *Looking after Heritage Places: The Basics of Heritage Planning for Managers, Landowners and Administrators*, Melbourne: Melbourne University Press.

Pressouyre, L. (1993) *La Convention du Patrimoine mondial, vingt ans après*. Paris, Éditions UNESCO [English version (1996) *The World Heritage Convention, Twenty Years Later*, Paris: UNESCO Publishing].

Sullivan, S. (1997) 'A planning model for the management of archaeological sites', in *The Conservation of Archaeological Sites in the Mediterranean Region*, M. de la Torre (ed.), Los Angeles: Getty Conservation Institute, pp. 15–26.

Teutonico, J.M. and G. Palumbo (eds) (2000) *Management Planning for Archaeological Sites*, Los Angeles: Getty Conservation Institute.

UNESCO (1994) 'Expert Meeting on the "Global Strategy" and thematic studies for a representative World Heritage List' (UNESCO Headquarters, 20–22 June 1994), World Heritage Committee Document WHC-94/CONF.003/INF.6, Paris: UNESCO World Heritage Centre.

UNESCO (2003) *The State of World Heritage in the Asia–Pacific Region: Periodic Report, 2003*, Paris: World Heritage Centre.

UNESCO (2005) *Operational Guidelines for the Implementation of the World Heritage Convention*, Paris: World Heritage Centre.

CHAPTER 9

PUBLIC ARCHAEOLOGY IN
THE TWENTY-FIRST CENTURY

Tim Schadla-Hall

Archaeologists ... must come to terms with the contemporary demands on the profession and with the complex setting in which it operates

(Ucko 1990, xx)

Archaeology, in terms of actively recovering and interpreting evidence of past material cultures is little more than 200 years old and arguably even more recent as a recognisable field of academic research. In most parts of the world for most of this period, it has been the province of the few rather than the many and its present form is fundamentally a development stemming from Western Europe. During the majority of this period it has been characterised, especially in recent years, as stemming from an imperialist and largely European view of the world (WAC 2005). This approach has also been presented as avowedly (but not actually) apolitical, scientific and objective, and distinctly unworldly. The image of the eccentric, absent-minded but also academic and authoritative, figure – invariably male – still exists and although it is now undergoing a significant change it continues to dominate the public consciousness. It is also clear that there are still those who approach the subject as if there had been no changes in this 'scientific objectivity' since archaeology was first practised. In the last 40 years, however, archaeology has undergone a transformation from being a relatively restricted area of interest, pursued by a few and interpreted by even fewer, towards having an increasingly extensive public profile. The relative exposure that archaeology receives varies from country to country but nevertheless recognition of the relevance of archaeology in an increasingly globalised world does appear to be on the increase for a variety of reasons that are political, social and economic. This increasing awareness has not always developed as a result of the activities of the archaeological profession, nor has it always been under the control of professional archaeologists.

Archaeology has increasingly become public – or at least more widely accessible – in recent years. For example, the growth of television in the UK, both terrestrial and satellite, has been considerable both in terms of numbers of channels and of broadcast hours, and archaeology has been one of the beneficiaries; over the last 15 years the increase in archaeologically related programmes on terrestrial television in the UK exceeds 600 per cent (personal communication Anna Gardiner). The archaeological establishment has not, however, reacted with universal joy at this increased exposure and has in some cases complained vociferously about its format, content and even its presenters (for example, see Mower 2000). Indeed, when *Time Team* launched the *Big Dig* in 2003 there were even rumours that one august society was intending to send representatives to protest to the Secretary of State at the Department for Culture, Media and Sport (personal communication D. Morgan-Evans). The important and significant point that some appear to miss is that in the 1990s over 4 million of the population a week watched archaeological programmes and became familiar with much of the practice of archaeology. I recently took a taxi, and on admitting I was an archaeologist was immediately asked, 'So where is your geophys?' – not a question I should have expected in the 1970s. Archaeology has been particularly adept at using the media, (see, for example, Ascherson 2004) and the mass media have been happy to take up archaeology because, presented appropriately by them, it does have public appeal. Likewise, one of the most successful books, in terms of sales, about British prehistory in the late 1990s was written by a former pop star with no formal archaeological training (Cope 1998); it was reviewed by *The Guardian's* Science correspondent – an honour rarely accorded to works by eminent archaeologists – and received lengthy review treatment in the *Times* magazine. It was not reviewed in any academic archaeological journals despite its sales.

Expansion of archaeology has also taken place in many European countries – although not always along the same lines – and in addition there has been a steady increase in national and international legislation to protect and maintain the archaeological heritage. This might be seen as a response to previous destruction, as an increasing recognition of the importance of the past or even as connected to the rise of a new post-colonial nationalism. For example, most of the emerging nation states outside Europe were quick to construct and develop national museums and recognise their past as a means of providing an identity. An ongoing development during the same period has been the growth of mass tourism, which has ensured that all parts of the world are increasingly accessible to increasing numbers in the developed world. Technological developments in television and electronic media, on the other hand, have offered accessibility to the past in the home, so that increasing numbers of those with sufficient income, mainly from the developed world have been able to 'visit' the archaeology of the world both virtually and actually. All of these factors have contributed to an increasing interest in the past and also in other cultures – the curiosity of the human race about others has always been insatiable.

Academic archaeology – as the study and interpretation of the past – also changed during this period, as it became increasingly clear to some that the subject could no longer continue within the narrow confines of a dead past, examining objects and placing them in neat boxes of typology in a limited academic field. There were, and are, several pressures on archaeology and archaeologists to recognise the need to look beyond their own immediate specialist interests.

First, if the subject is to have any relevance in the twenty-first century – and academic subjects can fade from the public interest – there needs to be recognition that archaeology, its results and activities are relevant to a wider society in several different areas.

Second – and partly as part of a general trend towards the increasing democratisation of knowledge and the development of education – there is a clear need to reach out to a wider audience.

Third, the growth of the sometimes much-derided heritage industry, often based on archaeological sites and the results of archaeological work, has created a demand from a non-specialist audience for more and more information, which will be provided by others unless archaeologists are prepared to assist and support what has increasingly become a key sector in the economy of many countries given its close relationship to the tourist industry. It is worth noting that archaeology has no direct economic product, but the results of archaeological activity can be relatively easily linked to economic activity.

Fourth, a desire has become increasingly apparent for people to assert and demonstrate their identity and origins in a clear and comprehensible way. This role for archaeology has always been present, although recognition of what is essentially a political element has only been acknowledged and seriously studied in the last 50 years. Recognition of this field is now clearly seen in studies of the misuse of archaeology and archaeological work in the later ninteenth and earlier twentieth centuries when, at various times and in several countries, archaeology was used to support nationalist and ethnic origin myths. For example, in Britain an important role for archaeologists during this period was to reinforce the myth of the English as an Anglo-Saxon nation, by producing archaeological evidence of the Anglo-Saxon presence to support the textual and linguistic claims. At the same time, the results of archaeology were also used to demonstrate the importance of the Romans in a society that relied on the links to and values of the classical world to reinforce its nineteenth century imperial role.

Finally, legislation relevant to archaeology and state involvement with the subject have expanded almost exponentially in the last 50 years at a national, intra-national and international level, and in a variety of areas, relating to the protection of archaeological sites and also of archaeological artefacts. The complexities of the art market, looting, repatriation etc. have become a topic in themselves. Nations have been forced to reconsider how to retain/reclaim and display both sites and artefacts.

These factors that impinge increasingly on archaeological activity are intertwined in complex ways and it is difficult to treat them as individual subject areas. However, taken together they provide the basis for examining archaeology in a far wider context. For example, if an expert archaeologist were to provide (as has happened in the past) a catalogue entry for an auction house of an object that he/she effectively authenticates, then there may well be an ethical issue about becoming involved in the sale of artefacts, as in this case the academic input will add to the value of the object as well as contributing to the corpus of archaeological knowledge. The archaeologist has thus entered into the realm of economic activity (in this case generated by the art market). The case becomes more serious, however, if it subsequently emerges that the object has been illegally removed from its country of origin. At this stage the archaeologist is now involved, albeit indirectly, in criminal activity, and potentially in politics. In turn, the object may become the subject of a request for repatriation from its originating country, perhaps as a result of a complaint from an indigenous group from within that country. At this stage the archaeologist is involved in international law, national identity and the issue of indigenous rights. The position of the archaeologist is no longer one of the isolated academic operating in a rarefied and unworldly neutral environment and there should be no way in which he/she should fail to recognise the wider ramifications of a simple act of identification.

The need to provide a forum for discussing and examining the many elements of public archaeology is critical; equally so is the training and education of archaeologists in this new area of the discipline. The first university graduate course to be developed in Public Archaeology was a Masters course conceived by Peter Ucko at the Institute of Archaeology, University College London (UCL) in 1997. In the same period he also introduced a compulsory element of Public Archaeology into the second year of the undergraduate degrees. The undergraduate component is taught to all archaeology undergraduates regardless of their archaeological specialism. This development reflected and underlined Ucko's longstanding commitment to ensuring that archaeology – and archaeologists – consider the wider implications of their academic work, recognising that archaeology is not and never has been a neutral scientific activity, devoid of political content. This does not preclude the use or value of scientific techniques but does analyse and ask questions about the interpretation of the scientific results and the wider implications of the work of archaeologists. It ensures that students are introduced to issues of nationalism, ethnicity, politics, media, illicit antiquities, education and globalisation of the past as part of their mainstream studies.

This movement towards a wider and more inclusive view of the study of the past was first clearly and internationally manifest at the World Archaeological Congress of 1986 (WAC1) (Ucko 1987; see Day, Chapter 5, Ascherson, Chapter 6, Stone, Chapter 7 in this book), where there was a conscious and deliberate attempt to involve not just archaeological professionals but also native and indigenous people who had an interest in their own identity and history from a non-traditional archaeological viewpoint. Indeed, one of the implicit aims of the Congress, and subsequent WACs, was to encourage an open approach to the study of the past, in which consumers and users as well as 'producers' were given equal weight. In a sense this first Congress formally recognised a development (still opposed by some who believe their studies are unaffected by real life and existence) that moved archaeology closer to the realities of the world and made archaeology relevant to the non- archaeological community. In doing so it accepted the pluralist, multi-vocal and political nature of archaeological work and recognised that archaeology needs to concern itself with the issues that are current in the study of public archaeology.

Remarkably, Ucko made few specific references to public archaeology – at least that have survived in print. Implicitly he defined what he wished to develop, writing retrospectively:

> the WAC was ... an exceptional event because it put great emphasis on giving equal status and weight to those interested in the past who were not professional archaeologists or anthropologists ... it included some from nations, tribes and cultural groups whose material culture has been, and indeed still is, excavated by archaeologists. The voices of these groups added a new dimension to the WAC proceedings, speaking ... as objects of archaeological investigation (often carried out by archaeologists of alien cultures) ... In them, the present and the past were fused, not because they were fully part of the modern world in 1986, but because they claimed for themselves a greater right to 'their' past than that of the archaeologist or anthropologist. (Ucko 1987: xi)

This comment indicates what had been his predominant concern – indigenous and non-archaeological communities – an area that continues to form an important element of public archaeology as it is currently conceived. He developed this definition implicitly in a book foreword (Ucko 1990), where he highlighted, as much of WAC 1 inevitably did, the subjective interpretation of the past and its political significance in terms of ownership As he argued then, 'For example, the archaeological "evidence" of cultural continuity, as opposed to discontinuity, may make all the difference to an indigenous land claim, to the right of access to a site or a region, or to the disposal of a human skeleton to a museum, as against its reburial' (Ucko 1990: xiii). The idea of injecting politics even with a small 'p' was anathema to many archaeologists.

Curiously, Ucko took a much more (then) conventional line in his glossary, where he defined public archaeology – 'see cultural resource management (refers to the protection and development of archaeological sites). It is also used to refer to the management of, and legislation concerning, sites' (Ucko 1987: 246, 249). This harks back to an archaeologically centred worldview that the development of public archaeology has attempted to counter in recent years, and it reflects the managerial component that has been central to monitoring and preserving the archaeological resource. It seems that he was also considering this managerial component when he commented on the way in which archaeologists had previously worked in the IUPPS (International Union of Prehistoric and Protohistoric Sciences): 'The IUPPS has no Commission dealing with "Public Archaeology", although this could be viable within a predominantly European and North American framework' (Ucko 1987: 222). It also echoes his foreword for Cleere's book in the *One World Archaeology series* (Cleere 1989), which hardly refers to Public Archaeology at all despite suggestions that the public is important! He nevertheless sounded a note of caution when dealing with the concept of World Heritage:

> For those whose traditions involve the correct performance of rituals at sacred localities to ensure their continuation, the assumption of rights by the 'world' will be seen as shocking and

will be accompanied by little, if any, understanding of such developments or of the supposedly related concepts of 'serene joy and pleasure of the national and international public'. (Ucko 1989: xiii; see also Cleere, Chapter 8, in this book)

However the scope of public archaeology is now drawn, Ucko's intention was to make it an arena of debate in which many of the cherished beliefs that professional archaeologists had been secure in, particularly as high priests, or as experts, needed to be questioned. An agenda had been set that effectively opened archaeology up to a far wider audience, and also to a new set of challenges, particularly in the university field.

The suggestion that archaeology and its results – the study of the past – suddenly became a matter of public interest in the 1980s is clearly an over-simplification; for example, the membership of archaeological societies, at a national and local level, in the UK in the 1890s was relatively much higher than it is today, (see e.g. Ebbatson 1999), but it was also much more elitist. In a sense it might be possible to argue that the early development of archaeology in nineteenth-century Britain was public, in that it was led by amateur or part-time archaeologists who were largely drawn from the middle and upper classes. Indeed, until the 1940s much of the archaeological activity was carried out by archaeological societies that were, in a majority of cases run by amateurs and part-timers. In fact, with the exception of a few government-employed archaeologists and a handful of university archaeologists, there were few professionals. It was only from the late 1950s that the concept of the professional, trained archaeologist began to take root, and only in the late 1960s and 1970s, in the RESCUE era (Jones 1984: 142–152), that there was an expansion in university places and departments of archaeology in the UK.

Since the 1970s archaeology in universities has developed considerably in terms of academic scope and size. This expansion has accompanied the creation of archaeologically related posts at both local and national government level, initially for field archaeologists, (as post-war economic development accelerated), but subsequently particularly in the field of planning and development control. Archaeology in the UK, and to some degree elsewhere in the world, has been able to move with some success into the heritage industry. Whilst there are still difficulties in promoting archaeology in the school sector in Britain, partly at least because of the constraints of the National Curriculum, archaeology is now more embedded in people's lives and to a greater degree that it was even 30 years ago. However, it is still questionable whether the issues that were raised at least partly as a consequence of WAC 1 have been embraced by professional archaeology.

This reluctance to embrace a 'red-blooded' approach to public archaeology is to some extent illustrated by Austin (1987) in his discussion of archaeology in British universities '… we might, as academic archaeologists, prove our relevance to the community if we more often found ways of working with units in our regions, both to enhance the research aspects of their field programmes and to raise the consciousness of the public to archaeology as a conservation issue.' And later

> … academic archaeology must come out of its ivory tower and explain its arcane mystery to a fascinated but bewildered public which can, for example, be taught the meaning and value of prehistoric landscapes, and which can help in conserving and understanding them. To this end universities must also think about the postgraduate professional training that they can offer and from which the community at large will benefit. (Austin 1987: 234–235)

Here the academic archaeologist as lofty pedagogue is writ large – the benefit *they* will give to the public by teaching them – an echo of what can be defined as the deficit model (see later in the chapter).

At this point it is worth returning to the use of the term *public archaeology* and its place both in academic circles and also in the wider world. The first published use of the term public archaeology was by McGimsey in 1972 when he published his bleak assessment of the future of archaeology in the USA at a time when development, destruction and looting of the past were a real concern to archaeologists there. McGimsey (1972) noted the lack of provision by both the State and Federal governments of legislative protection for antiquities and sites, and made a strong plea for legislation to protect US archaeology. This lack of protection was contrasted with the relative effectiveness of protective legislation in Western Europe, particularly in Scandinavia, where there is a long history of protecting visible monuments; even in the UK protective legislation for monuments had existed for over a century. He went on to make a plea for greater public involvement in the past and advocated the need for public education, which he believed was a key to engaging people with their past and ensuring that the past would be preserved for future generations to appreciate. Of course, it could be argued that one of the reasons that destruction had hitherto taken place was a result of the US public – and particularly those in government circles – having no real interest in the pre-eighteenth century indigenous past of North America, and that the development of concern was at least partly aided by the increasing post-colonial interest in indigenous people. The approach that McGimsey took was apolitical, managerial and educational – nothing inherently wrong with that, but it did imply that archaeologists were in a position to control and direct developments in the public sphere on the basis of their expertise and knowledge. Despite boldly stating that 'There is no such thing as "private archaeology" ' at the outset (McGimsey 1972: 5) his view of the public was clearly one that saw the public as represented by the state and officialdom.

Using the term *public archaeology* without defining what is meant by *public* is bound to cause difficulties. There will be those who, quite correctly, wish to define the term and meaning much more tightly than I should wish to, but such debates should not be allowed to undermine what the espousal of a more open and public archaeology has done for the subject as a whole. The issue of defining the public has become an area of debate. Matsuda (2004) and Merriman (2004) have both considered this problem and the debate could be summarised by accepting that there are 'two notions of public – the state and the people'. Merriman went on to point out that, 'In the literature, most often "public" archaeology means archaeology regulated by the state, discharging a generalised public interest, and only occasionally does it mean the archaeology "of the public", who pursue their own (different and competing) ways of understanding the past' (Merriman 2004: 2). The reasons for this are obvious; professional archaeologists, especially outside academic circles, but also within them, tend to pursue their own interests by promoting what Merriman describes as the deficit model of public archaeology. Thus they conceive public archaeology as a process in which they control consumption of archaeology. This is done through state control of the resource in terms of site management and cultural heritage management processes that can be exported across the globe and also by giving to the non-archaeologist, the public, more 'education', which will in turn allow the consumers to appreciate and support more archaeological work and research. This approach forms the core of McGimsey's definition, and it is clear that professional archaeologists have even recognised the need to consult with other 'stakeholders' on the use of the archaeological resource, although consultation appears to ensure that in many cases, for example when it comes to site and resource management, this is merely lip-service. By pursuing this approach to public archaeology archaeologists can remain secure in their monopoly of expertise and wisdom but run the risk of failing to recognise 'some possible inconsistencies between the theory we preach and the social function we [could] perform' (Grima 2002: 89).

In 2004 the publication of *Public Archaeology* (Merriman 2004), just over 30 years on from McGimsey's original work, indicates just how much the balance in approaching public archaeology has shifted. The collection of papers indicates a wide geographical and topic spread that in Merriman's view represents a development from the deficit model of public archaeology to the multiple perspective model. He is right. The papers overall do demonstrate the multiple perspectives from which archaeology can be approached, and they collectively and individually emphasise the potential that public archaeology has to make archaeology relevant in a wider world, outside the confines of academia and bureaucracy. It also shows implicitly, the effectiveness of WAC 1 in changing the archaeological agenda.

The study and interpretation of objects and material from a remote, or even a recent, past remains at the core of archaeology. The importance of public archaeology as an area of study is that it introduces a relatively narrow discipline into a far more complex world and ensures that archaeologists confront the implications of their work and the development of their studies. It may not be tidy, but this was never the intention of Ucko when he introduced a 'non-professional' element into WAC1. There are no 'right' answers to the values that are inherent in indigenous archaeology any more than there are to the various aspects of alternative archaeology (Schadla-Hall 2004). Public archaeology is aimed at dialogue and debate; it is political and not formulaic and it takes what might be termed mainstream archaeology into uncertain territory. It is about continuing to develop an understanding of the ongoing manipulation of the past for social and political purposes. Without examining the public archaeology agenda our subject of archaeology will be used and abused by others, and simply complaining that those who use our conclusions inappropriately are not archaeologists misses the essential point. If we do not examine archaeology in a wider context we shall never be able to influence the ways in which our data and information is used. That is why public archaeology owes so much to WAC 1 and why archaeology as the proper study of mankind needs to embrace the downstream results of its activities and understand them.

REFERENCES

Ascherson, N. (2004) 'Archaeology and the British media' in *Public Archaeology*, N. Merriman (ed.), London: Routledge, pp. 145–158.

Austin, D. (1987) 'The future of archaeology in British Universities', *Antiquity*, 61: 225–238.

Cope, J. (1998) *The Modern Antiquarian – A Pre-Millennial Odyssey through Megalithic Britain*, London: Thorsens.

Cleere, H.F. (ed.) (1989) *Archaeological Heritage Management in the Modern World*, London: Unwin Hyman.

Ebbatson, L. (1999) 'Context and discourse: Royal Archaeological Institute membership 1845–1942' in *Building on the Past. Papers Celebrating 150 years of the Royal Archaeological Institute*, B. Vyner (ed.), London: Royal Archaeological Institute, pp. 22–74.

Grima, R. (2002) 'Archaeology as encounter', *Archaeological Dialogues*, 9.2: 83–89.

Jones, B. (1984) *Past Imperfect. The Story of Rescue Archaeology*, London: Heinemann.

Matsuda, A. (2004) 'The concept of "the public" and the aims of public archaeology', *Papers from the Institute of Archaeology*, 15: 66–76.

McGimsey, C.R. (1972) *Public Archaeology*, New York: McGraw-Hill.

Merriman, N.J. (ed.) (2004) *Public Archaeology*, London: Routledge.

Mower, J.P. (2000) 'Trench warfare? Archaeologists battle it out', *Papers from the Institute of Archaeology*, 11: 1–6.

Schadla-Hall, R.T. (2004) 'The comforts of unreason: the importance and relevence of alternative archaeology', in *Public Archaeology*, N. Merriman (ed.), London: Routledge, pp. 255–271.

Ucko, P.J. (1987) *Academic Freedom and Apartheid. The Story of the World Archaeological Congress*, London: Duckworth.

Ucko, P.J. (1989) 'Foreword', in *Archaeological Heritage Management in the Modern World*, H.F. Cleere (ed.), London: Unwin Hyman, pp. ix–xiv.

Ucko, P.J. (1990) 'Foreword', in *The Politics of the Past*, P. Gathercole and D. Lowenthal (eds), London: Unwin Hyman, pp. ix–xxi.

WAC (2005) *The History of the World Archaeological Congress*, available at http://ehlt. flinders.edu.au/wac/site/about_hist.php, accessed 01.12.2005.

CHAPTER 10

INDIGENOUS HUMAN REMAINS
AND CHANGING MUSEUM IDEOLOGY

Cressida Fforde and Jane Hubert

Museums have collected, conserved, studied and displayed human remains for centuries. Their right to do this has gone unchallenged. Only recently, with the ever-widening and intensifying campaign for the repatriation of human remains has the concept of 'giving back' what has been considered museum property been considered. Since collecting began on a wide scale in the early nineteenth century, human remains were considered on a par with the flora and fauna collected and dispatched abroad, reflecting colonial attitudes to the indigenous peoples of the world.

Collections of indigenous human remains are to be found in many European museums and institutions. These commonly form part of larger collections amassed to bring together human skeletal material from all over the world. They provided representative samples of all the different 'races' for study by physical anthropologists and comparative anatomists interested in understanding human diversity and evolution. These studies were conducted within a racist paradigm which upheld, and were a product of, perceptions of other peoples as biologically and culturally inferior to Europeans.

Most of these remains were obtained in the nineteenth and early twentieth centuries and were collected in various ways. Doctors in the colonies sent remains to their old universities; officers on the crews of exploring ships collected skulls and brought them home, sometimes as part of their remit; amateur scientists, anthropologists, missionaries and Protectors of Aborigines, amongst others, all believed in the claimed scientific importance of remains and sent them back to Europe. Some were purchased direct from collectors or from specialised auction rooms, and some were provided by overseas museums (see, for example, Weatherall 2000; Turnbull 2002; Fforde 2002, 2004).

Also in the nineteenth and twentieth centuries, museums in the New World supplied indigenous human remains to institutions in Europe and elsewhere. Sometimes these were donated. For example, the Canterbury Museum in New Zealand presented two Maori skulls to Oxford University in 1871, Wanganui museum presented two Maori skulls to the Natural History Museum, London, in 1925, and the Peabody Museum presented two Native American skulls to the Royal College of Surgeons of England in 1879.

In other cases, museums offered indigenous remains to other institutions in exchange. Along with floral and faunal specimens, indigenous human and cultural remains were a unique currency that could be used to acquire specimens from other museums. Curators in New World institutions had access to items believed to be of high scientific importance at the time and very hard to acquire in Europe, thus making them extremely valuable. The Natural History Museum in London acquired two Aboriginal skulls (in exchange) from Perth Museum in Western Australia, and the catalogue of the University of Oxford collection (now also mostly in the Natural History Museum) lists nine Maori skulls acquired (in exchange) from H.D. Skinner of Otago Museum.

In the 1870s and 1880s, Thomas F. Cheeseman, Curator of the Auckland Museum, set up a considerable exchange programme, and in this way greatly increased the size of the Auckland Museum collections. He wrote to many overseas museums, offering a wide range of 'specimens'. For example, on 19 September 1877 he wrote to Enrico Giglioli at the Natural History Museum in Florence:

> Dear Sir, On the part of the Auckland Museum, I take the liberty of writing to you to ascertain whether it would not be possible to open an exchange of specimens with the Museum under your charge ... I hope in a short time to have a considerable number of duplicates available for exchanges. I could send: 1st New Zealand bird skins ... 2nd NZ insects ... 3rd New Zealand Shells ... 4th Ethnological specimens relating to the Maori Race – also a series of their crania etc. I could also on my own account send a very large collection of herbarium specimens of NZ plants ...
>
> We principally wish to have in return specimens of South European mammals and birds, but we should gladly receive specimens in all branches of Natural History ... (Auckland War Memorial Museum archives: MA 96/6 Letter book 1872–1882)

Cheeseman's exchange programme was highly successful and continued after his curatorship had ended. Between 1877 and 1919, specimens were received in exchange from at least 22 institutions and individuals in New Zealand, Australia, the USA, Canada, Germany, England, Switzerland, Italy and France.

Although by no means all of these institutions received Maori and Moriori crania, many were sent overseas to, for example, the Australian Museum in Sydney, the Smithsonian Institution in Washington, the Royal College of Surgeons of England and the Natural History Museums of Paris, London and Florence. 'Thank-you' letters from European curators demonstrated a high level of interest in Cheeseman's consignments. On 1 March 1876, Prof. Quatrefages wrote from the Paris Natural History Museum, thanking Cheeseman for the first part of a collection of Maori skulls noting that:

> we have in France a proverb that says that the appetite comes in eating and the arrival of this shipment has me desiring more. Sir, I therefore take the liberty of referring to your good care our anthropological collections. (Auckland War Memorial Museum archives: MA95/38/9 Av2.1.23)

In response Cheeseman sent more Maori and Moriori remains (as well as bird skins and a tuatara lizard) to the Paris Natural History Museum. In a letter to Cheeseman (29 April 1877) Quatrefages wrote:

> Your ancient [remains] from the area around Auckland area [are] ... very interesting. I have only examined them, not having had the time to study them at the moment. But when Mr. Hamy and I will get to the Study of the Polynesians, they will be the most precious of data.
>
> Thank you for your Moriori skull. But if you could send me others I would be very appreciative. To have some certitude relating to the anthropological affinities of a population, one needs to have a certain number of skulls. Here the thing is all the more necessary in that the Chatham Islands was definitely peopled in part by Maoris, but in part also by a population that preceded them. Several skulls are therefore necessary to have the certitude that the two groups are basically Polynesian.
>
> I can offer you for your museum casts of Polynesians and other Oceanics (including Maoris) from the Dumont d'Urville expedition, castings of prehistoric skulls from the quaternary era ...
>
> All the skulls and skeletons that you can send us, be they ancient or recent, will be of much interest to us. The same goes for weapons, utensils of the Maori, but especially if they come from the most ancient inhabitants of the islands and from those that [...] as having preceded the present Maoris. (Auckland War Memorial Museum archives; AWMM MS 58, Box 14, folder 3)

A short while later, on 23 July 1877, Cheeseman responded:

> I hope to visit many of the old burial places of the Maoris to the north of Auckland, and
> will send you a more extensive collection and also a number of the weapons & tools used
> by the Maoris. These latter articles once very common, are now becoming rare, as the
> manufacturer of them has long since ceased. I have also written to the Chatham Islands of
> the Morioiri skulls – but communication with the islands is so infrequent that it may be
> some time before I secure them. We shall be much obliged for the collections you so kindly
> offer to send us. The case of the prehistoric skulls, and those of the Polynesians collected
> by the expedition of Dumont D'Urville would be very valuable to us. (Auckland War
> Memorial Museum archives: MA 96/6 Letter book 1872–1882)

It is clear from nineteenth and early twentieth century reports that the human remains of
indigenous populations were collected and exchanged or sold in the same way as – and
often among – collections of faunal and floral specimens. Many of those who collected the
remains of the indigenous people of their country apparently saw no distinction between
them. However, there is an increasing amount of historical evidence which illustrates that
some collectors were aware of indigenous opposition to the theft of their ancestors'
remains. In one instance, at least, such opposition delayed Cheeseman's collecting and
exchange programme. In a letter to William Flower of the British Museum (Natural
History) (25 May 1885), he wrote:

> I have at last succeeded in obtaining a very good series indeed of 30 crania … from a Maori
> burial cave … in the Whangarei district. This cave is only a few miles distant from the one
> from which I obtained the skulls sent to the College of Surgeons. I have known of it for
> some time, but until very lately some Maoris resided in the immediate vicinity, and kept
> such good watch that it would not have been prudent to have made an attempt to secure the
> skulls. I believe that the cave was used for burial purposes until about 25 years ago. – but
> of course most of the skulls must have been deposited a much longer time. (Auckland War
> Memorial Museum archives: MA 96/6 Letter book 1872–1882, p. 211)

The collecting of human remains of indigenous people was not only taking place in New
Zealand and Australia. They were also being dug up, sold and exchanged for scientific
study or display all around the globe. Museums required representative samples of all the
different 'races' and a network of international contacts were used to achieve this.
Although grave-robbing and theft of bodies or skulls decreased in the first decades of the
twentieth century, the skeletal remains of indigenous peoples continued to be treated
differently from the bodies of 'white' populations. In the USA, for example, when graves
were exposed, either through archaeological excavation, or as a result of commercial
demolition and construction, Native American remains were sent to laboratories and
museums for scientific investigations or display, whereas the remains of white Americans
were taken away for reburial.

THE REBURIAL ISSUE

By the 1970s, indigenous people in North America, Australia and New Zealand had begun
to request the return of the human remains of their ancestors housed in museums and other
institutions. These claims, and the opposing arguments put forward by many
archaeologists, physical anthropologists and museum professionals, became what is
known as the 'reburial' or 'repatriation' issue.

In Australia, issues about the treatment of Aboriginal human remains became widely
known through publicity and publications about Truganini, the so-called last Tasmanian,[1]

who died in 1876. Truganini had feared that her body would be exploited after death and had requested to a close friend that her remains be buried at sea. Her fears were justified as, soon after her burial, her remains were dug up and sent for study in Melbourne. She was later put on public display in the Tasmanian Museum until 1947, when her skeleton was taken off display and stored in the museum, available for scientific study, although as Ryan (1974) reports there was little scientific analysis of Truganini's skeleton in all the years that it had been available for research.

A prolonged campaign by Aboriginal people, supported increasingly by the Church and public opinion, strove to have Truganini's remains laid to rest. As part of this process, in 1974, the Australian Institute of Aboriginal Studies (AIAS), under its then Principal, Peter Ucko, recommended to the Director of the Tasmanian Museum that Truganini's remains be disposed of immediately in accordance with her own wishes and those of her descendants (Ucko 1975). In 1976, Truganini was cremated and her ashes scattered in the D'Entrecasteaux Channel – one hundred years after her death.

In 1986, at the first World Archaeological Congress (WAC), attended by over 500 people from 62 countries, the reburial issue was brought home to archaeologists in a forceful and, for some, emotionally challenging way:

> At this Congress Native Americans from the USA, Canada and South America, Australian Aborigines and Inuit from Sweden and Norway came together with archaeologists, in formal and informal sessions, to present and discuss the issue of greatest concern to them in the context of the discipline of archaeology – their prior claim to the remains of their ancestors. This claim to the 'ownership' of these remains, whether or not they could satisfy any legal demands for them to demonstrate direct relationship to the skeletal remains in question, had clear implications: human remains should not be disturbed or removed from the ground without consultation and permission; those in museums should be removed at once from public display; 'ancestors' should not be used as the subject of research without permission; they should be returned from museums, university departments and laboratories for disposal by the indigenous peoples by whatever means they consider appropriate. (Hubert 1992: 107)

The late Jan Hammil (Bear Shield) a Mescalero Apache Native American, and Robert Cruz, a Tohono O'otham from Arizona, presented the views of American Indians Against Desecration, which had been formed in 1974 as a result of the 'Longest Walk', when Native Americans walked from California to Washington DC in support of 'Treaty Rights':

> As we crossed the country and visited the universities, museums and laboratories, we found the bodies of our ancestors stored in cardboard boxes, plastic bags and paper sacks. We found our sacred burial places stripped and desecrated, the bodies, and sacred objects buried with our dead, on display for the curious and labelled 'collections', 'specimens' and 'objects of antiquity'. (Hammil and Cruz 1989: 195)

Ernest Turner, an Athabascan from Alaska, after visiting the Smithsonian Institution in Washington, said:

> It is not respectful to the people ... I was horrified, I had no idea that they had [ancestral remains] in the museum ... I was shocked that that was happening. (Turner, personal communication, September 1986)

In 1989, at an Inter-Congress on 'Archaeological Ethics and the Treatment of the Dead', WAC drew up a position statement on human remains. Proving that archaeologists and indigenous people could come to agreement through debate and discussion, the Vermillion Accord called for respect for the mortal remains of the dead, irrespective of origin, race, religion, nationality, custom and tradition, and for the wishes of the local community and relatives of the dead, as well as respect for the scientific research value of human remains (for information about the Accord, and its impact, see Zimmerman 2002). The Accord was later followed by WAC's Code of Ethics, which set out members' obligations to indigenous peoples.

Through the 1980s and early 1990s, continued campaigns by indigenous groups had begun to be supported by legislation and to force a shift in museum policy. Recognition by those in charge of collections that human remains belonged to source communities began slowly to challenge, and in some cases replace, the conviction that scientific value was paramount. In the USA, the 1990 Native American Graves Protection and Repatriation Act (NAGPRA) demonstrated that Native American ownership of Native American human remains, housed in institutions that receive federal funds, was now recognised in law (McKeown 2002):

> The Native American Graves Protection and Repatriation Act of 1990 and the regulations (43 CFR Part 10) that allow for its implementation address the rights of lineal descendants, Indian tribes, and Native Hawaiian organizations (parties with standing) to Native American human remains, funerary objects, sacred objects and objects of cultural patrimony, cultural items. The statute requires Federal agencies and museums to provide information about Native American cultural items to parties with standing and, upon presentation of a valid claim, ensure the item(s) undergo disposition or repatriation. (www.usbr.gov/nagpra)

By the mid-1980s, indigenous groups from many parts of the world were making requests for the return of human remains from museums in Europe and particularly from the UK. Australian Aboriginal groups were particularly active, and some success was forthcoming in the early 1990s with the return of remains from a number of small collections as well as from the large collection at the University of Edinburgh. This was the first institution with a substantial collection of indigenous human remains in the UK to adopt a policy of repatriation. The other three institutions which held major collections of human remains, the Natural History Museum in London, Cambridge University and the Royal College of Surgeons of England, as well as many other museums with much smaller collections, continued to refuse indigenous requests, arguing that the scientific value of remains outweighed the ethical, moral and spiritual concerns of indigenous peoples.

Over the past five years, the reburial issue in Britain has been largely dominated by the interest shown in it by the UK Government (Hubert and Fforde 2002). While traditionally taking the view that the issue was one for consideration by individual museums, at the beginning of the new millennium the UK government signalled a more direct interest in two ways. The first was a Prime Ministerial Joint Statement on Aboriginal Remains, on 4 July 2000, by the Prime Ministers of Australia and Britain, in which they agreed

> to increase efforts to repatriate human remains to Australian indigenous communities. In doing this, the governments recognise the special connection that indigenous people have with ancestral remains, particularly where there are living descendants.

The second was the findings of a Department of Culture, Media and Sport (DCMS) select committee set up in 2000 to examine issues surrounding the return and illicit trade of cultural property (www.culture.gov.uk). Although the reburial issue was not initially supposed to be of specific concern to this Committee, having received submissions from various parties, including indigenous groups, it concluded that claims for the return of human remains were in a unique category and deserved further and more detailed attention. As a result, the UK government appointed a Working Group on Human Remains in 2001, under the chairmanship of Professor Norman Palmer, to focus specifically on this issue.

THE DEPARTMENT OF CULTURE, MEDIA AND SPORT (DCMS) WORKING GROUP ON HUMAN REMAINS

Published in late 2003, the Report of the Working Group on Human Remains (www.culture.gov.uk) details the findings of three years of discussion, information gathering, consultation and debate with a wide range of authorities by leading museum, anthropology and legal professionals. It is a significant document in many ways, not least because it recognises the validity of indigenous claims and judges the current situation with regard to UK collections to be untenable. The Working Group considered that the way forward for museums was to introduce a Code of Practice, supported by a licensing system. It recommended that museums should have no legal impediment to de-accessioning human remains, but held back from proposing legislation to force museums to accede to indigenous wishes. Instead, it believed that decisions about the future of human remains collections should be underpinned with the guiding principle of consent, that this should be set out in a Code of Practice and that resolution should be pursued through communication and dialogue. Fundamental to establishing communication with communities was the full provision of information about collections and the seeking of consent for their continued retention and scientific use. However, not all the members of the Working Group agreed, and the report is also instructive because it highlights a growing division within the UK museum community – between those who continue to believe that the scientific value of human remains is paramount and an increasing number of others who consider this not to be the case.

This division is apparent in the Working Group's deliberations over the issue of consent, or the lack thereof, by source communities, in the initial collection, and continued retention and use of human remains for scientific research. In broad terms, consent was unanimously accepted as a guiding principle as it pertained to the wishes of the deceased or had been invested in close kin or relatives whose genealogical connection could be proven. While this was as far as a minority of the Working Group would go, the majority went further, believing instead that consent must be a 'paramount and universal principle' and

> a threshold consideration in determining the legitimacy of *any* proposed treatment of human remains by museums. Once the principle is entrenched, attention can focus on the more important and delicate question of *who* is an appropriately interested person or group and *whose consent* must be given. (DCMS 2003: 102)

On a practical level, this returned to an old point of divergence in the non-indigenous debate about the reburial issue, namely whether or not the level of information associated with human remains (i.e. name, biological lineage, how 'ethical' were the circumstances of removal) should determine the success of indigenous claims. In the early stages of the reburial issue in Australia, similar 'categories' of remains were also the first to be suggested by scientists as appropriate for repatriation, suggesting that the issue had as much to do with Western perceptions of who (or what) could be legitimately claimed as 'the dead' as it did with any claimed scientific value. However, in the end such a position was considered untenable and was replaced with the view that appropriate representatives within the indigenous community should have pre-eminent rights to determine the future of all remains within collections.

The greatest indicator of division within the Working Group was the Statement of Dissent by Neil Chalmers, Director of the Natural History Museum, which appends the Working Group Report. While in support of many of its conclusions, Chalmers disagreed with 'several of the report's recommendations in their detailed formulation, and also with significant parts of the main body of the report'. He believed the report to be slanted heavily in favour of the wishes of claimant communities and did not provide a 'proper balance' between these and the 'public benefits deriving from medical, scientific and other research'. He also considered some of the report's recommendations to be overly complicated and unworkable. Those with views similar to Chalmers quickly had their opinions publicised in the national press, for example, the *Independent*, *Financial Times* and *Daily Telegraph* all ran stories on 16 May 2003 in which leading scientists stressed the importance of human remains for current and future research.

The seemingly unbridgeable gap between the perspectives and beliefs of some scientists and those of the indigenous peoples whose human remains are in contention is epitomised in the context of Tasmanian remains. Some scientists have questioned whether, at least in Tasmania, those requesting the return of remains had any acceptable mandate to do so. For example, according to the director of the Leverhulme Centre, as quoted in the *Observer* (McKie 2003), Tasmanian Aborigines no longer exist, thus those whose remains are in collections have no descendants. This view is in very stark contrast to the views of Tasmanian Aboriginal people themselves, who had already responded to a similar charge, made at that time by geneticists, as quoted in the Working Group's report:

> having read the offensive language used by the museum submission we must say it is little wonder there is an increasing lack of sympathy for scientific research of us as a people. We are not animals to be described as 'pure' or 'spoiled' by inter-marriage. The use of such language reminds us of the Nazi era.
>
> We cannot resist saying that the geneticists' claim that Aborigines have no mandate to deal with the rights of our dead must be one of the best examples of pure hypocrisy we have heard for some time. (DCMS 2003: 38)

But not all holding institutions in the UK believed that scientific valued outweighed indigenous concerns. In 2003, prior to the publication of the Working Group Report, three museums returned Aboriginal remains to Australia: the Manchester City Museum and Art Gallery, the Horniman Museum in London, and the Royal College of Surgeons of England. The Manchester Museum judged that the indigenous moral claim to the four Australian human remains in its collection overrode 'any scientific or interpretative value, or legal rights of possession vested in the University', and hoped that its offer to return remains would provide a new basis on which to build 'a more rewarding relationship based on mutual understanding and respect between our peoples in the future'. For the

Director of the Manchester Museum, the return of Aboriginal remains was an act which recognised 'our common humanity' (http://museum.man.ac.uk).

While the Manchester Museum and the Horniman both housed a relatively small number of Aboriginal human remains, the Royal College of Surgeons housed about 50 crania, most, if not all, donated after the Second World War. While providing information about its collection to indigenous organisations, for many years the College had declined requests for repatriation. In 2003, with the return of remains to Australia, a process undertaken with the involvement of Aboriginal people, the President of the College stated his recognition of the importance to Aboriginal people of returning remains to their homeland, explaining that 'understanding different cultures is the way forward and as our museum here in the College is currently undergoing a change of direction – I look forward to a continuing dialogue on cultural issues' (DCMS 2003: 47–48). More recently, an endorsement of Aboriginal concerns was forthcoming from The Royal Society which told a seminar in London that indigenous cultural issues overwhelming outweighed the cause of science (*The Age* 13 January 2005).

These very different views held by staff and directors of leading UK institutions are more than simply a matter of a difference in opinion about the scientific value of skeletal remains collections, and the rights of indigenous communities – and not scientists – to determine what should happen to indigenous human remains. They indicate an emerging shift in museum ideology and future direction that has been growing internationally for some time. It began over 20 years ago in Australia, New Zealand and North America, where the relationship between museums and indigenous communities has been steadily renegotiated.

In its submission to the Working Group on Human Remains, Te Papa Tongarewa, the National Museum of New Zealand, placed its own acknowledgement of indigenous pre-eminent rights to their ancestors' remains in the context of the changing role of museums in today's society:

> The concept of museums working more closely with communities is an increasingly occurring practice internationally, as organisations recognise that reconnecting communities with their treasures increases the organisation's knowledge base and enhances the museum experience. The recognition of communities as key stakeholders in museums has significantly altered museum practice in many institutions around the world, including Te Papa. This principle underpins much of the work that Te Papa does and how it operates in relation to this issue.
>
> Te Papa achieves increased community participation through a number of partnership approaches including exhibitions, research, events and in the care of *taonga* or treasures. The repatriation of ancestral remains, though controversial and complex at times, is also a key means of developing and maintaining important relationships. (Te Papa Tongarewa 2003: 4)

For Te Papa,

> Traditional museological practice in the area of human remains, and the value of continuing to hold these collections can now be questioned when examined in light of positive relationships with indigenous communities and the changing role of museums in society.

One critical shift in perception at Te Papa, as at the Auckland War Memorial Museum (see later in the chapter), is the view that human remains are not artefacts or collection items. Instead:

> Te Papa recognises that … human remains have an ongoing connection with the peoples and cultures from which they originate. These remains are regarded as ancestors and will remain in the care of Te Papa until such time as matters of provenance and long term care have been discussed and agreed upon with Mäori/Moriori.

> Te Papa acknowledges that most of the human remains in its care are Mäori and Moriori and are therefore committed to acknowledging the inherent importance of human remains to Mäori and Moriori people. This commitment has considerable implications for how these human remains are cared for and managed within Te Papa. The human remains held at Te Papa are stored and treated with dignity and in a manner sympathetic with cultural and scientific requirements. This includes access and research parameters established in partnership with Mäori. (Te Papa Tongarewa 2003: 9)

Te Papa's commitment to changing the way it deals with human remains is evidenced both by the specially built room or wahi tapu in the foundations of the new building which has been blessed by Maori elders to contain human remains, and in its continuing role in the repatriation of Maori and Moriori human remains from overseas institutions. This role has recently received New Zealand Government mandate and funding.

Auckland War Memorial Museum's Governance Policy on Human Remains sets out its responsibilities towards the human remains in its collections. The purposes of the policy are:

- to provide direction on the care and handling of human remains;
- to ensure that the Maori values associated with any *whakapakoko, uru moko or koiwi* (Indigenous Human Remains) in the possession of the Museum are protected until such time as they can be repatriated to source;
- to facilitate the repatriation of all Museum-associated Indigenous Human Remains back to source.

According to this policy, at the Auckland War Memorial Museum, the Maori committee or Taumata-a-Iwi are 'Customarily accountable to all *iwi* for the guardianship (kaitiakitanga) of Indigenous Human Remains held by the Museum'. The Auckland War Memorial Museum Act of 1996 provides for the Taumata-a-Iwi, which is founded upon the principle of *mana whenua* (customary authority of and over ancestral land). The Taumata-a-Iwi 'acts in a trustee role in representing the interests of Maori and advising the Trust Board on matters of custodial policy and guardianship of *taonga* (Maori ancestral treasures) and any *whakapakoko, uru moko* and *koiwi* (indigenous human remains) held by the Museum'. Acknowledging its role in having sent Maori and Moriori human remains to other (and particularly overseas) institutions in the past, the Auckland War Memorial Museum's governance policy states that it 'will seek the cooperation of identified international museums and institutions to assist in the return of Auckland Museum-associated Indigenous Human Remains back to source'. To this end it is currently engaged in a research project to locate and document the human remains that it sent overseas as exchange items, and will provide the results of this research to relevant *Iwi*. Once a supplier of indigenous remains to institutions throughout the world, Auckland War Memorial Museum is thus now seeking to reverse the collecting process that it began over a 100 years ago.

The perception by New Zealand's primary museums of their roles and responsibilities towards the remains in their collections, the indigenous community and the broader community is very different, therefore, to many museums in Europe. Both the Auckland War Memorial Museum and Te Papa see their roles as primarily safekeeping on the behalf of descendants, whose wishes as to the future of these remains will be sought, respected and facilitated whether this be in respect of return to source communities or requests for scientific research.

By contrast, the Natural History Museum's 'Policy on Human Remains' states that:

> The Museum has very limited power to return human remains to their countries of origin on a permanent basis, owing to the constraints on disposal of items from the collection … This is combined with a presumption against disposal that arises from the recognition of the scientific value of maintaining a collection of human remains as a resource for active research. (Natural History Museum 2001)

The development of new policy at Auckland Museum and Te Papa, and at other museums in New Zealand, Australia and North America is in great part because these countries have an indigenous population. Museums have an indigenous constituency and employ an increasing number of indigenous staff. As a result the museums have been forced to develop a new relationship with indigenous people and, in doing so, institutional perceptions about indigenous human remains have undergone a fundamental change.

Such an indigenous constituency is obviously lacking in the UK, although British museums have increasingly sought to be inclusive of the UK's own ethnic minorities. In addition, some UK museums have sought to establish relationships with foreign cultures whose collections they curate, and in some cases this relationship has been formulated around repatriation. The return of a Ghost Dance shirt by the Kelvingrove Museum in Glasgow to the Lakota Sioux is an example of this (Simpson 2002). The Kelvingrove had acquired the shirt from a member of Buffalo Bill's Wild West Show which had visited Glasgow in 1892. In the late nineteenth century many Lakota Sioux began to practise a new religion, that of the Ghost Dance, that would help them drive out the colonisers. Wearers of Ghost Dance shirts would be protected from gunfire. Fleeing their reservation to practise the banned Ghost Dance religion, hundreds of Lakota Sioux were massacred by the US cavalry at Wounded Knee in 1890.

In 1994 a request was made by the Wounded Knee Survivors' Association for the return of the Ghost Dance shirt at the Kelvingrove Museum. After initial refusal and later re-examination of the request, including a public hearing at which presentations were given by museum staff and members of the Lakota Sioux, Glasgow City Council's Arts and Culture Committee decided to return the shirt. However, this was done on condition that the shirt would continue to educate about the Lakota Sioux and its own history in Glasgow, that at times agreed by Glasgow City Council and the Wounded Knee Survivor's Association the shirt might be brought back to Glasgow for public display and that the Council and the Association would explore opportunities for developing educational and cultural links. The Lakota Sioux presented the Kelvingrove with a replica shirt and other items. These formed the centrepiece of a display at the Kelvingrove which presented information to the public about the shirt, the story of the Lakota people, Wounded Knee and the repatriation itself. As argued by Mark O'Neill, head of curatorial services, to the public hearing:

> If museums represent our better selves and humane values, then we have to admit the possibility that there may be other values, which are more important than that of possession. Possession is not an absolute value. If our values lead us to preserve an object because of what it tells us about the history of a particular human group, then it is inconsistent not to give that group the respect of at least taking their views seriously. (O'Neill 1998, quoted in Simpson 2002: 208)

There is evidence, therefore, that some UK museums now wish to establish a collaborative, inclusive relationship with the indigenous communities whose cultural heritage they curate and to do this must face and resolve indigenous requests for the return of their ancestors' remains. Increasing globalisation both facilitates and motivates this shift. Indigenous peoples campaign for their concerns and for their voices to be heard. Organisations such as the WAC have assisted communication by bringing archaeologists, museum people and indigenous people together. Its publications have sought to place information about collections in the public domain and include indigenous authors from both academic and non-academic backgrounds thus helping to breakdown the barriers between those who study and curate indigenous culture and those whose past is the subject of enquiry (and these groups are obviously not mutually exclusive).

Other factors have also been significant in changing perceptions about human remains. The significance of human remains to individuals and families in the UK, as a result of the 'stolen babies' and stolen organs episode, was brought home to families whose babies were stripped of their organs without their consent, and became evident to the rest of the population when it was reported that some 54,000 organs, body parts, still births and fetuses had been retained from post-mortems in the UK without parental consent (Department of Health 2002). The issue of consent was paramount. For example:

> During the inquiry into the management of the care of children receiving complex heart surgery at Bristol Royal Infirmary, it emerged that the retention of hearts removed (for teaching and research) during post-mortem examination of the child's body had been commonplace. In many cases it appears to have taken place without parental consent or indeed knowledge. Specifically, it emerged that a more extreme situation existed at Alder Hey Children's Hospital in Liverpool. The Alder Hey Inquiry has found that collections of children's hearts and other organs had been accumulated over several decades, in some cases as long as 50 years. The Inquiry established that it had been common practice to retain organs without express parental knowledge and agreement. (Department of Health 2000)

The public outcry about the treatment of human remains within British culture might have been expected to bring about a change in attitudes towards the human remains of other cultures. Nonetheless there is still resistance to change, particularly in those UK institutions which retain large collections of human remains.

The Report of the Working Group on Human Remains, published in November 2003 (www.culture.gov.uk), was a significant document, stressing the vital necessity for ethical consideration of the rights of indigenous communities claiming the repatriation of their ancestral remains. As we have seen, not all members of the group supported these views to the same extent, especially in the context of the need to obtain consent from descendant communities for the retention and scientific use of ancestral remains. Following the Report of the Working Group, a detailed consultation paper: 'Care of historic human remains' (DCMS 2004) opened a consultation period from July to October 2004. The main points of the consultation were:

- whether current laws relating to the holding of human remains by UK museums, taken together with the new provisions of the Human Tissues Bill, are sufficient;
- whether museums holding human remains should be subject to some form of Code of Practice or regulation;
- whether the Government should establish a Human Remains Advisory Panel to mediate claims for repatriation;

- how museums should handle claims for restitution of human remains and what model of consent should be adopted in dealing with any claims.

Over 40 representatives of UK institutions – about half of whom were museums or research centres – responded to the consultation (see www.culture.gov.uk for individual responses). As a result of the responses received, the DCMS has convened a Human Remains Code of Practice Drafting Group, whose brief is to produce a Code of Practice for the keeping of human remains in museums and, where appropriate, other human remains collections in England, Wales and Northern Ireland, in accordance with the Human Tissue Act 2004.

In response to one of the Working Group's key recommendations, the government has moved to change the law to allow nine national museums to move human remains out of their collections (through Section 47 of the Human Tissue Act 2004). Previous to this (and see the Natural History Museum's statement on return quoted earlier in this chapter) some museums had argued that the British Museum Act (1963) made it illegal for them to de-accession items from their collections, although this had been argued against by Aboriginal authorities, amongst others (see Simpson 2002). However, there will be no introduction of a licensing system, as recommended by the Working Group, to support the Code of Practice, which will thus be at the discretion of museums to endorse and follow.

The Committee drafting the Code of Practice is chaired by the Museum of London and consists of representatives from a range of institutions: the British Museum, English Heritage, the Horniman Museum, the Leverhulme Centre of Evolutionary Studies (Cambridge), the Museums Association, the Natural History Museum (London), National Museums and Galleries of Wales, the Petrie Museum (University College London (UCL)) and the Wellcome Trust. Despite the emphasis placed by the Working Group on including indigenous people in the decision-making process, there are no indigenous representatives on this committee.

Although many of the institutions represented on the committee expressed support for a Code of Practice, the majority were predominantly unsympathetic to the majority view on consent as set down in the report of the Working Group on Human Remains. Only UCL (Petrie Museum) and the Museums Association responded in support (although it should be noted that the Horniman Museum has responded positively to requests for the repatriation of human remains). All others supported the minority view. For example, in response to the question in the consultation document relating to the view of the majority of the Working Group:

> Do you agree with the view of the majority of the Working Group that where no family or descendants are identified, there should be a requirement to obtain consent from those who have within the deceased person's own religion or culture a status or responsibility comparable to that of close family or direct genealogical descendants? (DCMS 2004: 28)

the Leverhulme Centre of Evolutionary Studies (Cambridge University) responded:

> We would most strongly agree with the minority report. The majority report is not only impractical, but is based on a very essentialist notion of human communities – as static entities with unified perspectives … It would be completely impossible to ask curators to seek out those who, according to their particular community's cultural values, might have a religious, or cultural position of responsibility for that community's historical human remains. The most straightforward and effective way forward would be to develop a code of practice which would place the responsibility on the Curator to respond to claims and to do his/her best to ensure that consultation across a wide cultural spectrum takes place. (Leverhulme Centre for Evolutionary Studies 2004: 6)

This is despite over a decade of experience by national museums in Australia, North America and New Zealand of consulting with indigenous groups about the continued retention or return of human remains in museum collections. The majority view in the Working Group's Report demonstrated a keen awareness of the complexities involved in consent issues, including issues of distance in time and distance of personal relationship, but in relation to these, it adds: 'But that will be judged by the standards of the belief system at issue, and not by Western standards' (DCMS 2003: 113). Crucially, the majority believed that:

> Consent should therefore be a starting principle for all museum holdings of human remains. In conformity with the approach of the DH towards future-acquired material, but subject to the qualifications that we have outlined, consent should be the cardinal legitimising principle for the retention and treatment of existing holdings of human material by all museums: in lawyer's terms, a condition precedent. (DCMS 2003: 115)

Museums worldwide clearly perceive human remains, their value, relevance and meaning in very different ways. This difference is in large part one of ideology. Over the past five years, the UK Government has strongly signalled its interest in the reburial issue. The removal of legislation that impedes the de-accessioning of remains is a step forward, as may be the direction provided by the Code of Practice – in draft at the time of writing. However, the majority of responses to the consultation document, the composition of the Code of Practice Drafting Group and the brief announcement from Government (21 March 2005) suggest a very real danger that, despite the comprehensive analysis by the Working Group on Human Remains, indigenous communities requesting the return of their ancestral remains will have no more power to achieve this than they have now.

It is clear, however, that the repatriation issue has changed the perspectives of many, including museum curators and scientists, regarding the individual, social and cultural significance of human remains. As a result, and in a very real sense, museums will never be the same again.

ACKNOWLEDGEMENT

We are very grateful to the Auckland War Memorial Museum for permission to reprint letters from their archives.

NOTE

1 Despite ongoing assertions, particularly in the anti-repatriation camp, that Tasmanian Aborigines became 'extinct' with the death of Truganini, there are many Tasmanian Aboriginal people today descended from the pre-contact population of Tasmania.

REFERENCES

The Age (2005) 'Museums face court if they keep remains'. Melbourne 13 Journey. Department of Culture, Media and Sport (DCMS) (2003) *Report of the Working Group on Human Remains*, available at www.culture.gov.uk. Accessed 29.11.2005.

Department of Culture, Media and Sport (DCMS) (2004) *Care of Historic Human Remains*, available at www.culture.gov.uk. Accessed 29.11.2005.

Department of Health (2000) *Report of a Census of Organs and Tissues Retained by Pathology Services in England*, London: The Stationery Office.

Department of Health (2002) *Retention and Use of Human Tissue and Organs*, London: The Stationery Office.

Fforde, C. (2002) 'Yagan' in *The Dead and Their Possessions: Repatriation in Principle, Policy and Practice*, C. Fforde, J. Hubert and P. Turnbull (eds), London: Routledge, pp. 229–241.

Fforde, C. (2004) *Collecting the Dead: Archaeology and the Reburial Issue*, London: Duckworth.

Hammil, J. and Cruz, R. (1989) 'Statement of American Indians against desecration before the World Archaeological Congress', in *Conflict in the Archaeology of Living Traditions*, R. Layton (ed.), London: Unwin Hyman, pp. 195–200.

Hubert, J. (1992) 'Dry bones or living ancestors?', *International Journal of Cultural Property*, 1 (1) 105–127.

Hubert, J. and Fforde, C. (2002) 'Introduction: the reburial issue in the 21st century', in *The Dead and Their Possessions: Repatriation in Principle, Policy and Practice*, C. Fforde, J. Hubert and P. Turnbull (eds), London: Routledge, pp. 1–16.

Leverhulme Centre of Evolutionary Studies (2004) 'Response to DCMS Care of Human Remains Consultation', available at www.culture.gov.uk. Accessed 29.11.2005.

McKeown, C.T. (2002), 'Repatriation in the USA: a decade of federal agency activities under NAGPRA', in *The Dead and Their Possessions: Repatriation in Principle, Policy and Practice*, C. Fforde, J. Hubert and P. Turnbull (eds), London: Routledge, pp. 108–132.

McKie, R. (2003) ' Scientists fight to save ancestral bone bank. Aborigines demand return of skeletal remains'. *The Observer*. 28 September.

Natural History Museum (2001) *Policy on Human Remains*. Submission to the Working Group on Human Remains: Appendix I, available at www.culture.gov.uk. Accessed 29.11.2005.

Ryan, L. (1974) *Report to the Australian Institute of Aboriginal Studies on Truganini*, Canberra: AIAS.

Simpson, M. (2002) 'The plundered past: Britain's challenge for the future', in *The Dead and their Possessions: Repatriation in Principle, Policy and Practice*, C. Fforde, J. Hubert and P. Turnbull (eds), London: Routledge, pp. 199–217.

Te Papa Tongarewa (2003) ' Working group on human remains. Submission by The Museum of New Zealand, Te Papa Tongarewa'. London: Departmnet of Culture, Media and Sport, UK Government.

Turnbull, P. (2002) 'Indigenous Australian people, their defence of the dead and native title', in *The Dead and Their Possessions: Repatriation in Principle, Policy and Practice*, C. Fforde, J. Hubert and P. Turnbull (eds), London: Routledge, pp. 63–86.

Ucko, P.J. (1975) 'Review of AIAS activities 1974', *AIAS Newsletter*, 3, 6–17.

United States Government: Bureau of Reclamation. The Native American Graves Protection and Repatriation Act (NAGPRA) 1990, available at www.usbr.gov/nagpraj. Accessed 29.11.05.

Weatherall, R. (2000) '1989: Aborigines, archaeologists, and the rights of the dead', paper presented at 1989 WAC Inter-Congress, Vermillion, South Dakota, available at www.faira.org.au/lrq/archives/200102/stories/dead_rights.html. Accessed 29.11.2005.

Zimmerman, L. (2002) 'A decade after the Vermillion Accord: what has changed and what has not?', in *The Dead and Their Possessions: Repatriation in Principle, Policy and Practice*, C. Fforde, J. Hubert and P. Turnbull (eds), London: Routledge, pp. 91–98.

CHAPTER 11

'THE MAN WHO WOULD BE MOSES'

Beverley Butler and Michael Rowlands

'Moses' will not let my imagination go.
(Freud quoted in Raphael-Leff 1999: 310)

INTRODUCTION

The point of departure for our paper is two collectors. The first, Professor Sigmund Freud, has famously been photographed surrounded by his collection of antiquities, including, for example, a Greek Sphinx, the Egyptian god Thoth and a Chinese sage, which one critic described as Freud's 'ancestors of choice' (Gamwell 1989: 29). The second, Professor Peter Ucko, also a self-confessed collector (Ucko 2001: 302), has been photographed surrounded by what another set of critics (Museum Studies students) describe as 'One World Archaeology' objects. The latter photograph currently hangs in the staff room of the Institute of Archaeology (IoA), University College London (UCL), with a sample of these objects in a glass case. An interesting link between the two men occurs with Ucko's recent challenge to a dominant genre of critique which argues that one can psychoanalyse Freud using his 'antiquities as so many surgical knives to probe mysteries' (Gay 1989: 19: cf. Corcoran 1991; Forrester 1994; Ucko 2001). Instead he argues that, with honourable exceptions, Freud made no explicit statements that his collections held 'meaning' and, as such, they cannot legitimately be used to issue statements about Freud's relationship to what are now regarded as 'Freudian subjects' of origins, identification, transference and other psychoanalytic themes. Perhaps ironically, Freudian theory itself issues the same critique of presumed systems of meaning ['a cigar is just a cigar'] by challenging stated reasons for actions and behaviours and instead using 'archaeological' techniques to access into 'buried', 'repressed' 'meanings' via the interpretation, for example, of 'slips' and 'dream-work'.

A further feature that these two collectors hold in common is that their objects provide a link between collections and commemoration (an apt topic for a *Festschrift*). A number of Freud's objects were gifts (Ucko 2001: 282) (some to commemorate birthdays, for example); similarly, the label in the IoA staff room points out that to a large extent these objects are gifts, the intention of which is to commemorate Ucko. In what follows, our purpose is to pursue these connectivities further. We seek to discuss the potency of collecting, collections and commemoration not only as concepts and practices but also as methodological frameworks of analysis. As such we discuss the deconstructive potency of the intellectual as the 'collector' of disparate facts who challenges, destroys – thus engages in an 'archaeology of the deconstruction' of – the presumed system of meaning. We also use this to bring into view a further dynamic: the 'Moses syndrome' (as Freud illustrates earlier in the text he has an enduring preoccupation and/or empathetic/ sympathetic identification with Moses/the 'ancestors') which directs us to the status of our two collectors as 'founders' of a discipline (that of psychoanalysis and of 'One World Archaeology' respectively) and not only offers up the question of how one engages in acts of reconstruction and of alternative interpretation but takes on the task of both creating and also sustaining a vision of a transformed future.

EUROCENTRIC 'REGIMES OF MEMORY' – COMMEMORATING THE ANCESTORS

The Western genealogy of commemoration is realised in forms of collective memory objectified in public spaces such as museums, monuments and memorials. Fearful of the general impulse of modernity to permeate identity with a sense of instability and anxiety ('all that is solid melts into air'), commemorative acts project into a past a sense of stability and fixity through the sacralisation of key ancestral tropes/ origins. The communitarian Christian ethos in which this figures is scarcely accidental since, by calling on such sacrificial metaphors, the reality of an anxious present is projected into a more stable past. The impulse to both commemorate and collect is based on a project, therefore, which aims not only to introduce a system of meaning but also to stabilise collective memory and identity by appearing to respond to active appeals of the ancestors and their remembrance by the living.

Commemoration as a process is therefore dominated both by the idea that it is the living in the present that actively remember, and the view that culture and history are not just something created by people but that which creates persons and their capacity to remember. This is a fairly straightforward understanding of why tangible heritages of objects, archives, museums, monuments and memorials exist, in order to make us believe in the permanence of identity and an authenticity of 'pure' origins (typically collectively 'Greek'). Moreover, following Nora's now classic work on 'lieux de memoires', these regimes of memory are self-consciously held ideas of the past, constructed usually in the midst of upheaval (Nora 1989). As Lowenthal suggests, the projection of an image of permanence on to a landscape is more important than accuracy in historical detail (Lowenthal 1996). As history destroys the capacity for 'real memories', Nora argued that it constructs instead regimes of memory as a social and encompassing symbiosis maintained through objects and performances (cf. Nora 1989; Connerton 1989).

Nineteenth-century Western commemoration is dominated by the idea that the actions of the present can redeem the violent acts of the past, that is, the Western genealogy of commemorating suffering and imaginative reliving lies within the Christianity of the Via Dolorosa. The more general point is that commemoration has a 'theological implication', bound up as it is in a spirit of *communitas* as part of a secularising modernity and in the display of its triumphs, underpinned by ideas/ideals of progress. By the twentieth century, this had come to narrativise a perception of consciousness and mortality that, rather than commemorating God, now commemorates what it is to be human. The effects of twentieth century war transformed the significance of the museum/monument from patriotic nationalism to a more frightening suggestion that the shades of the dead are alive and can have an effect on the living. Commemoration became imbued with a belief in social justice which insisted that not only should sacrifice be recognised but also that not to do so would be evocative of a 'bad death'. Recognition of the obligation of the present to the violent deaths of the past was therefore acceptance that more than homage by the present was required but also of the need to stabilise it in the face of profound loss of social cohesion. Empathy, initially conceived as an aesthetic experience, offered a means to experience the suffering of others without explicitly claiming to imaginatively relive modernity's violences. Such obligations to ancestors/ origins shift the practice of commemoration from a process of remembering transmitted pasts to an active engagement with the consequences of past actions in the present. Monuments and memorials are neither fully past nor present, to cite Maleuvre's argument on the uncanny nature of commemoration; the ceremonial aspects of commemoration move backwards and forwards in sacrificial time (Maleuvre 1999: 22).

In the Western genealogy, the motive for the collection, monument and museum is to create a safe ancestral 'home', 'origin', or 'refuge' where a politics of belonging can be identified as a way to be redeemed. But the essentialising of empathy on which this depends is always only partial and the extent to which its redemptive/curative aspects can be recognised are limited. The extremes of this scenario are, according to one critic, that, 'Sympathy is performed with altruistic ends, but empathy may or may not be motivated by good intentions. Indeed one may empathise solely with narcissistic ends. It is said, for example, that Hitler empathised with the Jews in order to annihilate them.' (Wispe 1991: 5)

'DISTURBANCES OF MEMORY': THE RETURN OF 'OTHER' ANCESTORS

'Freud, hesitant and a little embarrassed, wants to suggest that Moses was perhaps an Egyptian.' (Bennington 1992: 106)

This 'disturbance' is based on Freud's experience of visiting the particular 'Greek' icon of the Acropolis. His experience of a 'disturbance' (a feeling of 'de-realisation' when his literal confrontation with what had previously been a literary landscape/ 'object of the imagination' (and as such housed in the timeless landscape of the 'unconscious')) brought about the possibility of accessing the unconscious (Freud 1984: 443–456). This, it has been claimed, offered Freud a 'moment' of radical alterity – a crisis/ breakthrough in the recognition of repressed memories, identities, origins, genealogies and new interpretations of self/world. The analogue we wish to draw is with a more general disturbance of memory or a disruption of confidence in the Eurocentric framework of commemoration. At the most obvious site to sustain the integrity of the empathetic identification with a European ancestry/ origin and its capacity to sustain the integrity of identity in the face of the dissolving onslaught of modernity, Freud's vision fails and the self-imposed fixity of identity is exposed.

The idea that heritage is unstable and cannot be controlled is pursued further by Derrida who challenges, in his discussion of the Freudian archive, the assumed stability of the Western' 'Greek' archive by drawing out the archival dramas, repressions and violences which underpin it. The archive is thus recast as the scene of epic Oedipal violences which are underpinned by the destructive forces of the 'death-drive', which manifests as a force of evil and malice (Derrida 1996: 80). This Derridean thesis thus has a clear identification with a 'trauma in the archive' according to Rapaport (2003: 81), who emphasises that 'archives occur at that moment when there is a structural breakdown in memory' and by way of a comparative illustration reiterates 'where there is regularity and efficiency in Foucault's archive, there is trauma in Derrida's' (Rapaport 2003: 76). The dominant 'Greek' control of the archive and their status as the pre-eminent 'hospitality-givers' (Rapaport 2003: 84) is also disturbed by Derrida's account of the figure of the 'Jew' within the archival domain and the 'acting out' of a 'Jewish story' of 'exile' and exodus/Exodus (Rapaport 2003: 81). As such, Freud's texts of *Totem and Taboo* (1986a [1913]) and of *Moses and Monotheism* (1986b [1939]) are positioned as the emergent foundational/originary scripts of archival dramas (Derrida 1996: 59), both of which are underpinned by the trauma of an originary act of murder (Derrida 1996: 65).

For Derrida, this crisis/breakthrough affords further destabilisations in the form of the re-emergence of other archival spectres, lost ancestors, forgotten genealogies, 'aboriginal' figures, alternative origins and 'traces' of 'the other' which come (partially) into view (Derrida 1996: 34; see also Feuchtwang 2000). A Eurocentric fixity of identity becomes irremediably lost and for Freud and Derrida it is a Jewish/Egyptian repressed 'other' that comes back to haunt and to claim a space in the alternative archaeologies available to explore origins. Again, the issue is of neglected ancestors erupting into the present to claim a place in dissolving a narrative of origins that excluded their contribution. Crucially too, Derrida's text can also be understood as an alternative (though ultimately unresolved and irresolvable) commemoration of Freud. As such Derrida combines his search for and deconstruction of the 'Greek' 'origins' and control of archive with a parallel search for the 'secrets' of Freud's personal 'archive'/ identity-work.

It is H.D., the poet and Freud's analysand, however, who, in her own commemorative volume – her *Festschrift*-like 'Tribute to Freud' (1974 [1956]) – offers a means to link Freud to his collection. Ucko points to 'exceptional category to her insights', suggesting that in H.D.'s case her 'treatment' as analysand was based upon a recognition that this was 'part of a situation, which includes the analyst's and the patient's personalities.' (Ucko 2001: 285). H.D.'s characterisation of Freud as the 'Blameless physician' leads her to see Freud in a liminal position between life and death, and as controller of the 'pharmacy' and 'pharmakon' which sees psychoanalysis as the ambivalent poison/cure and gift/ burden (Chisholm 1992: 27). She characterises him not only within an earlier, original identity as 'Egyptian' but also with reference to more alchemical and even totemic images and meanings. A return to Derrida clarifies the extent deconstruction owes to this search for alternative 'personas' and 'concepts'. It is, therefore, with Freud as a Moses/ Muse figure that Derrida powerfully takes up 'Egypt' as an emblem and also as what is perhaps best described as a speculative synonym for deconstruction (Bennington 1992). In a complex schema (or non-schema as Derrida might have it) 'Egypt', like 'deconstruction' itself is subsequently staged as a liminal 'site'/'non-site', a 'beyond', a 'between', and a 'beneath' and as an 'undecided', which is always enigmatic, and therefore never fixed (Bennington 1992: 116; Derrida 1997). Moreover, the key dramas that Derrida seeks to return to in order to both 'destabilise' and 'unfix' are nothing less than the foundation moments of Western metaphysics.

Deconstruction then reclaims 'Egypt' as the 'unnameable necessity', which is capable of confronting Western 'logos' culture with its own fears, distress, confusion and blindness with regard to the nature of its own origin (Bennington 1992). It is here that alternative 'readings' of the central themes of origins, traumatic loss, separation, and reattachment and the dynamics of cosmopolitanism and 'othering' can be extracted and the final possibility of a movement into what Freud termed the 'dark continent'. The synonym of Egypt as Africa here is scarcely accidental, nor the implication that Africa once again is the mediation that enables the West to accede to its own subconscious and give a public account of its subjectivity (cf. Mbembe 2001: 3). In this case, Derrida's use of the 'zombie' to provoke an anxious encounter as a third space in between, is intended to short-circuit the usual logic of distinction (see Collins and Mayblin 2001). Ancestors, as neither alive nor dead, return to affect the living through objects, illness and violent acts as well as through ensuring the conditions of fertility and cultural reproduction. The Africanist turn is taken therefore precisely in order to subvert the Freudian theme of internalised memory and identity as fixed in a particular trajectory. A Western subjectivity is deemed to be confronted by an exteriority; the world of objects and things that instils an agency for good or bad purposes depending on context.

RECONSTRUCTION OF WORLDS: EMPATHETIC IDENTIFICATION/SYMPATHETIC MAGICS

At this point we need to bring into play the notion of empathy/sympathy. The first, commonly understood to embrace 'the ability to imagine oneself in another's space', is often considered to be the cornerstone of morality (i.e. a gauge for understanding goodness) and a form of social awareness and of moral reasoning (Basch 1983: 110). The counter view would be that which sees empathy as relative and sees morality reduced to a set of meaningless private languages. A further critical position would be that 'empathy has little to do with the other person (the empathee); in other words, when we hurt somebody, we don't experience his [her] pain. We experience OUR pain ... So we experience pain whenever another person claims to experience it as well. We feel guilty.' (Rogers 1999) The commemoration of origins/ancestors and empathetic identification with the 'other' is assumed to be a moral act and by default will mean that history will not repeat itself if we 'remember' (empathise with) the cruelties of the past. As Elie Wiesel stated at the visit of Clinton and the inauguration of the Washington Holocaust Museum (Channel 4 2001), to identify perhaps with your own suffering and not necessarily that of the suffering of others is often a substitute for action (in this case Wiesel refers to Bosnia and the suffering there; that is, it is easier morally/ethically to remember the horrors of the past in museological form than to deal with their contemporary and future manifestations); or as Sontag reminds us: the museum/photograph will not *per se* stop repetitious cycles of cruelty/ violence (Sontag 2003).

> The extremes of this position have, however, drawn out the potential amorality of empathy and its relationship to the term 'sympathy'.
>
> In empathy the self is the vehicle for understanding, and it never loses its identity. Sympathy, on the other hand, is concerned with communion rather than accuracy, and self-awareness is reduced rather than enhanced ... In empathy one substitutes oneself for the other person; in sympathy one substitutes others for oneself. To know what something would be like for the other person is empathy. To know what it would be like to be that person is sympathy. In empathy one acts "as if" one were the other person. The object of empathy is understanding. The object of sympathy is the other person's well-being. In sum, empathy is a way of knowing; sympathy is a way of relating. (Wispe 1991: 5)

The extremes of this scenario are according to one critic, 'Sympathy is performed with altruistic ends, but empathy may or may not be motivated by good intentions.' (Wispe 1991:5)

We can now associate the limits of empathy and an understanding of it as a substitute for action with Derrida's designation of the 'zombie' within his lexicon of deconstruction. Derrida is credited with exposing a dilemma/intimacy in the (potentially) redemptive idea that an archival acting out can be repeated in such a way that the trauma can be mastered (Rapaport 2003: 89). Significantly, this archival dilemma is expressed by Rapaport as the difference between a mastery of trauma as played out, for example, in the museological realm (he cites the Washington Holocaust Museum as an example of this potential) while also exploring the crisis of empathetic identification which is also bound up in such domains (Rapaport 2003: 89). The latter crisis is detailed as a risk to an 'empathetic moment in which [occurs] a transferential contamination of trauma [which one] might call 'secondary trauma' (Rapaport 2003: 88). He argues further, 'Apparently, from a Derridean perspective, one does not simply inherit or share the trauma of others; one encounters trauma as something that is Other on a horizon that is not predictable.' (Rapaport 2003: 88)

The dilemma has been expressed as the difference between the mastery of trauma, as for example played out in the museological realm, and the risk involved in the fact that one does not simply inherit or share the trauma of others. Again the dilemma is between the discourse that 'destroys' and that which 'holds': discourse can also be destroyed by the traumatism. When the discourse holds in some way, it is at once because it has been opened up on the basis of some traumatizing event, by an upsetting question that doesn't let one rest, that no longer lets one sleep, and because it nevertheless resists the destruction begun by its traumatism" (Derrida quoted in Rapaport 2003: 88–89). This relates to the claims he makes vis-à-vis UNESCO that it needs to respond and give recognition to the archive of the 'other' and of 'difference' and thus define an archival economy that holds rather than 'destroys' (Derrida 2000a).

Always the third space is a resource that will neither repeat nor destroy but promises a 'return to the real'; a means of being responsive to 'others' and to their aspirations for a future. But this does not resolve the problem of empathy as a potentially narcissistic, colonising urge and also as a resource for imposing on others how they should think and feel about the conditions within which they live and aspire for a future. This relates to the fact that there is a cruelty to stripping people of meaning if one accepts (as the majority would) the necessity of human beings expressing themselves through story-telling as a key focus of identity, memory-work and meaning-making and its use as a fundamental resource of asserting the dignity of self.

Derrida's hope for the agency of a third space, therefore, will not open up this scenario for critical thought to promote the needed radical ambivalence and the destruction of meaning precisely because it does not fully escape the Western logic of empathetic identification. Said's alternative 'excavation' of Freud's 'Moses' similarly looks to the 'openings' and 'fissures' responsive to 'non-European' identity-work using these as a resource to articulate a 'just' future for Palestine (Said 2003). His broader 'archaeology of identity' draws out alternative 'cosmopolitan' and 'besieged identities' (Said 2003: 53–54) as alternative strategies of 'othering'. Said sees these as fundamental to the creation of 'just' futures through the recognition of mutual experiences: notably those of suffering and marginalisation. As such the potential applications for those who remain 'exiled' outside the realms of institutional-archival hospitality – the archive's originary constituency – are evident. A solution to the apparent failure of empathetic identification, or rather its Western underpinnings of tolerance and compassion, instead involves returning to our two collectors and, in the process, imagining that we get to the 'promise' that Derrida says is the messianic aspect of the archive. This is also the route towards the recognition and re-conceptualisation of alternative 'sympathetic heritage magics' across and within North and South.

CONCLUSION: THE RETURN HOME AND PROMISED LANDS

The final preoccupations of Freud during the last year of his life were not only to finish *Moses and Monetheism* (1939), his last great book, but to secure a future for psychoanalysis, the 'science' he founded. In a letter to Jung written years before, Freud's unease manifested itself in his sense that, as 'Moses the founder', all he could do was to 'glimpse from afar' yet never enter or return to the 'promised land of psychiatry'; this in turn is underpinned by a moment of anxiety that he and Jung 'may have strayed onto the wrong path' (Freud quoted in Blum 1994: 116). Yet in the final backdrop of Freud fleeing from persecution in Vienna and led by his desire to 'die in freedom' in what he referred to as 'Egypt-London', the possibility of stability and peace emerges (Davies 1998). Derrida, using Freud's former London home now museum/archive as illustration, however, crystallises the continued instability of context by highlighting the, 'diasporic condition of the archive', in terms of, 'its founding being a consequence of exile' (Rapaport 2003: 78).

Derrida identifies a further element to the condition of the archive pertinent to Freud's predicament – that of a revelatory moment described by Derrida as a 'spectral messianicity at work' which he further argues is 'nothing less than a promise of having a future' (Derrida 1996: 36). It is this right to a future that Freud defined in many different ways – through his work, his family, his objects. His collection of antiquities famously accompanied him in exile as a consolation; as a passive inheritance whose metaphysical genealogy remains to be interrogated. Political responsibility here therefore lies in the active, critical acceptance of an inheritance or a tradition which will remember us if we do not remember it (cf. Bennington 2001: 197). But a politics is not Freud's purpose in having a collection. As a source of stability or security in troubled times, it provided him with a self-indulgence; the relationship with reality might not be always one of transgression and politics, but by being ingeniously extra-discursive and extra-textual, one can avoid the chance to engage with reality, with 'the thing itself'. Freud, by consoling himself with antiquities, put promise in a future when their use as objects of analysis would be restored in the developed field of psychoanalysis. This would follow the common sense view that a certain amount of critical reflection is a prerequisite for action and hence inseparable from political decisions, whilst Derrida's point in relation to Freud is that theorising and interpretation are structurally interminable and 'can never prepare for the interruptive and precipitate moment of decision and action' (Bennington 2001: 200). The decision to act makes an exception of the subject and is thus event-like; what Derrida calls spectral, or within the structure of undecidability, where the decision is not given, comes as a surprise but must be taken. For our second collector, gifts are a promise of future undecidability or interruption to a sense of purpose since, as overtly political gifts, they avoid the reflective and interrupt the promise of a definite future.

This is where we need to conclude on the point about the power of objects/ancestors to define a future. If we surrender the notion of a controlling centre of meaning then we also surrender the Western genealogy of a will to empathetic identification. Instead, if it's not the subject that makes decisions, then the undecidability of events is figured in both of our collectors. Whether a radio from a South African township or a penis sheath or a model Chinese terracotta warrior, Ucko's objects are active agents of the future which both commemorate him but also insist that a One World Archaeology will demand that the future will act on the past and act on behalf of the 'besieged subject' in order that they gain justice and are 'justly remembered'. Objects as fetish, pharmakon and as good/bad gifts (i.e. capable of absorbing and removing pollutions from the past (cf. Parry 1986)) occur with the performative force of a promise, opening the possibility of whatever comes to pass but without in any way guaranteeing it. This Africanisation of the West and the recognition of a 'one world' ancestry bound up in aboriginal heritages in turn reveals not only the metaphysical void at the heart of a Western philosophy but also the means of healing the wound. When the mother of a friend Jo, who was murdered, promises her daughter she would find out who murdered her, she empowers herself through a desire to empower the dead. We recognise that what is called for is some kind of response (hence responsibility) in answering the call of the other. This means we all take on the moral load ourselves: in this sense we should all wish to be Moses.

ACKNOWLEDGEMENTS

In memory of Joanna Parrish and her family and friends' struggle to achieve their promise to her and see her 'justly' remembered and commemorated.

REFERENCES

Basch, M.F. (1983) 'Empathic understanding: a review of the concept and some theoretical considerations', *Journal of the American Psychoanalytic Association*, 31: 101–126.

Bennington, G. (1992) 'Mosaic fragment: if Derrida were an Egyptian ...', in *Derrida: A Critical Reader*, D. Wood (ed.), Oxford: Blackwell, pp. 97–119.

Bennington G. (2001) 'Derrida and Politics', in *Jacques Derrida and the Humanities: A Critical Reader*, T. Cohen (ed.) Cambridge: Cambridge University Press, pp. 193–212.

Blum, H. (1994). *Freud and the Figure of Moses: the Moses of Freud*. London: Faber.

Channel 4 (2001) 'Battle for the Holocaust', [transcript of video].

Chisholm, D. (1992) *H.D.'s Freudian Poetics: Psychoanalysis in Translation*, Ithaca: Cornell University Press.

Collins, J. and B. Mayblin (2001) *Introducing Derrida*, London: Icon Books.

Connerton, P. (1989) *How Societies Remember*, Cambridge: Cambridge University Press.

Corcoran, L.H. (1991) 'Exploring the Archaeological Metaphor: The Egypt of Freud's Imagination', *The Annual of Psychoanalysis*, 19: 19–32, London: Analytic Press.

Davies, E. (1998) *20 Maresfield Gardens: A Guide to the Freud Museum,* London: Serpent's Tail Publications.

Derrida, J. (1996) *Archive Fever: A Freudian Impression*, (trans.) E. Prenowitz, Chicago: University of Chicago Press.

Derrida, J. (1997) [1981] *Disseminations*. (trans.) B. Johnson, London: Athlone Press.

Derrida, J. (2000) *Ethics, Institutions and the Right to Philosophy* (trans.) P. Pericles Trifonas New York: Rowman and Littlefield Publishers.

Derrida, J. (2002) *On Cosmopolitanism and Forgiveness*, London and New York: Routledge.

Feuchtwang, S. (2000) 'Reinscriptions: commemorations, restoration and the interpersonal transmission of histories and memories under modern states in Asia and Europe,' in *Memory and Methodology*, S. Radstone (ed.), Oxford: Berg Publications, pp. 59–78.

Forrester, J. (1994) "Mille e tre": Freud and collecting,' in *The Cultures of Collecting*, J. Forrester and R. Cardinal (eds), London: Reaktion Books, pp. 224–51.

Freud, S. (1984) [1936] 'A disturbance of memory on the Acropolis', in *On Metapsychology*, A Richards (ed.) London: Penguin Books, pp. 443–456.

Freud, S. (1986a) [1913] 'Totem and Taboo,' in *The Origins of Religion*, Albert Dickson (ed.), Harmondsworth: Penguin Books, pp. 53–226.

Freud, S. (1986b) [1939] 'Moses and monotheism: three essays,' in *The Origins of Religion*, A. Dickson (ed.), Harmondsworth: Penguin Books, pp. 243–386.

Gamwell, L. (1989) 'The Origins of Freud's Antiquities Collection', in *Sigmund Freud and Art: His Personal Collection of Antiquities*, L. Gamwell and S. Barker (eds), London: Thames and Hudson, pp. 21–32.

Gay, P. (1989) 'Introduction', in *Sigmund Freud and Art: His Personal Collection of Antiquities*, L. Gamwell and S. Barker (eds), London: Thames and Hudson, pp. 15–19.

Gregory, E. (1997) *H.D and Hellenism*, Cambridge: Cambridge University Press.

H.D. (1974) [1956] *Tribute to Freud*, New York: New Directions Books.

Lowenthal, D. (1996) *The Heritage Crusade and the Spoils of History,* London: Viking.

Maleuvre, D. (1999) *Museum Memories: History, Technology, Art,* Stanford: Stanford University Press.

Mbembe, A. (2001) *On the Postcolony*, Berkeley: University of California Press.

Nora P. (1989) 'Between memory and history: les lieux de memoires', *Representations*, 26, Spring: 1–10.

Parry J. (1986) 'The gift, the Indian gift and the 'Indian gift', *MAN* (ns) 21.3: 453–474.

Radstone, S. (ed.) (2000) *Memory and Methodology*, Oxford: Berg Publications.

Rapaport, H. (2003) *Later Derrida: Reading the Recent Work*, London and New York: Routledge.

Raphael-Leff, J. (1990) 'If Oedipus was an Egyptian' in *International Review of Psychoanalysis*, vol. 17, London: Institute of Psycho-Analysis Publications, pp. 309–35.

Rogers, C. (1999) 'Empathy' available at *Encyclopaedia Britannica.com*. Accessed 28/11 2004.

Said, E.W. (2003) *Freud and the Non-European*, London: Verso.

Sontag, S. (2003) *Regarding the Pain of Others* New York: Farrar, Straus & Giroux.

Ucko, P.J. (2001) 'Unprovenanced material culture and Freud's collection of antiquities', *Journal of Material Culture*, 6(3): 269–322.

Wispe, L. (1991) *The Psychology of Sympathy*, New York: Plenum Press.

CHAPTER 12

'THEY MADE IT A LIVING THING DIDN'T THEY …'

The Growth of Things and the
Fossilisation of Heritage

Siân Jones

Christine:	[…] I think everything has feelings. Even a piece of stone that was carved all those years ago. I feel that it's, well they made it a living thing didn't they?
Siân:	Mmmm
Christine:	When they did that.
Siân:	Yes, when they created it?
Christine:	Yes. They made a living thing. So I feel, yes, I think when it goes back into the ground it will be home.
Siân:	Yes, that's really interesting.
	Christine laughs.
Christine:	I do, I feel it's waiting to go back. We've taken it out, disturbed it, we've looked at it and it, I mean I know it has to have lots of things done to it to preserve it erm, but I think once it goes back I feel it'll shine in its own …
Siân:	In its place?
Christine:	Yes. And I hope it goes back where it was found. Because I feel that that's right.[1]

The piece of stone at the heart of this conversation is the long-lost lower section of a famous Pictish sculpture dating from around AD 800 (Figure 12.1). It was re-discovered one bitterly cold afternoon in February 2001 by three archaeologists excavating a ruined medieval chapel in the small village of Hilton of Cadboll, where Christine lives on the northeast coast of Scotland (Kirkdale 2001; Figures 12.2 and Map 12.1). Hailed as one of the most exquisite and important examples of early medieval sculpture in Scotland, and indeed Western Europe, the upper section of the Hilton of Cadboll cross-slab was the focus of an acrimonious 'repatriation' debate in 1921, when it was offered to the British Museum by the landowner and sent to London. Within the same year it was returned to Scotland to be incorporated into the collection of the National Museum of Antiquities in Edinburgh, and it is now a cherished exhibit in the new Museum of Scotland (Figure 12.3). However, the lower section and thousands of carved fragments from the cross-face had been lost since the seventeenth century, broken and dressed off the upper section by a 'barbarous mason' commissioned to convert the stone into a burial memorial (Miller 1835 [1994]: 40). Their excavation in August 2001 (James 2002) re-ignited tensions between the local community and national heritage bodies about ownership, conservation and presentation of the monument (see Jones 2004; 2005a, b). Most of the heritage professionals involved with the monument argued that the conservation needs and research potential of the new finds justified their removal to the National Museum in Edinburgh. This position was also in keeping with national guidelines for the allocation of excavated remains, which privilege the integrity of the object or assemblage and recommend that fragments from the same object or assemblage be kept together (Scottish Executive 1999: 6; Foster 2001: 16). Yet, Christine and many others within the local community were opposed to this course of action. From

Figure 12.1 The lower section of the Hilton of Cadboll cross-slab, *in situ* during excavations in 2001 at the Hilton of Cadboll chapel (photograph by the author).

Figure 12.2 Hilton of Cadboll Chapel site in the late 1980s prior to erection of the reconstruction (Crown Copyright, Historic Scotland).

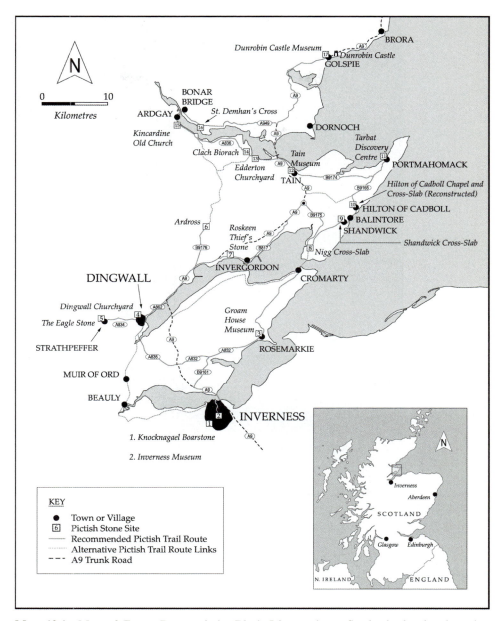

Map 12.1   Map of Easter Ross and the Black Isle, northeast Scotland, showing key sites mentioned in the text (drawn by A. Mackintosh).

their perspective, as Christine eloquently explains, the monument is conceived as a 'living thing', and, as many others pointed out, it 'belongs' in Hilton, because, as far as they are concerned, that was where it was 'born' and where it 'grew'. Furthermore, for Christine at least, although the lower section 'has to have lots of things done to it to preserve it', it will only 'shine' and 'breathe' when in the ground.[2] The well-publicised conflict that emerged

Figure 12.3   The Hilton of Cadboll cross-slab in the Museum of Scotland (photograph by the author, with kind permission of The National Museums of Scotland).

around the excavation of the lower section thus revealed the monument's ongoing symbolic, economic and political value. It also highlighted the perplexities and challenges facing archaeologists and heritage managers when conservation principles and practices come into conflict with contemporary meanings and values.

The contested meanings and identities surrounding the Hilton of Cadboll stone capture a theme at the heart of Peter Ucko's work: the role of the past in contemporary society. Only two to three decades ago this was an area of apparent irrelevance for most archaeologists and Ucko was one of the leading figures in bringing it to the forefront of the discipline. Through his research and publications he has emphasised the social and political contexts of archaeology and the importance of engaging with issues of ownership, power and identity, particularly with respect to the archaeology of indigenous communities and non-Western societies (e.g. Ucko 1983a, b, 1985, 1987, 1994, 1997, 2000). Importantly, he has combined this concern with a critical examination of the ultimately Western principles, assumptions and methods that are so often taken for granted in archaeological enquiry and heritage management. Without such challenges regarding, for instance, the objectivity of archaeological interpretation (Ucko 1983a, 1989a, b) or the ability of archaeologists to distinguish past ethnic groups from material culture (1989a, b, 1997), research on the contemporary socio-politics of the past is artificially divorced from the nature of archaeological enquiry, and hence limited in its insights and impact. Equally important is Ucko's (1983b, 1985, 1987, 1994) recognition of the need to review institutional and legislative systems that structure archaeological enquiry and heritage management so that decision-making can be opened up to a wider range of communities whose interests, identities and values are not always served by Western academic principles and practices. Above all this wide-ranging body of work is driven by the argument that:

> To isolate a remote past investigated by archaeology from the more recent past (to which archaeology is not considered relevant) may be useful for government and the elite of a country, but it runs the risk of either leaving the study of archaeology where it so often is – outside public consciousness – or of disenfranchising the more distant past from any living reality or contemporary relevance. (Ucko 1994: 238)

CONSERVATION AND SOCIAL VALUE: THE FOSSILISATION OF HERITAGE

Here, I intend to explore one specific sphere of heritage management that often contributes to this disenfranchisement: the intersection of conservation and social value and the tensions and problems that surround it (for related discussions see Johnston 1994; Walderhaug Saetersdal 2000; Foster 2001). There is an important thread *within* the philosophy of conservation, which emphasises the organic life of historic remains and I will return to this below. Nevertheless, as Ucko (1994: 261–263) has argued, the traditional Western approach to the conservation and presentation of archaeological remains has been to isolate them from contemporary social life and create static protected sites and artefacts, valued primarily with relation to their original meaning and use, and actively conserved with respect to specific, usually distant, points in time. This situation is the product of a number of key principles underlying Western discourses of conservation, which underpin international heritage charters (see Bell 1997; McBryde 1997: 94; Clavir 2002: xxi). First, that the preservation of cultural heritage for posterity is a moral imperative and beneficial to both present and future generations. Second, that the authenticity of heritage is primarily associated with the fabric of artefacts and monuments, even though intangible dimensions are increasingly acknowledged. Third, that the original meanings and uses of artefacts and monuments are of primary importance in determining the significance of cultural heritage and appropriate modes of conservation, despite long-standing arguments that later developments also contribute to their authenticity. Thus, on the one hand, heritage management is suffused with rhetoric about our responsibilities to a faceless abstract public who, it is assumed, will derive meaning and value from cultural heritage. On the other hand, the authenticity and significance of cultural heritage, as defined by heritage management practices, becomes frozen at particular points in time, abstracted from ongoing social and cultural processes, and of necessity only subject to expert assessment and stewardship (see Walderhaug Saetersdal 2000 for a similar argument).

Over the last few decades, research in multi-ethnic contexts, usually non-European nation-states with colonial histories, has highlighted the contradictions inherent in this situation. Meanings, values and identities produced in relation to cultural heritage do not necessarily coincide with the expert assessments of heritage managers and conservators. Furthermore, attitudes towards permanency and appropriate ways of looking after heritage places and objects are culturally specific, thus leading to considerable complexity in multicultural contexts (see Mellor 1992; Larsen 1995; Ryne 2000; Clavir 2002). Ucko (1994) highlighted this complexity in his study of the treatment of sites and monuments in Zimbabwe. For instance, Great Zimbabwe, a site of immense national symbolic significance and a focus of international cultural tourism, has been subject to extensive conservation and reconstruction schemes. However, up until the early 1990s at least, conservation reports had been concerned exclusively with method and technique, apparently based on the assumption that it is self-evident which particular moment in the history of the monument should be preserved (Ucko 1994: 271). As Ucko points out, this is not straightforward as the monument has a dynamic social life and is subject to a multiplicity of meanings (Ucko 1994: 272). A survey at the monument, for example, found that some visitors would like its collapsed walls reconstructed in what they perceive to be an 'authentic' manner. Yet such reconstruction would disregard the beliefs of rural Zimbabweans that such wall collapses are the result of the deliberate actions of spirits destroying their own homes just as living people do when they wish to move to a new area (Ucko 1994). How such competing social values should be dealt with is not at all clear-cut, but in 1992 it seems the dynamic social life of Great Zimbabwe was not prominent on the agenda of the National Museums and Monuments Service, whose Master Plan still referred to the site as an ancient medieval structure (Ucko 1994: 275).

Arguments in favour of an approach to conservation that recognises the dynamic social lives of objects and monuments have been evident in some of the literature on heritage and authenticity since at least the mid-nineteenth century. For instance, reacting against the restoration of historic buildings through the removal of later accretions, the Victorian anti-restoration movement associated with Ruskin and Morris held that authenticity lies in the sequence of developments associated with buildings or monuments and that they should not be tampered with except for essential repairs (Lowenthal 1995: 129; Stanley Price *et al.* 1996: 309–11). Nevertheless, with the ratification of the *Venice Charter* in 1964, a respect for authenticity in the sense of the 'genuine', the 'original', uncontaminated by intrusions of another age held sway (Pye 2001: 58). The same emphasis also underlay the development of the 'test for authenticity' as a key tool in evaluating nominations for the World Heritage List (McBryde 1997: 94). Similarly, in museum conservation there has been an emphasis on the integrity or 'true' nature of objects defined in relation to their origins, original fabric and the intentions of their makers (Pye 2001; Clavir 2002: xxi). Over the last two decades, however, Western approaches to authenticity and conservation have been seriously challenged by alternative perspectives derived largely, though not exclusively, from non-Western contexts that highlight diverse approaches to conservation and deterioration. In the case of some monuments or artefacts, it is acceptable or appropriate that they deteriorate and decay, for instance, as with Great Zimbabwe, North-West Coast Native American totem poles (Ryne 2000; Clavir 2002: 153–157) or Zuni Ahayu:da (Merrill and Ahlborn 1997). In other instances, rather than preserve the original fabric of a site, building or artefact, it is deemed appropriate to rebuild or retouch it, as in the case of the Aboriginal tradition of repainting Wandjina sites to renew the spiritual power of the image (Mowaljarlai *et al.* 1988; Ward 1992).

Increased recognition of this cross-cultural diversity has brought about the modification of conservation principles as expressed in codes of ethics and heritage charters (Lowenthal 1995: 129; McBryde 1997: 94; Clavir 2002: xxi). There is increasing emphasis on the ongoing social and spiritual value of heritage, such as in the *Burra Charter*

(Australia ICOMOS 1979, latest revised version 1999). In this document the emphasis on the present is clear: 'Places of cultural significance enrich people's lives, often providing a deep and inspirational sense of connection to community and landscape, to the past and *to lived experiences*' (Australia ICOMOS 1979, latest revised version 1999: 3; my emphasis). Furthermore, whilst upholding the Venice Charter, the *Nara Document on Authenticity*, arising from a UNESCO World Heritage Conference in 1994, stresses the need to acknowledge diverse cultural beliefs in conservation practice, including how it is safeguarded, presented, restored and enhanced:

> All judgements about values attributed to heritage [...] may differ from culture to culture, and even within the same culture. It is thus not possible to base judgements of value and authenticity on fixed criteria. On the contrary, the respect due to all cultures requires that cultural heritage must be considered and judged within the cultural contexts to which it belongs. (Larsen 1995: xxiii)

Despite these developments, there are a number of unresolved problems in bringing together conservation principles and practices with the new emphasis on present-day meanings and values. Research has shown that the meanings and values attached to monuments are often heterogeneous and contested. Furthermore, in the ongoing social life of any particular monument the meanings and values surrounding it tend to be transient, fluid and 'in the making'. Thus, for instance, Native American attitudes to the care of totem poles have been subject to considerable change over the course of the twentieth century (Ryne 2000; Clavir 2002: 153–157), and the revival of repainting Wandjina art in the western Kimberly region of Australia in 1987 took place in a radically altered social, cultural and political context (see Ward 1992). In contrast, conservation practices still involve the identification of specific points in time almost always *prior to the present*, which are deemed worthy of preservation, in some cases with reference to a traditional 'source' culture which is often constructed as static and homogeneous. This was highlighted at the UNESCO conference in Nara by conservation practitioners who argued that critiques of definitions of authenticity do not remove 'the need for practical tools to measure *the wholeness, the realness, the truthfulness of the site* on which they work to improve the effectiveness of proposed treatments' (Stovel 1995: 396, my emphasis). Thus, despite recent developments, conservation practices still lead to a fossilisation of the past, and are consequently often at odds with acknowledging the diverse and often transient meanings and values that are associated with historic places. Here, I will argue that issues of contemporary cultural significance and social value cannot merely be recorded and tacked onto existing frameworks. Instead, these issues require a more radical rethinking of the principles of conservation underpinning heritage management. Should we be preserving particular points in the life of monuments or artefacts and thus inevitably arresting further developments? Or should they be allowed to grow, change, rejuvenate, collapse and decay if these processes are integral to the ongoing meanings and values surrounding them?

THE CONSERVATION OF EARLY MEDIEVAL SCULPTURE

I want to turn now to the conservation of early medieval sculpture in Scotland. Perceived as a product of a formative period in the history of the Scottish nation, many such monuments have been attributed national and international significance (Foster 2001: 1; Historic Scotland 2003: 3). Indeed, the role of early medieval sculpture in the construction of Scottish national identity was highlighted in the late nineteenth century by Joseph

Anderson, Keeper of the National Museum of Antiquities (1869–1913), who argued that the formation of a gallery of such 'indigenous' art materials would 'restore to the native genius of the Scots the original elements of that system of design which are its special inheritance' (Anderson 1881: 134). Given this significance, it is not surprising that such sculpture has been subject to a lengthy history of attempts to conserve and present it. As with parietal rock art and carved stone on buildings, preservation has been a particular concern. In the case of early medieval sculpture it is vulnerable to a range of naturally occurring threats, particularly from water, frost action and storm damage, as well as to a lesser extent accidental and deliberate human actions (see Muir 1998; Historic Scotland 2001, 2003). Over the course of the last two centuries, private individuals, charitable and subscription bodies, as well as heritage institutions have engaged in a range of preservation strategies involving removal to private houses or museums, relocation to historic buildings (usually churches), enclosure in purpose-built shelters (Figure 12.4), and maintenance in the landscape. Replicas, reconstructions, and scale models have also been used for the purposes of recording, displaying and studying early medieval sculpture (see Foster 2001). Usually these are housed in museums or visitor centres, but in cases where historical processes have resulted in removal of sculpture from a site, reconstructions or replicas can provide a powerful substitute, as indeed with Barry Grove's carving of the Hilton of Cadboll sculpture[3]. Nevertheless, these strategies frequently arouse varying degrees of conflict and controversy (see Foster 2001).

In Scotland, as elsewhere, conservation policies and charters, such as the *Stirling Charter* (Historic Scotland 2000: 3), stress the importance of preserving historic remains for posterity. Yet, in keeping with the international developments discussed earlier, recent documents also emphasise the significance of all phases of development (Historic Scotland 2003: 4), and the importance of present-day social, economic, recreational and

Figure 12.4 The Shandwick cross-slab displayed in its original location within a glass case (photograph by the author).

educational values (Historic Scotland 2003: 1). Similarly, in Historic Scotland's (2003: 6) revised policy guidance notes for the conservation of carved stone (including early medieval sculpture),[4] there is an emphasis on social value alongside historic and aesthetic value: 'The cultural significance of a carved stone is embodied in its fabric, design, context and setting; in associated documents; in its use; in people's memories and associations with it'. Furthermore, setting is attributed particular significance in the policy guidelines with a presumption in favour of maintaining the association of monumental carved stone with its locality (Historic Scotland 2003: 6–7). Here too it is stressed that the history of the monument is important and secondary locations can accrue significance of a social and economic nature as well as for historical reasons:

> Where a carved stone still possessing monumental qualities is believed to be *in situ* or in a place of significance, the presumption is that it will not be moved unless the importance of retaining it there is outweighed by demonstrable conservation needs that cannot be satisfied in any other way. Such considerations need to take into account not simply archaeological and historic factors, but also social and economic ones. (Historic Scotland 2003: 7)

Nevertheless, despite this acknowledgement of social value, the overriding emphasis in the conservation of carved stone in Scotland is still focused on the historic significance of any particular monument and on the preservation of the original fabric of the stone. In part this is because methodologies for assessing social value have yet to be embedded in routine heritage management processes, with the result that social value is often outweighed by historic and economic value (Bell 1997: 14; de la Torre and Mason 2002: 3; Jones 2004: 5–6, 66–67). More fundamentally, as the above quotation highlights, the overriding emphasis is still placed on the 'demonstrable conservation needs' of the carved stone itself (Historic Scotland 2003: 7). The implication is that ultimately authenticity is assumed to lie in the fabric of the monument and only secondarily in setting, use, meaning and value. The physical fossilisation which results from techniques aimed at addressing 'demonstrable conservation needs' can thus conflict with the contemporary meanings and values associated with monuments. This tension, which is inherent in current conservation policies and practices, often underlies the controversy surrounding early medieval sculpture and the critical public response.[5]

MONUMENTS AS 'LIVING THINGS': THE CASE OF HILTON OF CADBOLL

The Hilton of Cadboll cross-slab, with its complex and fragmented biography, arouses conflict equal to, if not exceeding, other examples of early medieval sculpture. As we have seen earlier, the excavation of the lower section of the cross-slab along with thousands of small carved fragments in 2001, resulted in tensions between local residents and national heritage agencies over its conservation and presentation. Local residents claimed ownership of the new discoveries and strongly resisted first the excavation of the lower section from the ground and later its removal from the village. In response, heritage professionals emphasised the threats facing the lower section whilst it remained in the ground and the historical knowledge that could be gained from research in a museum context. A heated public meeting between local residents and representatives of the funding bodies[6] at the excavation resulted in an agreement that the lower section could be excavated, as long as it subsequently remained in the village until such time when ownership had been established through legal channels.[7] During 2003 the National Museums of Scotland (NMS) were eventually attributed ownership and have subsequently proposed long-term display in the village. However, ownership is still contested by the local Historic Hilton Trust and to date the lower section remains in Hilton of Cadboll in a secure location. Here I do not intend to focus on the complex issues surrounding ownership (for a detailed discussion see Jones 2004; 2005b). Instead I wish to draw on field research carried out in Hilton of Cadboll to explore the tensions between conservation principles and practices on the one hand and the contemporary meanings and values surrounding the monument in local contexts on the other.[8]

At the heart of the meanings and values surrounding 'the Stone' in local contexts is the way in which it is conceived of as a living thing. Sometimes such meaning is produced through the use of metaphors. For instance, it is referred to as having been '*born*', '*growing*', '*breathing*', having a '*soul*', '*living*' and '*dying*', having '*charisma*' and '*feelings*'. A few informants were more explicit about this symbolic dimension drawing direct similes rather than relying on metaphor. For instance, after it had been uplifted Christine noted that the lower section of the cross-slab:

> was like something that was born there and it should go back [...]. It's like people who emigrate or go away, they should always come back where they were born and I feel that that stone should go back.

Another local resident, Duncan, remarked that if the upper part of the cross-slab returned from Edinburgh:

> There'll be a party maybe and there'll be things going on here that'll be absolutely unbelievable like a, how would I put it now, an ancient member of the village coming back, if that came through here on a trailer and everybody would be here. [...] Coming home where it's always been [...] If the stone had a soul it would be saying oh there's the Port Culac you know, there's so and so's house you know. I'm going over to the park and there's, there's the other bit of the stone and it broke off a hundred and fifty years ago or whatever.

Furthermore, as the last quote highlights, the monument is seen not merely as a living thing, but crucially as *a living member of the community*. Not only is a direct analogy drawn between the cross-slab and an 'ancient member of the village', but it is also attributed the kind of social knowledge that is essential to establishing a person's membership within the community.

The application of discourses of kinship and 'belonging' also reinforces the cross-slab's place as a living member of the community. 'Belonging' is a key concept in the identification of kinship relationships in the Highlands of Scotland (see Macdonald 1997), particularly amongst people who are born and brought up there. Thus the term regularly crops up in conversation, for instance, in an interview with Maggie: 'she belongs, they're both Sutherland in their name', or 'it was the first of the Sutherlands that belong to my granny'. Such statements do not simply relate to actual kin, but are also extended to others who are considered part of the community. Indeed, rather than a reflection of static relationships they provide a means of articulating and negotiating 'who is and who is not "part of the place", and who is and is not authentically "local" ' (Macdonald 1997: 131). Given such usage, the extension of the concept of belonging to the cross-slab carries a connotation of kinship. For instance, one woman noted in an interview, 'I still think that the stone belongs to the people here' (Mary), and another, '... it's still not where it should be, it should be back up home where it belongs' (Janet). Birth place is also important in 'placing' people and negotiating degrees of 'belonging'. Being born in Hilton, or related to someone who was born there, is central to being accepted as an insider or a 'local'. Again, like people, the cross-slab 'belongs' in Hilton because, as Christine puts it, it is 'like something that was born there', and 'that's where it was created'.

Thus, the body of metaphorical and symbolic meaning surrounding the monument in local discourse concerns its place within the community. In this way the monument provides a medium for the expression and negotiation of identities and boundaries. Categories of 'local' and 'incomer', and through them the boundaries of community as a whole, were continuously negotiated in relation to the monument at the height of the conflict in 2001.[9] Conceived of as a living member of the community, the monument also provides a mechanism for expressing the relationship between people and place; a relationship that is fraught and contested in the Scottish Highlands where the dislocation and alienation wrought by the Clearances remain prominent aspects of social memory (see Jones 2005a). The monument acts as an icon for the village as a whole, as expressed metaphorically by one local activist in the statement: 'it belongs to the village, it is Hilton'. Indeed, it is sometimes even positioned as constitutive of place and therefore part of the fabric of people's existence. Associations between the monument and features such as rocks and sea, serve to place it as an ontological component of the landscape as expressed by Màiri:

> the Hilton stone, you almost feel attached to it, it's almost like being attached to rocks or the sea or it's always been here, it's part of the place and for generations, I don't know, it was a close community you know.

So how does this body of symbolic meaning surrounding the monument in local contexts come into conflict with conservation principles and practices? I should first stress that the symbolic conception of the monument as a living thing is not a product of a static and homogeneous framework of meaning uniformly shared throughout the local community. Rather it is a dynamic discourse that draws upon existing frameworks of meaning concerning community and the relationships between people and places in the Highlands. Such meanings are particularly resonant amongst people with long-term, often multi-generational family connections to the Highlands. It is also these individuals, particularly those historically associated with the village of Hilton, who came to occupy positions of authority regarding the local campaign to keep the lower section and in representing the relationship between monument and community. Paradoxically, the excavation itself was particularly important in the crystallisation of local discourses in which the cross-slab is conceptualised as a living member of the community. Being able to witness the lower portion of the cross-slab being revealed in the ground through excavation reinforced a sense of intimacy and kinship as expressed by Màiri, a woman in her forties who was born and brought up in the village:

> When I was up on the [excavation viewing] platform there on Saturday and looking down on it ... and I was able to see it, and the fact [she laughs] it's in there, it's in the earth and it's been there for so long ... you actually feel for it, you have a feeling for it. I can't put it any other way. It's part of your culture and therefore it's part of the people, its part of the community.

Similarly, Duncan, another Hilton 'local', recounted how he felt an intimate connection with the base of the cross-slab tied into feelings of ancestry:

> ... they were excavating all round it for a few weeks and I didn't ask anyone because I thought it would be stupid [...] but the one thing I really wanted to do was just to touch it, put my hands on it. [...] I think we were connected with it, going back down the years they were connected with it. [...] to know that my people were here and that stone is there just to touch it you know they must have seen it, they must have touched it, you know going back these years, it was like something holy I just, I just needed to touch it.

The excavation also reinforced people's belief that the cross-slab was 'born' there, irrespective of the fact that archaeological evidence revealed it to be in a secondary context (probably of medieval date) (James 2002). For some the close association between the lower section and the soil was also important in terms of the life-force metaphorically attributed to the cross-slab, by references to it being able to 'breathe' and 'grow'. Indeed, in this sense the soil seemed to offer protective qualities. For instance, one local resident noted that 'the elements are killing the stone' once the soil around the lower section had been removed through excavation. And Christine metaphorically hinted at the positive qualities of the soil:

Christine: I think being in the ground gave it something [...] whatever was in the ground was good for it [...] I feel if it is back in the ground it'll breathe.

Siân: You think it can't breathe when it's out here.

Christine: It's just a cold piece of stone.

Ironically, the very same processes of discovery and excavation brought the lower section, and smaller fragments, squarely within the sphere of conservation principles and practices. Not surprisingly, within this framework primary emphasis was placed on conserving the physical fabric of the lower section, which, once exposed, was threatened by the action of water and the leaching of salts. Acute conservation needs were addressed on site (see Figure 12.5), but many heritage professionals also stressed that it was in the best interests of the stone to uplift it and take it to the Museum of Scotland in Edinburgh where it could receive expert conservation.[10] Despite the metaphorical safety offered by the soil, most local residents accepted that the lower section had to *have lots of things done to preserve it* and there was high level of consensus about the sources of threat, including ice, frost, wind, air blown sand and salt. Tensions surrounding conservation thus stemmed from the broader implications attached to it, that is, the dislocation of the relationship between monument and community wrought through the historic removal of the upper section in the mid-nineteenth century and now by the threatened removal of the lower section to Edinburgh. As Alan remarks with respect to the upper section of the cross-slab in Edinburgh:

I look at the Hilton stone when it's in the Edinburgh museum and it's just a dead headstone among other headstones, just a dead you know, whereas in Hilton it could be a living stone, hopefully as a focus for a living community again and also indirectly basically the catalyst for more development in the place.

Thus, by dislocating its relationship with community, physical displacement of the monument thereby negates its social life. For some, uplifting the stone for conservation purposes resulted in a form of symbolic violence to the social life of the monument, as it is the soil itself that provides a metaphorical source of protection and life for the lower section. For others, however, the relationship between monument and community appears to be preserved whilst the lower section remains physically present within the village, which may well be achieved by NMS's proposal that the lower section be lent to the community for long-term display, although ownership remains a problem (see Jones 2005b).

Another problematic aspect of conservation is the tension that exists between those with professional conservation expertise and those who have 'feeling' for the monument on the basis of relationships of kinship and 'belonging' (as expressed by Màiri in the interview citation earlier). Inevitably there was considerable suspicion amongst local residents about the possible manipulation of conservation in the conflict over ownership and presentation of the new discoveries. More subtly though, members of the local community, again particularly those with long-term family associations, are imputed a privileged role in the protection of the stone, in possessing 'feeling' for what it needs. Thus, the authority vested in conservation experts and heritage professionals from without the community can create tensions, as these individuals cannot be located in local sets of social relationships and hence by definition cannot possess the same 'feeling' for the stone. Such tensions were expressed by Alan, first in commenting on the landowner's decision to take the upper

Figure 12.5   Conservation taking place during the excavation of the lower section at the Hilton of Cadboll Chapel site in August 2001 (photograph by the author).

portion to his castle grounds in Invergordon in the mid nineteenth century, an action partly legitimated, at least retrospectively, on conservation grounds:

> Well I think what really came across [in the stories told within the village] was just the negativity of the fact that the people that moved the stone had no feelings for the stone themselves you know and they'd no feelings for the people in the place, and I think that's the sort of feeling that came through is that, eh, it was something that was important to the place, but basically those that had the power basically had, it's like, it's like a lot of these people that come into the place can be interested and whatever, but well one thing about Hilton, eh, you can be here fifty years and if you're no' born here you're still an outsider.

And later with relation to the heritage professionals currently involved with the new discoveries:

> You know Historic Scotland as far as I'm concerned is a faceless quango. I mean I would like to basically know the guys. I wouldn't mind a list of them so I know what they are, who they are, where they're from, eh, that are making decisions about our stone.

Hence, in the process of taking care of the stone and making decisions about it, there is a need to 'place' people and locate them within sets of social relationships. This concern, I suggest, is not merely a mechanism for establishing trust, but more fundamentally stems from the conception of the monument as a living, breathing, thing embedded in social relationships and conceived as *an ancient member of the village*.

CONCLUSIONS

Earlier, I asked whether monuments and artefacts should be allowed to grow, change, rejuvenate, collapse and decay if these processes are integral to the ongoing meanings and values surrounding them. The answer to this question depends, in part, upon what we want to prioritise through conservation practices; the physical integrity of objects, or their wider cultural significance and conceptual integrity, which may be linked to intangible and transient values (Clavir 2002). If the emphasis is shifted towards the latter then the answer will be yes in the case of some objects. However, as we have seen cultural context is of the utmost importance. Traditionally, in North-West coast Native American cultures some totem poles, erected as memorials, were allowed to decay and return to the earth, and in the Kimberly district of North-West Australia Wandjina rock art was retouched in order to renew its spiritual power. But neither cultural tradition is static or homogeneous, both being subject to discontinuity, revival and transformation in colonial and post-colonial contexts, in part, through engagement with Western conservation policies and practices (see Clavir 2002 and Ward 1992).

In the case of the Hilton of Cadboll cross-slab, its significance in local contexts does not depend upon the gradual deterioration of the monument. Indeed, local residents often express concern over the well-being of the stone, and, as we have seen, identify similar environmental hazards as heritage and conservation professionals themselves. However, members of the local community also identify other threats, namely dislocation of the physical relationship between monument and community[11] and removal of control and care of the monument from the sphere of authorised 'locals' into the hands of 'outsiders'. These threats are not primarily harmful to the material integrity of the monument as far as local residents are concerned, although this is implied at times. They do, however, endanger the intangible cultural significance of the monument in terms of the meanings and values created through it in local contexts. As indicated above, the Hilton Stone is only 'alive' when it is in Hilton. Out of the ground, and certainly in Edinburgh, it becomes just a 'cold dead stone'. Thus, prolonging the object's existence materially is not necessarily equivalent to continuing its social 'life'; sometimes these two things coincide, but all too often they can run counter to one another.

There are many, perhaps surprising, parallels between the Hilton of Cadboll case and the conflict often surrounding the conservation of First Nations heritage. In her book, *Preserving What is Valued*, Miriam Clavir (2002: 145) compares First Nations' and museum conservators' perspectives and concludes that:

> Both perspectives value 'preservation'; however, this term has two different meanings: (1) that favoured by museums, which involves using physical and intellectual means to ensure that material fragments from the past do not disappear, and (2) that favoured by First Nations, which involves continuing and/or renewing past traditions and their associated material culture; that is preserving the culture's past by being actively engaged in it and thereby ensuring that it has a living future. Within Western culture, heritage is often described materially, in terms of a cultural product or production; within First Nations cultures, heritage is often described culturally in terms of 'process' rather than 'product'.

Clavir's distinction between heritage as 'product' and as 'process' is a useful one, but the Hilton of Cadboll case challenges the idea that Western culture is characterised by a uniform tradition or set of values as regards the conservation of cultural heritage. In many ways, this commonplace notion is preserved by the assumption that European nation-states are for the most part culturally homogeneous (with the exception of immigrant communities) and that there are no minority indigenous 'source' communities. As a result, those who conserve and present national heritage are assumed to represent a homogeneous majority culture, and likewise the historic and aesthetic expertise and assumptions that inform their decision-making are regarded as part of the core values of the wider culture. I am not suggesting that the local population of Hilton of Cadboll or the wider region be regarded as a minority or indigenous community equivalent to First Nations communities of Canada, New Zealand and Australia.[12] Rather, if we look more closely at the meanings and values attached to monuments and artefacts in many parts of Britain and Europe we will find a similar emphasis on their social lives, and on heritage as 'process' rather than 'product' (see, for instance, Bender 1998; Holtorf 1996; Riegl 1903 [1996]; Walderhaug Saetersdal 2000).

Of course, the authenticity of meanings and values surrounding heritage today can often be challenged if they are judged with respect to cultural continuity and the original intentions of those who produced the remains in question, as is still the current heritage orthodoxy. It is unlikely that current conceptions of the Hilton of Cadboll cross-slab as a living thing reflect the symbolic meanings attached to it in early medieval contexts. The Reformation wrought a significant dislocation in the religious beliefs and traditions associated with early medieval and medieval Christianity, thus undermining claims to cultural continuity between 'source' and present-day populations. Moreover, the forced population movements of the late eighteenth and early nineteenth centuries brought about massive dislocation of communities and were largely responsible for the creation of marginal fishing villages, such as Hilton of Cadboll, in the west and far northeast of Scotland (Richards 2000). The point is that such processes of dislocation accompanied by the transformation and (re)invention of tradition are present in almost all cultural contexts to a greater or lesser degree; they lie at the heart of people's engagement with the material remains of the past, and ensure their continuing significance.[13] Indeed these processes are even part and parcel of the development of Western traditions of collecting and preservation that underpin modern conservation principles. Rather than constituting universally-relevant values, these principles represent historically and culturally specific modes of engagement with historic remains, deriving from the landowning and 'polite' classes of eighteenth- and nineteenth-century European societies, and intimately tied to political movements such as nationalism and imperialism.

Thus, I suggest that we need to shift our approach to conserving cultural heritage away from the current emphasis on the material fossilisation of heritage as 'product', towards a focus on heritage as 'process', whether dealing with the historic remains of disenfranchised indigenous and post-colonial cultures or those of European nation-states. If heritage conservation is redirected towards 'process', towards the dynamic and transient (re)making of meaning and tradition, then this will go some way towards addressing the contradiction inherent in current frameworks, which stress the importance of social value and contemporary cultural significance, whilst still privileging preservation of the material fabric of historic remains. Indeed, it will be necessary to break down the artificial dichotomy that is often created between the conservation of physical fabric using specialised scientific techniques and the conservation of meanings and values as if the latter were simply applied to the surface form of objects. As the Hilton of Cadboll Stone reveals, the social lives of objects are not merely created through the attribution of new layers of meaning and value that are wrapped around them in changing social and historical circumstances. The materiality of artefacts and monuments is implicated in, indeed lies at the heart of, their biographies: things are born, they grow, breathe, live and die; they are conceived as having a soul and a personality, and as being nourished and harmed by other substances such as air, soil and water. Their substance and identity is no longer discrete but related through birth, kinship and belonging to other things and to people. They are often implicated in the fabric of place and community, and like organic things, the materiality of artefacts and monuments is expected to change with time. The material fabric of artefacts and monuments must therefore be considered an integral part of their social lives and should not be frozen in perpetuity at a particular moment in time. That is not to suggest that monuments should be abandoned in a blanket fashion to 'the continuous and unceasing cycle of change in nature' as argued by adherents to the late nineteenth century cult of monuments (Riegl 1903 [1996]: 73–74). Instead, each case should be contextualised in terms of the dynamic, culturally specific meanings and values attached to it. Furthermore, to do so it will be necessary to open up the preserves of significance assessment and conservation planning to greater dialogue and negotiation. This may not be a consensual process; the creation of meaning is often heterogeneous and contested. However, as Ucko (1994: 247) has argued with respect to Zimbabwean 'culture houses', tensions and disputes can be seen as signs of success, demonstrating genuine involvement in heritage and highlighting its role in the reproduction *and* transformation of cultural traditions.

ACKNOWLEDGEMENTS

I am indebted to many people and organisations without whom this paper would not have been possible. The Hilton of Cadboll research was generously supported by grants from Historic Scotland, the University of Manchester and the Arts and Humanities Research Leave scheme. Thanks to Sally Foster for introducing me to the fascinating biography of the Hilton of Cadboll cross-slab and for her unflagging support. Thanks also to individuals in the following organisations for their important contributions: Groam House Museum, GUARD, Historic Scotland, The Highland Council, National Museums of Scotland, RACE, Seaboard 2000, Tain Museum and Tarbat Discovery Centre. In writing this chapter, I have benefited greatly from discussion with Stuart Jeffrey, Bob Layton, Colin Richards and Louise Tythacott. Although he was unaware of this chapter, I would also like to thank Peter Ucko for the inspiration, support and incisive criticism he has provided over the past 15 years; this work is very much a product of his influence on the way I see things. Finally, thanks to Dolly Macdonald, and the other residents of Hilton and the seaboard area of Easter Ross, for their insight and candid reflections. They tolerated my intrusion in their lives with patience, humour and generosity.

NOTES

1   Citations from fieldwork interviews are in italics. To protect the identity of those concerned, all names used in relation to interview citations and fieldwork are pseudonyms. This does not apply to individuals speaking or acting in an official capacity either in (or in relation to) public forums, as their identity is intimately tied to that official position. See note 7 for further information on the fieldwork itself.

2   The lower section of the cross-slab was uplifted during the excavations in the summer of 2001 (on 10th September), about a week before this interview with Christine took place.

3   The Hilton of Cadboll reconstruction is a full-size sculpture commissioned from artist Barry Grove in the mid-1990s following a failed request to the National Museums of Scotland for the repatriation of the original. The project was spearheaded by the late Mrs Jane Durham, a Commissioner for the Royal Commission for Ancient and Historic Monuments who lived in Easter Ross, in conjunction with Tain and Easter Ross Civic Trust. However, the Hilton of Cadboll community were also actively involved, and became more so once carving began in the village itself. The sculpture was erected at the Hilton of Cadboll Chapel site in 2000, accompanied by much ceremony and celebration. The reconstruction is highly valued by the community and there is no question of it being dismissed as an inauthentic copy; indeed, many of the meanings and values attached to the original which will be discussed here are also applied to the reconstruction (see Jones 2004). Nevertheless, the reconstruction has only a minor impact on the desire of most local residents to keep the lower section in the village. The two monuments, original and reconstruction, are perceived as different kinds of object, each with their own spheres of meaning and authenticity, at once overlapping but also incommensurable (Jones 2004).

4   Historic Scotland (2003: 4) estimate that there are about 1,600 early medieval carved stones surviving in Scotland today. About one-third of these come under Historic Scotland's jurisdiction, 350 as properties in the care of Scottish Ministers and a further 180 or more as scheduled ancient monuments (Historic Scotland 2003: 4). Furthermore, Historic Scotland's operational policy on carved stone is designed to provide guidance to local authorities, landowners and third parties with an interest in carved stones.

5   In the sphere of heritage management there has been a persistent debate about whether such sculptures should be treated as art objects and placed in museums or regarded as monuments and preserved within the landscape (Foster 2001). In many instances this issue also intersects with the wider cultural significance and social value attached to early medieval sculpture (see Jones 2004: 56–58). However, as we shall see there are other conceptual and symbolic issues at stake.

6   Four organisations funded the excavation in the summer of 2001: Historic Scotland, National Museums of Scotland, Ross and Cromarty Enterprise, and the Highland Council. Local protest in Easter Ross largely focused on the former two Edinburgh-based, as opposed to Highland, organisations. As Withers (1996: 328) points out, these two regions maintain a core-periphery relationship associated with oppositions in many aspects of social and political life, including the construction of identity.

7   Initially, it had been anticipated by heritage managers that future ownership would be legally determined by Treasure Trove. However, in early 2002 the Queen's and Lord Treasurer's Remembrancer (the Crown's representative regarding Treasure Trove) declared it to be outwith Treasure Trove, as he did not regard the new finds as 'ownerless', being derived from an object that is already owned. Although, the identity of the 'owner(s)' was not initially specified, in 2003 the Queen's and Lord Treasurer's Remembrances declared that they belong to the National Museums of Scotland on the basis that the organisation already owns the upper portion of the monument.

8   The field research took place between 2001 and 2003 and involved participant observation and in-depth qualitative interviews (52 in total) carried out whilst living in Hilton of Cadboll and the adjacent village of Balintore for a period amounting to six months in total. The research was grant-aided by Historic Scotland and aimed to investigate 'the meanings, values and interests associated with the Hilton of Cadboll cross-slab, and the ways in which these are manifested in the debates and commentaries concerning its conservation, location and presentation'. Funding was also provided by the University of Manchester. See Jones (2004) for a full discussion of the results.

9   For instance, in the debates over the new discoveries in 2001, 'locals' could negotiate relative positions of authority and status through their association (and their parents' and grandparents' connections) with the biography of the monument. 'Incomers' on the other hand, could

negotiate greater degrees of 'insiderness' through adopting, or respecting, the socially constructed authoritative community position, demanding that the new discoveries remain in Hilton. For other studies illustrating similar processes see Macdonald (1997) and Nadel-Klein (2003).

10 Interestingly, this argument was often more prevalent amongst heritage managers than professional conservators who were prepared to consider a wider range of conservation options (for further discussion see Muir 1998).

11 Dislocation of the relationship between monument and community was posed by the proposed removal of the new discoveries to Edinburgh at the time of excavation. The agreement between Historic Scotland and the local community that the lower section would not be removed from the village until ownership had been legally established postponed this event. However, a sense of the threat of imminent removal remained strong and has not been alleviated by the proposal by the National Museums of Scotland to facilitate local display.

12 Although, it can be argued that eighteenth- and nineteenth-century political and economic relationships between the English/southern Scottish and the Gaelic-speaking Highlanders were framed by the same discourses of race and primitivism that informed the colonial conquest of non-European peoples.

13 For a discussion of the ways in which eighteenth- and nineteenth-century processes of dislocation and displacement associated with the Highland Clearances inform the symbolic and metaphorical significance of the Hilton of Cadboll cross-slab see Jones (2005a).

REFERENCES

Anderson, J. (1881) *Scotland in Early Christian Times (Second Series), The Rhind Lectures in Archaeology for 1880*, Edinburgh: David Douglas.

Bell, D. (1997) *The Historic Scotland Guide to International Conservation Charters*, Edinburgh: Historic Scotland.

Bender, B. (1998) *Stonehenge: Making Space*, Oxford: Berg.

Clavir, M. (2002) *Preserving What is Valued: Museums, Conservation, and First Nations*, Vancouver: UBC Press.

de la Torre, M. and R. Mason (2002) 'Introduction', in *Assessing the Values of Cultural Heritage* M. de la Torre (ed.), Los Angeles: The Getty Conservation Institute, pp. 3–4.

Foster, S.M. (2001) *Place, Space and Odyssey: Exploring the Future of Early Medieval Sculpture*, Inverness: Groam House Trust.

Historic Scotland, (2000) *The Stirling Charter: Conserving Scotland's Built Heritage*, Edinburgh: Historic Scotland.

Historic Scotland (2001) *The Carved Stones of Scotland: A Guide to Helping in Their Protection*, Edinburgh: Historic Scotland.

Historic Scotland (2003) *Carved Stones: Historic Scotland's Approach*, Edinburgh: Historic Scotland [Draft, available at http://www.historic-scotland.gov.uk/carved_stones_hs_approach.pdf, Accessed 01.12.2005].

Holtorf, C.J. (1996) 'Towards a chronology of monuments: understanding monumental time and cultural memory' *Journal of European Archaeology*, 4: 119–152.

ICOMOS (1964) *The Venice Charter: International Charter for the Conservation and Restoration of Monuments and Sites*. Venice: ICOMOS.

Australia ICOMOS (1979) [1999] *Charter for the Conservation of Places of Cultural Significance* (*The Burra Charter*), Deakin, Australia: Australia ICOMOS.

James, H. (2002) *Investigation of the Setting and Context of the Hilton of Cadboll Cross-slab, Recovery of the Stump and Fragments of Sculpture*, Unpublished Report, Glasgow University Archaeological Research Division.

Johnston, C. (1994) *What is Social Value? A Discussion Paper*, Australian Heritage Commission Technical Publications, Series No. 3, Australian Government Publishing Service, Canberra.

Jones, S. (2004) *Early Medieval Sculpture and the Production of Meaning, Value and Place: The Case of Hilton of Cadboll*, Edinburgh: Historic Scotland.

Jones, S. (2005a) 'Making place, resisting displacement: conflicting national and local identities in Scotland,' in *The Politics of Heritage: 'Race', Identity and National Stories*, J. Littler and R. Naidoo (eds), London: Routledge.

Jones, S. (2005b) ' "That stone was born here and that's where it belongs": Hilton of Cadboll and the negotiation of identity, ownership and belonging', in *Able Minds and Practised Hands: Scotland's Early Medieval Sculpture in the 21st Century*, S. Foster and M. Cross (eds), Edinburgh: Society for Medieval Archaeology.

Kirkdale Archaeology (2001) *Hilton of Cadboll Chapel Site Archaeological Excavation. 7th March 2001*, Unpublished Report for Historic Scotland.

Larsen, K.E. (ed.) (1995) *NARA Conference on Authenticity in Relation to the World Heritage Convention*, Paris: ICOMOS.

Lowenthal, D. (1995) 'Changing Criteria of Authenticity', in *NARA Conference on Authenticity in Relation to the World Heritage Convention*, K.E. Larsen (ed.), Paris: ICOMOS, pp. 121–135.

McBryde, I. (1997) 'The ambiguities of authenticity – rock of faith or shifting sands?', *Conservation and Management of Archaeological Sites*, 2: 93–100.

Macdonald, S. (1997) *'Reimagining Culture: Histories, Identities and the Gaelic Renaissance*, Oxford: Berg.

Mellor, S.P. (1992) 'The exhibition and conservation of African objects: considering the intangible', *Journal of the American Institute for Conservation*, 31(1): 3–16.

Merrill, W.A. and R.E. Ahlborn (1997) 'Zuni archangels and Ahayu:da: a sculpted chronicle of power and identity', in *Exhibiting Dilemmas: Issues of Representation at the Smithsonian*, A. Henderson and A.L. Kaeppler (eds), Washington, DC: Smithsonian Institution Press, pp. 176–203.

Miller, H. (1835) [1994] *Scenes and Legends of the North of Scotland*, Edinburgh: B&W Publishing.

Mowaljarlai, D., P. Vinnicombe, G.K. Ward and C. Chippindale (1988) 'Repainting of images on rock in Australia and the maintenance of Aboriginal culture', *Antiquity*, 62: 151–153.

Muir, C.A.C. (1998) 'The containment of Scottish carved stones in situ: a study into the efficacy of this approach', Unpublished MSc dissertation, University of Bournemouth.

Nadel-Klein, J. (2003) *Fishing for Heritage: Modernity and Loss along the Scottish Coast*, Oxford: Berg.

Pye, E. (2001) *Caring for the Past: Issues in Conservation for Archaeology and Museums*, London: James and James.

Richards, E. (2000) *The Highland Clearances*, Edinburgh: Birlinn.

Riegl, A, (1903) [1996] 'The modern cult of monuments: its essence and its development', in *Historical and Philosophical Issues in the Conservation of Cultural Heritage*, trans. and reprinted in N. Stanley Price, M.K., Tally and A.M., Vaccaro (eds), Los Angeles: The Getty Conservation Institute, pp. 69–83.

Ryne, C.S. (2000) 'Changing approaches to the conservation of northwest coast totem poles', in *Tradition and Innovation: Advances in Conservation*, A. Roy and P. Smith (eds), London: The International Institute for Conservation of Historic and Artistic Works, pp. 155–160.

Scottish Executive (1999) *Treasure Trove in Scotland: Information on Treasure Trove Procedures, Criteria for Allocation and the Allocation Process*, Edinburgh: Scottish Executive.

Stanley Price, N, Talley, M.K. and Vaccaro, A.M. (eds.) (1996) *Historical and Philosophical Issues in the Conservation of Cultural Heritage*, Los Angeles: The Getty Conservation Institute.

Stovel, H. (1995) 'Considerations in framing the authenticity question for conservation', in *NARA Conference on Authenticity in Relation to the World Heritage Convention*, K.E. Larsen (ed.), Paris: ICOMOS, pp. 393–398.

Ucko, P.J. (1983a) 'The politics of the indigenous minority', *Journal of Biosocial Science Supplement*, 8: 25–40.

Ucko, P.J. (1983b) 'Australian academic archaeology: Aboriginal transformation of its aims and practices', *Australian Archaeology*, 16: 11–26.

Ucko, P.J. (1985) 'Australian Aborigines and academic social anthropology', in *The Future of Former Foragers in Australia and Southern Africa*, C. Schire and R. Gordon (eds), Cambridge, MA: Cultural Survival Inc, pp. 63–73.

Ucko, P.J. (1987) *Academic Freedom and Apartheid: The Story of the World Archaeological Congress*, London: Duckworth.

Ucko, P.J. (1989a) 'Foreword', in *Archaeological Approaches to Cultural Identity*, S.J. Shennan (ed.), London: Unwin Hyman, pp. ix–xx.

Ucko, P.J. (1989b) 'Foreword', in *Conflict in the Archaeology of Living Traditions*, R.H. Layton (ed.), London: Unwin Hyman, pp. ix–xvii.

Ucko, P.J. (1994) 'Museums and sites: cultures of the past within education – Zimbabwe, some ten years on', in *The Presented Past: Heritage, Museums and Education*, P.G. Stone and B.L. Molyneaux (eds), London: Routledge, pp. 237–282.

Ucko, P.J. (1997) 'Archaeological interpretation in a world context', in *Theory in Archaeology*, (ed.) London: Routledge, pp. 1–27.

Ucko, P.J. (2000) 'Enlivening a 'dead' past', *Conservation and Management of Archaeological Sites*, 4: 67–92.

Ward, G.K. (ed.) (1992) *Retouch: Maintenance and Conservation of Aboriginal Rock Imagery*, Melbourne: Australian Rock Art Research Association.

Walderhaug Saetersdal, E.M. (2000) 'Ethics, politics and practices in rock art conservation', *Public Archaeology*, 1: 163–180.

Withers, C.W.J. (1996) 'Place, memory, monument: memorializing the past in contemporary Highland Scotland,' *Ecumene*, 3 (3): 325–344.

CHAPTER 13

THE ARCHAEOLOGY OF LOCAL MYTHS AND HERITAGE TOURISM
The Case of Cane River's Melrose Plantation

Kevin C. MacDonald, David W. Morgan, Fiona J.L. Handley,
Aubra L. Lee and Emma Morley

BACKGROUND

The archaeology of the African Diaspora and the relationship between archaeology and the tourist industry are two strands of archaeological investigation that have only recently become subjects of academic research. In the USA, the archaeology of African Americans and indeed the historical archaeology of all non-European peoples was largely neglected until the 1980s, when there was a shift to investigating the pasts of those traditionally left out of American historical narratives. The discipline of public archaeology developed concurrently, with one of its aims being to understand the discursive effect that interpretation to the public had on the creation of archaeological knowledge. This chapter draws together these two strands by examining the way that our archaeological work into the Coin Coin/Metoyers, a family of African descent, was influenced by its location at Melrose, the house built by the Metoyers and now a prominent tourist attraction on the Cane River, Louisiana. The fascinating history of the Coin Coin/Metoyers – one of the Creole of Color families – drew us to work in the area and created immense interest in the archaeology we undertook. With this interest came a tremendous amount of information – some academic, some folkloric – us to unravel, and it also gave an emotional weight that added a significant dimension to the work we did. The traditional stories of the history of Melrose and Marie-Thérèse Coincoin formed the public interest in the material we surveyed and excavated, but also created a narrative that our findings had to engage with and sometimes argue against.

INTRODUCTION

Melrose Plantation, a United States National Historic Landmark since 1974, is one of the main foci for cultural tourism in northern Louisiana (Map 13.1). It plays an important role in the Cane River National Heritage Area because of a number of factors:

- It is associated with the legendary free 'woman of color' Marie-Thérèse Coincoin and her children.
- Its architecture is unique and diverse, including notional African influences and structures pre-dating the Louisiana Purchase of 1803.
- It has more recent associations with the literary and artistic circle of Cammie Henry, including the celebrated folk artist Clementine Hunter.

The origins of Melrose are said to go back as far as 1796, when it is claimed that a freed slave of African descent named Marie-Thérèse Coincoin acquired this property on behalf of her mixed race son, Louis Metoyer, who was then still a slave (Mills and Mills 1973: 39–43). Marie-Thérèse herself may have been born in West Africa – the most convincing

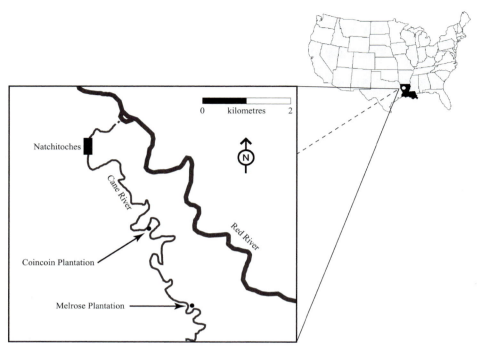

Map 13.1   The location of the Melrose and Coincoin plantations within the Cane River region, and within the USA.

source for her birth being family oral tradition that she was born in 'Guinea' (Woods 1972), though others have guessed at Nago/Yoruba (Hall 2000) or Ewe (G. B. Mills 1977) origins on the basis of her name alone. G. B. Mills (1977) has argued that she was born in Louisiana of first generation African parents, rather than being native to Africa, but his claim is based on rather shaky archival evidence (see MacDonald *et al.* 2002). Regardless, Coincoin was originally a slave of Louis Juchereau de St. Denis, founder of Natchitoches (MacDonald *et al.* 2002). She remained a slave until 1778 when she was purchased and freed by Claude Thomas Pierre Metoyer, a French bourgeois by whom she had borne several children. He ended their alliance in 1786 with a gift of 68 acres of land astride the Cane River at Cedar Bend (about 10 miles from Melrose). Coincoin, as a wealthy, slave-owning African American, has attracted a great deal of literary attention, including novels by Lyle Saxon (*Children of Strangers* 1937), Norman German (*No Other World* 1992), and Elizabeth Mills (*Isle of Canes* 2004). As Coincoin's story becomes more widely known the attraction of heritage sites associated with this remarkable woman will undoubtedly continue to grow.

As a tourist site, Melrose is presented as a tale of three women: Marie-Thérèse Coincoin, Cammie Henry, (the Anglo owner responsible for Melrose's 'renaissance' in the early twentieth century) and Clementine Hunter (the celebrated African-American artist who lived and worked at Melrose during the Cammie Henry era). The basic narrative of the property begins with the construction of a relatively modest half timber structure, Yucca House, in 1796. This structure, and the grain store or 'slave jail', Africa House, are of particular importance because they have been associated with the Marie-Thérèse legend, and are claimed to have been built under her direction. From there the tour progresses to the more luxurious 'Big House' built in 1833 by Marie-Thérèse's grandson Jean Baptiste Louis Metoyer, shortly after his father Louis' death. The tale then moves on to the sale of the plantation by the partly-African Metoyer family in 1847 to the Euro-American Hertzog family, who owned it in the decades straddling the Civil War. The story culminates with the restoration of the property, beginning in 1899, by John and Cammie Henry, who gave the plantation its present name of Melrose. It is from Cammie Henry, and the artists' colony that she created around her, that the legend of Melrose grew.

As archaeologists working over the past three years at Melrose and the other plantations of Coincoin and her family, we have lived in the shadow of this narrative and the Marie-Thérèse legend. Unsurprisingly, expectations born of the stories about Marie-Thérèse have influenced our investigations at both Melrose and her own plantation a few miles away. Indeed, these stories and the local interest in this past were some of the key reasons why our project was initiated. However, little by little archaeological and archival findings have unravelled the links between traditional narratives and the history of these properties, obliging us to renegotiate their pasts (see MacDonald *et al*. 2002/2003 and for the story of the *Maison de Marie-Thérèse*).

MELROSE: THE BIRTH OF A LEGEND

Louisiana's 'Creoles of Color' – free people of a mixed African, European and Native American ancestry – coalesced as a distinct cultural group early in the colonial period. Like others in the area, and more successfully than many, Cane River's free Creoles of Color profited from the cotton boom in the first decades of the nineteenth century. By the 1830s and 1840s the Creoles, especially the Metoyer descendents of Marie-Thérèse Coincoin, were amongst the wealthiest people in Louisiana. For example, at the height of their prosperity the Metoyers owned more slaves then any other free African-American family in the USA (Louisiana State Museum 2003). However, the Creole of Color community was the first to suffer in times of financial hardship and social change. After the failed Reconstruction of the South in the late 1860s, new 'Jim Crow laws'[1] categorised Creoles as 'black' and subjected them to 100 years of American Apartheid. The history of the Cane River Creoles of Color is one of a people who were respected, hard working and sometimes wealthy, yet restricted in their interaction with the white 'high society' with whom they shared genetic heritage. Paradoxically, they were simultaneously keen to distinguish themselves from the African slaves that they owned. Even today they maintain their distinctive identity.

The heritage of the Creoles of Color has long attracted the interest of outsiders. The great travel writer and abolitionist Frederick Law Olmstead wrote about the Cane River community in 1856. Not long after the Civil War, George Washington Cable set his novels and short stories amongst Louisiana's Creoles of Color, including *Old Creole Days* (1879) and *The Grandissimes* (1880). Part of the fascination is the inter-racial sexual component of this history, which questions later American stereotypes of romantic/sexual relationships between black and white. Most of Louisiana's Creoles of Color communities stem from semi-illicit but accepted antebellum relationships – often common law marriages – between wealthy white men and African slaves or free women of mixed-race. A portion of such relationships derived from the *plaçage* system, where free women of color were 'placed' by their families as permanent mistresses or 'second wives' to the white gentry and established in their own households (Ingersoll 1999). Thus, Marie-Thérèse Coincoin's liaison with the white Frenchman Pierre Metoyer, who subsequently freed her and eventually their illegitimate children, is merely one relationship among many – but it is a well remembered one.

It was Lyle Saxon (1937), a folklorist and member of Cammie Henry's artist commune, who first hinted at the story of Marie-Thérèse, but it was another member of that community – the self-styled Frenchman François Mignon – who did the most to popularise her tale. He did so first as writer of a regionally syndicated column, 'The Cane River Memo' (1957–1970), and then as author of the book *Plantation Memo* (1972). Mignon was the first to associate the name 'Yucca' with the earliest plantation at the property and, indeed, he may have invented it. He also claimed that Marie-Thérèse Coincoin, a freed slave 'from the Congo', was the first owner of Yucca Plantation and in 1750 built Yucca House and Africa House (Mignon 1972:1–2). A bronze plaque to this effect was set in the brick front porch of Yucca House and still exists today. Mignon claimed Louis Metoyer inherited Yucca from his mother, and that Louis' son (Jean Baptiste Louis) built the main house in 1833, at which point Yucca House was turned into a home 'for indigent slaves' (Mignon 1972: 1–2). Mignon (1972: 5, 30–31) also claimed that the two-story Africa House was 'a replica of tribal houses on the Congo river in Africa', and that it served simultaneously as both a jail for Coincoin's recalcitrant slaves and as a storeroom.

Meanwhile, at this same time local folk historian Louis R. Nardini Sr was pouring scorn on the writings of Mignon. He wrote in the *Natchitoches Times* on 22 October 1972 that, 'Marie-Thérèse Coin Coin never owned the plantation known as Melrose in Natchitoches Parish … she was not the builder of the buildings designated as the Yucca House, the Africa House, or the Ghana House … she never received a land grant [for the Yucca/Melrose property] from the King of France.' He went on to assert that previous writers of the story of Marie-Thérèse and Melrose wrote 'with their imagination and the pretense that the records are now missing from the courthouse'. Instead, Nardini presented the outline of what has become one perspective on the disputed past of Cane River: that Marie-Thérèse Coincoin lived in her own plantation at Cedar Bend until at least 1816, and that her son Louis Metoyer alone was involved with the construction of Yucca – and much later than Mignon had claimed.

In 1973, amid growing controversy, the owners of Melrose – the Association for the Preservation of Historic Natchitoches (APHN) – hired the genealogists and historians Gary and Elizabeth Mills to write a proper account of the origins of the plantation (Mills and Mills 1973). The Mills' work developed into the book *The Forgotten People* by Gary Mills (1977), and now defines the conventional story of Melrose's origins.

Gary and Elizabeth Mills laid aside Mignon's claim that Coincoin's ownership of Yucca/Melrose dated back to 1750, because records plainly showed that Marie-Thérèse would have been only a girl at that time and that she was not freed until 1778. They focused instead on documents regarding a Melrose property dispute that raged in 1806 and 1807. Louis Metoyer, the son of Marie-Thérèse and Pierre Metoyer, filed claim to the land in December 1806. Sylvestre Bossier, the original 1789 grantee, contested the claim and argued that Metoyer was squatting on the land without title. Louis Metoyer replied that Bossier's right to the land had lapsed, since he had not made required improvements, and that the land had then been deeded to Metoyer in 1796. This was convenient, since the Natchitoches Parish surveyor had gone blind in 1795 and was not replaced until 1803. Thus, there was no record. Ultimately, Louis Metoyer was awarded the land. In hindsight the Mills' saw one flaw in Metoyer's story: he was legally a slave until May 1802, and slaves could not be deeded land. To bridge this logical gap, Gary and Elizabeth Mills (1973: 41) asserted that Marie-Thérèse acquired the land in 1796 for her son, then technically still a slave. However, this does not make logical sense, because if Marie-Thérèse *had* owned the property, Bossier's challenge to the claim would have been directed at Marie-Thérèse, not her enslaved son.

Thus the association of Marie-Thérèse with Melrose is founded upon gaps in the documentary record, rather than any actual written proof of her presence. Indeed, Nardini (1972) claimed there were other documents that would draw an even greater separation between Coincoin and the ownership and management of Melrose. This is supported by a recently located 1820 Census entry that shows Coincoin was still the head of her own household near Cedar Bend and was not dwelling in the Melrose area (MacDonald *et al.* 2002/2003).

The 1974 documents which registered Melrose as a United States National Historic Landmark are only slightly more conservative than Mignon's fanciful writings and continue to reflect his influence. The papers state that, 'Architecturally its buildings illustrate the changes and variations in local building forms and techniques from the earliest French Colonial times to the 1830s period of the Big House' (document on file with APHN). Mignon's 1750 date is thus implied, but not stated. Marie-Thérèse also is not explicitly mentioned, yet it is written that, 'Melrose [was] established and developed by free people of color through several generations. This fact lends credence to the assumption that the design of the Africa House and Ghana House at Melrose are actually African.' No further details on Ghana House are provided, but, regarding Africa House, it is said that, 'The absence of supporting columns gives the building a curious umbrella-like appearance that is believed to be of African derivation.' Of Yucca House little is firmly asserted, but it is 'said to be the original plantation house.'

After several decades the myths of Melrose have crystallised as fact in the many tourist brochures, websites and academic papers that take an interest in Marie-Thérèse and Melrose plantation. 'The story of romantic Melrose Plantation', proclaims the Melrose Plantation tourist brochure printed in 2002, 'begins with the legend of Marie Thérèse Coincoin'. The APHN (2004), the site's owners and managers, lead off their website with a quote from Mignon: 'According to ... tradition, Marie-Thérèse Coincoin was the recipient of the grant known as Melrose Plantation.' By choosing this particular quotation they exploit the allure of oral history and the Coincoin myth without violating documented history. Others are not so circumspect. For instance, the State of Louisiana's Department of Culture, Recreation and Tourism (2003) advertises that Coincoin 'was the matriarch' of Melrose plantation until her death in 1816 [sic], and that 'Yucca (Melrose) Plantation was the first plantation owned and operated by a freed African woman.' The myth also has made its way into more academic sources. For instance, Barbara Allen (2003) presents 'The Story of Marie Thereze Coin-Coin' and asserts that Coincoin earned the funds with which to manumit her children through a slave-run plantation: in 1816 she 'owned twelve thousand acres of land and thirty nine slaves all part of what is now known as Melrose Plantation'. The list goes on.

The Coincoin myth overlaps with interpretations of Ghana House and Africa House – supposed examples of African-inspired architecture. Ghana House, however, is a simple log cabin, like many other slave or sharecropper cabins known along Cane River in the nineteenth century. Indeed, several local informants have told us that it was re-located from another property along the river by Cammie Henry in the 1920s. More attention has been given to Africa House. Jones (1985: 202), for example, writes that, 'Marie-Thérèse Coincoin, said [by Mignon] to have been from the "Congo," possibly fashioned her structures [Yucca and Africa House] as she or her older relatives remembered their first home.' He then goes on to provide an illustrative comparison to Bamiléké houses in Cameroon (Jones 1985: 202:

Figure 9.4). In a recent study of Creole building practice, Edwards (2002: 66) argues persuasively against such an association for Africa House. He writes:

> nothing about this building can be directly related to African tradition. The builders of Africa House employed no customary African methods or design principles, but rather those of France. It was built as a utilitarian structure by craftsmen at least indirectly familiar with French farmhouse forms and construction technology. Such skills were well-learned by African and Creole apprentices early in the history of the Louisiana colony.

Edwards (2002: 66, figure 44) goes on to supply illustrations of French farm structures closely resembling Africa House.

In short, Coincoin has become firmly associated with the story of Melrose Plantation's origins on the basis of no positive evidence and in the face of some contrary evidence (MacDonald *et al.* 2002; MacDonald *et al.* in press). Yet, it is interesting to note that *another* Marie-Thérèse *was* resident at Melrose until at least 1838. Marie-Thérèse Metoyer, the widow of Louis Metoyer, was still alive at the time of her son Jean Baptiste Louis' death in 1838. Since Marie-Thérèse Metoyer was probably only in her fifties or early sixties, she may well have continued to live there. As a widow used to keeping the main house, a very suitable residence for her in 'retirement' would have been a house on the grounds where she could live attended by a few servants, such as Yucca. A memory of *a* Marie-Thérèse Metoyer living in Yucca House could easily become a memory of *the* Marie-Thérèse Coincoin living there, hence the persistent association of a Marie-Thérèse with Melrose Plantation in oral tradition.

It thus seems most likely that Louis was responsible for the founding and initial development of Melrose Plantation, and no documentary evidence supports the legendary association of Coincoin with the founding of the plantation. Regardless, one large question remains: when were the core structures of the plantation built?

DOCUMENTARY EVIDENCE FOR THE HISTORIC LANDSCAPE

As we began our archaeological investigations of Yucca/Melrose, we sought past survey maps of the property in local archives. The earliest that we found in Natchitoches was an 1877 survey undertaken for the Hertzog family, showing the historic core of the property situated north of the river, much as it is today. Further research at the State Land Records Office in Baton Rouge located maps, heretofore unstudied, indicating that the original structures of the plantation were not even in the vicinity of the current historic core and, indeed, were located *south* of the river.

On 15 March 1813, Deputy Surveyor Joseph Irwin surveyed two land tracts held separately by Augustin Metoyer and Louis Metoyer. Then, on 19 October 1814, Irwin recorded another tract of Augustin Metoyer's land situated alongside the two recorded in the previous year. Together these three tracts encompass modern Melrose Plantation, as well as contiguous property to the south and east.

The largest tract (certificate B No. 1953) was Louis' plantation property sitting astride Red River. The surveyor reckoned that 858.98 acres lay north of the river, and that 52.62 acres lay south of it. The northern territory was surveyed using six reference points, all of which were posts positioned relative to witness trees. Reference mark A, for instance, was 'a Post, an Elm tree bears S.38E. dist. 31 links, & a Hackberry tree S.17E. dist. 47 Links'. The southern portion of the property was surveyed using four reference points. In contrast to the northern portion, two of the survey marks for the southern portion are structures. Survey mark H was a 'Mulberry Post, whence the house of Louis Metoyer bears N.89W', and survey mark I was 'a Post, the house of Augustin Metoyer bears N.85W. & the house of Louis Metoyer N.15W'.

The second tract was Louis' brother Augustin's (certificate B No. 1952), and it too straddled Red River. The portion south of the river was surveyed using four survey marks. One, mark G, apparently was the same survey post as mark H from the survey of Louis' territory, as it, too, lists Louis' house as lying on a bearing of 89 degrees west of north. The second mark, F, was 'a Post, the house of Augustin Metoyer bears N.69W. & the house of Louis Metoyer N.11W'.

Lastly, in the 1814 survey six marks were used to record a second 157 acre piece of property owned by Augustin Metoyer (certificate B No. 1960). This tract lay on both sides of the Red River west of, and adjacent to, Louis' property. Again, of the six marks, two are posts whose positions are given relative to houses. One refers to Augustin's dwelling, and the other, again, is to 'the house of Louis Metoyer N.15W'.

Using the five survey marks and their reference bearings it is possible to triangulate the position of Louis' house (Map 13.2). Without doubt, Louis' house in 1813 sat south of Red River near the eastern edge of Augustin's land, almost due south of modern Melrose Plantation. Not coincidentally, an 1877 map of the plantation under Hertzog family ownership depicts three structures still extant in the Melrose property south of the river: a stable, a gin, and a 'dwelling' (Map 13.3).

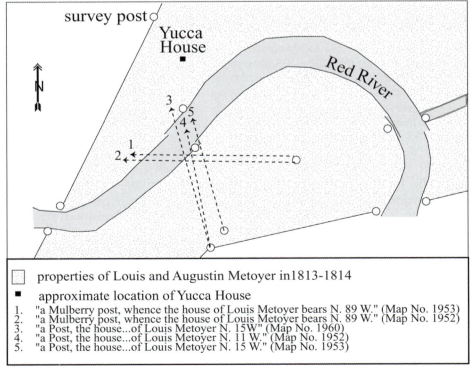

properties of Louis and Augustin Metoyer in1813-1814

approximate location of Yucca House

1. "a Mulberry post, whence the house of Louis Metoyer bears N. 89 W." (Map No. 1953)
2. "a Mulberry post, whence the house of Louis Metoyer bears N. 89 W." (Map No. 1952)
3. "a Post, the house...of Louis Metoyer N. 15W" (Map No. 1960)
4. "a Post, the house...of Louis Metoyer N. 11 W." (Map No. 1952)
5. "a Post, the house...of Louis Metoyer N. 15 W." (Map No. 1953)

Map 13.2   Composite of the 1813–1814 survey maps showing triangulation to 'the House of Louis Metoyer [ca.1813–14]' versus the location of Yucca House.

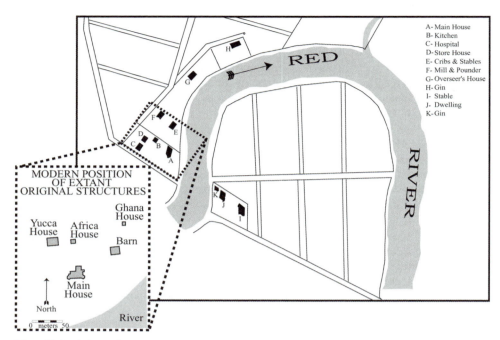

Map 13.3   Schematic reproduction of the 1877 Hertzog map, with an inset (oriented magnetic north) of the current layout of the historic core of the property.

There are three possible interpretations: (1) structures existed north of the river, but they were not used in the 1813–1814 surveys for reasons that are unclear; (2) structures existed north of the river, but Irwin perceived none of them as permanent enough to be used as a survey reference; and (3) no structures existed north of the river in 1813. We feel that the second and third options are the most likely because of the way the surveyor recorded his marks. Every time a witness tree was used Irwin provided a bearing and a distance to it. Every time he used a structure it was a dwelling, and no distances were provided, only bearings. We interpret this as the surveyor seeing house locations as obvious and permanent to anyone using his work. Thus, it would have seemed preferable for both cartographic and legal reasons to record the locations of dwellings whenever possible.

This archival finding, made while we were excavating at Yucca house, obliged us to look carefully for information that might bear upon its date of initial construction and use. Unfortunately, the land to the south of the river where dwellings were recorded in 1813–1814 has been heavily developed for modern housing, making it probable that the remains of any historic structures there have been heavily disturbed or destroyed. Thus evidence for early occupation at Yucca, whether positive or negative, became very important for understanding the historical development of the plantation.

SURVEY AND EXCAVATION AT MELROSE 2002

We began a programme of geophysical survey and excavation at Melrose Plantation in 2001, concentrating mainly on areas where we believed we would find slave quarters (MacDonald *et al.* in press). However, in December 2002 an opportunity arose to excavate in and around

Yucca House. The APHN was concerned about standing water under and around the structure. In the course of assessing the condition of the building, the wooden floor was removed, exposing the hearth beds and earthen sub-floor. It was decided that a drainage scheme was needed and that mitigation archaeology was required. To this end the Institute of Archaeology of University College London (UCL) and the Cultural Resource Office of Northwestern State University of Louisiana worked with Earth Search, Inc. to excavate areas likely to be disturbed. We systematically placed 21 shovel tests and seven auger tests around the perimeter of the house, and also excavated three units outside of the structure and six within it (Figure 13.1). Our excavations were strategically placed to sample a variety of potential discard areas: at a front doorway, within a hearth, in the area outside the back porch and in other less likely areas beneath and beside the structure.

To arrive at an initial date for the structure we assessed the following diagnostic aspects of excavated material culture:

Pottery   Our analysis found that manufacture dates for the majority of sherds falls between the mid nineteenth century and the present day. In terms of wares of European or Euro-American manufacture, this recent period is represented by whitewares and ironstones (n = 358), semi-porcelains (n = 24), yellow wares (n = 20), terracotta flower pots (n = 7)

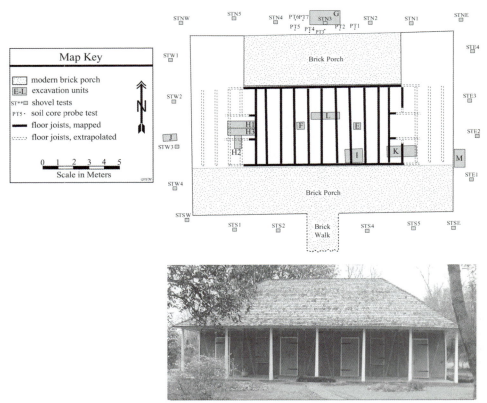

South Side of Yucca House, Facing North

Figure 13.1   Scale plan of the December 2000 excavations at Yucca House with inset photograph of the façade of Yucca House.

and fiesta wares (n = 2). Two ware types are problematic in terms of the broad span of their potential manufacture dates. First is porcelain, which is represented in the excavations by three undecorated sherds. Second is stoneware, of which we found 19 sherds. Most of the stoneware vessel fragments bear an Albany glaze on one or both surfaces, which suggests a manufacture date somewhere between the 1840s and the 1920s (Guilland 1971; Gums 2001). Five, however, are either clear glazed, unglazed or salt glazed. All three decorative techniques could predate the nineteenth century and could date anywhere between the 1770s – the initial surge in American stoneware production – and the 1920s.

The ambiguous stoneware sherds aside, there are some early ware categories that are important for interpreting the initial occupation of this site: clear lead glazed redware (n = 3), black glazed redware (n = 2), creamware (n = 8) and pearlware (n = 57). These date to the late 1700s and the 1820s. Lead glazed redwares were imported to North America as early as the 1500s, but their local production probably did not begin until the early 1600s, when it is documented from sites on the east coast (e.g. Turnbaugh 1985: 21; Ketchum 1991; Erickson 2004). Very little is known of the ware's history in the Gulf South, but appears to be a relatively late phenomenon. Redware production did not begin in southern Louisiana until the late eighteenth century (Lee 1997), in Alabama the earliest kiln was built in the 1820s and Mississippi's earliest kiln dates to 1856 (Ketchum 1991:101–108). Even less is known about clear glaze redwares in northern Louisiana, but the closest documented clear lead glaze redware potter to Melrose was J.R. Tanner, whose kiln in Marshall, Texas (on the Louisiana border), operated in the 1830s and 1840s (Ketchum 1991: 120). Projecting an analogous age to the sherds from Yucca house is not unreasonable. The two black glazed redware sherds are of a type known as 'Jackfield', manufactured in England c. 1740–1790 (Noël Hume 1969: 123). The latter were thus produced prior to the house's earliest hypothesized construction date of 1796 and may well represent a single curated vessel.

Creamwares are only slightly more numerous, making up 1.4 per cent of the assemblage. Creamware production in England began by the 1760s, and creamware vessels were being imported to the USA by the 1770s (Hughes 1960:107; Noël Hume 1973: 219, 224). Creamware sherds are found most commonly at archaeological sites dating between the 1760s and 1790s, particularly along the northern coast of the Gulf of Mexico (Waselkov and Gums 2000: 146). Pearlware manufacture, by contrast, began slightly later, in the 1770s, and pearlware vessels were being shipped to the USA in small quantities in the 1780s and in much larger quantities between 1790 and 1830 (Noël Hume 1973: 236). The two co-existed, but pearlware surpassed creamware in popularity relatively quickly, becoming the predominant American tableware by about 1810 (Lockett 1972: 36). Most manufacturers moved away from creamware production by this date, and Lockett (1972: 36) suggests 'there is little true creamware that one could date to after 1815'. Pearlware remained in vogue until increasingly numerous whitewares and ironstones brought about its decline by c.1830 (Price 1982). Pearlware sherds at Yucca House represent 10.3 per cent of the total collection and outnumber creamware sherds by a factor of roughly 7 : 1. This may be a conservative ratio, too, as we follow Price (1982) and others in identifying as pearlware only those sherds with an overall bluish cast and not just cobalt pooling at vessel inflection points.

It is possible that the eight creamware and five redware sherds could represent the debris from a household dating to the 1790s, with the sparse quantities either echoing the small number of household occupants at that time or reflecting sample bias. But we do not believe this to be the case. We argue that the number of occupants of Yucca House would not have changed markedly over time, as its two rooms could only ever have held a few occupants. We also think that our systematic shovel testing around the house's perimeter and our placement of test units at strategic interior and exterior discard locations militates against sample bias (see Figure 13.1). Given the rarity of the creamwares and the relative abundance of the pearlwares that replaced them c. 1810, an initial occupation date of post 1810 for Yucca House is indicated by the Euro-American ceramic evidence.

Another category of ceramic debris includes low-fired coarse earthenwares of probable Native American manufacture. The two sherds of this type recovered in our excavations provide another insight into Yucca House's probable age. Using samples from 10 colonial and early American period sites in the Cane River area we have demonstrated a clear decline in the presence of this ware type over the course of the late 1700s and early 1800s (Morgan and MacDonald in press). In the late 1700s such unrefined earthenwares account for roughly 40 per cent of the pottery at the inspected plantations, and this figure dwindles to zero by about 1830, at which point the local Caddo Indians were removed to reservations in Oklahoma. At Melrose, in two years of widespread excavation and survey, we have only ever recovered the two bone-tempered body sherds unearthed just outside Yucca House. While inferential, this earthenware signature more closely resembles plantation sites post-dating 1815 than it does those dating to the late 1700s or first decade of the 1800s.

Window Glass   Over the past 20 years or more, window glass thickness has been used increasingly as a dating tool for historical structures in North America (e.g. Roenke 1978; Moir 1987; Ison 1990; Day 2001). In essence, it has been found that window glass tended to increasingly thicken from the early nineteenth century through to c. 1915 when panes reached their modern dimensions. Moir (1987) produced a regression formula on the basis of window glass from structures of known date:

Glass Manufacture Date = 84.22 × Glass Thickness in mm + 1712.7

This formula is said to be accurate to ± 7 years in 60 per cent of the cases studied. If effective, thickness distributions of glass should show peaks when there were new installations of windows on structures – showing periods of initial construction and subsequent periods of refurbishment. Work with early window glass by Earth Search, Inc. in Louisiana indicates that Moir's formula may need to be recalibrated for the region, and that it tends to produce dates which are earlier than known samples by around 10 years or more. Thus, the evidence presented below may well be more recent than described, but certainly not older.

We applied Moir's formula to the flat window glass excavated at Yucca, utilising both raw fragment counts and total fragment weights to quantify it. The former will bias in favour of thinner, more friable glasses and the latter will bias in favor of heavier thicker panes. Taken together they give a more realistic picture of glass distribution (Figure 13.2).

The results of this analysis show three peaks corroborated by both weight and thickness counts: 1.2 mm (dating to c. 1814), 2 mm (dating to c. 1881) and 2.5 mm (dating to c. 1923). A fourth peak at 3 mm (dating to c. 1965) may be real, but it is discounted as it falls well outside Moir's (1987) stated 1810–1915 best accuracy range for his method. The results are fascinating and may indeed reflect the original building of the structure (c. 1807–1821), a renovation during the Hertzog ownership (c. 1874–1888) and another during the Cammie Henry era (c. 1916–1930).

Nails   Much to the benefit of Louisianan historical archaeologists, Edwards and Wells (1993) have studied nails from well-dated historical structures to create a useful morphological typology and associated dating system. We employed their typology for wrought, cut and wire nails in our study and discovered that the vast majority (62.4 per cent)

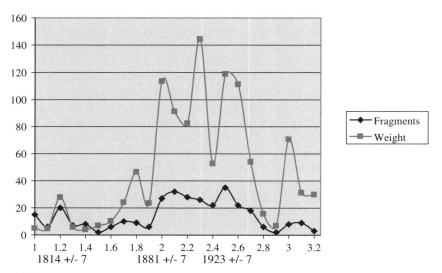

Figure 13.2 Distribution of thickness of window glass recovered from Yucca House by number of fragments and weight. Date ranges for peaks at 1.2mm, 2mm and 2.5mm are given at the base of the graph.

of identifiable nails recovered by our excavations (n = 431) were of the modern wire variety – Types 11 and 12, dating from the 1870s to the modern day (Figure 13.3). Next most common were standard cut nails (Type 8) that were supplied to the area between 1828 and 1920. Only one forged nail was recovered from the excavations. A Type 1/2f, it is thought to date between c. 1730 and 1820. This nail was located in one of the test excavations situated outside of the dwelling (Unit J, Context 2). With this single exception the nails recovered at Yucca give no indication of building debris pre-dating the 1820s. However, it should be noted on the basis of work at other French Colonial structures in Louisiana by Earth Search, Inc., that early (forged) nails are rarely numerous in the excavation of eighteenth century half timber structures due to the more common use of pegs in their construction. Yet their virtual absence at Yucca is still most parsimoniously explained by the structure being built in the 1820s or afterwards.

HISTORY AND MYTH MAKING AT MELROSE

In summary, the archival and archaeological evidence indicate a later date for the building of Yucca and Melrose's historic core than has previously been believed. Our findings indicate that:

- it was not Marie-Thérèse Coincoin who built Yucca, but rather her son Louis Metoyer;
- the structure was not constructed in 1796, but was more likely built in the 1820s;
- it is likely that Yucca, and by extension Africa House, were not the first structures built on the plantation. Rather, it appears such structures are no longer extant and were situated on the opposite side of the river.

It remains possible that Marie-Thérèse did live at Melrose in her extreme old age, perhaps in Yucca House, between the 1820 Census and her death, but there is no evidence whatsoever to support this contention.

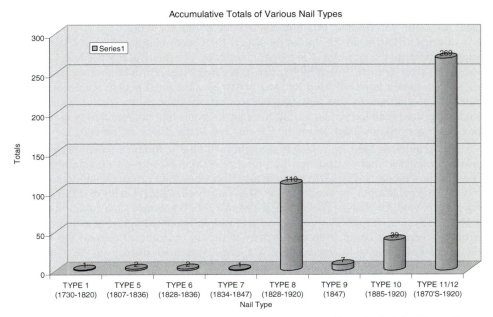

Accumulative Totals of Various Nail Types

Figure 13.3   Total identified nail types from excavations both within and adjoining Yucca House.

For many years the myths of Melrose were a suitable explanation for how, when, and by whom these structures were built. As such they have played an important role in creating and sustaining public interest in this property, and in the past of the region as a whole. While the seeds of these myths can be traced back to oral history and community memory of the Creoles of Color and other local people, the 'packaging' of these myths into a narrative can be dated to the Cammie Henry years at Melrose. This was a period when the gardens, house and its history were recreated into a suitable, romantic version of the past. Along with this was the 'rediscovery' and dissemination of the story of the Creoles of Color.

The first histories of local 'Creoles of Color' by writers such as Lyle Saxon and François Mignon served to preserve and popularise the history of the Creoles. Yet, they also challenged the stereotypical roles of white master and black slave in the American South. It goes without saying that this is still a highly relevant topic. While Cammie Henry provided the location, and Saxon the gravitas to show that this was valuable history, it was François Mignon who spun these together to create the backbone of the Melrose mythos. The irony of this is that Mignon's biggest myth was in fact himself. Rather than being a French *savant*, as he claimed to be, Mignon actually was born in Cortland, New York as Frank Mineah (Cammie G. Henry Research Center 2004). It is a matter of speculation as to whether he actually ever even visited France.

Mignon's recreation of Melrose's past was not only dubious, it also subtly remolded the history of the Creoles of Color. Melrose was the property of Louis, Marie-Thérèse's second son, who although wealthy and respected in the Cane River, lived in the shadow of his elder brother Augustin, who owned more land, more slaves, had more children and lived a much longer life. Augustin died in 1856, leaving a legacy of respect, a church that he built in his name and generations of Creoles of Color who looked up to 'Grand pere

Augustin'. Many people in the 1940s, and even 1960s, would have known people who knew Augustin. Yet Mignon, as a privileged white living in the pre-Civil Rights era, was able to create Melrose as the 'point of origin' for Creole culture without contestation. Augustin became a lesser player in Mignon's version of events, partly because his home across the river burned in the 1880s, partly because Augustin had nothing to do with Mignon's adopted home of Melrose, and partly because local people were not writing their own past. It was by this rewriting of local history through the lens of Melrose that Mignon secured both the importance of his adopted home and became during his lifetime the gatekeeper of knowledge about the Creoles and Marie-Thérèse Coincoin.

Interpretation at Melrose is slowly changing with the findings of recent research, but guides continue to make claims for the presence of Marie-Thérèse Coincoin and earlier dates for the structures. The Melrose myth also lives on in their promotional literature, and in two very visible signs on Yucca House: Mignon's bronze plaque with its 1750 date and more recent wooden plaque proclaiming a date of 1796. What makes the situation difficult at Melrose is that, despite the progressive archival and archaeological questioning of its narrative, there is a compelling reason why it should continue to present the story of Marie-Thérèse Coin Coin: there are few places where the history of the Creoles is interpreted for tourists. There are only self-guided driving tours that permit one to see small houses (e.g. Badin Roque); churches (especially St. Augustine, built by Augustin) and the St. Augustine graveyard. The site of Marie-Thérèse's own plantation is private property, set back on an unpaved road. Effectively, Melrose is to date the only place where the story of Marie-Thérèse Coincoin is physically interpreted – a dilemma addressed by the Cane River National Heritage Area's Master Interpretive Plan (Martin 2003: 44).

In theory, one would expect that academic challenges to the myths of Melrose would over time cascade down into site interpretation, popular publications and tourism websites. However, it is not just archaeologists and historians who contribute to the public understanding of Marie-Thérèse. Writers of fiction have no reason to restrain themselves to fact. For example, it is probably just a matter of time before the novel *Isle of Canes*' 'historically accurate' characterisation of Marie-Thérèse as the granddaughter of 'African kings' becomes incorporated in the Coincoin/ Melrose myth. In many respects, the myths move faster and in more disparate ways than mere archaeological and historical research can counter. Whether as a proud African woman, a romantic character in a hopeless love affair, the founder of a dynasty of powerful African Americans or as an example of local character in French colonial culture Marie-Thérèse's importance goes beyond being a straightforward agent in a historical narrative. As the Cane River becomes increasingly visible at national level through the efforts of the Cane River National Heritage Area and the Cane River Creole National Historical Park, Marie-Thérèse's prominence will continue to grow and, inevitably, so will the myths that surround her name.

ACKNOWLEDGEMENTS

The work of the Cultural Resource Office and the Institute of Archaeology along Cane River has been funded by grants from the British Academy, The Institute of Archaeology (UCL), the US National Park Service's Delta Initiative, and the Cane River National Heritage Area.

The senior author would also like to acknowledge with gratitude Peter Ucko's generous and caring support of African archaeology, whether on the continent or amongst the Diaspora, over his years at the Institute and, indeed, before.

NOTE

1 'Jim Crow laws' – from the 1880s to the 1960s many American states enforced segregation through legislation which ordered businesses and public institutions to separate blacks and whites, and forbid mixed race marriages.

REFERENCES

Allen, B. (2003) 'Reconstituting the vanished: gender, memory, and placemaking in the Delta South' *Architronic*, 5(1.02), available at http://architronic.saed.kent.edu/v5n1.02a.html, accessed on 5 March 2003.

APHN (Association for the Preservation of Historic Natchitoches) (2003) 'Official Websites for Melrose Plantation and Kate Chopin House', available at http://www.natchitoches.net/melrose/, accessed on 5 March 2003.

Cable, George W. (1879) *Old Creole Days*, New York: Charles Scribner's Sons.

Cable, George W. (1880) *The Grandissimes*, New York: Charles Scribner's Sons.

Cammie G. Henry Research Center, Northwestern State University Libraries (2004) 'Francois Mignon Collection Biographical Sketch', available at http://www.nsula.edu/watson_library/cghrc_core/mignon.htm, accessed on 15 February 2004.

Cane River National Heritage Area Commission (2003) *Cane River National Heritage Area Management Plan*, Denver: National Park Service, Denver Service Center.

Day, G.L. (2001) 'Window glass dating: When was McConnell's homestead built?', paper presented at the 4th annual South Central Historical Archaeology Conference, Little Rock, October 2001, available at www.crai-ky.com/education/reports/reports-online.htm, accessed, on 7 October 2004.

Edwards, J.D. (2002) 'Vernacular vision: the gallery and our Africanized architectural landscape', in *Raised to the Trade: Creole Building Arts of New Orleans*, J.E. Hankins and S. Maklansky (eds), New Orleans: New Orleans Museum of Art, pp. 61–94.

Edwards, J.D. and T. Wells (1993) *Historic Louisiana Nails: Aids to the Dating of Old Buildings*, The Fred B. Kniffen Cultural Resources Laboratory Monograph Series No. 2, Baton Rouge: Geoscience Publications.

Erickson, H.A. (2004) 'Early New England Redware Pottery Research Site', available at http://www.people.fas.harvard.edu/~ericks/redweb/index.htm, accessed on 21 June 2004.

German, Norman (1992) *No Other World*, Thibodaux (LA): Blue Heron Press.

Guilland, H.F. (1971) *Early American Folk Pottery*, Philadelphia: Chilton Book Company.

Gums, B.L. (2001) *Made of Alabama Clay: Historic Potteries on Mobile Bay*, Archaeological Monograph 8, University of South Alabama Center for Archaeological Studies, Mobile.

Hall, G.M. (ed.) (2000) *Databases for the Study of Afro-Louisiana History and Genealogy 1699–1860: Computerized Information from Original Manuscript Sources*, CD-ROM. Baton Rouge: Louisiana State University Press.

Hughes, G.B. (1960) *English and Scottish Earthenware 1660–1860*, London: Lutterworth Press.

Ingersoll, T.N. (1999) *Mammon and Manon in Early New Orleans: The First Slave Society in the Deep South 1718–1819*, Knoxville: University of Tennessee Press.

Ison, B.S. (1990) *Window Glass in Kentucky 1790 to 1940: Potential Characteristics and Variation of the Archaeological Assemblage as Produced by the Processes of Manufacture, Distribution, Use, and Deposition*, Unpublished MA Thesis, University of Kentucky, Lexington.

Jones, S.L. (1985) 'The African-American tradition in vernacular architecture', in *The Archaeology of Slavery and Plantation Life*, T. A. Singleton (ed.), Orlando: Academic Press, pp. 195–213.

Ketchum, W.C., Jr (1991) *American Redware*, New York: Henry Holt and Company, Inc.

Lee, A.L. (1997) 'Colonial Redware production on the Acadian Coast', paper presented to the 54th Annual Meeting of the Southeastern Archaeological Conference, Baton Rouge, Louisiana.

Lockett, T.A. (1972) *Davenport Pottery and Porcelain 1794–1887*, Rutland: Charles E. Tuttle Inc.

Louisiana State Museum (2003) 'The Cabildo–Antebellum Louisiana: agrarian life', web page: *Louisiana State Museum Online Exhibits*, available at http://lsm.crt.state.la.us/cabildo/cab9.htm, accessed on 24 February 2003.

Martin, Brenden (2003) *Cane River National Heritage Area Master Interpretive Plan*, Denver: National Park Service, Denver Service Center.

McConnell, K. (1988) *Redware: America's Folk Art Pottery*, West Chester: Schiffer Publishing Ltd.

MacDonald, K.C, D.W. Morgan and F.J.L. Handley (2002/2003) 'Cane River: the archaeology of 'Free People of Color' in Colonial Louisiana', *Archaeology International*, 6: 52–55.

MacDonald, K.C, D.W. Morgan and F.J.L. Handley (in press) 'The Cane River African Diaspora Archaeological Project: Prospectus and Initial Results', in *African Re-Genesis: Confronting Social Issues in the Diaspora*, J. Haviser and K. MacDonald (eds), London: UCL Press.

Mignon, F. (1972) *Plantation Memo: Plantation Life in Louisiana 1750–1970 and Other Matters*, Baton Rouge: Claitor's Publishing Division.

Mills, E.S. (2004) *Isle of Canes*, Provo: MyFamily.com (in press).

Mills, G.B. (1977) *The Forgotten People: Cane River's Creoles of Colo*, Baton Rouge: Louisiana State University Press.

Mills, G.B. and E.S. Mills (1973) *Melrose*, Natchitoches: The Association for the Preservation of Historic Natchitoches.

Moir, R.W. (1987) 'Socioeconomic and chronometric patterning of window glass in historic buildings', in *Material Culture and People of the Prairie Margin*, D.H. Jurney and R.W. Moir (eds), Richland Creek Technical Series, Volume 5, pp. 73–81, Dallas: Southern Methodist University Department of Anthropology.

Morgan, D.W. and K.C. MacDonald (in press) 'Colonoware in Western Colonial Louisiana: makers and meaning', in *The Historical Archaeology of French America: Louisiana and the Caribbean*, K. Kelly and M. Hardy (eds), Gainesville: University of Florida Press.

Nardini, Louis Sr (1972) 'Legends' about Marie Therese Disputed, *Natchitoches Times*, 22 October, 1972, p. 8-A.

Noël Hume, I. (1969) *A Guide to Artifacts of Colonial America*, Philadelphia: University of Pennsylvania Press.

Noël Hume, I. (1973) 'Creamware to Pearlware: A Williamsburg perspective', in *Ceramics in America*, I. B. Quimby (ed.), Charlottesville: The University Press of Virginia, pp. 217–254.

Olmstead, F.L. (1856) *Journey in the Seaboard Slave States, With Remarks on Their Economy*, New York: Dix & Edwards.

Price, C.R. (1982) *19th Century Ceramics in the Eastern Ozark Border Region*, Center for Archaeological Research, Southwest Missouri State University Monograph Series No. 1. Springfield: Southwest Missouri State University.

Roenke, K.G. (1978) *Flat Glass, Its Use as a Dating Tool for Nineteenth Century Archaeological Sites in the Pacific Northwest and Elsewhere*, Northwest Anthropology Research Notes, Memoir No 4, Moscow: Idaho.

Saxon, L. (1937) *Children of Strangers*, Boston: Houghton Mifflin Co.

State of Louisiana's Department of Culture, Recreation, and Tourism (2003) 'Louisiana: Our Culture Abounds' available at http://www.crt.state.la.us/crt/tourism/ourcultureabounds/ocacenla.htm, accessed on 5 March 2003.

Turnbaugh, S.P. (1985) 'Introduction', in *Domestic Pottery of the Northeastern United States: 1625–1850*, S.P. Turnbaugh (ed.), Orlando: Academic Press, Inc, pp. 1–28.

Waselkov, G.A. and B.L. Gums (2000) *Plantation Archaeology at Rivière aux Chiens, ca. 1725–1848*, Mobile: University of South Alabama Center for Archaeological Studies.

Woods, Sister F.J. (1972) *Marginality and Identity: A Colored Creole Family through Ten Generations*, Baton Rouge: Louisiana State University Press.

CHAPTER 14

PRACTISING ARCHAEOLOGY IN EASTERN AND SOUTHERN AFRICA

Coming of Age or the Indigenisation of a Foreign Subject?

George H. Okello Abungu

SETTING THE CONTEXT

Africa is an ancient continent: one that is rich in resources and unique in its great diversity of plant and animal life, geology and geography. It goes without saying that Africa has a long and rich history. Like any other continent, the history of Africa is that of achievements as well as losses, of great civilisations and their decline, of good and bad times; it is indeed a history of mixed fortunes. It is a continent that has attracted various unflattering descriptions such as 'Darkest Africa' and 'The Dark Continent'; there are repeated references to the continent as mysterious or unknown. No other continent has had so many other mysteries created around it. Yet it is Africa that saw the beginnings of humanity with abundant associated evidence. It is also the same continent that has contributed in many areas to the domestication of various plants. These more positive roles have often been down-played and even at times taken away from it.

For centuries Africa was engaged in trade with Europe and the Mediterranean, the Red Sea, Asia, the Far East and the Arabian Peninsula, exporting many rare commodities beyond its borders. After the coming of the Portuguese and other Europeans, Africa ceased to produce only rare and valuable commodities in the form of raw materials, but sadly also became a major exporter of human beings to the Americas, Europe and Arabia, a dark period indeed in the historical experience of humankind.

By the mid nineteenth century, Africa was not just a 'Dark Continent' and a source of raw materials and markets, but also an adventurer's paradise, attracting a range of diverse people with diverse interests, from discovering the sources of great rivers such as the Nile and studying its natural phenomena – its extraordinary plants and animals and such unique geological formations as the Great Rift Valley – to investigating cultural landscapes with monumental architecture of various forms and scales. The end of the nineteenth century brought colonialism, resulting in the division of the continent and its apportionment among the various European powers. For the first time, the continent had been totally opened to the world. With this opening came great interest in Africa as a land that could hold the answers to many questions. Africa now had a new-found position as the cradle of humankind that was not only romanticised but attracted a concerted effort by Western scholars; this set in motion the human origins studies/debates that were to be associated with, and dominate, much of the research and practice of palaeontology and archaeology in Eastern and Southern Africa up to the present.

Today, the continent is still referred to as 'Developing', with all the associated problems – poverty, disease, illiteracy, conflict etc. Despite all these, the continent has continued to charm humanity with its rich cultural and natural heritage, relaxed lifestyle and a sense of community relations and friendship that its people exhibit up to today in many places. The list of visitors to the continent in the last 200 years reads like a *Who's Who* in the fields of science and adventure in world history. Unfortunately, the innocent romantic attitude of the past still prevails in various forms, depicting the history and culture of the continent as that still worthy of 'discovery'. 'Discovery' is one of those terrible words that has permeated African historiography and has been part of the vocabulary of African studies; not even liberated African minds have managed to evade it. The archaeology of Africa itself for a long time remained the 'archaeology of discovery'. In fact, for decades, the archaeology of Africa remained by and for a few white elites from both within and outside Africa; this has been the context in which archaeological and palaeontological studies have taken place, particularly in the archaeologically and palaeontologically rich Eastern and Southern African regions.

ORIGINS OF ARCHAEOLOGY AND PALAEONTOLOGY IN EASTERN AND SOUTHERN AFRICA

Archaeology and palaeontology – as practised by the West – were never part of indigenous African thought systems. Introduced on the continent at the turn of the twentieth century, the subjects became the preserve of a few elite white scholars and adventurers who in the process perfected the art of fundraising for their work through public talks and appeals directed at inquisitive and interested audiences in both Europe and America. To be able to carry out research, one needed large sums of money to maintain camps, organise transport and ensure pre- and post-field research work. Even though Africans did all the manual work, they were not even paid enough to run a modest home. Despite the fact that archaeological and palaeontological research involved huge sums of money and the generation of knowledge meant to unearth a people's history, the Africans remained passive and silent participants from the start and were always relegated to diggers and fossil hunters without any hope of climbing the ladders of success or knowledge.

Some of the earliest areas of interest for foreign students of archaeology in Africa were the magnificent architectural feats including, but not restricted to, Great Zimbabwe, the Swahili city-states and the extensive earthworks of West Africa. The problem was not just the presence of such phenomenal architectural masterpieces in what was perceived as the 'Dark Continent' but the need for an explanation that would put the inhabitants and builders of such feats squarely outside the continent. Wasn't Africa being colonised because it was backward and because its people were naïve tribal entities who were only capable of simple technologies and subsistence farming? Then how could anything so complex be attributed to Africans? This would negate the core belief in 'positive' European intervention and render colonialism unwarranted. Naturally, archaeology became a tool for investigations into the origins of complex societies in Africa from the very beginning.

The negative and paternalistic attitude that influenced early archaeology on the continent is still felt today. The practice of archaeology in Africa was for a long time not only one of appropriation of a people's memory and history by outsiders, but also one of disenfranchising the indigenous people through denying them the opportunity to take part in the formulation and production of their history. The colonial system not only denied local people the right to political and economic freedom, but the freedom to be who one was. This of course had implications and influenced the way most later scholars came to do their archaeology and even their choices of areas within the wider field of African archaeology. Just as it had been used to negate the continent's achievements and assign anything seen as complex to outside sources, so archaeology became a tool of protest and self-assertion by the locals.

In the past two decades, many indigenous archaeologists in Eastern and Southern Africa have, to a large extent, been preoccupied with disproving the past interpretations and practice of archaeology on the continent with the aim of not only correcting past histories, but also of carving a niche for themselves in the hitherto white-dominated field. In the process, too much attention has been paid to perceived 'discoveries' as opposed to breaking new ground and opening up new frontiers in theoretical discourse. The practice has at times been more Reaction rather than Action, with too much discussion of terminologies, as many archaeologists tend to think that baptising old things with new names is one way of making a mark. This has often led to confusion, as names of pottery or traditions change as often as does the number of archaeologists in the field.

In the past, there was a tendency among some researchers to be too site-specific; many archaeological sites were treated as personal properties that held all the information the researcher required. Often this was done at the expense of a regional approach and so one ended up with fragmented research that was devoid of any relation to the surrounding areas except by inference. This is not to say that good work has not been done. On the contrary, African archaeologists have restored honour to the continent by returning the true history of the continent to its owners, as expounded later in the chapter. There has been much rigorous archaeological research by scholars that has transcended the previous artificial boundaries, thus resulting in information that has fundamentally transformed our understanding of African history.

However, it is important to note that the biases of the colonial past have persisted until recently. It is the denial of a right to partake in the exercise of knowledge production as equals, and the lack of recognition and appreciation of the African's contribution to the production of his history, that formed until recently the basis of archaeological studies. Most of the current crop of archaeologists working in Eastern and Southern Africa, both Africans and non-Africans, lack these earlier biases. However, nothing has changed in the field of palaeontology over the decades. It is still dominated by non-Africans or Africans of colonial descent, who continue to have a stranglehold on the subject. Various scholars and their collaborators have carved niches for themselves and the struggle for control in this field remains intense.

A CENTURY-OLD DIALOGUE WITH THE PAST

In 1891, in the southern part of the continent at Great Zimbabwe, one of the earliest archaeological expeditions in Africa took place. The aim of the expedition led by the archaeologist J. Theodore Bent was to explain the origins of what were then seen as the 'mysterious' stone settlements in the interior of the so-called Dark Continent. At a period when the colonial powers controlled the purse-strings and the contemporary belief was that Africans were incapable of building stone structures or establishing complex societies, Bent's (1902) results were bound to be influenced by the then-current views of his surroundings. He, like many others, was a product of his time. It was within the framework of the colonial mentality and biased literary sources that were available and fashionable that Bent declared that the Great Zimbabwe monumental architecture was the work of some ancient race of settlers from the Near East (Hall and Neal 1902; Hall 1905, 1909). He further based his belief at the time on written sources and on some imported ceramics from the coast of East Africa referred to as 'very fine pieces of pottery which would not disgrace a classical period in Greece or Egypt' (Bent 1902: x).

The scholars also read geometry into the constructions and Bent (1902: xiii–xiv) notes that

> from this mass of fresh evidence as to the curves and orientation of the Mashona land ruins we may safely consider that the builders of these mysterious structures were well versed in geometry, and studied carefully the heavens. Beyond this nothing, of course, can really be proved until an enormous amount of careful study has been devoted to the subject. It is however, very valuable confirmatory evidence, when taken with the other points, that the builders were of a Semitic race and of Arabian origin, and quite excludes the possibility of any Negroid race having had more to do with their construction than as slaves of a race of higher cultivation; for it is a well accepted fact that the Negroid brain never could be capable of taking the initiative in work of such intricate nature.

With this statement, archaeology had been compromised and a terrible injustice had been committed to the historiography of the continent of Africa yet again.

Reiterating his conviction on the theory of foreign origins, Bent – writing in 1894 (Bent 1902: xvii–xviii) – stated that

> … no one of the many reviewers of my work has criticised adversely my archaeological standpoint with regard to these South African remains: on the contrary, I continue to have letters on the subject from all sides which make me more than ever convinced that the authors of these ruins were a northerner race coming from Arabia – a race which spread more extensively over the world than we have at present any conception of, a race closely akin to the Phoenicians and the Egyptians, strongly commercial, and eventually developing into the more civilised races of the ancient world.

This racist attitude had great impact for a long time on the interpretation of all archaeological finds perceived to be unique; this concept of diffusion from outside as an explanation permeated all levels of archaeological periods, including the Neolithic, and further came to influence the focus and practice of archaeology on the continent to the present.

It took another decade before the damage could be corrected for Great Zimbabwe. The work of David Randall-McIver (1969) told a different story when he concluded that Great Zimbabwe was constructed by unknown African people of relatively recent times. This did not go down well with the colonial governments and within the settler community, which still preferred an interpretation that would suit their biased views. The view that these monuments were of African construction was further confirmed through the work of G. Caton-Thompson who carried out her research at Great Zimbabwe at the turn of the twentieth century. With one of her terms of reference being 'To supervise the distribution of portable objects from excavations to museums or otherwise', a preposterous term of reference that could only be carried out in Africa, she set out to undertake the archaeology in what were seen as conditions of extreme adversity, despite the fact that she stayed in the newly opened Great Zimbabwe Hotel.

The research by Caton-Thompson (1931) went further to confirm that the monumental architecture was indigenous in origin:

> I was indeed fortunate that within reach of my work at Zimbabwe was one whose scientifically-oriented mind, whose understanding of native mentality and tradition, provided a store of knowledge sympathetic to my archaeological conceptions of the ruins' native origin.'

A view consistent with the findings on the ground can be discerned; however, the language of even liberal-minded archaeologists rarely saw the Africans they worked with as stakeholders in the process of archaeological research. To the contrary, the locals were seen as 'different', with a different mentality, more of beasts of burden. This attitude had great implications for the practice of archaeology and palaeontology, as Africans are still seen by many Western researchers as no more than handymen whose job is to dig for a little cash and food rations.

Caton-Thompson (1931) herself had this to say about her own staff:

> in another land I am used to directing my native labour without assistance; a white man is not an indispensable adjunct to discipline and I prefer to deal directly with my workmen. In Rhodesia while maintaining my presence in this respect, there were difficulties inseparable from unfamiliarity with local native habits and language. I was therefore, while in Zimbabwe, the more grateful to Mr. Wallace not only for actually recruiting workers, but also for issuing to them weekly rations and helping me with them when difficulties arose.

There was a clear-cut division between the whites and blacks, with the latter recognised only for their labour, but not seen either as contributors or as part of the collective whole in the process of the research and interpretation of archaeological data. At best, the African was the handyman, something that discouraged any archaeological training of Africans until long after independence. Even then, the discipline and its associated instruments, such as museums and other heritage institutions, continued to be controlled by the small elite, whose sympathies lay with the West.

There is no doubt that Great Zimbabwe is probably the most studied historic site in the whole of sub-Saharan Africa. During much of this period of study that coincides with colonial occupation, those who were engaged with it were the same elite group whose obsession was with finding evidence of origins. Rarely did they look at the site as one among many and as a dynamic space with different variables, including active political, social and economic discourses. However, Great Zimbabwe is a good example of a site that has undergone a complex interpretation and reinterpretation of its history, proving a good laboratory for examining the development of the subject of archaeology and related studies on the continent. It has attracted the attention of scholars in the region who have used various theoretical analyses and systems to try to understand the historical dynamics that have operated at the Great Zimbabwe site and other associated type-sites.

Since the 1970s and 1980s, Great Zimbabwe and other Zimbabwe-type have attracted more attention, particularly in the interpretation of what can be seen as a phenomenon. While its origins and the indigenous nature of the sites and tradition are no longer in doubt, the explosion of such magnificent and complex societies in this general area from around the eleventh century AD has been an interesting subject of research. Their subsequent decline and collapse in the lower part of the Zimbabwe plateau from around the fourteenth to fifteenth centuries and their continuity during the historical period as exemplified by the Monomutapa state have added more interest as various hypotheses and theoretical frameworks have been put forward to explain the concept of development and decline.

The many scholars who have attempted to explain the evolution, development and subsequent collapse of the Zimbabwe tradition and sites include Tom Huffman (1972, 1986), Peter Garlake (1973, 1982, 1983), Paul Sinclair (1987), Gilbert Pwiti (1996), Webber Ndoro (1994), Innocent Pikirayi (1993) and Edward Matenga (1996). While Huffman has extensively used ethnographically derived models to explain the spatial arrangements and ceramic styles of the Zimbabwe sites, Sinclair has applied more of a Geographical Information Systems (GIS) approach that involves analysis of cored materials to identify not only the areas of activity and occupation but also material types and concentrations and the mapping of resources and activity areas within and beyond the site. Oral traditions and historical records have been used to supplement the archaeological records. Except for some of the obvious weaknesses that come with ethnographic analogies, especially the attempt to infer a wide-ranging cultural continuity between these sites and the present living societies, there is much common ground between the various researchers. There is no disagreement that the Zimbabwean tradition was to a large extent based on a cattle culture, that the inhabitants had trade contacts with the coast of East Africa (trading in gold and other items) and that there was a strong spiritual component, with sacred areas probably located on the highest ground, particularly for the site of Great Zimbabwe. More so, there is no argument that the site is indigenous and locally founded and based.

The coast of East Africa, with its stone built town settlements and elaborate trade networks, posed another challenge to academia. Based on the same premise that Africans were incapable of invention, the towns of the coast of East Africa were all assigned foreign origins. James Kirkman (1964) and Neville Chittick (1965, 1974) saw these settlements as having been built by the Arabs who came to trade with local Africans and as such they were interpreted as sea-facing Arab settlements that had their backs to the African interior. The Swahili culture was portrayed as an alien coastal culture of Muslim civilisation that was separate from the cultures of the indigenous Africans. The settlements were therefore often treated as fragmented foreign settler outposts devoid of any indigenous roots.

Although both Kirkman and Chittick were good scholars who dedicated themselves to researching coastal settlements, notably through large-scale excavations, they were people of their times influenced by the colonial set-up that accredited everything unique to foreign origins. The two were relentless in their interpretation of coastal civilisations as foreign, basing their argument on architectural styles. They were however not the first. Justus Strandes (1968), writing about the Swahili of Mombasa in the 1890s, observed that,

> As is natural, the centuries which have passed, and the continued intermarriage with the native African have done much to efface the characteristics of the original stock. They are not, however, pure Bantu and it is indeed remarkable how frequently the Aryan physiognomy and bearing distinguishes these people from the Africans amongst whom they live.

This argument borders on racism. Many scholars, including Western scholars of the later period, have since disputed this construction of alternative histories.

Nurse and Spear in their book *The Swahili: Reconstructing the History and Language of an African Society, 800–1500* (1985) stated that

> The history of the Swahili has long been tangled in the web of their own and other people's perception and misperception of them. At its most extreme, they have been seen as cultural aliens, Caucasian Arabs who brought civilization to a primitive continent. Just as state formation across the continent was seen as the product of Hamitic (Caucasian) invaders from the north, so the Muslim trading towns of the eastern coast were seen as cultural transplants from the Arabian Peninsula. This view is not simply racist; it also implies an understanding of history that sees all cultural innovation in Africa as the result of diffusion of people and ideas from elsewhere, thus denying African historical actors roles in their own histories.

This is indeed an accurate observation of the situation in Africa up to the 1980s.

Even Nurse and Spear were unable to categorically state that the Swahili were Africans without qualification. To them (Nurse and Spear 1985: viii):

> The Swahili are an African people, born on that continent and raised of it. This is not to say they are the same as other African peoples, however, for in moving to the coast, participating in Indian Ocean trade and living in towns, their culture has developed historically in directions different from those of their immediate neighbours. It is not to say

they have not borrowed freely from others. Arabs have been trading along the coast for a long time, and ... the result has been neither African nor Arab but distinctly Swahili.

These complexities of African historiography are a result of the reluctance to let Africans partake in the interpretation of their history.

The Swahili are in many cases, but not all, a cosmopolitan and urban group that has had global interaction for centuries. It is therefore inevitable that they would influence and be influenced by those they come across. The borrowing and lending does not make them less what they are. The internal contradictions that may prevail are not unique to them alone and therefore denying the Swahili their identity, and particularly their indigenous identity, in the name of research findings previously geared towards confirming their foreignness or mixed nature was a failure on the part of the researchers and their research methodology.

The archaeologists working in the mid-1980s had a role to play by pushing forward the frontiers of knowledge through new research and re-interpretation of the hitherto accepted 'facts'. However, even this has not been easy until recently; as late as 1990, the publication *A History of African Archaeology* (Robertshaw 1990) has no African among its contributors. Instead, the list of contributors is again a *Who's Who* of white American and European Africanist archaeologists. Did this mean that there was not a single black African capable of writing about the development of archaeology on his or her doorstep in 1990?

The archaeology of East and Southern Africa was, however, not just about the monuments and towns, and the development of complex societies, but encompassed the study of humans from the beginning to the present. Although the present chapter may appear to be biased towards the complex societies, the majority of African archaeology lies outside this realm of study and those other areas too had their doses of discrimination.

For example, the rich rock art of Eastern and Southern Africa that dates to the earliest period (the site of Apollo 9 in Namibia dates to 27,000 years ago), was for years not taken as an African achievement (Agnew and Bridgland in press). On the contrary, early scholars, who were comparatively few, always looked at the rock art as a Western-introduced concept and art form, as the indigenous people were seen as incapable of innovation without external intervention. When this art was grudgingly accepted as African, the colonialists termed it 'primitive' or children's art. Attributed mostly to hunter-gatherers, this art-work was seen as inconsequential and made by bored individuals with nothing else to do (Ranger 1999).

Ranger (1999) writing about the Matopos area at the beginning of the colonial era notes that a missionary, D. Carnegia, did not even believe that Africans appreciated the beauty and variety provided by nature. Carnegia believed that, to the African, 'the book of nature is shut up and sealed; there is no music in the moaning of the winds ... nor loveliness in the golden-tinted sunsets. Nature's messengers only inspire fear and distrust' (Ranger 1999: 16). This attitude of course had an impact on the study and conservation of rock art in Africa. It showed a lack of understanding on the part of the missionary as to the African view and appreciation of nature as the mother of everything. On the contrary, the art itself reflected a deep understanding of the environment. Walker (1996: 23) has stated that the rock paintings of the Matopos '... were at times ways of mastering nature rather than being subjected to it'. Furthermore, Garlake (1987: 3, 9, 63) states that, 'Paintings do not set out to mirror nature, but to control it ... they express 'supernatural potency' and the urge to control many aspects of the natural world, from rain to animals'.

Many early scholars failed to see that the environment of their archaeological studies and interpretation was a landscape sculpted by human actions over generations and that the interpretation of the same environment must take into consideration this interaction and dialogue between man and nature that at times may not be too obvious. Any interpretation worthy of note should take into consideration not only the views of the shapers of the environment but the sculptures they have created in the form of symbolic and religious spaces, areas of ideological as well as social values.

Even today, rock art remains the preserve of a comparatively few professionals. Although hunter–gatherers created the majority of the rock art, particularly in Southern Africa, the Bantu and other groups have also contributed to this heritage, a fact hardly acknowledged by many of the practising researchers. To the contrary, the Bantu are portrayed in written records as fast moving iron-using farmers who often subdued the hunter–gatherers and had nothing to do with the ritually oriented paintings of the latter. More than that, as benevolent occupants of the land and environment, the Bantu iron users were seen as wasteful, wreaking wanton destruction upon the environment. They were considered a group incapable of striking a balance between man and nature.

Archaeological and anthropological research so far carried out suggests that rock art has been of great importance to the well-being of many African societies going back into the prehistoric periods (Garlake 1995). As a spiritual medium, rock art has helped them to understand their environment and the forces that interact with it and to interpret those things beyond the human realm. It ensured the ordered process of society and in some cases was used for initiations and ceremonies. Even today many Bantu societies, such as those found around the rock art site of Domboshawa, near Harare in Zimbabwe, still believe in carrying out rain rituals at the rock art sites (Pwiti and Mvenge 1996).

In some cases, and in recent times, rock art has been used for political purposes such as land claims (Abungu in press). In Southern Africa for example, because rock art was perceived to have been the preserve of the Khoisan, who had been more or less wiped out, those new powerful and colonial settlers who occupied the land considered themselves, rather than the Bantu, the rightful owners. Thus, in this situation, sites were used to claim ownership of land in the absence of the original owners whose trademark or signatures were seen to be the rock art. It is no coincidence that rock art studies were dominant in South Africa in the 1970s and 1980s (Abungu in press), during apartheid, despite the fact that overall, systematic studies and formal government protection had come late in Africa.

The later Neolithic and iron age archaeology of Africa, particularly in Eastern Africa, is another good example of the inherent contradictions and controversies associated with the subject. Here too the question of human origins has proved elusive, beginning as early as the 1920s. At times, however, the discussions have centred on trivial things such as changing names of sites, traditions etc. by individuals working at a site; occasionally, scholars have failed to agree even on what attributes are to be taken into consideration in the classification of ceramics or wares, only adding more confusion.

Practically, however, this later archaeology of East Africa, as Kiriama (2001: 5) has noted,

> … ranged from the need to understand the later Pleistocene and Holocene artefact traditions and linguistic groups in the region, the reconstruction of the environmental changes for the period based on analysis of pollen cores from highland lakes and limnological analysis of lakes in the area, to the techniques of artefact making and the collection of oral traditions to verify the existence of various archaeological entities.

The majority of the studies have taken a culture-historical and ecological construction approach. Many years of research have resulted not only in the definition of major cultural entities in the region but have also demonstrated climatic and vegetation shifts in the late Pleistocene and early Holocene periods.

Louis Leakey's work in the Nakuru–Naivasha basin of Kenya that started in the 1920s was the first systematic study of later prehistory in East Africa (1931, 1970; M. Leakey 1945), and he was later joined by his wife, Mary Leakey. In Uganda, T.O. O'Brien and E.J. Wayland's (1939) work in the Kagera was the first of its kind there, while in Tanzania Hans Reck had excavated burial mounds in the Ngorongoro Crater as early as 1915–1916, and found material evidence, particularly beads, that were similar to what Leakey found at the Njoro site near Nakuru (Leakey and Leakey 1950). Louis Leakey, however, was the first to coin the term Neolithic, based on the presence of stone bowls, polished axe heads, pottery and human burial sites that he compared to the European finds of the Neolithic period (1931). Louis Leakey's interest at the time was to reconstruct the region's cultural history through archaeological evidence, the main aim being the investigation of the origins of food production in the region. Leakey concluded that there was evidence for the domestication of cereals and that the culture could have been a Sudanic one that had intruded into this area. This was to be a major point of discussion for many years until John Sutton and others' work (Sutton 1973, 1974; Onyango-Abuje 1976, 1980; Bower 1991) showed no link between the area and the so called Hamitic/Cushitic intervention. The name Neolithic also had to undergo change in the 1950s only to be restored in the 1970s, but this time with specific definitions such as 'Pastoral Neolithic' (Bower 1991; Onyango-Abuje 1976).

The following decades saw frantic research and expeditions in this period and general area by American, European and, eventually, indigenous African scholars. It also saw different theories and hypotheses developed, mostly touching on the origins of food production and domestication of animals, based on specific sites rather than regionally except for Sutton's work (1974) and Onyango-Abuje and Simiyu Wandibba's (1979) among others.

Kiriama (2001: 5–16) has captured the prevailing situation related to the classification of the Neolithic period in East Africa at that time by stating that

> … the main centres of these studies revolve around the issue of indigenous versus foreign origins of the culture. One group composed mainly of indigenous archaeologists such as Onyango Abuje and Wandibba (1979) argues for a local origin. The archaeologists believe that the indigenous population of East Africa domesticated at least some of the livestock and a majority of the crops (millet, sorghum, yam etc.) that are currently grown in Africa. The other group, composed almost exclusively of foreign archaeologists, argue that the Neolithic cultures of East Africa intruded into the region. The intruders, who may have come from the northeast, were Caucasoid and brought with them the art of animal husbandry and perhaps crop production as well.

While this can be said to have been true in the 1970s and 1980s, the same is not true today. Peter Robertshaw gives great credit to the British Institute in Eastern Africa for this change when writing about the Institute's contribution; he states that 'An active programme of field-work soon led to substantive results, including the demise of the "Hamitic myth" in all its forms' (1990: 88). Whatever the case, it is clear that young upcoming indigenous archaeologists were always fighting the diffusionist theories and when the time came, under attack from all directions, theories died a natural death, as was the case in other areas, including the discussions surrounding monumental heritage.

The Iron Age in sub-Saharan Africa was also not without controversy and, if anything, it came to focus an area of intense discussion based on who the iron makers were, what were their origins and how iron-making spread across the continent. While one group sees the introduction of iron technology in the area under discussion as mostly the work of one group, the Bantu spread across the continent as evidenced by ceramic similarities (Soper 1967a,b, 1971; Phillipson 1976a,b, 1977, 1985), another group argues that ceramic affinities do not necessarily reflect an ethnic or linguistic uniformity or cultural group. On the contrary, they argue that ceramics and their styles are entities that have utilitarian functions and can be used to negotiate social relations at individual level. It is further argued that groups of individuals at village level may use ceramic styles to show their relations with one another and not necessarily ethnic affiliations (Schmidt 1978; Kiriama 1987). Whatever the case, there is no doubt that controversy has been part of the archaeology of East and Southern Africa for a century now.

CONCLUSION

While a lot of the controversies were a result of the way archaeology was practised in the colonial period, later approaches to doing archaeology were fuelled by the gaining of independence and a need on the part of the indigenous African scholars to rediscover their true history – and quickly. In the need to correct the mistakes of the past, there was urgent need to give more emphasis to local history that had hitherto been neglected or assumed not to exist. There was a need to reconstruct African history, and archaeology offered the physical evidence to do this.

In the hurry to prove indigenous achievements and to create a sense of identity, there was a tendency to marry archaeology to oral tradition, linguistics and ethnographic data among others. At times one saw an attempt on the side of African archaeologists and some 'apologetic western sympathisers' to try and see only local inventions and nothing foreign; diffusion became an unacceptable terminology. While this was incorrect, it was understandable; the reason partly being that, even long after independence, across the continent historical and archaeological practice was still in the hands of a small clique of Western scholars, some of whom continued to construct Africa's history and interpret its archaeology entirely from a diffusionist point of view. Science even then decided not to give to Africa what was Africa's by classifying everything complex as 'unique and mysterious', and accrediting such heritage to people of foreign origins.

It is no wonder that even with all the discoveries and intense research work carried out in South Africa in archaeology and palaeontology, there was no black African trained archaeologist or palaeontologist before the collapse of the apartheid system. In Kenya and Tanzania, home to world renowned archaeological and palaeontological sites, there were no indigenous Africans holding PhDs until the end of the 1970s and beginning of the 1980s, over 20 years after independence. It was therefore obvious that this denial would translate into a particular way of looking at archaeology, once the local professionals became empowered; it would be the archaeology of protest, one of wanting to be heard and to 'own' the instruments of the production and interpretation of 'local' knowledge.

One of the most important developments, however, was in the late 1980s and 1990s: the very active training of African archaeologists who have revolutionised the practice of the subject and taken control of their own destiny and the destinies of their countries. This is clearly seen in the magnificent work and results of work carried out by indigenous African scholars in Botswana, Zimbabwe, Tanzania and Kenya among others. The rapid growth in numbers of qualified and well-trained archaeologists in this region has been to a certain extent a statement of protest by the hitherto voiceless majority. It is a statement made possible by a new consciousness that came with the founding of the World Archaeological Congress (WAC) through the work of scholars like Peter Ucko, when the previously voiceless majority and the discriminated minority were given an opportunity to participate on an equal footing. Through the WAC publication series 'One World

Archaeology', African professionals not only obtained an accepted platform to openly air their views, but also got much-needed hands-on training in editing and publication. More than any other forum, WAC empowered the previously voiceless to stand up against any academic domination. More so, the generous support for African archaeology that came from the Swedish Government through Uppsala University from the end of the 1980s to the present, totally transformed the archaeological landscape of this region. For the first time in the history of academia, there was a well-planned, and well-executed programme of training for Africans on the subject of archaeology that also came with financial support to empower the participants to engage in research. The results are obvious – an empowered and competent body of researchers who, through their work, have been able to reclaim Africa's rightful place in the historical annals and to place themselves squarely with the best in the international arena.

Today, even with the difficult economic situation in the areas where the archaeologists of the region continue to practice and write, they have moved from looking at single sites – as was the case in the past – to regions. The sophistication of practice and the development of the subject are not only measured in the techniques of investigation that now include GIS and other information technologies, but also in the quality of data and the resultant products. Today, the archaeologists have formed a network called The African Archaeological Network with numerous ongoing projects. Among these are projects looking at issues such as wetland and riverine resource exploitation and the resultant settlements as well as the development of urbanism and of trade systems. Twenty years ago, this was not even imaginable.

It has been a long, winding and bumpy road, with a few casualties along the way. After one century, however, African archaeology has finally come of age.

ACKNOWLEDGEMENTS

I want to thank the Getty Conservation Institute for the resources they made available to me during the writing of this paper, to Lorna Abungu and Ajuma Kayo Abungu for their support and patience and Jane Hubert and Peter Ucko for their motherly and fatherly care and ever ready advice that saw some of us start taking the discipline of archaeology seriously as one with a human face.

REFERENCES

Abungu, G.H.O. (in press) 'Rock art management in Eastern Africa: whose responsibility?', in *Of the Past, For the Future: Integrating Archaeology and Conservation*, N. Agnew and J. Bridgland (ed.) Los Angeles: Getty Trust Publications.

Agnew, N. and J. Bridgland (eds.) (in press) *Of the Past. For the Future: Integrating Archaeology and Conservation.* Los Angeles: Getty Trust Publications.

Bent, T.J. (1902) *The Ruined Cities of Mashonaland*, London: Longmans.

Bower, J. (1991) The Pastoral Neolithic of East Africa, *Journal of World Prehistory*, 5: 49–82.

Caton-Thompson, G. (1931) *The Zimbabwe Culture: Ruins and Reactions*, Oxford: Clarendon.

Chittick, N. (1965) 'The "Shirazi" colonization of East Africa', *Journal of African History*, 6: 275–294.

Chittick, N. (1974) *Kilwa: An Islamic Trading City on the East African Coast*, Vol. II, Nairobi: British Institute in Eastern Africa.

Garlake, P.S. (1973) *Great Zimbabwe*, London: Thames and Hudson.

Garlake, P.S (1982) *Great Zimbabwe: Described and Explained*, Harare: Zimbabwe Publishing House.

Garlake, P.S. (1983) 'Prehistory and ideology in Zimbabwe', in *Past and Present in Zimbabwe*, J. Peel and T.O. Ranger (eds), Manchester: Manchester University Press.

Garlake, P.S. (1987) *The Painted Caves: An Introduction to the Prehistoric Rock Art of Zimbabwe*, Harare: Modus Publications.

Garlake, P.S. (1995) *The Hunter's Vision: The Prehistoric Art of Zimbabwe*, Harare: Zimbabwe Publishing House.

Hall, R.N. (1905) *Great Zimbabwe*, London: Methuen.

Hall, R.N. (1909) *Prehistoric Rhodesia*, London: F.T.Unwin.

Hall, R.N. and W.G. Neal (1902) *The Ancient Ruins of Rhodesia*, London: Methuen.

Huffman, T. (1972) 'Rise and fall of Zimbabwe', *Journal of African History*, 13: 353–366.

Huffman, T. (1986) 'Iron Age settlement patterns and the origin of class distinction in Southern Archaeology', *Advances in World Archaeology*, 5: 291–338.

Kiriama, H. (1987) 'Archaeo-metallurgy of iron smelting slag from a Mwitu tradition site in Kenya', *South African Archaeological Bulletin*, 42: 125–130.

Kiriama, H. (2001) 'The history of the later archaeology of East Africa', in *Encyclopaedia of Archaeology: History and Discoveries*, T. Murray (ed.), Santa Barbara: ABC-CLIO, pp. 5–16.

Kirkman, J. (1964) *Men and Monuments on the East African Coast*, London: Lutterworth Press.

Leakey, L.S.B. (1931) *The Stone Age Cultures of Kenya Colony*, Cambridge: Cambridge University Press.

Leakey, L.S.B. (1970) *The Stone Age Races of Kenya*, Oosterhut: Anthropological Publications.

Leakey, M.D. (1945) *Report on the Excavations at Hyrax Hill, Nakuru, Kenya Colony, 1937–1938*, Cape Town: The Society.

Leakey, M.D. and L.S.B. Leakey (1950) *Excavations at the Njoro River Cave: Stone Age Cremated Burials in Kenya Colony*, Oxford: Clarendon Press.

Matenga, G. (1996) 'Conserving history of the Great Enclosure, Great Zimbabwe, with reference to proposed restoration of a lintel entrance', in *Aspects of African Archaeology*, G. Pwiti G. and R. Soper (eds), Harare: University of Zimbabwe Publications.

Ndoro, W. (1994) 'Preservation and presentation of Great Zimbabwe', *Antiquity*, 68 (260): 616–623.

Nurse, D. and T.T. Spear (1985) *The Swahili: Reconstructing the History and Language of an African Society, 800–1500*, Philadelphia: University of Pennsylvania Press.

O'Brien, T.O. and E.J. Wayland (1939) *The Prehistory of Uganda Protectorate*, Cambridge: Cambridge University Press.

Onyango -Abuje, J.C. (1976) 'Reflections on culture change and distribution during the Neolithic period in East Africa', *Hadith*, 6: 14–30.

Onyango -Abuje J.C. (1980) 'Temporal and spatial distribution of Neolithic cultures in East Africa', in *Proceedings of the 8th Panafrican Congress of the Prehistory and Quaternary Studies*, R.E. Leakey and B.A. Ogot (eds), Nairobi: International Louis Leakey Memorial Institute for African Prehistory.

Onyango-Abuje, J.C. and S. Wandibba (1979) 'The paleoenvironment and its influence on man's activities in East Africa during the latter part of the Upper Pleistocene and Holocene', *Hadith*, 7: 24–40.

Pikirayi, I. (1993) *The Archaeological Identity of the Mutapa State: Towards a Historical Archaeology of Northern Zimbabwe*, Uppsala: Societas Archaeologica Upsaliensis.

Phillipson, D.W. (1976a) 'The Early Iron Age in Eastern and Southern Africa: a critical re-appraisal', *Azania*: Journal of the British Institute in Eastern Africa, 11: 1–23.

Phillipson, D.W. (1976b) *The Prehistory of Eastern Zambia*, Nairobi: British Institute in Eastern Africa.

Phillipson, D.W. (1977) *The Later Prehistory of Eastern and Southern Africa*, London: Heinemann.

Phillipson, D.W. (1985) *African Archaeology*, Cambridge: Cambridge University Press.

Pwiti, G. (1996) *Continuty and Change: An Archaeological Study of Farming Communities in Northern Zimbabwe, AD 500–1700*, Studies in African Archaeology, 13, Uppsala: Acta Arkeologica Upsaliensis.

Pwiti, G. and G. Mvenge (1976) 'Archaeologists, tourists and rainmakers: problems of the management of rock art sites in Zimbabwe, a case study of Domboshava national monument', in *Aspects of African Archaeology*, G. Pwiti and R. Soper, Harare: Zimbabwe Publishing House.

Randall-MacIver, D. (1969) *Medieval Rhodesia*, New York: Negro University Press.

Ranger, T.O. (1999) *Voices from the Rocks: Nature, Culture and History in the Matopos Hills of Zimbabwe*, Bloomington: Indiana University Press.

Robertshaw, P.T. (1990) *A History of African Archaeology*, London: James Currey Ltd.

Schmidt, P.R. (1978) *Historical Archaeology: A Structural Approach in an African Culture*, Intercultural Comparative Studies No. 3, Westport: Greenwood Press.

Sinclair, P.J.J. (1987) *Space, Time, and Social Formation: A Territorial Approach to the Archaeology and Anthropology of Zimbabwe and Mozambique, c. 0–1700*, Uppsala: Societas Archaeologica Upsaliensis.

Soper, R. (1967a) 'Kwale: An Early Iron Age site in south-eastern Kenya', *Azania*: Journal of the British Institute in Eastern Africa, 1: 1–17.

Soper, R. (1967b) 'Iron Age sites in north-eastern Tanzania', *Azania*: Journal of the British Institute in Eastern Africa, 2: 19–36.

Soper, R. (1971) 'Early Iron Age pottery types from East Africa: a comparative analysis', *Azania* 6: 39–52.

Strandes, J. (1968) *The Portuguese Period in East Africa*, trans. J.F. Wallwork, Nairobi: East African Literature Bureau.

Sutton, J.E.G. (1973) *Archaeology of the Western Highlands of Kenya*, Memoir 3, Nairobi: B.I.E.A.

Sutton, J.E.G. (1974) 'The aquatic civilisation of middle Africa', *Journal of African History*, 15(4): 527–546.

Walker, N. (1996) *The Painted Hill: Rock Art of the Matopos*, Gweru: Mambo Press.

CHAPTER 15

CENTRAL EUROPEAN ARCHAEOLOGY AT THE CROSSROADS

Arkadiusz Marciniak

INTRODUCTION

Central European archaeology has never been a coherent entity with clearly defined boundaries and this remains the case to this day. It is composed of a number of distinct national schools but interestingly the overall way in which research is conducted and the explanatory devices employed seem astonishingly similar (Sommer and Gramsch forthcoming). It is often defined in terms of shared research traditions, objectives pursued and methods applied (Bertemes 2002, forthcoming). It is dominated by German archaeology but should certainly not be equated with it. Labelling the Central European tradition as German is based on the fact that the German language has dominated discourse in this intellectual milieu.

Central European archaeology as an independent category, however, is hardly recognised outside the region, a state of affairs inherited from the political conflict after the Second World War, when a sharp East/West divide left no space for any entity in-between. Consequently, the political situation flattened out this highly diverse region of great archaeological richness. The countries on the western edge of the Soviet empire such as Czechoslovakia, Hungary and Poland, which were politically dominated by it, were included in the East. At the same time, the category of *Mitteleuropa* continued to retain its significance in these countries to stress their distinctiveness and opposition to the Soviet hegemony (see also Sommer and Gramsch forthcoming).

It is not my intention to explore here the different trajectories of development of national archaeologies contributing to Central European archaeology (see various contributions in Biehl *et al.* 2002a). There is no doubt, however, that critical and effective evaluation of the current status of this archaeology can only be possible when we explicitly address its theoretical and epistemological traditions as well as the historical and political embeddedness of its practice (e.g. Bernbeck 1997; Lech 1997–1998; Ostoja-Zagórski 1997; Härke 2000; Veit *et al.* 2003). A turmoil of political and social changes over the decades contributed to the peculiar condition of this archaeology (see also Hodder 1991:7). The Kossina syndrome and Soviet domination, in particular the imposition of Marxism, are believed to be two decisive factors that have shaped the way that archaeology in Central Europe has been practised (see e.g. Barford 1993; Lech 1997). These affected an enormous range of aspects, including the academic structure of the discipline, preferred research objectives, funding structure and its relation to the public (see Lozny 2002: 146). Because of different historical and social conditions in different settings, archaeology developed distinctively in different places (see e.g. Barford 1993 analysing the case of Polish archaeology). The historical circumstances of post-war Germany led archaeology in a unified Germany to struggle with the legacy of the Nazi period and a communist state (Arnold 1997–1998: 251; Bloemers 2002: 380).

The period following the revolution of 1989 brought about a number of changes in all spheres of practising archaeology. Central Europe as a geopolitical entity is in the process of rapid social, political and cultural transformation associated with the integration of the continent and globalisation. All countries in the region have undergone dramatic transformations affecting all aspects of archaeological practice, although their intensity has varied from country to country (see Schild 1993: 146–150). The face of archaeologies that had battled under harsh regimes, political division, closed borders and individual unscrupulousness has been rapidly changing. Increased communication and co-operation have brought about greater openness and less marked borders between different national archaeologies. This chapter outlines the major developments resulting from these dramatic changes in the context of the inherited theoretical and historical features of the region.

In 1995 Peter Ucko published an article entitled 'Archaeological interpretation in a world context', which exemplifies many of the virtues I have in mind. He stressed that any interpretive framework in archaeology is adopted within a socio-political context and rightly postulated that recognition of the theoretical and conceptual framework of doing archaeology is of the utmost significance. He further stressed the importance of collaboration – interaction that leads to 'the mingling of archaeological traditions of investigation and interpretation'. The aim of this chapter is to address these issues in Central European archaeology, not in the world context but within the highly diverse context of Europe. It is my intention to show that, despite the vested interests of particular societies, they share common interests that are regional in scope. In addition, as Ucko pointed out, Central European archaeology is an example of a tradition which is often patronised and stereotyped by a mainstream discourse and the chapter also aims to challenge a number of unjustified claims and opinions in this regard.

THEORETICAL TRADITIONS

A specific version of the culture-historical approach dominated Central European archaeology after the war. It comprised inductionism, empiricism, typological methods, relative chronology modelling, description and cataloguing of empirical material, diffusion (so called influences) as the major causative factor and migration (e.g. Barford and Tabaczyński 1996; Lech 1996; Minta-Tworzowska and Rączkowski 1996; Bertemes 2002, forthcoming; Neustupný 2002a; Sommer and Gramsch forthcoming). It focused on archaeological cultures, their origins and dispersal, as well as spatial and cultural relations with similar entities (see e.g. Milisauskas 1997–1998: 227). Archaeological cultures were interpreted in ethnic terms (Mamzer 1997: 41–42). The research process was focused exclusively on observable phenomena in accordance with 'practical' positivism, as defined by Topolski (1983). This was further supplemented by interests in paleoenvironment, settlement studies and, to a limited degree, in ethnicity (see e.g. Laszlovsky and Siklódi 1991: 275; Neustupný 2002a: 285).

Despite political circumstances and expectations, the impact of Marxism remained limited and Central European archaeologies were mainly culture-historical in scope (e.g. Barford and Tabaczyński 1996). In countries like Poland political pressure related to the imposition of Marxism was especially strong in 1950–1955 (Lech 1996: 186; Kobyli´nski 1998: 225). In the beginning a rather shallow "declarative" Marxism predominated. As a result of the enormous pressure of the Stalinist regime, this was soon replaced by a "dogmatic" Marxism (Lech 1997: 183).

The reluctance to engage in any substantial theoretical debate in the post-war period in Central European archaeology is striking. It had a number of interconnected historical, sociological and academic causes. One of them was the politicisation of archaeology (Biehl et al. 2002b: 27). Political circumstances in Central Europe – the misuse of archaeology by the Nazis in Germany and the necessity of constant compromising with communist rule in other Central European countries – resulted in a search for a secure position for the discipline. This was provided by an escape into supposedly 'objective' scholarship, which guaranteed security and refrained from involvement in any political struggle (see e.g. Härke 2002: 28; Wolfram 2002: 187). It was particularly evident in Germany, where the Nazi experiences clearly strengthened a desire to embed the discipline in empiricism and inductionism (Wolfram 2002: 184).

This declared objectivity and a need to create something that defined German archaeology led in the long run to the creation of a *Vorsprung durch Technik* (advance through technology) idea (Arnold 2002: 403; Wolfram 2002), which corresponded well with the declared objectivity and industrial superiority that were stressed in post-war Germany. This concept emphasised uses of quantitative techniques, computers and the contribution of 'hard' sciences such as zoology or soil science (Wolfram 2002: 185).

However, just as Anglo-Saxon archaeology cannot be portrayed exclusively as highly theoretical, its Central European counterpart cannot be viewed exclusively as traditional, with little theoretical debate. Theoretical issues were raised, but they were marginalised and not addressed explicitly. Consequently, various interesting issues have never entered into mainstream debate. At the same time, earlier theoretical interests were explicitly abandoned. They were hidden and practised to a limited degree in the first post-war period and then largely forgotten. Substantial debate on the aims, methods and theory of archaeology did not take place until the beginning of the 1990s (see Härke 1991: 191,198).

At the same, methodological advances and scientific methods such as radiocarbon dating, archaeometry techniques, non-invasive methods of prospection, environmental sampling, etc. were introduced into Central European archaeologies at a similar pace to Western Europe. Interestingly, these were easily accommodated within the dominant paradigm and did not lead to immediate changes in the theoretical and conceptual framework of archaeological practice.

RELATIONS AMONG ARCHAEOLOGIES OF CENTRAL EUROPE

When seen from outside, Central European archaeology, if recognisable at all, may appear as a relatively small entity. Thus, considerable differences in the archaeology practised within the region go unnoticed and it is viewed as a single, coherent and homogeneous milieu (see Barford 1993: 258). It is, however, considerably differentiated. Undoubtedly, the dominant position in this circle is occupied by the archaeology practised in Germany, or rather German archaeology. German archaeology as a "majority archaeology" (Neustupný 2002a) has had a considerable influence on its neighbours, due to its sheer size and economic, political and cultural potency, in addition to its language.

The culture-historical tradition in the period before the fall of the Iron Curtain encouraged and stimulated contacts among archaeologists in the region pursuing supranational relations and connections, searching for analogies and synchronising chronological schemes, etc. In this sense the communication network among Central European archaeologists was never really broken by the post-war borders. The relations among national archaeologies in the region, however, are not easy to capture.

Evžen Neustupný (1997–1998, 14–15; also 2002a: 284–285) has coined a distinction between 'mainstream' and minority archaeologies, as self-contained and largely homogenous entities, as a means of capturing the variability of archaeology in Europe. The mainstream archaeological communities are self-sufficient in terms of their practice of all kinds of archaeologies; they tend to be inward looking, closed and isolated. The size of the mainstream universe is large enough that its members are not forced to rely on and refer to the publications published in other circles and communities. Mainstream archaeologists in general are not capable of reading literature in the languages of the minority countries in their immediate vicinity (Neustupný 1997–1998: 20). Their publications have to be published in the language of the mainstream community. Nevertheless, even when their work is accessible linguistically, reference to authors outside the community is largely limited. This self-sufficiency often leads to a self-inflicted isolation. These communities come from large and economically strong countries and include in particular German and British archaeologies but also Polish as well (see also Bogucki 2002). Particularly significant in this respect is German (especially West-German) archaeology, which formed a stable and self-contained universe of discourse. There was not felt to be any need to pay much attention to developments in remote areas like the USA.

On the contrary, archaeology in smaller countries like the Czech Republic or Hungary belongs to the minority. These communities have insufficient numbers of specialists and import concepts from outside. Their achievements are not considered and recognised in mainstream communities. However, this is not because of their 'minority' status but because of the self-isolation and self-sufficiency of the majority communities. Even publishing in one of the major languages does not contribute to being recognised by mainstream colleagues. Accordingly, on this view, the potential of non-mainstream archaeologies to contribute to the development of global archaeology is minimal (Neustupný 2002b: 162).

This distinction, however, is not altogether valid as it defines the mainstream community as a closed and coherent entity. However, it is in a state of flux and this internal differentiation is not sufficiently noticed. This is particularly true with reference to German archaeology, whose constitutive elements are difficult to define (Barford 2002: 80). The 'German' school is commonly viewed as including 'empiricist work; a preference for description over interpretation; technical excellence, but little reflection on basic questions; hierarchical attitudes; an absence of lively debate; and self-imposed isolation from the intellectual mainstream' (Bloemers 2002:381; Härke 2002:18).

There is no doubt that the distinctiveness of German archaeology is created and manipulated to meet certain ends in the practice of Central European archaeologies. Its perception is often simplified, modified and caricatured by those for whom it is a frame of reference, believed to be the only 'good and solid' approach and used to build up their power and dominance in the academic system of their countries. Advocates of such a simplistic picture of German archaeology do not want to notice its internal developments in recent years, which make its coherent definition increasingly difficult. If the diversity is scrupulously reported, reference to this tradition as a means of creating and maintaining academic identity, in opposition to a number of new developments of the last decades, will cease.

CENTRAL EUROPEAN ARCHAEOLOGY AND
BEYOND – ISOLATION AND COMMUNICATION

There is no doubt that post-war Europe suffered from a lack of communication and exchange of ideas which resulted in a vast gap in understanding between different traditions (Biehl et al. 2002b: 26). It contributed to the emergence of increasingly divergent national traditions which eventually ceased to understand each other (Härke 2002: 16).

One of the major causes of this situation was the isolation of countries in Central Europe from the external world, which defined the conditions for practising archaeology in this region before 1989. The restrictions on foreign travel and free contact with the international community were particularly irritating (Kobyliński 1991, 1998; Marciniak and Rączkowski 1991). Only a very small section of the scientific community was allowed to travel and participate in international exchange without limitations, for a number of reasons, of which political circumstances were one of the most significant (see also Neustupný 1991: 261). However, this did not contribute to any significant changes in local archaeologies (for a different opinion see Milisauskas 1997–1998:229). The post-war period was also marked by restricted access to foreign literature, which did not encourage knowledge of other traditions (Marciniak and Rączkowski 1991: 62; Barford and Tabaczyński 1996: 166–167).

The degree of isolation from the outer world, together with indoctrination and oppression, clearly differed in the successive phases of the post-war period (Marciniak and Rączkowski 1991:57; Tabaczyński 1995: 70). It was particularly strong in the first decades after the war and was gradually eased through the 1970s and 1980s. This is evident in the incorporation of some concepts and theories from outside into the actual practice of archaeology in the countries of the region (see e.g. Laszlovsky and Siklódi 1991: 281–283). These were the first attempts aimed at introducing elements of these foreign concepts into traditionally (in the Central European sense) designed research projects.

A consequence of the break in communication between different traditions is a widespread tendency on the part of its practitioners to identify various achievements of the archaeologies of Central Europe that arguably emerged there prior to their appearance in the Anglo-Saxon milieu. The latter is often accused of reinventing the wheel and ignoring research undertaken in a different language area. It is argued, for example, that British environmental archaeology was preceded by German research in this domain (Härke 1991: 202). Similar arguments are put forward with regard to American ethnoarchaeology. Another interesting example is the division of historical records into ergotechnic, sociotechnic and psychotechnic proposed by Labuda (1957), anticipating the later proposal by Binford (1962) or the conceptualisation of formation processes put forward by Eggers (1951) foreshadowing work by Schiffer (1987). Other topics include the discussion of analogy by Smolla (1964). For various reasons, as discussed by Wolfram (2002: 192–195), these developments have not received sufficient attention within the German archaeological milieu. Similarly unknown and potentially challenging are East-German experiments with the application of Marxism (Jacobs 2002: 351–353). Equally inspiring may be Polish attempts to set up a research agenda in relation to historical disciplines as proposed by the 'Poznań School' of Marxist philosophy of Jerzy Kmita and Leszek Nowak (see more in Kobyliński 1991: 224–230, 1998: 227; Marciniak and Rączkowski 1991: 60; Tabaczyński 1995: 72). However, the parallel approaches to similar issues on both sides of the Iron Curtain, as well as the heuristic potential of their Central European conceptualisations, remain largely unexplored.

Continuous integration within the European Union and between the EU countries and their neighbours has contributed to increased communication between the various traditions of archaeology (Härke 2002:16). This involves in particular the recognition and understanding of their respective historical, political, social and ideological background, as well as their trajectories of development, and differences in terminology, concepts, paradigms and research pursuits (Marciniak 1996; Biehl et al. 2002a, b). This better understanding of the various European archaeologies and their mutual background is a prerequisite for successful future development (Biehl et al. 2002b: 25) and as such is absolutely necessary (Bloemers 2002: 393–394). Increasing communication, manifested by intensified international contacts and joint projects, easier access to literature, the possibility of studying abroad and the availability of ever-growing resources on the web will undoubtedly contribute to the transformation of Central European archaeology in the years to come (see e.g. Laszlovsky and Siklódi 1991: 291).

Communication problems both within Central European archaeologies and outside are also caused by language barriers (Bertemes 2002: 104). A new tendency apparent in recent years is an increased shift towards English. The significance of German, the previous *lingua franca* of Central European archaeology, has decreased (see also Härke 1991: 202, 2002: 33; Neustupný 1991: 259; Bernbeck 1997: 12; Bertemes 2002: 103). As a result it is mostly the older generation that speaks German and communicates in this language. Analysis of citations in papers in *Archaeologia Polona* – a leading Polish journal – revealed a drastic change in the language of references in bibliographies. English references increase from 20 per cent in 1984 to 45 per cent in 1994 (Kristiansen 2001). The increasing dominance of English contributes to further exclusion of those whose English is faulty (Biehl *et al.* 2002b: 31). Kristiansen (2001: 38–40) showed that smaller countries tend to be characterised by a more international environment, as revealed in international and multi-language references and books chosen for review in local journals. This stands in marked contrast to large archaeological communities like those of Germany, France or the UK. Language division continues to play a significant role in maintaining Central European archaeology. Although they are announced as international, professional gatherings attended by a small number of foreign specialists are always dominated by discussion conducted within the conceptual traditions of the organisers, whether they are Germans or Poles. Communication problems, however, are not limited to simple language barriers. They are caused to a considerable degree by the incompatibility of the concepts, categories and definitions used by other archaeological communities.

PUBLIC ISSUES AND THE
COMMERCIALISATION OF ARCHAEOLOGY

In many domains current archaeology in Central Europe is very dispersed and is in a state of flux. The political changes of the recent past have resulted in previously unknown dangers, such as commercialisation, isolation and loss of public interest in archaeology, greater destruction of the archaeological heritage due to large-scale developments and intensive agriculture leading to the destruction of archaeological sites (Lozny 1998; Kobyliński 2001a: 17). The previously solid system of state sponsorship and the high status of scientists has collapsed (Tabaczyński 2001: 43; Kobyliński 2002: 421). Archaeologists are slowly becoming aware that the security of the ivory tower of university chairs provided by state sponsorship is gone and they need to confront the demands and expectations of society in order to survive. This remains a tough situation to confront.

The characteristic feature of Central European archaeologies in the past was their separation, both in principle and in practice, from the general public (see the review of the situation in Germany in Schmidt 2002; see also Wolfram 2002). In Arnold's (2002: 415) words, archaeologists were 'hyper-intellectual pinheads out of touch with reality'. The changes initiated by the 1989 revolution brought about new social, political and economic conditions that have shaped the whole discipline and continue to do so. It is clear that in these new circumstances, Central European archaeology can no longer be practised and understood from a purely scientific perspective.

Despite these significant changes, however, public archaeology, understood as the social context of the work of archaeologists and its relation to the public – a consumer of archaeological 'production' (Lozny 1998) – still remains a relatively unknown concept in Central Europe. At the same time, there is a lack of social awareness of archaeology and its aims and role in constructing social entities. There are, however, significant attempts to create more effective ways of informing the public of the need for conservation and the protection of the culture heritage.

This tendency is accompanied by an increasing awareness of threats to the substance of the archaeological heritage (Kobyliński 1991: 19) and the fast pace of its destruction. Some of the causes existed before 1989 but they have clearly intensified in the new situation. Some others, however, have emerged as a result of the dramatic social and political changes in this period. Despite many attempts, an effective strategy for dealing with threats to the Central European archaeological heritage is still lacking (these threats are enumerated and discussed in detail by Barford and Kobyliński 1998: 461–464).

As I have mentioned, archaeology after the war was practised as a purely scientific enterprise and issues of heritage preservation and protection did not attract any interest (Wysocki 1997–1998: 447). The period after 1989 brought about considerable changes in the organisation of the system for the protection and management of the archaeological heritage in the context of a free market economy, and the significance of these issues has increased dramatically. Archaeologists are becoming more aware of their own responsibility to protect the archaeological heritage; this was not so self-evident in the past. This new attitude is well epitomised in a departure from terms such as 'archaeological record' and its replacement by 'archaeological heritage'. This is a fundamental shift that marks a recognition of the cultural and social dimensions of archaeological sites and objects rather than their purely scientific content (Kobyliński 2001b: 77). Archaeology is to become a form of cultural activity, actively participating in public life, engaged in the socially understood and accepted processes associated with the preservation of the human environment (Kobyliński 2001b p. 80). The accessibility of the knowledge produced to many segments of the society has become a matter of debate. Preservation of the archaeological heritage in countries like Hungary is even defined as a major task of local archaeology (Bökönyi 1993). Equally important is the fact that in many countries the heritage sector, broadly understood, today creates the majority of archaeological jobs.

It is clear that archaeological heritage is no longer perceived within the borders of national states. Globalisation processes are resulting in dangers to the heritage that are Europe wide (Biehl *et al*. 2002b: 26). At the same time, the increasing political integration of the continent has created a need for resolving these problems on a European level. It does not mean that 'European archaeological heritage' is an independent category but rather that local 'heritages' need to be approached and dealt with in the light of experiences and solutions elaborated elsewhere. However, there are difficulties in the application of Western models of archaeological heritage management in Central Europe (Barford and Kobyliński 1998). The co-operation of heritage management organisations on a European scale was seen in the creation of the *Europeae Archaeologiae Consilium* in 1999, intended to co-ordinate these activities at the European level. Central European authorities responsible for archaeological heritage found this body very useful and were actively involved in its creation and activities (see e.g. Kunow 2002: 176).

The other challenge Central European archaeology has to face is the commercialisation of archaeological activities. Instead of confronting explicit political or ideological pressure it needs to face the demands of consumer society (Kobyliński 2002: 421). A new element in this respect are large-scale infrastructure projects that demand large-scale rescue excavations in association with pan-European investments, such as pipelines from Russia to Western Europe and the network of highways built mainly by private investors in the Build, Operate, Transfer system (Lech 1997–1998: 151). Poland has never had so many large-scale excavations as in the 1990s (Kobyliński 2002: 422). These processes have led to a dramatic increase in commercial archaeology, which is manifested in a large number of German *Grabungsfirmen* (Härke 2002: 20), a trend that intensified in the 1990s. Similarly, the commercial sector in Poland is composed of an increasing number of private firms and consortia consisting of universities, research institutions and museums. The emergence of private archaeological firms working on rescue projects has led to the rapid creation of a quite new professional group on the market (Kunow 2002: 174) and caused considerable changes in the panorama of Central European archaeologies (Lech 1997–1998: 152). The effects of these changes remain largely unexplored and may result in consequences for the condition of archaeology in Central Europe that are currently unforeseen.

Rescue archaeology has significantly shaped the character of Central European archaeology (see Arnold 2002: 410) and created many unforeseen problems. It is responsible for the production of a vast body of material, which in turn has created still unresolved problems for their study, publication and storage (see Brzeziński 2001: 183). This huge amount of data remains largely undigested at the moment, but when it has been processed it will contribute significantly to modification of our knowledge of various aspects of the past.

Rescue projects on pipelines and highways, as huge logistic operations, have also forced institutional transformation (Kobyliński 1998: 232). Not surprisingly, this has generated a conflict between state bodies responsible for the protection and management of archaeological heritage (themselves in a constant flux as political and administrative changes proceeded – changes in this domain in Poland are presented in detail by Barford and Kobyliński 1998) and various consortia of private or semi-private firms, set up to run rescue excavations on a large scale. This conflict in Poland, still unresolved today, indicates that legislation in this domain has been ineffective in the face of the quantitatively and qualitatively significant changes brought about by the first years of a free market economy. Another challenge is to mobilise and effectively incorporate other resources such as non-destructive methods into the investigation and protection of archaeological and historical heritage (Barford and Kobyliński 1998: 477).

The Valetta convention raised the complex issue of contract archaeology, with its aims, standards and relations with existing bodies and regulations. The bringing together of heritage requirements, public expectations, contract archaeology, research strategies and archaeological education is far from complete, if indeed it has begun at all. In fact, almost all the elements of this puzzle are in states of flux of different intensity. This divide is wide open and we can only hope that the elements will get closer to each other in the years to come.

In addition to rescue excavations, popular, open-air festivals and fairs are another symptom of commercialisation. Recent years have brought a rapid increase in their number. The largest of them takes place in Biskupin and it has become a model for similar events organised by local museums across Poland (Brzeziński 2001: 187). The first festival in Biskupin was organized in 1995 and was attended by around 50,000 visitors (Brzeziński 1998: 499) and the following years brought an increasing number of guests. A decade of their existence clearly shows that it has been impossible to avoid their commercialisation, and the educational functions originally stressed have been largely unmet. Instead, there is a tendency to create collages and a mixing up of various episodes from the past in one performance in order to attract visitors. Thus, the Egyptians interact with the Slavs, who themselves stand next to flint knappers.

CENTRAL EUROPEAN ARCHAEOLOGY TODAY AND THE TRANSFORMATION OF ARCHAEOLOGY IN EUROPE

The current state of academic archaeology in Central Europe is diverse and complicated as a result of openness to the external world after 1989 and global changes in this period. A number of previously unknown and alien categories and concepts have been introduced into research agendas. Initially this incorporation was rather superficial, resulting in incoherent collages. If we want to incorporate new concepts, theories and models into our research agendas, we need to raise the question of whether they are applicable to the local research tradition and the specificity of its material evidence (Lozny 2002: 142). It is clearly unfeasible to directly import ready-to-use models from the West. Rather, archaeologists in Central Europe should be more self-aware of their own methodological and theoretical background when they try to combine it with foreign theoretical traditions (Barford and Tabaczyński 1996: 174). Since this self-awareness still remains to be achieved, a number of foreign concepts, categories and methods have been uncritically added to the known and inherited traditions. The coherence of the result has hardly been explicitly addressed; 'add foreign models and stir' would be an accurate description of what has happened. However, as a result of these developments, one could argue that in most cases a threshold of self-consciousness has been reached in Central European archaeology. The following issues are more obvious than previously: (1) archaeological evidence is not an objectively given set of 'pure facts', (2) archaeology is a political enterprise and (3) the passive collection of facts will not result in objective knowledge of the past.

The research practice of the majority of contemporary Central European archaeologists is characterised by a large-scale level of explanation and a lack of satisfactory attention paid to the complex relations between the nature of the categories of archaeological evidence and the explanatory framework they are believed to refer to. These attempts lack methodological rigour as self-reflexivity in research practice has never been a strong part of Central European archaeology. Pressure to build up grand narratives is even stronger than in the previous period. A lack of theoretical knowledge justifies jumping freely between various levels of social and economic complexity. Examples of these unreflective practices are omnipresent and are manifested in a return to grand narrations such as the origin of the Slavs, the emergence of statehood, large-scale migrations, etc. Changes in material culture on a small scale are referred to these large processes, forgetting about the complexity of the factors responsible for the formation of archaeological evidence.

Another characteristic feature of modern Central European archaeology is an 'integrated' approach to culture in its landscape setting, as indicated by a number of works aimed at the integration of the natural sciences with the interpretation and explanation of the prehistoric past. An interdisciplinary approach was regarded in the 1990s as a sign of good archaeology. Equally significant is social archaeology (Kuna 1994). At the same time, prominent representatives advocate sticking to a material-based type of practice and the avoidance of any theory-based discourse. Interestingly, they also participate in this new climate and adopt some scraps of this debate. It was predicted that removing political pressure and ideological indoctrination would result in the development of multiple approaches to the past, including an application of Marxism free of external pressure (Kobyliński 1991: 238; Barford and Tabaczyński 1996: 173–174; Tabaczyński 1998: 557). Other issues discussed have included reasoning procedures, the interpretation of material culture and the reintegration of different schools as well as growing awareness of the philosophical and theoretical implications of archaeological practice. Unfortunately, little exchange between these different enterprises has taken place so far.

Changes after 1989 brought about significant, albeit unexpected, changes such as shrinking governmental funding for science (Barford and Tabaczyński 1996: 169). At the same time, however, more money is being spent on education. The number of students has increased dramatically, in particular in Poland. This has resulted in the emergence of enormous departments of archaeology. The Institute of Archaeology of the University of Warsaw, with its nearly 1,500 students, is probably the largest department of archaeology in the world. As a result, it is calculated that in the 1990s, 90 per cent of the classical archaeologists in Europe were educated in Poland (see Lech 1997–1998: 146–147). In general, this new period is marked by an ever-growing number of places to study archaeology, resulting in an increasing number of practising archaeologists. It is also accompanied by increasing 'specialisation' (Parzinger 2002: 48).

The dynamic transformations in European archaeology need to be brought to the fore and taken into consideration in the ongoing debate in Central Europe. New conditions for the practice of archaeology after the 1989 transformation forced archaeologists from this region to define their identity by explicitly addressing their relations to archaeologies in other parts of the world, in particular the West. First, however the state of the latter needs to be defined.

I would argue that contemporary European archaeology is characterised by the disappearance of monolithic research agendas; the previously coherent traditions of some academic centres are now gone. Today, categories overlap and crosscut each other. To paraphrase Fletcher's (1989) words it 'has too many cross-cutting conceptual axes to possess a middle position with a defined identity'. The borders of national archaeologies are increasingly blurred. Thus, there is no justification for talking about national schools or clearly delimited paradigms anymore (see Biehl *et al.* 2002b; Kadrow forthcoming). In particular, we need to overcome simple dichotomies like processual versus postprocessual or theoretical versus traditional. Thus, any attempt to conceptualise the condition of contemporary archaeology on the basis of normatively defined entities (as postulated e.g. Minta-Tworzowska 2002: 61) fails to capture the very nature of the changes we are witnessing at this moment. I have no doubt that we need to see the richness of European archaeologies as beyond the bounds of paradigms – defined as coherent entities. They are clearly unable to grasp the variety and richness of European archaeology and give a simplistic and untrue picture. European archaeology is becoming increasingly pan-European, with students and researchers studying in different settings and creating a mosaic of approaches. This tendency will clearly intensify in the future.

One major tendency in Central Europe of the 1990s was catching up with the supposed backwardness of its archaeology, as seen from the Anglo-Saxon perspective. This was believed to be a never-ending pursuit of reputedly more advanced archaeological thought. However, others argued that Central European archaeologists should avoid what Vilfredo Pareto called the 'trap' (Tabaczyński 2002: 75). This implies the impossibility of catching up with any paradigm and research agenda, as this point of reference is constantly changing. Consequently, no 'transition' from one paradigm to the other is possible. What has been proposed instead is a 'transformation' model stressing 'the relatively autonomous internal development of theoretical self-reflection in collaboration with the other disciplines' (Tabaczyński 1998: 560). This model does not specify any predefined state to be achieved, but rather describes a process of incorporating various experiences and deepening critical reflections (Tabaczyński 2002: 75). From this perspective, to catch up with the West and its paradigms is both unrealistic and naïve (Kuna 1994; Tabaczyński 2002: 75). Moreover, such an uncritical imitation of other concepts and paradigms is not a means of achieving a comparable status to other archaeologies. Another proposal has been to introduce local ideas and concepts, which is particularly feasible for smaller archaeological communities (Neustupný 2001: 37–38).

As indicated above, contemporary archaeology does not develop along a single axis but rather incorporates elements from various research strategies, schools, practices and paradigms, creating an ever-increasing pool of potential archaeological resources. Accordingly, the most effective relation, and the most valuable contribution, of Central European archaeology to this pool would be to explore the richness of local traditions. In this respect, the pluralism and diversity of today's European archaeology may turn out to be a chance and an asset in this process rather than a burden (Parzinger 2002: 36). In other words, the aim is to overcome the schemes that dominated the practice of archaeology after the Second World War and return to some of the now apparently dead and frozen issues examined in the 1930s or 1940s. However, returning to these largely forgotten concepts and paradigms as if they were intact is clearly unfeasible and impossible. They need to be debated within the climate of modern archaeology. German environmental archaeology, Polish ethnoarchaeology or material culture studies are potentially very valuable resources in this respect. Unfortunately, voices from this part of Europe need to be more persuasive to be heard. Conceptual debate in the mainstream communities is in a circular, self-referential stage and there are no signs of getting out of this circle with a newly inspiring agenda. Thus, one way to move forward may be by adding new ingredients of Central European origin.

Unfortunately, however, the input of Central European archaeology to the European pool remains unsatisfactory despite the increased number of publications in English in the region. These works are rarely cited and used. In other words, the language barrier can no longer be used to explain the relative insignificance of Central European archaeology's impact. The causes of this situation are numerous and include the fact that the politics of citation in the mainstream communities, especially US archaeology, are largely self-sufficient, as well as the fact that difficulties exist in incorporating conceptually alien ideas and concepts from outside one's own circle. Thus, Central European publications, if read and used at all, are referenced mainly for empirical materials. Discussions of more general issues are treated with disrespect.

FINAL REMARKS

If we want to describe the state of Central European archaeology as being in crisis, it is undoubtedly not greater and deeper than in the West. The current situation is an intertwined consequence of the openness resulting from the post-1989 changes as well as rapid changes in the humanities on a global scale. This does not mean that national archaeologies do not exist anymore or will disappear in the immediate future. The context of their existence, however, will be marked by this rapidly changing world, different from that in the past.

The future of Central European archaeology remains unclear. Today Central Europe experiences rapid social, political and cultural transformations connected with European integration and globalisation. These changes have caused innovations in many Central European archaeologies. Czech, German, Polish archaeologies and the like face a changed climate which now allows them – or even demands them – to ask neglected questions. One cannot predict whether this entity will survive and preserve its distinctiveness, given the multiscalar and multidirectional development of European archaeology. This is particularly the case now that smaller countries from the region no longer need to identify themselves as non-Soviet, for which a category such as Central European archaeology seemed to be ideal. When one looks at the conceptual debate in recent years e.g. in Polish and Czech archaeologies, there is hardly any significant attempt to look for inspiration from each other. Interestingly, there was no debate in the post-1989 period focused exclusively on mutual inspirations within the region and undertaken within its scientific milieu. Paradoxically, they are only discussed at pan-European gatherings. I predict that archaeology in Central Europe, as in other parts of the continent, will not develop along a single axis. There is a tendency to incorporate elements from different research strategies, schools and paradigms. The pool of potential archaeological resources widens, but the relations between them remain poorly developed and their foundations largely imprecise and undefined. This eclectic tendency must be accompanied by deep discussion on the epistemological and social identities of various national archaeologies.

REFERENCES

Arnold, B. (1997–1998) 'The power of the past. Nationalism and archaeology in 20th century Germany', *Archaeologia Polona*, 35–36: 237–252.

Arnold, B. (2002) 'A transatlantic perspective on German archaeology', in *Archaeology, ideology and society. The German experience*, H. Härke (ed.), 2nd revised edition, Peter Lang: Frankfurt am Main, pp. 401–425.

Barford, P.M. (1993) 'Paradigms lost. Polish archaeology and post-war politics', *Archaeologia Polona*, 31: 257–270.

Barford, P.M. (2002) 'East is East and West is West? Power and paradigm in European archaeology', in *Archaeologies of Europe. History, Methods and Theories*, P.F. Biehl, A. Gramsch and A. Marciniak (eds), Münster: Waxman, pp. 77–99.

Barford, P.M. and Z. Kobyliński (1998) 'Protecting the archaeological heritage in Poland at the end of the 1990s', in *Theory and Practice of Archaeological Research. Volume III. Dialogue with the data. The Archaeology of Complex Societies and Its Context in the '90s*, W. Hensel, S. Tabaczyński and P. Urbańczyk (eds), Warsaw: Institute of Archaeology and Ethnology Polish Academy of Sciences, pp. 461–482.

Barford, P.M. and S. Tabaczyński (1996) 'Polish archaeology. Reality and challenges of the 1990s', in A. Marciniak (ed.), Section 2: Poland, *World Archaeological Bulletin*, 8: 153–176.

Bernbeck, R. (1997) *Theorien in der Archäologie*, Tübingen & Basel: A. Francke Verlag.

Bertemes, F. (2002) 'Die mitteldeutsche Archäologie. Eine Standortbestimmung zwischen Ost und West', in *Archaeologies of Europe. History, Methods and Theories*, P. Biehl, A. Gramsch and A. Marciniak (eds), Münster: Waxman, pp. 99–118.

Bertemes, F. (forthcoming) 'Prehistoric Archaeology in Central Europe', in *A History of Central European Archaeology. Theory, Methods and Politics*, A. Gramsch and U. Sommer (eds),

Biehl, P., A. Gramsch and A. Marciniak (eds) (2002a) *Archaeologies of Europe. History, Methods and Theories*, Münster: Waxman.

Biehl, P., A. Gramsch and A. Marciniak (2002b) 'Archaeologies of Europe: histories and identities. An introduction', in *Archaeologies of Europe. History, Methods and Theories*, P. Biehl, A. Gramsch and A. Marciniak (eds), Münster: Waxman, pp. 25–31.

Binford, L.R. (1962) 'Archaeology as anthropology', *American Antiquity*, 11: 198–200.

Bogucki, P. (2002) 'Polish archaeology as world archaeology' *Archaeologia Polona*, 40: 125–135.

Bloemers, J.H.F. (2002) 'German archaeology at risk? A neighbour's critical review of tradition, structure and serendipity', in *Archaeology, Ideology and Society. The German experience*, H. Härke (ed.), 2nd revised edition, Frankfurt am Main: Peter Lang, pp. 378–399.

Bökönyi, S. (1993) 'Recent developments in Hungarian archaeology', *Antiquity*, 67: 142–145.

Brzeziński, W. (1998) 'Museum archaeology and the protection of the archaeological heritage in Poland', in *Theory and Practice of Archaeological Research. Volume III. Dialogue with the Data. The Archaeology of Complex Societies and Its Context in the '90s*, W. Hensel, S. Tabaczyński and P. Urbańczyk (eds), Warsaw: Institute of Archaeology and Ethnology Polish Academy of Sciences, pp. 496–503.

Brzeziński, W. (2001) 'Archaeology in the museum. Presenting the past to the general public', in *Quo vadis archaeologia? Whither European Archaeology in the 21st century?*, Z. Kobyliński (ed.), Warsaw: Institute of Archaeology and Ethnology Polish Academy of Sciences, pp. 181–190.

Eggers, H.J. (1951) *Der römische Import im freien Germanien*, Atlas der Urgeschichte 1, Hamburg: Museum für Völkerkunde und Vorgeschiche.

Fletcher, R. (1989) 'Social theory and archaeology: diversity, paradox and potential', *Mankind*, 19(1): 65–75.

Härke, H. (1991) 'All quiet on the Western front? Paradigms, methods and approaches in West German archaeology', in *Archaeological Theory in Europe. The Last Three Decades*, I. Hodder (ed.), London and New York: Routledge, pp. 187–222.

Härke, H. (ed.) (2000) *Archaeology, Ideology and Society. The German Experience*, Frankfurt am Main: Peter Lang.

Härke, H. (2002) 'The German experience', in *Archaeology, Ideology and Society. The German experience*, H. Härke (ed.), 2nd revised edition, Frankfurt am Main: Peter Lang, pp. 13–40.

Hodder, I. (1991) 'Archaeological theory in contemporary European societies. The emergence of competing traditions', in *Archaeological Theory in Europe. The Last Three Decades*, I. Hodder (ed.), London and New York: Routledge, pp. 1–24.

Jacobs, J. (2002) 'German unification and East German archaeology', in *Archaeology, Ideology and Society. The German Experience*, H. Härke (ed.), 2nd revised edition, Frankfurt am Main: Peter Lang, pp. 342–355.

Kadrow, S. (forthcoming) 'The German influence on Polish archaeology', in *A History of Central European Archaeology. Theory, Methods and Politics*, A. Gramsch and U. Sommer (eds),

Kobyliński, Z. (1991) 'Theory in Polish archaeology 1960–90. Searching for paradigms', in *Archaeological Theory in Europe. The Last Three Decades*, I. Hodder (ed.), London and New York: Routledge, pp. 223–247.

Kobyliński, Z. (1998) 'Theoretical orientations in archaeology in Poland (1945–1995)', in *Theory and Practice of Archaeological Research. Volume III. Dialogue with the Data. The Archaeology of Complex Societies and its Context in the '90s*, W. Hensel, S. Tabaczyński and P. Urbańczyk (eds), Warsaw: Institute of Archaeology and Ethnology Polish Academy of Sciences, pp. 225–258.

Kobyliński, Z. (2001a) 'Quo vadis archaeologia? Introductory remarks', in *Quo vadis archaeologia? Whither European Archaeology in the 21st Century?*, Z. Kobyliński (ed.), Warsaw: Institute of Archaeology and Ethnology Polish Academy of Sciences, pp. 17–20.

Kobyliński, Z. (2001b) 'Archaeological sources and archaeological heritage. New vision of the subject matter of archaeology', in *Quo vadis archaeologia? Whither European Archaeology in the 21st Century?*, Z. Kobyliński (ed.), Warsaw: Institute of Archaeology and Ethnology Polish Academy of Sciences, pp. 76–82.

Kobyliński, Z. (2002) 'Archaeology on the ruins of ivory towers. What sort of theory do we need?', in *Archaeologies of Europe. History, Methods and Theories*, P. Biehl, A. Gramsch and A. Marciniak (eds), Münster: Waxman, pp. 421–424.

Kristiansen, K. (2001) 'Borders of ignorance. Research communities and language', in *Quo vadis archaeologia? Whither European Archaeology in the 21st Century?*, Z. Kobyliński (ed.), Warsaw: Institute of Archaeology and Ethnology Polish Academy of Sciences, pp. 38–43.

Kuna, M. (1994) Česká archeologie v postmoderní době. Prádnáška k 75.vývocí zalozání ústavu (ARUP). Unpublished manuscript.

Kunow, J. (2002) 'Die Entwicklung von archäologischen Organisationen und Institutionen in Deutschland im 19. und 20. Jahrhundert und das "öffentliche Interesse" – Bedeutungsgewinne und Bedeutungsverluste und deren Folgen', in Archaeologies of Europe. History, Methods and Theories, P. Biehl, A. Gramsch and A. Marciniak (eds), Münster: Waxman, pp. 147–183.

Labuda, G. (1957) 'Próba nowej systematyki źródeł historycznych' Studia Źródłoznawcze, 1: 3–48.

Laszlovsky, J. and Cs. Siklódi (1991) 'Archaeological theory in Hungary since 1960 Theories without theoretical archaeology', in Archaeological Theory in Europe. The Last Three Decades, I. Hodder (ed.), London and New York: Routledge, pp. 272–297.

Lech, J. (1996) 'A short history of Polish archaeology', in A. Marciniak (ed.), Section 2: Poland, World Archaeological Bulletin 8: 177–195.

Lech, J. (1997) 'Małowierni. Spór wokół marksizmu w archeologii polskiej lat 1945–1975, Archeologia Polski, 42, 175–232.

Lech, J. (1997–1998) 'Between captivity and freedom. Polish archaeology in the 20th century', Archaeologia Polona, 35–36: 25–222.

Lozny, L. (1998) 'Public archaeology or archaeology for the public?', in Theory and Practice of Archaeological Research. Volume III. Dialogue with the data. The archaeology of complex societies and its context in the '90s, W. Hensel, S. Tabaczyński and P. Urbańczyk (eds), Warsaw: Institute of Archaeology and Ethnology Polish Academy of Sciences, pp. 431–459.

Lozny, L. (2002) 'Far outside, looking in. Polish archaeology and looking-glass self', Archaeologia Polona, 40: 137–148.

Mamzer, H. (1997) 'Pytanie o archeologię', in Jakiej archeologii potrzebuje współczesna humanistyka? J. Ostoja-Zagórski (ed.), Poznań: Instytut Historii UAM, pp. 13–49.

Marciniak, A. (1996) 'Introduction', in A. Marciniak (ed.), Section 2: Poland, World Archaeological Bulletin, 8: 151–152.

Marciniak, A. and W. Rączkowski (1991) 'The development of archaeological theory in Poland under conditions of isolation' World Archaeological Bulletin, 5: 57–65.

Milisauskas, S. (1997–1998) 'Observations on Polish archaeology 1945–1995', Archaeologia Polona, 35–36: 223–236.

Minta-Tworzowska, D. (2002) 'Between a community of inspiration and the separateness of archaeological traditions', in Archaeologies of Europe. History, Methods and Theories, P. Biehl, Peter, A. Gramsch, and A. Marciniak (eds), Münster: Waxman, pp. 54–64.

Minta-Tworzowska, D. and W. Rączkowski (1996) 'Theoretical traditions in contemporary Polish archaeology', in A.Marciniak (ed.), Section 2: Poland, World Archaeological Bulletin 8: 196–209.

Neustupný, E. (1991) 'Recent theoretical achievements in prehistoric archaeology in Czechoslovakia', in Archaeological theory in Europe. The Last Three Decades, I. Hodder (ed.), London and New York: Routledge, pp. 248–271.

Neustupný, E. (1997–1998) 'Mainstream and minorities in archaeology', Archaeologia Polona, 35–36: 13–23.

Neustupný, E. (2001) 'Archeologia w trzecim tysiącleciu', in Archeologia na progu III tysiąclecia, J. Lech (ed.), Warszawa: Komitet Nauk Pra-i Protohistorycznych PAN, pp. 31–38.

Neustupný, E. (2002a) 'Czech archaeology at the turn of the millennium', in Archaeologies of Europe. History, Methods and Theories, P. Biehl, A. Gramsch and A. Marciniak (eds), Münster: Waxman, pp. 281–287.

Neustupný, E. (2002b) 'A few remarks on my relationships with Polish archaeology', Archaeologia Polona, 40: 159–162.

Ostoja-Zagórski, J. (ed.) (1997) Jakiej archeologii potrzebuje współczesna humanistyka?, Poznań: Instytut Historii UAM.

Parzinger, H. (2002) ' "Archäologien" Europas und "europäische Archäologie" – Rückblick und Ausblick', in *Archaeologies of Europe. History, Methods and Theories*, P. Biehl, A. Gramsch, and A. Marciniak (eds), Münster: Waxman, pp. 35–51.

Schiffer, M.B. (1987) *Formation Processes of the Archaeological Record*, Albuquerque: University of New Mexico Press.

Schild, R. (1993) 'Polish archaeology in transition', *Antiquity*, 67:146–150.

Schmidt, M. (2002) 'Archaeology and the German public', in *Archaeology, Ideology and Society. The German Experience*, H. Härke (ed.), 2nd revised edition, Frankfurt am Main: Peter Lang, pp. 244–274.

Smolla, G. (1964) 'Analogien und Polaritäten', in *Studien aus Alteuropa*, vol. 1, R.V. Ulstar and K.J. Narr (eds), Beihefte der Bonner Jahrbücher 10/1, Cologne: Böhlau, pp. 30–35.

Sommer, U. and A. Gramsch (forthcoming) 'German Archaeology in Context. An Introduction to History and Present of Central European Archaeology', in *A History of Central European Archaeology. Theory, Methods and Politics*, A. Gramsch and U. Sommer (eds),

Tabaczyński, S. (1995) 'A future for the Marxist paradigm in Central European archaeology? The Polish case', in *Whither Archaeology? Papers in Honour of Evžen Neustupný*, M. Kuna and N. Venclová (eds), Prague: Institute of Archaeology, Academy of Sciences of the Czech Republic, pp. 69–81.

Tabaczyński, S. (1998) 'Concluding remarks', in *Theory and Practice of Archaeological Research. Volume III. Dialogue with the Data. The Archaeology of Complex Societies and Its Context in the '90s*, W. Hensel, S. Tabaczyński and P. Urbańczyk (eds), Warsaw: Institute of Archaeology and Ethnology Polish Academy of Sciences, pp. 555–561.

Tabaczyński, S. (2001) 'Archeologia na progu XXI wieku', in *Archeologia na progu III tysiąclecia*, J. Lech (ed.), Warszawa: Komitet Nauk Pra-i Protohistorycznych PAN, pp. 39–51.

Tabaczyński, S. (2002) 'From the history of eastern and western archaeological thought. An introduction to discussion', in *Archaeologies of Europe. History, Methods and Theories*, P. Biehl, A. Gramsch and A. Marciniak (eds), Münster: Waxman, pp. 67–76.

Topolski, J. (1983) *Teoria wiedzy historycznej*, Poznań: Wydawnictwo Poznańskie.

Ucko, P.J. (1995) 'Archaeological interpretation in a world context', in *Theory in Archaeology. A World Perspective*, P.J. Ucko (ed.), London and New York: Routledge, pp. 1–27.

Veit, U., T.L. Kienlin, Ch. Kümmel and S. Schmidt (2003) *Spuren und Botschaften: Interpretationen materieller Kultur*, Münster: Waxman.

Wolfram, S. (2002) ' "*Vorsprung durch Technik*" or "Kossinna syndrome"? Archaeological theory and social context in post-war West Germany', in *Archaeology, ideology and society. The German experience*, H. Härke (ed.), 2nd revised edition, Frankfurt am Main: Peter Lang, pp. 183–204.

Wysocki, J. (1997–1998) 'The protection of the archaeological heritage in Poland in the 20th century. Concepts and practices', *Archaeologia Polona*, 35–36: 427–452.

CHAPTER 16

THEORETICAL AND ETHICAL ISSUES OF ARCHAEOLOGY IN SOUTH AMERICA

Gustavo G. Politis

INTRODUCTION

In the last 10 years I have published my view about the development of archaeology in South America, its current theoretical and methodological structure and the sociopolitical factors that have affected its historical trajectory and development (Politis 1995, 2001, 2002, 2003; Politis and Pérez Gollán 2004). Although few other archaeologists have debated this subject from a regional perspective (e.g. Dillehay in press), similar analyses for specific countries have proliferated in the last few years (e.g. Gnecco 1996, Langebaeck 1996, Llanos Vargas 1999, Lima 2000, López Mazz 2000, Eremites de Oliveira 2002). In this chapter, I will summarise and present an update of the most relevant issues I have discussed elsewhere in order to characterise current trends in South American archaeology. I will also refer to some ethical and political dimensions of professional practice regarding the so-called re-burial issue and the always difficult interaction between archaeologists and indigenous people.

CURRENT THEORETICAL SCENERY

As I have argued elsewhere, current archaeology in South America is the result of a myriad of traditions, foreign influences and socio-political trajectories. However, some common traits can be recognised in the current theoretical scenario. The first trait is the strong persistence to date of its culture-history framework, albeit updated and transformed to take into account a variety of research problems and themes. The culture-history that is popular in South America is the North American version, despite the fact that until the 1960s it was the 'Kulturkreise' school that shaped the archaeology of hunter–gatherers most strongly. The influence of the culture-historical approach remains strong not only because of its epistemological stability, but also because of its ability to organise diverse archaeological records in terms of comparable units. It has provided a powerful descriptive tool that could synthesise existing data at a regional scale and offer methods to investigate unknown areas. Influenced by this essentialist, culture-historical foundation, South American archaeologists have recently developed three major strategies for studying the past that include the adoption of new scientific methods and concerns. These strategies are: (1) improved methods for the empirical identification and temporal and spatial organisation of archaeological remains; (2) environmental archaeology and (3) problem-oriented research. These are now part of South American archaeological practice, although it is often difficult to divide them into discrete theoretical–methodological trends (see discussion in Politis 2003: 247–249).

The second trait that can be recognised in the theoretical panorama is the impact of the different trends labelled as 'processual archaeology', with a greater emphasis on the North American style inspired by Lewis Binford's influential papers (e.g. 1980, 1981, 1983, 1989). Behavioral archaeology (Schiffer 1995) is much less represented. When

Latin American archaeologists analyse site formation processes, especially natural ones, they approach them via geoarchaeology (e.g. Oliver and Alexander 2003) or vertebrate taphonomy (e.g. Borrero 1990, 2001), rather than embracing the methodological and conceptual corpus of this trend. I doubt that any of these archaeologists seek to contribute to a programme whose objective is to accumulate 'a corpus of well-confirmed laws and theories (expressed in behavioral terms) for inferring and explaining human behavior' (Schiffer 1995: 253). In South America, the impact of processualism has been more moderate. It occurred years after the initial optimism disappeared and when the first wave of criticism had already passed. In the case of Colombia, Piazzini (2003: 77) has stated, 'neither the hypothetic-deductive model nor "general systems theory", which was also proposed to combat induction and imagination, were adopted extensively by researchers, nor were they introduced into the academic syllabus' (translated by the author).

Processual approaches had a major and earlier impact in the Southern Cone. This was associated with the archaeology of hunter–gatherers from Patagonia and the Pampean Plains (see for example revision in Lanata and Borrero 1999). In countries such as Peru, Mexico and Venezuela the impact of this trend was buffered by the local development of 'Latin American social archaeology'. Of course, many North American archaeologists worked in the Nuclear Areas in the 1970s under the early processualism umbrella but at the time their work did not have a significant influence on local researchers. As I have argued before (Politis 1995), the different degrees of influence of processual archaeology in the region were partially a consequence of political conditions during the 1970s and 1980s. During these decades, the processual approach had a lesser impact and 'Latin American social archaeology' was strong in such countries as Mexico, where the democratic government hosted exiled Marxist scientists from different South American countries. In nations with military or right-wing oriented governments, Marxism was persecuted and its followers fled the country.

'Latin American social archaeology' (Lumbreras 1974; Bate 1977, 1978, 1998; Vargas and Sanoja 1992, 1999) is the best regional representative of Marxist thinking in archaeology. It not only reacted at an early stage against processual archaeology (see Gándara 1980, 1982) but also emerged independently from the Anglo-American Marxist approach in archaeology. It is considered to be one of the most genuine and independent theoretical approaches produced in the region. However, some critics take issue with its theoretical structure (Oyuela et al. 1997; Valdez 2004), the absence of a well-developed methodology (Gnecco 1995) and its application on an empirical level, basically to the archaeology of South American hunter–gatherers (Lanata and Borrero 1999). Its importance and significance in the region has been the subject of ongoing debate (see Patterson 1994, 1997; Oyuela et al. 1997; McGuire y Navarrete 1999; Benavides 2001; Politis 2003; Valdez 2004).

Post-processual archaeology is still marginal in the region in spite of the fact that subjects such as the role of regimes of power in the construction and legitimisation of knowledge and the importance of archaeology in the building of identities – both ethnic and social – could be of especial interest to South American archaeologists. The problem with post-processualism is that few local archaeologists agree with the extreme relativism of some of the post-processual approaches (e.g. Tilley 1991) or consider that this school does not offer the appropriate methodological tools for research topics dependent on an incomplete data base and without the help of written sources (as occurs in the majority of cases in South America). However, some issues derived from post-processual archaeology are increasingly percolating into local research projects, such as studies of the perception of landscape (e.g. Curtoni 2000, Gianotti 2000), material culture and identity (Funari 1999) and the deconstruction of archaeological discourse (Gnecco 1999).

Gender archaeology is one of the worldwide hallmarks of the post-processual endeavour since its defenders argued for the importance of gender issues in archaeological research (Wylie 1991). Nonetheless, gender archeology has not been widely developed in South America, and it is basically restricted to North American archaeologists working in the Andean region (e.g. Silverblatt 1987; Gero 1991, 1999; Hastorf 1991). A provocative example of the construction of archaeological knowledge and gender bias has been put forward by Gero (1996), based on her 'ethnographic' data gathered in 1992 in the excavation of Arroyo Seco 2, a Palaeoindian site located in the Pampas region of Argentina. However, a methodological critique of this work and alternative interpretations have been proposed by the director of the excavation (see Politis 2001: 94–96). South American archaeologists themselves have barely researched this field. The few studies in the area have been focused on the sociology of knowledge (e.g. Bellelli *et al*. 1994), and the identification of the sexual division of labour as represented in dwellings, ceremonial spaces and settlement patterns (Oyuela 1991). Schaan's recent gendered and contextual perspective on the Marajoara female figurines is a contribution to this direction (Schaan 2001).

More recent theoretical trends are less popular in the region. For example, discussion of evolutionary archaeology is almost exclusively restricted to Argentina (basically to Buenos Aires University), with perhaps a few isolated researchers in other countries. Explorations in Historical Ecology are even less popular, despite their great influence on the anthropology of Amazonia.

As I have noted elsewhere, Latin Americans generally give less attention to theoretical issues than North Americans and some Europeans (see also Dillehay in press). Undoubtedly, in the majority of cases conceptual production in the region has not been aimed at generating high-level theories but mostly low-level theories and related models. This output, however, is still limited. The reasons for the lack of long-term and sustained theoretical thinking are difficult to assess, especially because of the historical, scientific, economic and socio-political factors involved. Some have explained the scarcity of theoretical production as arising from the absence of a 'critical mass' of researchers. It has been claimed that it is necessary for there to be a minimum number of archaeologists, based on the assumption that a percentage of them may then start to produce theory. I am not convinced by this argument, and I will briefly summarize what I consider to be the most significant factors affecting theory production in the region.

There are several features that conspire against a more original and sustainable production of 'grand theory'. First, a primary concern of South American archaeologists is the accumulation of essential data from the region (see also Ucko 1995 for a comparative view). Many areas have seen no systematic archaeological excavations at all, and many others are poorly known. Second, the conditions under which archaeologists have to develop their research, both in the field and in the laboratory and office, have been generally unstable, and the socio-political situation in which archaeological investigation occurs not only fluctuates but can also turn violent (e.g. military coups). Moreover, the reduced funding for archaeological investigation in most countries, as well as inconsistent research and educational policies, are also negative factors for theoretical production. The subordination of academic and research institutions to political powers has also made the direction of archaeological research difficult and uncertain. Third, poor libraries and difficulties in obtaining complete and up to date information have always produced limitations for those researchers with theoretical inclinations.

Although most of the above-mentioned causes have resulted in a reduction of theoretical and methodological creativity, they are, nonetheless, secondary. The lack of a clearer theoretical inclination among Latin American archaeologists is in part the consequence of their intellectual subordination. This is, in turn, the reflection of the political–economic dependency of the countries of the region (see a more detailed discussion in Politis 2003). The archaeologists who work in South America are basically 'consumers' of theory, models and concepts developed in the central countries. It means that they use imported theoretical and methodological tools developed elsewhere, produced in other contexts and with other concerns in mind. In some ways, this is the result of the neo-colonial order in which Third World countries occupy a dependent position not only politically and economically but also scientifically. There is a direct connection between the country of origin of the archaeological theoretical resources and the colonialist (or neo-colonialist) position of this country with regard to South America. The most important influence comes from the USA, which has clearly dominated the region since the Second World War. The second is from England and the third from France, which were both colonial powers during the nineteenth and part of the twentieth-century. Although in such fields as literature and arts South American production displays a more independent trajectory, in archaeology the theoretical and methodological reliance is quite obvious.

Nevertheless, I do not want to neglect the theoretical and methodological production of South American researchers, nor do I want to say that local archaeologists are passive consumers of foreign theory and methods. Theoretical and methodological developments in the region are still limited but do exist. Many 'pure' theoretical papers can be found in the Boletín de Antropología Americana (in print for over 20 years), among other Latin American journals, and in recent proceedings from International Meetings of South American Theoretical Archaeology (D'Agostino Fleming 1999; Martinez and Lanata 2002; Curtoni and Endere 2003; Funari and Zarankin 2004; Haber 2004; Politis and Peretti 2004; Alberti and Williams in press). Some edited books published in recent years are also oriented to the promotion of theoretical discussion (e.g. Zarankin and Acuto 1999).

Apart from the 'pure' theoretical papers, there are also those that raise theoretical issues as they arise in factual contexts. Among several cases, I will select two areas/themes that I believe are representative of original, high quality, regional research strategies. One is the 'core' of symbolic and cognitive research particularly in the archaeology of metallurgy, sacred architecture and ritual offerings in northeastern South America (e.g. Falchetti 1999, 2000; Llanos Vargas 1995; Lleras-Pérez 2000). The 'nucleus' of this research effort is essentially made up of Colombians and has been clearly influenced by the ethnographic work and the interpretative strategies of G. Reichel-Dolmatoff (1978, 1985, 1986, 1988). This is a positive influence that has introduced an original mode of inquiry, although at the same time it has led to biases in interpretation due to the pervasive effect of Tukano and Kogi Indian cosmologies (the best and most-developed ethnographic sources studied and used by Reichel-Dolmatoff). Based on mythologies and ethnohistorical sources, this research trend has tried to capture the meaning of the metal objects and monumental architecture as well as to understand their symbolic context. In addition to these Colombian examples, other regional cases are focused on cognitive-symbolic topics (e.g. González 1992, 1998; Alconini 1995). Although these cases could be considered closely related to British post-processualism, they seem to have evolved independently from this theoretical trend. However, they overlap one another in terms of research topics and methodologies.

Other innovative advances have been made in the study of complex societies under the umbrella of political economy, including ideology (e.g. Pérez Gollán 2000). In the Central Andes, recent research on Moche and associated cultures on the North Coast of Peru has gone beyond the dominant horizon-intermediate period chronology and explored the role played by ideology in the materialisation, consolidation and centralisation of political power (e.g. Alva 1992; Alva and Donnan 1993; Castillo 1993; Uceda and Mujica 1994;

Uceda *et al.* 1995). Other recent research on political economy pays less attention to ideology, focusing rather on the social implications of economic control (e.g. Gassón 1997, 1998).

Beyond these original studies, current South American archaeology is devoting great efforts to developing methodologies for a better interpretation of the archaeological record. Although these methods are intertwined with world-wide developments, I believe that South American archaeologists are producing relevant and original contributions in the fields of zooarchaeology, lithic studies, vertebrate taphonomy and ethnoarchaeology (see a detailed discussion in Politis 2003: 255–257).

ETHICS AND PRAXIS IN SOUTH AMERICA

Archaeology is a product of modernity (Hernando 2002), and it has been used as a means of social subordination. The Western world derives its notions of legitimate knowledge from science. That which does not fit into the standards of science is not considered admissible, legitimate or recognisable. Indigenous cosmovision and myths are seen as exotic products and as the object of scientific inquiry but not as another legitimate way of perceiving reality and producing knowledge. Archaeology in fact started as a scientific discipline carrying on its Western and colonialist heritage: the search for the exotic for scientific enquiry and the appropriation of the past of the colonised 'other'. This foundational legacy accompanied the discipline throughout the twentieth-century and in one way or another has permeated the theory and the practice of archaeology. For this reason, archaeological praxis in South America must be understood within its global and 'postmodern' context, following Jameson's understanding of the postmodern condition as a globalising cultural project which reflects the logic of the multinational phase of capitalism (Jameson 1984); hence the suggestion that the praxis of scientific archaeology has been converted into a hegemonic exercise in accordance with this globalising project (Gnecco 1999: 23).

However, in recent decades indigenous claims for their rights have started an unstoppable spiral. The indigenous voice can be heard increasingly loudly and clearly these days. Indigenous groups are currently in the process of organising themselves and claiming rights to their lands and resources, to make their own decisions, to maintain their culture and language and to dispose of their dead and ancestors in their own way. The rights of indigenous peoples have already been enshrined in national and international conventions and laws. The ownership of many 'wild' plants and domesticated crops and the right to control genetic modifications to these materials in the future have been hotly debated (Ucko and Sillar 2001).

In South America, the indigenous claims and achievements in terms of rights target a variety of issues. The demands include many topics, from the right to decide whether or not they want a dam for hydroelectric energy (which is happening in Southern Chile with the Mapuche Indians) to total autonomy to spend the state and municipal budgets (which is happening in the Estado Amazonas in Venezuela). In countries such as Bolivia indigenous people are increasingly controlling political power and their demands are discussed daily in the Congress. By the early 1980s, there were already two indigenous representatives in Bolivia and one in Brazil (Ontiveros Yulquila 1988). The South American indigenous struggle has achieved important successes, such as the new constitutions of Colombia (1991) and Venezuela (1999), which are good examples of how new laws can respect cultural diversity and recognise the rights of indigenous people. Although putting these constitutions into practice means confronting the logical difficulties of articulating different cultural categories and cosmologies, it is undoubtedly a step forward.

Among the claims that indigenous people are increasingly presenting, one is that their rights of ownership over their 'heritage' should be recognised (Ucko 2001). Part of this 'heritage' is composed precisely of archaeological sites and objects that archaeologists find in them, especially human remains (Carmichael *et al.* 1994). Conflicts have emerged, arising from the fact that some archeologists regard themselves as the stewards of the archaeological heritage.

For generations archaeologists have excavated human remains in South America (and throughout the world) without paying the slightest attention to the opinions and feelings of indigenous peoples, including some who are the living descendants of those exhumed. Two decades ago the situation started to change. This change occurred at the same time that The American Indians Against Desecration (AIAD) began to pronounce in favour of the re-burial of indigenous remains that had been stored in museums and university collections. It also happened at the time when Australian Aborigines opposed the excavation of burial sites (Hubert 1989). Susequently, indigenous people from several parts of the world gained recognition of their rights particularly concerning human remains (see review in Hubert 1989, 1992; Fforde 1997, 2002; Ucko 2001; Zimmerman 2002). It may be thought that with the setting up of the World Archaeological Congress (WAC), the return of many human remains and cultural property around the world and appropriate laws, significant issues would already have been resolved. But the increasing political power of indigenous people, the wide diversity of their demands and expectations, as well as the diversity of ways in which external groups have reacted to these demands have resulted in a far more complex range of legal and ethical considerations (Ucko and Sillar 2001). A clear-cut example of this complexity is the legal battle over the property of Kennewick man in the USA (see among many other sources Chatters 2001).

In South America the situation is different and relatively backward in comparison with the USA, Canada, Australia or New Zealand. First of all, indigenous people's rights are not yet fully recognized in the majority of countries, and indigenous communities are still exploited and browbeaten in many places. In the majority of cases (the exception would be Venezuela) they have not achieved the goals obtained by their Australian and North American counterparts. Second, it is important to note that the dialogue between archaeologists and indigenous peoples in the region has always been difficult, erratic, distant and basically absent. Tombs, monuments and sacred places have been excavated in the name of science without any consideration for the people culturally and historically related to them (Mamami Condori 1989). They were passive and suffering observers of how archaeologists treated their dead; they were disinterred and sent to city museums. In Argentina, as in most countries of South America, the construction of a single nation with one only 'true' national identity, was considered central to the consolidation of national unity (Slavsky 1992) and to the placing of the country on the world stage (Barre 1983).

The conflict with the archaeologists stems from the discussion about the ownership of archaeological human remains, the property of the archaeological heritage and the control of the excavation and management of archaeological sites. In some places, the tension between archaeologists and indigenous peoples has reached unprecedented heights. In the northwest of Argentina indigenous people stopped on-going excavations and wanted to expel archaeologists from the archaeological sites. In San Pedro de Atacama (Northern Chile), a few years ago, a radical indigenous group started a fire at night in the church and in the archaeological museum (which contains one of the bigger Andean archeological collection). This was a clear message against those whom they consider to be the icons of domination and colonialism. The situation was later mitigated as a result of the negotiation of local open-minded archaeologists, but tensions still persist.

In the entire region, only Peru, Argentina and Uruguay have a record of recognising rights and claims for the return of indigenous human remains, yet this occurs in a variety of ways and for different purposes. In other countries, notably those with significant and widespread indigenous populations, such as Brazil, Venezuela and Colombia, there has not been a single known case in which an indigenous community has asked for the return or the re-burial of human bones. By contrast, in recent decades in Argentina there have been a number of claims for indigenous human remains (see review in Endere 2002). There are two cases that show the complexity of the issue and the erratic positioning of archaeologists: the re-burial of the skeleton of the cacique (chief) Inakayal and the re-burial of the skull of Panguithruz Güor, a Rankülche chief.

Inakayal was an Indian chief from Patagonia who was captured in the military campaigns bitterly known as the 'Conquista del Desierto' in 1884 and died in the Museo de La Plata (where he and his family were taken in captive) in 1888. He was not buried; his bones, brain, scalp and death mask became part of the museum collection. His skeleton was displayed in the Anthropological Galleries of the museum until 1940 when it was withdrawn to the storerooms. In 1994, the remains of Inakayal returned to his homeland and were buried in the small Patagonian town of Tecka in a mausoleum. The event was made possible by a law proposed by the National Senator of the Patagonian Province of Chubut, Dr H. Solari Irigoyen and supported by indigenous organisations that had been unsuccessfully trying to bury Inakayal in his land. The National Congress approved the law in 1991, number 23,940, and the Museum of La Plata had to return the remains of Inakayal to his descendants.

However, not all archaeologists and physical anthropologists agreed with the return of Inakayal's remains to his descendants. Some of them still consider human remains, even those with close, 'scientifically' proven living descendants, as an indivisible part of a museum's collection. Over 25 years ago, the Australian Institute of Aboriginal Studies (AIAS) proposed that the remains of Truganini (the so-called last Tasmanian) should be disposed of immediately in accordance with her own wishes and those of her descendants, because '[i]t was felt that the case of Truganini, a known historical person, is an exceptional one and that the moral issue involved overrides any other consideration' (Ucko 1975: 7). In the case of Inakayal, which has similar characteristics, one would have expected a comparable reaction from the archaeological and anthropological staff of the Museo de La Plata, but even today, at least in Argentina, archaeology cannot free itself from its colonial background and several scientists still consider themselves the owners of the remains of the colonised 'other'.

The second example of re-burial is the case of the skull of Chief Panguithruz Güor, also known as Mariano Rosas. The skull was buried in the province of La Pampa (the homeland of Panguithruz Güor) after a struggle to bring it back again from the Museo de La Plata. Panguithruz Güor was a Rankülche chief who died before the final military campaigns against the Indians. His burial was looted by soldiers who gave the skull to the scientist who accompanied the campaign. The return of the remains was a long indigenous struggle that included lobbying the provincial and national congresses to obtain a law for the repatriation of the remains, which was finally enacted in 1998 (Curtoni et al. 2003). The objections of some archaeologists and physical anthropologists to the return of the skull were one of the many obstacles that delayed the re-burial of Panguithruz Güor. However, the mausoleum where the remains were placed seems to be the result of a Western strategy to alienate the symbolic value of the skull but retain some control over it (see discussion in Curtoni et al. 2003).

Another interesting case is the return of the Charrúa chief Vaicama Peru (or Pirú), in Uruguay. At the end of the nineteenth-century he was sent to France along with other three Charrúas and died there. His remains were kept in the Musée de L'Homme in Paris. However, some years ago, an indigenous association that claimed to be descendants of the Charrúas demanded the remains back (Endere 2000, López Mazz 2000, Martinez Barbosa 2002). The Government of Uruguay supported the demand and included it in the agenda during President Jacques Chirac's visit to the country in 1997. The remains were finally returned in 2002 and were buried in the 'Panteón Nacional' along with the national 'criollos' heroes, many of whom fought against the Indians. As in the case of Panguithruz Güor, this strategy again alienated the emblematic value of the bones. Uruguayan archaeologists backed the repatriation process, arguing for the symbolic and scientific value of the remains, and took DNA samples in order to confirm the certainty of the identity of the bones. However, in May 2004 the Uruguayan Parliament approved law 17.767 which prohibits any scientific study of the remains of Vaicama Peru, so he can 'rest in peace'. The scientific community expressed its disagreement with this law (López Mázz, personal communication, 2004). The archaeologists did not go along with the indigenous organisations and cast some doubts on their legitimacy. In fact, the Charrúa descent of most of the members of this organisation was suspect and therefore, they do not seem to have more rights than other groups (including the archaeologists themselves) to decide where the remains were buried and to appropriate and use the symbolic value of Vaicama Peru.

These few examples demonstrate that archaeologists in South America need to promote a strong debate among themselves to resolve ethical contradictions and to reflect on the colonial implications of their practices. At the same time, South American archaeologists need to engage in a mature discussion with indigenous people and other subordinated segments of society in order to negotiate rights and develop compatible interests. This has to be done soon before the political dimension of these issues leaves archaeologists aside, without a voice and without room for research. As Gnecco (1999) has stated, archaeology must critically reflect on its contemporary role if it does not want to lose its legitimacy for the production of knowledge of the past.

FINAL CONSIDERATIONS

The current situation of archaeology in South America shows a scientifically mature discipline. Although it is still quite dependent on Anglo-American theoretical trends, it has begun a process of reflection and is developing a more original and genuine theoretical and methodological vision. Although an updated and revitalised version of the culture-historical paradigm still dominates, there are a variety of approaches in the current regional theoretical scenario. This diversity, especially the recent deconstruction of archaeological discourse and self-reflection on its praxis, is producing a lively and fruitful debate and making the discipline more dynamic and provocative.

In terms of ethical issues, South American archaeology lacks a deep discussion about the implication of its praxis and its relationship with the indigenous people of the region. It is far behind other parts of the world (e.g. Australia and New Zealand), where the tension between archaeologists and indigenous people has been reduced throughout debates and negotiation. Archaeologists should be aware of the intense effects that some of their practices, ideologies and assumptions may have on indigenous groups whose identity and livelihood may depend on places that frequently become fossilised archaeological sites due to research processes and preservation management (Ucko 2001; Ucko and Sillar 2001).

The archaeology of South America finds itself with a dual role. On the one hand, with very few exceptions, its theoretical development is subordinated to the central, developed countries. It follows the agenda advanced in the Anglo-Saxon world. On the other hand, South American archaeology cannot escape the essence of its origin, which manifests itself in the form of a tool for the domination of indigenous groups through the appropriation of a socially legitimised discourse on their past. Archaeology retains and controls objects from the past of indigenous societies, not only because of the value they hold as sources of information, but also because of their symbolic content, which is co-opted by the development of the Western hegemonic globalising model. Without doubt, South American archaeology needs a deep debate to discuss the ethical implications of the praxis of the discipline and to make its interests compatible with the indigenous peoples of the region. Only through this mutual understanding can archaeology free itself from its colonial legacy and develop the great potential that it has for the vindication of indigenous rights. If common agreements could be reached, archaeology would be the great ally of indigenous claims since issues such as the longevity of occupation and the continuity of cultural practices all rest on archaeological and historical evidence.

ACKNOWLEDGEMENTS

I would like to deeply thank Peter Ucko for his positive input throughout my career. In this chapter I summarised my ideas about the ethical issues related to archaeology and my view about how socio-political contexts have affected the development, both in the past and in the present, of the discipline in South America. My interest in these issues has been brought to me by Peter, not only through the reading of his books and articles but also during endless nights of discussion in his home, fuelled by abundant red wine.

Thanks also to Mónica Espinosa for her useful comments and help with the translation. Also to José M. López Mazz and María Luz Endere for their comments and suggestions. This chapter is a product of the INCUAPA Research Program (Investigaciones Arqueológicas y Paleontológicas del Cuaternario Pampeano), sponsored by the Universidad Nacional del Centro de la Provincia de Buenos Aires, the CONICET (PIP 2940/01), the Agencia Nacional de Promoción Científica y Tecnológica (PICT nro.04–12776) and the Fundación Antorchas.

REFERENCES

Alberti, B. and V. Williams (in press) *Género y Etnicidad en la Arqueología Sudamericana*, Serie Teórica nro.4. Olavarría: Ediciones INCUAPA.

Alconini, N. S. (1995) *Rito, Simbolismo e Historia en la Pirámide Acopana Tiawanaku: Un análisis de la cerámica Ceremonial Prehispánica*, La Paz: Acción.

Alva, W. (1992) 'El Señor de Sipán', *Revista del Museo de Arqueología*, 3: 51–64, Universidad Nacional de Trujillo, Perú.

Alva, W. and C.B. Donnan (1993) *Royal Tombs of Sipán*, Los Angeles: Fowler Museum of Cultural History, University of California.

Barre, M. Ch. (1983) *Ideologías indigenistas y movimientos indios*, México City: Siglo XXI Editores.

Bate, L.F. (1977) *Arqueología y materialismo histórico*, México City: Editorial de Cultura Popular.

Bate, L.F. (1978) *Sociedad, formación económico social y cultura*, México City: Ediciones de Cultura Popular, México.

Bate, L.F. (1998) *El proceso de investigación en arqueología*, Barcelona: Editorial Crítica.

Bellelli, C., M. Berón and V. Scheinsohn (1994) 'Gender and Science: Demystifying Argentine Archeology', in *Equity Issues for Women in Archaeology*, M.C. Nelson, S. M. Nelson and A. Wylie (eds), Arlington: American Anthropological Association (Archaeological Papers 5), pp. 131–137.

Benavides, H.O. (2001) 'Returning to the Source: Social Archaeology as Latin American Philosophy', *Latin American Antiquity*, 12: 355–370.

Binford, L. (1980) 'Willow Smoke and Dogs Tails: Hunter Gatherer Settlement Systems and Archaeological Site Formation', *American Antiquity*, 45: 4–20.

Binford, L. (1981) *Bones: Ancient Men and Modern Myths*, New York: Academic Press.

Binford, L. (1983) *Working at Archaeology*, New York: Academic Press.

Binford, L. (1989) *Debating Archaeology*, New York: Academic Press.

Borrero, L. (1990) Taphonomy of Guanaco Bones in Tierra del Fuego, *Quaternary Research*, 34: 36–371.

Borrero, L. (2001) 'Regional Taphonomy: The Scales of Application to the Archaeological Record', in *Animals and Man in the Past: Essays in Honour of Dr. A.T. Clason*, H. Buitenhuis and W. Prummel (eds), Groningen: ARC- Publicatie 41, pp. 17–20.

Carmichael, D., J. Hubert and B. Reeves (1994) 'Introduction', in *Sacred Sites, Sacred Places*, D. Carmichael, J. Hubert, B. Reeves and A. Schanche (eds), London and New York: Routledge, pp. 1–8.

Castillo, L.J. (1993) 'Prácticas funerarias, poder e ideología en la sociedad Moche tardía: El proyecto arqueológico San José de Moro' *Gaceta Arqueológica Andina*, 7(23): 67–82.

Curtoni, R.P. (2000) 'La percepción del paisaje y la reproducción social de la identidad en la Región Pampeana Occidental', *Tapa*, 19: 115–125.

Curtoni, R.P. and M.L. Endere (2003) *Análisis interpretación y gestión en la Arqueología de Sudamérica*, Serie Teórica nro. 2, Olavaria: Ediciones INCUAPA.

Curtoni, R., A. Lazzari and M. Lazzari (2003) 'Middle of nowhere: a place of war memories, commemoration, and aboriginal reemergence', *World Archaeology*, 35(1): 61–78. La Pampa, Argentina.

Chatters, J. (2001) *Ancient Encounter: Kennewick Man and the First Americans*, New York: Simon and Schuster.

D'Agostino Fleming, M.I. (ed.) (1999) *Revista do Museu de Arqueologia e Etnologia. Anais da I Reuniao Internacional de Teoria Arqueológica na América do Sul*, Suplemento 3, Universidad de São Paulo, São Paulo, Brasil.

Dillehay, T. (in press) 'Latin American Theories and Methods', in *Contemporary Theory and Method*, H. Maschner and C. Chippendale (eds), Aldine Press.

Endere, M.L. (2000) 'Patrimonios en disputa: acervos nacionales, investigación arqueológica y reclamos étnicos sobre restos humanos', *Trabajos de Prehistoria*, 57(1): 1–13.

Endere, M.L. (2002) 'The Reburial Issue in Argentina: A Growing Conflict', in *The Dead and Their Possessions: Repatriation in Principle, Policy and Practice*, C. Fforde, J. Hubert and P. Turnbull (eds), London: Routledge, pp. 266–283.

Eremites de Oliveira, J. (2002) 'A Arqueología Brasileira da década de 1980 ao início do século XXI', *Estudos Ibero-Americanos PUCRS*, 28(2): 25–52.

Falchetti, A.M. (1999) 'El poder simbólico de los metales: la *tumbaga* y las transformaciones metalúrgicas', *Boletín de Arqueología*, 14(2): 53–82.

Fforde, C. (1997) 'Controlling the dead: an analysis of the collecting and repatriation of aboriginal humans remains', unpublished PhD Thesis, University of Southampton, UK.

Fforde, C. (2002) 'Collection, repatriation and identity', in *The Dead and their Possessions: Repatriation in Principle, Policy and Practice*, C. Fforde, J. Hubert and P. Turnbull (eds), London: Routledge, pp. 25–46.

Funari, P.P. (1999) 'Etnicidad, identidad y cultura material: un estudio del cimarrón Palmares, Brasil, Siglo XVII', in *Sed Non Satiata. Teoría Social en la Arqueología Latinoamericana Contemporánea*, A. Zarankin and F. Acuto (eds), Buenos Aires: Ediciones del Tridente, pp. 77–96.

Funari, P. and A. Zarankin (2004) Arqueología Histórica en América del Sur. Los desafíos del Siglo XXI, Santafé de Bogotá: Universidad de los Andes.

Gándara, M. (1980) 'La vieja Nueva Arqueología (primera parte)', *Boletín de Antropología Americana*, 2: 7–45.

Gándara, M. (1981) 'La vieja Nueva Arqueología (segunda parte)', *Boletín de Antropología Americana*, 3: 7–70.

Gero, J. (1991) 'Genderlithics: women's roles in stone tool production', in *Engendering Archaeology. Women and Prehistory*, J. Gero and M. Conkey (eds), Oxford: Blackwell, pp. 163–193.

Gero, J. (1996) 'Archaeological practice and gendered encounters with field data', in *Gender and Archaeology*, R. Wright (ed.) Philadelphia: University of Pennsylvania Press, pp. 251–280.

Gero, J. (1999) 'La iconografía Recuay y el estudio de género' *Gaceta Arqueológica Andina*, 25: 23–44.

Gassón, R. (1997) 'Locational analysis and elites activities in a prehispanic chiefdom of the Western Venezuelan Llanos', *Antropológica*, 88: 3–32.

Gassón, R. (1998) 'Prehispanic intensive agriculture, settlement pattern and political economy in the Western Venezuelan Llanos', unpublished PhD dissertation, University of Pittsburgh, Pittsburgh.

Gianotti G.C. (2000) 'Monumentalidad, ceremonialismo y continuidad ritual' *Tapa*, 19: 87–102.

Gnecco, C. (1995) '*Praxis* científica en la periferia: Notas para una historia social de la arqueología Colombiana', *Revista Española de Arqueología Americana*, 25: 9–22.

Gnecco, C. (1999) *Multivocalidad histórica. Hacia una cartografía postcolonial de la arqueología*, Santafé de Bogotá: Universidad de Los Andes.

González, A.R. (1992) *Las placas metálicas de los Andes del Sur. Contribución al estudio de las religiones precolombinas*, Mainz am Rhein: Phillipp von Zabern.

González, A.R. (1998) *Arte Precolombino. Cultura La Aguada. Arqueología y Diseño*, Buenos Aires: Filmediciones Valero.

Haber, A. (ed.) (2004) *Hacia una Arqueología de las Arqueologías Sudamericanas*, Santafé de Bogotá: Universidad de los Andes.

Hastorf, C. (1991) 'Gender, space and food in prehistory', in *Engendering Archaeology*, J. Gero and M. Conkey (eds), Oxford: Blackwell, pp.132–162.

Hernando, A. (2002) *Arqueología de la identidad*, Madrid: Editorial Akal.

Hubert, J. (1989) 'A proper place for the dead: a critical review of the "reburial" issue', in *Conflict in the Archaelogy of Living Traditions*, R. Layton (ed.) London: Unwin Hyman, pp. 131–166.

Hubert, J. (1992) 'Dry bones or living ancestors? Conflictive perception of life, death and the universe', *International Journal of Cultural Property*, 1: 105–127.

Jameson, F. (1984) 'Postmodernism or the cultural logic of late capitalism', *New Left Review*, 146: 53–92.

Lanata, J.L. and L. Borrero (1999) 'The archaeology of hunter-gatherers in South America', in *Archaeology in Latin America*, G. Politis and B. Alberti (eds), London: Routledge, pp. 76–89.

Langebaeck, C. (1996) 'La arqueología después de la arqueología en Colombia', *En Dos Lecturas Críticas. Arqueología en Colombia*, Santafé de Bogotá: Fondo de Promoción de la Cultura, pp. 9–42.

Lima, T. Andrade (2000) 'Teoria e método na Arqueología Brasileira: avaliação e perspectivas', in *Anais do IX Congreso da* Sociedade de Arqueologia Brasileira, Souza, S.M.F.M. de (Org) Rio de Janeiro SAP. (CD Rom).

López Mazz, J.M. (2000) Investigación arqueológica y usos del pasado: Las tierras bajas del Este de Uruguay, *Tapa*, 19: 63–74.

Lumbreras, L. (1974) *La Arqueología como ciencia social*, Lima: Ediciones Hista.

Llanos Vargas, H. (1995) *Los chamanes jaguares de San Agustín: génesis de un pensamiento mitopoético*, Santafé de Bogotá: H. Llanos Vargas.

Llanos Vargas, H. (1999) Proyección histórica de la arqueología en Colombia, *Boletín de Arqueología*, 14 (2): 5–24.

Lleras-Peréz, R. (2000) 'The iconography and symbolism of metallic votive offerings in the Eastern Cordillera, Colombia', in *Precolumbian Gold. Technology, Style and Iconography*, Colin McEwan (ed.), London: British Museum Press, pp. 112–131.

Mamami C.C. (1989) 'History and prehistory in Bolivia: what about the Indians?', in *Conflict in the Archaeology of Living Traditions*, R. Layton (ed.), London: Unwin Hyman, pp. 46–59.

Martinez B.R. (2002) 'One hundred and sixty years of exile: Vaimaca Pirú and the campaign to repatriate his remains to Uruguay', in *The Dead and their Possessions: Repatriation in Principle, Policy and Practice*, C. Fforde, J. Hubert and P. Turnbull (eds), London: Routledge, pp. 218–221.

Martínez, G. and J.L. Lanata (eds) (2002) *Perspectivas integradoras entre arqueología y evolución. Teoría, Método y Casos de Aplicación*, Serie Teórica nro. 1. Olavaria: Ediciones INCUAPA.

McGuire, R. and R. Navarrete (1999) 'Entre motocicletas y fusiles: las arqueologías radicales anglosajona e hispana' *Revista do Museu de Arquelogia e Etnologia, Suplemento*, 3: 181–199.

Oliver, J. and C.S. Alexander (2003) 'Ocupaciones humanas del Pleistoceno terminal en el occidente de Venezuela', *Maguaré*, 17: 83–246.

Ontiveros Y.A. (1988) 'Hacia la consolidación de la indianidad', in *La cara india, la cruz del 92. Identidad étnica y movimientos indios*, J. Contreras (ed.) Madrid: Editorial Revolución, pp. 185–194.

Oyuela-Caycedo, A. (1991) 'Ideology And structure of gender spaces: the case of the Kaggaba Indians', in The Archaeology of Gender, D. Walde and N. Willows (eds), Calgary: The Archaeological Association of the University of Calgary, pp. 327–335.

Oyuela-Caycedo, A., A. Anaya, C.G. Elera and L. Valdez (1997) 'Social archaeology in Latin America? Comments to T. C. Patterson', *American Antiquity*, 62: 365–374.

Patterson, T.C. (1994) 'Social archaeology in Latin America. An appreciation', *American Antiquity*, 59: 531–537.

Pérez Gollán, J. (2000) 'El jaguar en llamas (la religión en el antiguo Noroeste Argentino)', in *Nueva Historia Argentina*, M. N. Tarragó (ed.), Buenos Aires: Editorial Sudamericana, pp. 229–256.

Piazzini, C.E. (2003) 'Teoría en la arqueología de Colombia: Un ejercicio a propósito de los umbrales epistemológicos', *Revista de Estudiantes de Arqueología de la Universidad Nacional de Colombia,* Universidad Nacional de Colombia, Santafé de Bogotá, Colombia, 1: 72–88.

Politis, G. (1995) 'The socio-politics of archaeology in Hispanic South America', in *Theory in Archaeology. A World Perspective*, P. Ucko (ed.), London: Routledge, pp. 197–235.

Politis, G. (2001) 'On archaeological praxis, gender bias and indigenous peoples in South America', *Journal of Social Archaeology*, 1(1): 90–107.

Politis, G. (2002) 'South America: in the garden of forking paths', in *Archeology: The Widening Debate*, B. Cunliffe, W. Davies and C. Renfrew (eds), Oxford: Oxford University Press, pp. 193–244.

Politis, G. (2003) 'The theoretical landscape and the methodological developments of archaeology in Latin American', *American Antiquity*, 68(2): 247–272.

Politis, G. and J.A. Pérez Gollán (2004) 'Latin America archaeology: between colonialism and globalization', in *A Companion to Social Archaeology*, L. Meskell and R. Preucel (eds), Oxford: Blackwell, pp. 353–373.

Politis, G. and R. Peretti (2004) *Teoría Arqueológica en América del Sur*, Serie Teórica nro.3. Olavarría: Ediciones INCUAPA.

Reichel-Dolmattoff, G. (1978) 'Desana animal categories, food restrictions, and the concept of color energies', *Journal of Latin American Lore*, 4: 249–291.

Reichel-Dolmattoff, G. (1985) *Los Kogi*, Bogotá: Nueva Biblioteca Colombiana de Cultura. Procultura.

Reichel-Dolmattoff, G. (1986) *Desana. Simbolismo de los indios Tukano del Vaupés*. Bogotá: Procultura. Presidencia de la República.

Reichel-Dolmattoff, G. (1988) *Orfebrería y chamanismo. Un estudio iconográfico del Museo del Oro*, Medellín: Editorial Colina.

Schaan, D. (2001) 'Estatuetas Antropomorfas Marajoara: o simbolismo de indentdades de gênero em uma sociedade complexa Amazónica', *Boletín Museu Paranaense Emilio Goeldi, sér. Antropología*, 17 (2): 437–477.

Schiffer, M.B. (1995) *Behavioral Archaeology: First Principles*, Salt Lake City: University of Utah Press.

Silverblatt, I. (1987) *Moon, Sun and Witches*, Princeton: Princeton University.

Slavsky, L. (1992) 'Los indígenas y la sociedad nacional. Apuntes sobre políticas indigenistas en la Argentina', in *La Problemática Indígena. Estudios Antropológicos sobre Pueblos Indígenas en Argentina*, A. Balazote and J. Radovich (eds), Buenos Aires: Centro Editor de América Latina, pp. 67–79.

Tilley, C. (1991) *The Art of Ambiguity: Material Culture and Text*, London: Routledge.

Uceda, S. and E. Mujica (eds) (1994) *Moche: Propuestas y perspectivas*, Lima: Travaux de l'Institut Français d'Etudes Andines 79.

Uceda, S., E. Mujica and R. Morales (eds) (1995) *Investigaciones en la Huaca de la Luna*, Perú: Universidad Nacional de Trujillo.

Ucko, P. (1975) 'Review of AIAS activities 1974', *AIAS Newsletter*, 3: 6–17.

Ucko, P. (1995) 'Introduction: archaeological interpretation in a world context', in *Theory in Archaeology. A World Perspective*, P. Ucko (ed.), London: Routledge, pp. 1–27.

Ucko, P. (2001) ' "Heritage" and "Indigenous peoples" in the 21st century', *Public Archaeology*, 1: 227–238.

Ucko, P. and B. Sillar (2001) *Indigenous Peoples and 'Patenting' the Past: The Developing Relationship between the Rights of Indigenous Peoples and the Work of Archaeologists in the 21st Century*. Institute of Archaeology's Research Seminars.

Valdez, L. (2004) 'La "filosofía" de la Arqueología en América Latina', in *Teoría Arqueologica en America del Sur*, G. Politis and R. Peretti (eds), Serie Teórica 3, Olavarría: Ediciones INCUAPA, pp. 129–140.

Vargas Arena, I. and M. Sanoja Obediente (1992) 'Revisión crítica de la arqueología sudamericana', in *Prehistoria Sudamericana. Nuevas Perspectivas*, B. Meggers (ed.), Taraxacum, Washington: México, pp. 35–44.

Vargas Arena, I. and M. Sanoja Obediente (1999) 'Archaeology as a social science', in *Archaeology in Latin America*, G. Politis and B. Alberti (eds), London: Routledge, pp. 59–75.

Wylie, A. (1991) 'The interplay of evidential constraints and political interests: recent archaeological research on gender', *American Antiquity*, 57: 15–35.

Zarankin, A. and F. Acuto (eds) (1999) *Sed Non Satiata. Teoría Social en la Arqueología Latinoamericana Contemporánea*, Buenos Aires: Ediciones del Tridente.

Zimmerman, L.J. (2002) 'A decade after the Vermillion Accord: what has changed and what has not?', in *The Dead and Their Possessions: Repatriation in Principle, Policy and Practice*, C. Fforde, J. Hubert and P. Turnbull (eds), London: Routledge, pp. 91–98.

CHAPTER 17

THE IDEA OF PREHISTORY IN THE MIDDLE EAST

David Wengrow

ARCHAEOLOGY AS FORGETTING

The transformation of particular places is an inevitable consequence of archaeological excavation, central to the way in which archaeology, as a distinct form of historical and material practice, creates, alters and destroys memory. To expand upon this, and as a way of introducing my wider topic, I would like to draw upon a personal recollection of one of the first excavations in which I participated, before beginning my formal education in archaeology and anthropology. The name and precise location of the site are of secondary importance here, as I do not wish to make any direct moral or political point. Rather I wish to highlight the way in which political considerations may enter, more or less consciously, into the very methods and practice of excavation, if we take the time and trouble to find out about the people whose landscapes we are altering, and their more immediate histories.[1]

With hindsight, the very status of this particular place as a subject of archaeological excavation could be considered highly contentious. Little more than half a century prior to our arrival it had been a living village, the houses and cemetery of which were still clearly visible over parts of the site. The residents of this village were displaced, along with many others, during a conflict which resulted in the region's resettlement by a largely foreign population. An accurate history of this conflict is only now beginning to be written, and neither they nor their descendants have since been allowed to return. There had in fact been a battle on the site of the village, and in preparing new areas for excavation we would occasionally stumble across rusted bullets and cartridges. None of these recent objects were recorded in any way, but simply disposed of.

It was the descendants of this new, incoming population who hosted us during the expedition, in a settlement originally established on the site of the old village, but subsequently moved to an adjacent plot of land. A handful of them could still remember the earlier village as a living settlement, and most of the older generation had been involved in some way in the wider conflict of identity, of which its destruction formed a part. Many had themselves been, or were descended from, refugees, victims of earlier and often brutal displacements. In forging a sense of belonging in their newly won home, this incoming community had, over the decades, attached a new set of historical associations to the overgrown remains of the village, linking the ancient site on which they lay with a remote mythical time: a heroic time, long preceding the memory of the conflict in which the village was destroyed.

The investigation of that remote time, and the discovery of its tangible remains, was a primary aim of the archaeological expedition, and the local residents made us very welcome. While there was no telling what might be found, traces of a monumental building had already been noted, and rumours of an ancient palace were in the air. Although few people acknowledged it openly at the time, we were engaged in a process of giving material reality to a local past which had previously existed only in legends, festivals and children's songs. And in the process of digging down into that past, we were effacing the physical remains of a more recent past that few of the current inhabitants wished to dwell upon, either literally or in their thoughts. Excavation, as every good textbook will tell you, is destruction; but it is the destruction of memory, and of the potential for future memories, as well as the destruction of historical evidence. With each house or burial of the village that was removed in order to access a more ancient reality, the possibility of reviving some other, more recent and disruptive memory of this particular place was diminished.

In the process, the commemorative character of the site was itself transformed, for what we discovered, deep below the earth, was a vast stone building belonging to the time of an ancient royal dynasty. There was no telling whether it was a palace or not, and scholarly debate on this point is ongoing. Regardless of this, the tangible memory of the place as a location of particular houses, families and individuals was replaced by that of a more monumental past, documented in religious texts as well as academic and popular publications and integrated into national and global frameworks of historical awareness and identity, not to mention a well-trodden tourist trail. When the excavations were over, the site was declared a national heritage park. A scenic walkway was installed leading from the ancient remains down to a nearby spring.

Archaeological excavation may then be understood as a praxis through which the forms in which past reality can be comprehended are irreversibly altered and rearranged. In channeling personal memories down certain pathways and closing off access to others, it creates new material environments for social memory to inhabit. Archaeology, notwithstanding the metaphorical usage made of it by Foucault (1972), is as much about forgetting as remembering. In the remainder of this chapter I will attempt to explore this formulation on a much broader canvas. My concern will be the relationship between remote material pasts and notions of political modernity and the different ways in which this relationship has been played out between Europe and the Middle East over the last few centuries. I conclude with some observations concerning the future of prehistory in the Middle East.

THE MULTIPLE HISTORIES OF 'WORLD PREHISTORY'

Today it is more or less taken for granted that prehistory, in the sense of an investigation into pasts without written records, can and ought to be pursued on a global scale. This forms part of the commitment to a total understanding of the human and hominid past that underpins the teaching of world history in Western (and many non-Western) institutions. The *possibility* of grasping the human story in its entirety is introduced at an early stage of schooling, and to deliberately exclude some part of that story tends increasingly to be seen as prejudicial. Global prehistory is definitely 'out there', but this should not blind us to the different processes through which prehistory has come into being in different parts of the world; the markedly varying extent to which it pervades local, national and continental views of the past or its equally variable role in shaping the perception of any given region's past by the outside world. Among the many achievements of the *One World Archaeology* Series has been to demonstrate how the factors that elevate prehistory in one area and mask its existence in another are as much social, historical and political as academic. This chapter is dedicated to its editor-in-chief who has, amongst many other things, made lasting contributions to the prehistory of the Middle East.

A historical perspective on these matters may be particularly useful in highlighting the extent to which concerns internal to Europe, the birthplace and still a leading patron of world archaeology, have set the agenda for historical consciousness on other continents. Such a perspective seems increasingly necessary if we are to understand what, if anything, ordinary people (as well as governments and academics) throughout the world have found to be of value in what archaeologists do. The establishment of prehistory in the Middle East is a case in point. As I will try to show, to consider its early development is to confront a very different historical and social reality from that which brought European prehistory into being. It is a reality which commences on the coattails of capitalist expansion and imperial conquest and follows a long period of archaeological exploration during which prehistory was largely overlooked in favour of the investigation of royal tombs, palaces, monuments and inscriptions. This may not in itself be surprising, and yet the broader cultural and historical implications of this chosen emphasis upon a deep, monarchical past have barely begun to be explored.

At much the same time that the antiquaries of northern Europe were piecing together local evidence for the Three Age System of human prehistory (Stone, Bronze, Iron), the birth of Egyptology and Assyriology was heralded by the decipherment of royal proclamations such as the Rosetta Stone, found by French military engineers in 1799 and subsequently surrendered to the British (Daniel 1950; Pope 1975). Nobody, in those early days of exploration, was looking for or thinking about a prehistory of the Middle East. The primary concern was, rather, to reveal, study and appropriate the cultural remnants of ancient and exotic forms of sacred kingship, and the civilisations where, as described in biblical and Graeco-Roman sources, they first rose and fell. Would it be far-fetched to seek some resonance here with later attitudes towards the possibilities for effective government in the Middle East, particularly among the more conservative elements of British imperial administration? David Cannadine (2002: 71, 102), for instance, has described the British Middle East of the twentieth century (politically organised through a process of what Gertrude Bell called 'creating kings') as saturated with images of timeless hierarchy:

> The First World War may (or may not) have made the world safe for democracy; for another generation, and in yet another part of the world, it certainly made the British Empire safe for hierarchy.
>
> ... Indeed, from the generally egalitarian-cum-republican perspective of the early twenty-first century, it is easy to forget the extent to which, in its heyday, the British Empire was a *royal* empire, presided over and unified by a sovereign of global amplitude and semi-divine fullness, and suffused with the symbols and signifiers of kingship, which reinforced, legitimated, unified and completed the empire as a realm bound together by order, hierarchy, tradition and subordination.

When significant quantities of prehistoric remains were eventually excavated in the Nile valley, at the close of the nineteenth century, it was more by accident than design, and the finds were not unanimously recognised as dating to a time before kingship. It was with a polite dismissal that W.M.F. Petrie, who subsequently went on to demonstrate almost single-handedly the existence of a 'predynastic' cultural sequence in Egypt, responded to the first volume of J. de Morgan's (1896) *Recherches sur les origines de l'Égypte* (see Drower 1985: 225). It is a further irony that a number of Petrie's own prehistoric discoveries, including the famous colossal statues of Min from Coptos, were subsequently rejected by the British Museum on grounds that they were 'unhistoric rather than prehistoric', a fit of pique for which Oxford's Ashmolean Museum and University College London (UCL) have been grateful ever since (see Petrie 1931: 153–157). Egypt 'before the pharaohs' was therefore a material object, or rather an assemblage of objects and unloved human remains, long before it became a historical idea. By 'a historical idea' I mean something more than just a subject of study for professional archaeologists or another gap filled along the chronological spectrum of human development. I mean something which resonates in the present and is generally felt to have been a formative, or at least distinctly meaningful, episode in the making of our contemporary world. Such a status can hardly yet be claimed for the funerary remains of predynastic Egypt, those unwilling Jeremy Benthams, uprooted from their places of rest.

The general state of affairs was aptly summed up by Michael Hoffman (1979: xvi), who observed that 'Unlike Egyptologists, prehistorians of Egypt do not now and never have possessed a conscious unity of purpose.' The beginnings of prehistoric archaeology in Iraq and neighbouring regions of the Middle East present a similarly fragmented narrative, driven along by tenacious individuals, personal and national rivalries, and a dogged sense of vocation that led a handful of excavators to dig extraordinarily deep trenches into ancient tells, cutting through the palaces and temples to obtain a full chronological sequence of material remains (see Daniel 1950: 199–213). The cast of actors is a disparate one, their agendas varying from the art historical (de Morgan again at Susa, Herzfeld at Samarra) to the reconstruction of prehistoric environments (Pumpelly and Schmidt at Anau). In his memoirs, Max Mallowan recounts how Reginald Campbell Thompson turned against the idea of a prehistoric sounding at Kuyunjik (Nineveh) once it was discovered 'to our amazement' that 'more than four-fifths of this great mound were pre-Assyrian and prehistoric' (Mallowan 1977: 81; although Thompson did concede, in a private letter to a sponsor, that 'It is great fun watching the men at work in this deep pit'; reproduced in Gut 2002: 27, figure 3).

My aim in making these points is not to criticise the excavators in question. On the contrary, without their work there would be no prehistory of the Middle East to speak of. It is simply to point out that they were bringing to light a past for which no existing framework of historical understanding was available. The debates that initially emerged to fill this vacuum, such as the so-called Sumerian Problem (Frankfort 1932), are now regarded by most scholars as interpretative blind alleys, although certain, still earlier ideas, adopted from Victorian anthropology (notably that of a common substratum of religious belief based upon the worship of a single Mother Goddess) have proved remarkably durable (e.g. Cauvin 2000), even in the face of contradictory evidence (see Ucko 1968; cf. Moorey 2003).

All was to change during the mid-twentieth century with Robert Braidwood's expedition to the 'hilly flanks' of the Iraqi Zagros, which demonstrated that V. Gordon Childe's accounts of the origins of farming in the Fertile Crescent could be substantiated with empirical data from prehistoric settlements (see Braidwood and Howe 1960). For both Childe and Braidwood, the importance of telling that particular story resided in its global implications for understanding the evolution of *all* human societies, rather than in changing perceptions of long-term social development in the Middle East (see, for example, Childe 1936; Braidwood 1952). As the American anthropologist Robert Redfield was quick to point out, in his Messenger Lectures on the Evolution of Civilization, prehistoric communities were characterised in these narratives mainly by what they were thought to lack (writing, trade, cities, organised government), rather than positively, in terms of the 'largely undeclared but continually realized' concepts through which they reproduced and transformed themselves. The criticism may seem harsh, given the limited data then available to interpreters. Redfield's (1953: 111) comments on Childe's *Man Makes Himself* are nevertheless revealing with regard to the overall theoretical orientation of prehistoric studies in the Middle East at that time, and for some decades to follow:

> The 'making of man' with which Childe is concerned is unplanned. It is that making of man in which a future is made that men do not foresee or strive to bring about. The consequences of agriculture and of the building of cities were not intended. They just happened ... In the early and very much longer part of his history man did not see himself as maker of either his future world or of himself. It is Childe, looking backward upon what happened in history, who sees man as the maker of himself.

To put things in more contemporary terms, the prehistory of the Middle East entered broader streams of historical consciousness as a story of technological change in the absence of social agency, shorn of any particular emotional, political or ethical connection to the Middle Eastern present.

THE ANCIENT CONSTITUTION AND ITS OTHER

The brief, foregoing survey is intended to highlight certain contrasts with the earlier emergence of prehistory in Europe, which had the character of a purposeful social and ideological movement, the ramifications of which extend far beyond the disciplinary history of archaeology. In considering this contrast, and some of its wider implications, I would like to delve into what George Stocking (1987: 71) has called the 'doldrums of antiquarianism', and to suggest that – from the perspective of contemporary, politicised archaeology – they were not quite so dull, comical or insignificant as is sometimes suggested. In particular I wish to draw attention to a phenomenon defined by John Pocock as 'constitutional antiquarianism', although he himself preferred the Italian terms 'cultura storico-giuridica' and 'tradizione giuridica'.[2] The setting is north-western Europe during the sixteenth to seventeenth centuries AD. The protagonists are jurists, interested in protecting popular sovereignty against the growing encroachments of absolute royal power. The mode of argumentation in defence of rights and privileges is not the familiar one of human or natural liberties (a later development), but one of appealing to a remote past and to the test of customary usage. Pocock (1957: 16–17) explains:

> In this way there grew up – or rather, there was intensified and renewed – a habit in many countries of appealing to 'the ancient constitution', of seeking to prove that the rights it was desired to defend were immemorial and therefore always beyond the king's power to alter or annul … If the constitutionalists could show that the laws were as old as, or older than, the kings, they might go on to assert a contractual or elective basis for kingship; but if the laws had come into being at a time when there was already a king, then nothing but the king's authority could have sanctioned them or made them law, and the king might assert a sovereign right to revoke what his predecessors had granted. The constitutionalists were therefore always being driven to argue that the laws were of a practically infinite antiquity, immemorial in the sense of earlier than the earliest king known.

The battle was fought not simply on the grounds of more or less extreme claims to antiquity, but between two quite different conceptions of the past and its hold upon the present and future. As their primary weapon, kings and their supporters employed textual criticism, principally of Roman Law, in order to trace back each existing law to the actions of a royal originator. Jurist-antiquarians, by contrast, located the institutions that enshrined their liberties on a continuum of customary usage extending from the present into ever more remote pasts. Written laws, they perceived, could always be shown to originate in a particular time and setting, such as ancient Rome, that on inspection could be shown to differ in important ways from the society they now inhabited. Accordingly their authority could be questioned on grounds of historical relevance. In place of codified laws they elaborated a notion of custom that owed much of its popularity to its unwritten character:

> all its emphasis was on gradual process, imperceptible change, the origin and slow growth of institutions in usage, tacit consent, prescription and adaptation. We may never know how much of our sense of history is due to the presence in Europe of systems of customary law, and to the idealization of the concept of custom which took place towards the end of the sixteenth century. To it our awareness of process in history is largely owing. (Pocock 1957: 19)

The heyday of constitutional antiquarianism during the sixteenth century was also the time of William Camden in England and Nicolaus Marschalk in Germany, a time in which the prehistoric landscapes of Europe, and in particular megaliths, tumuli and urn-fields, were receiving renewed attention. The recognition of material remains as independent means of reconstructing past ways of life was a slightly later development, associated with figures of the mid-seventeenth century such as the Danish scholar, Ole Worm and the Frenchman, Jacques Spon (Schnapp 1996: 139–218). By that time the flame was already going out of constitutional antiquarianism. For libertarian philosophers of the eighteenth century Enlightenment, such as Locke and Rousseau, the basis of popular sovereignty was to be found in the individual's adherence to abstract principles of nature and reason, rather than appeals to a collective past (Pocock 1957: 235–237). The patriotic writings of antiquarians such as Worm and Spon nevertheless retained a combative stance towards the world of ancient texts (biblical and Graeco-Roman), which continued to circumscribe their sense of chronology and led back, inexorably, to an external (Eastern) origin for some of their most important social and political institutions:

> Because our antiquities seem intractable most of us turn aside from our patriotic duty and, neglecting our local antiquities devote ourselves to the foreign, but to neglect the home ground in favour of that which is far away, to adhere to the distant at the expense of the familiar, is vice not virtue. So it naturally follows that the actions, rituals, customs, institutions, laws, victories, triumphs, and all those Danish achievements would be swallowed in darkness and be consigned to oblivion for eternity. (Ole Worm, from *Danicorum Monumentorum Libri Sex*, published in Copenhagen in 1643, cited in Schnapp 1996: 162)

There is no need here to rehearse the well-known events that led, during the eighteenth and early nineteenth century, to the abandonment of the short biblical chronology for human history and the establishment of Victorian anthropology (see Stocking 1987; Trautman 1992). What is worthy of comment, however, is the initial lack of impact that the expanded, secular framework of human time had upon the development of archaeology in the Middle East. As Mogens Larsen (1996: xii) observes, fascination with Near Eastern antiquities during the mid-nineteenth century was fuelled by an overriding sense that 'archaeologists were hunting for the very beginnings of human history, as perceived in the light of sacred writings'. The spell of the primordial that was being woven around new discoveries in Mesopotamia is vividly evoked in Alfred William Hunt's poem 'Nineveh', recited in the Sheldonian Theatre at Oxford on 3 July 1851 (cited in Larsen xii):

> The Arab knows not, though round him rise
> The sepulchres of earth's first monarchies;
> … Cities arose – enchanted hall revealed
> Treasures untold by primal kings concealed:
> It is no dream, though such as dreams alone
> Could ever paint – but all is very stone
> Calm all and grey. – Before the entranced eyes
> The world's primeval palaces arise.

To summarise, the initial outcome of parallel advances in European prehistory and Oriental philology was not, it seems, to unify these regions into an enlarged and unified framework of historical enquiry. Rather it was to consign them to separate domains of historical knowledge, each with a distinct point of departure and each oriented around a different perception of the forces responsible for change in human societies. In terms both of substantive content and ethical overtones, there is a marked continuity between these opposed modes of historical perception and the earlier dichotomy of Customary and Roman Law in European juridical thought. What I am suggesting, then, is that, to a greater extent than is often realized, the political values and interests of the constitutional antiquarians may have shaped the development of modern archaeology and its cognate disciplines in the western Old World.[3]

HEARTS, MINDS AND MUSEUMS

Egypt must be remembered in order to know what lies in the past, and what must not be allowed to come back. (Jan Assmann 1997: 8)

In drawing together the threads of this discussion so far, I wish to consider a little more closely the retention of a 'rootless' Oriental past – one form of tyranny rising up, phantom-like, upon the ruins of another – and its role in the European imagination of political modernity. I have already noted, following Pocock, that the bonds between antiquarianism and constitutional law in Europe were effectively severed by an Enlightenment discourse that mounted the case for popular sovereignty in terms of reason, nature and the universal rights of the individual citizen. The transformation of subjects into citizens – that is, active participants in their own systems of government – is not, however, a solely intellectual or abstract process. As Dipesh Chakrabarty (2000: 11) observes, 'the "nation" and the political are also *performed* in the carnivalesque aspects of democracy: in rebellions, protest marches, sporting events' and so on. Enfranchisement is invariably based, not just upon commitment to abstract principles, but on a shared sense of past sacrifice that legitimates further sacrifices on the part of the individual for the benefit of the collective. Wherever it is said to exist, 'freedom' cries out for concrete forms of expression which, if they are to have force in the present, can only be drawn from the disturbed remnants of a shared past. Accordingly, a central challenge for democracy since the great revolutions of the eighteenth and nineteenth centuries (echoing the earlier challenges faced by Renaissance republicanism, which addressed them through a dialogue with ancient Greece and Rome) has been to resolve the paradox of its own, recent origins, by resorting to memories of a past that threatens to overwhelm it with the sense of its own fragility and ephemerality.

As Peter Hughes (1995) and others have noted, this dual project of remembering in order to forget would seem to account for the prominence of ancient ruins in the revolutionary literature, art and festivals of eighteenth century France. He recalls, in particular, Constantine de Volney's meditation on the ancient cities of the Orient as an allegory for the fall of European monarchy. *Les ruines, ou, Méditation sur les révolutions des empires* was published in 1791, in the wake of the French Revolution and translated into English in 1800. It relates the reflections of a traveller passing through the lands of the Near East during the declining years of Ottoman rule:

Hail solitary ruins, holy sepulchres and silent walls! … When the whole earth, in chains and silence, bowed the neck before its tyrants, you had already proclaimed the truths which they abhor; and confounding the dust of the king with that of the meanest slave, had announced to man the sacred dogma of Equality. (Volney, 1991: 1; from the 1890 English translation)

In Volney's premonition that the banks of the Seine and the Thames might one day become a landscape of monumental ruins, like those of the Nile and the Euphrates, Hughes detects a sense of nostalgia for what had barely begun to pass. Drawing upon Kubler (1962), he observes that ruins serve to commemorate past desires, offering 'a way of overcoming the absence of the past when it is limited to paper and ink or condemned to fading memory' (Hughes 1995: 284). Their materiality brings the past into the sensory domain of the present, even as their weathered and fragmented forms summon the sensations aroused back into a ruptured past.

Much of the imagery evoked by Volney was given tangible form in the festivals of the French Revolution which, as Mona Ozouf (1988: 9) has demonstrated, were 'an indispensable complement to the legislative system, for although the legislator makes the laws for the people, festivals make the people for the laws':

> Time was not merely the formal framework within which the Revolution took place; it was also the raw material on which it obstinately worked … The first thing to be done was to manifest the discontinuity brought about by the Revolution in the flow of time, to signify, quite unequivocally, that the era of the Republic was no longer the era of kings, and to mark this absolute beginning. (Ozouf 1988: 158–159)

There can be few more direct materialisations of this dual process of remembering and distancing than the Egyptian galleries of the Louvre (see also, Wengrow 2003). Andrew McClellan (1994: 7, 91–123) describes how, in its transformation from royal palace into modern museum (an 'imposing school' of the nation) the Louvre became a shrine to 'popular sovereignty and the triumph over despotism', shaping republican identity in a manner comparable to the revolutionary festivals. The Egyptian galleries opened in 1826, under the restored monarchy of Charles X (Humbert 1997), just as Thomsen, in the Copenhagen Museum, was organising the displays of European pots, tools and weapons that subsequently led to the recognition of a three-age structure for world prehistory. Displays of ancient, exotic objects were installed in the former apartments of the queens of France and organised didactically according to general themes: two galleries for royal funerary practices, one for precious items and materials, and a fourth for religious beliefs. The ceiling of the latter chamber was adorned with an allegorical painting portraying the transition from the decadence of tyranny to the rewards of enlightened government as *L'Étude et le Génie des arts dévoilant l'Égypte à la Gréce*. Contemporary oil paintings depict Napoleon Bonaparte during his conquest of Egypt in 1798, directing the excavation of royal mummies (whose unwrapping and dissection had been a popular spectacle on the streets of Paris since the seventeenth century; Aufrère 1990: 166) from their subterranean tombs (see e.g. Ikram and Dodson 1998: 67, figure 58; Humbert *et al.* 1994: 226–227).

Here, then, in the abandoned corridors of royal power, were laid to rest what Michelet called the 'vampires of the ancien régime', and Volney the 'men who devour the substance of others', proof concrete that the time of kings had passed full circle, and returned to its exotic source of origin. What had been forgotten in the midst of all this were the people of the Middle East, where the European powers now prepared to install a revitalised network of Arab kingdoms in place of a decadent Ottoman Empire.

CONCLUSION: THE FUTURE OF PREHISTORY IN THE MIDDLE EAST

In a recent survey of the textbooks used to teach American college courses on Western Civilisation (or 'Western Civ' as it's known), Daniel Segal (2000) suggests that the 'Near East' – including ancient Iraq (Mesopotamia) and Egypt – still tends to be represented not so much as a place (or series of places) but as a stage of global history. Specifically, it is made to stand for 'early civilisation': a transitional phase between the simple life of Stone Age peoples and modern civilisation in its Western, secular form. During that phase, so the story goes, human societies achieved some important technical advances (e.g. the invention of writing and monumental architecture) but at the expense of submission to exploitative, religiously motivated and economically dysfunctional regimes. The prehistories of Egypt and Iraq are not presented as histories of what happened to societies there before the appearance of kingship, cities and writing systems. Rather they are absorbed into a generic prehistory of all humankind, during which 'people' achieved the transition from a hunter–gather lifestyle to early farming societies. The Neolithic, in particular, is conceived as a crucial episode of economic development, which of course it was, but – like all human transformations – it was a lot of other things as well and these tend to be excluded (cf. Sherratt's 1995 critique of 'periodisation by stereotype' in archaeology and evolutionary theory). In this established narrative, a change in *economic* conditions precipitates a change in *political* relations, such that the overall transformation of coherent life-words (always simultaneously economic, political and ideological) is obscured from view, and a genuine long-term history of social power in the Middle East rendered inconceivable.

The conclusion seems, on the face of it, to be a depressing one. Instead of a prehistory rooted in temporal development and encompassing multiple trajectories of social and cultural change, students and the public at large are still, for the most part, being offered a pastiche: a symbolic prehistory of humankind, which also acts as a repository – or rather graveyard – for aspects of the present deemed 'pre-modern'. In the present climate, with 'civilisation' firmly back on the political and intellectual agenda of the West, the retention of this topography of values has particularly strong implications for the Middle East, which hardly need to be spelt out in detail. On a more positive note, accepting the reality of this status quo may provide suitably minded archaeologists working in that region with something approaching a 'conscious unity of purpose'; the purpose being to change or at least question it. The idea of prehistory in the Middle East remains, in more senses than one, a subversive and 'disorienting' one.

NOTES

1 I first presented the account that follows at a meeting of the Association of Social Anthropologists in Arusha, Tanzania. The theme of the conference was 'social qualities of time'. After the presentation, a number of participants informed me that they knew the part of the world I was referring to, or at least somewhere very like it. The suggestions, no doubt influenced by the conference setting, included regions of Ethiopia, Kenya, Egypt and Sudan. I was finally exposed by an ethnographer with some experience in the Middle East, who identified the site (in the north of Israel) to within a 5 km radius.

2 I am grateful to Paul Treherne for drawing my attention to Pocock's work.

3 I make no attempt here to address notions of, or appeals to, prehistoric times in Arabic historical thought (for a general introduction, see Khalidi 1994). A comparison with the European trends outlined here would be of enormous value, but is far beyond my competence (my thanks to Yossi Rapoport, Robert Hoyland and Jeremy Johns for helpful advice on this subject).

REFERENCES

Assmann, J. (1997) *Moses the Egyptian. The Memory of Egypt in Western Monotheism*, Cambridge, MA and London: Harvard University Press.

Aufrère, S. (1990) *La momie et la tempête. Nicolas-Claude Fabri de Peiresc et la 'curiosité égyptienne' en Provence au début du VIIe siècle*, Avignon: Éditions A. Barthélemy.

Braidwood, R.J. (1952) *The Near East and the Foundations for Civilization: An Essay in Appraisal of the General Evidence*, Condon Lectures, Eugene: Oregon State System of Higher Education.

Braidwood, R.J. and B. Howe (1960) *Prehistoric Investigations in Iraqi Kurdistan*, Studies in Ancient Oriental Civilization 31, Chicago: University of Chicago Press.

Cannadine, D. (2002) *Ornamentalism. How the British Saw Their Empire*, London: Penguin.

Cauvin, J. (2000) *The Birth of the Gods and the Origins of Agriculture*, Cambridge: Cambridge University Press.

Chakrabarty, D. (2000) *Provincializing Europe. Postcolonial Thought and Historical Difference*, Princeton: Princeton University Press.

Childe, V.G. (1936) *Man Makes Himself*, London: Watts & Co.

Daniel, G. (1950) *A Hundred Years of Archaeology*, London: Duckworth & Co.

De Morgan, J. (1896) *Recherches sur les origines de l'Égypte. L'Age de la pierre et les métaux*, Paris: Ernest Leroux.

Drower, M. (1985) *Flinders Petrie. A Life in Archaeology*, London: Victor Gollancz Ltd.

Foucault, M. (1972) *The Archaeology of Knowledge* (translated by A.M. Sheridan Smith), London: Tavistock.

Frankfort, H. (1932) *Archaeology and the Sumerian Problem*, Oriental Institute of the University of Chicago Studies in Ancient Oriental Civilization, No. 4. Chicago: University of Chicago Press.

Gut, R. (2002) 'The significance of the Uruk sequence at Nineveh', in *Artefacts of Complexity. Tracking the Uruk in the Near East*, J.N. Postgate (ed.), Warminster: British School of Archaeology in Iraq, pp. 17–48.

Hoffman, M. (1979) *Egypt before the Pharaohs: The Prehistoric Foundations of Egyptian Civilization*, New York: Knopf.

Hughes, Peter (1995) 'Ruins of time: estranging history and ethnology in the enlightenment and after', in *Time. Histories and Ethnologies*, D.O. Hughes and T.R. Trautman (eds), Ann Arbor: University of Michigan Press.

Humbert, J-M. (1997) *L'Egypte à Paris*, Paris: Action Artistique de la Ville de Paris.

Humbert, J-M., M. Pantazzi, W. Seipel, and C. Ziegler (1994) *Ägyptomanie. Ägypten in der europäischen Kunst, 1730–1930*, Vienna: Kunsthistorisches Museum.

Ikram, S. and A. Dodson (1998) *The Mummy in Ancient Egypt*, London: Thames and Hudson.

Khalidi, T. (1994) *Arabic Historical Thought in the Classical Period*, Cambridge: Cambridge University Press.

Kubler, G. (1962) *The Shape of Time. Remarks on the History of Things*, New Haven and London: Yale University Press.

Larsen, M.T. (1996) *The Conquest of Assyria. Excavations in an Antique Land, 1840–1860*, London and New York: Routledge.

McClellan, A. (1994) *Inventing the Louvre. Art, Politics, and the Origins of the Modern Museum in Eighteenth-Century Paris*, Cambridge: Cambridge University Press.

Mallowan, M. (1977) *Mallowan's Memoirs*, Collins: London.

Moorey, P.R.S. (2003) *Idols of the People. Miniature Images of Clay in the Ancient Near East*, The Schweich Lectures of the British Academy 2001, The British Academy, London: Oxford University Press.

Ozouf, M. (1988) *Festivals and the French Revolution* (translated by Alan Sheridan), Cambridge, MA and London: Harvard University Press.

Petrie, W.M.F. (1931) *Seventy Years in Archaeology*, London: Sampson Low, Marston & Co.

Pocock, J.G.A. (1957) *The Ancient Constitution and the Feudal Law. A Study of English Historical Thought in the Seventeenth Century*, Cambridge: Cambridge University Press.

Pope, M. (1975) *The Story of Decipherment, from Egyptian Hieroglyphic to Linear B*, London: Thames and Hudson.

Redfield, R. (1953) *The Primitive World and Its Transformations*, New York: Cornell University Press.

Schnapp, A. (1996) *Discovery of the Past. The Origins of Archaeology*, London: British Museum Press.

Segal, D. (2000) ' "Western Civ" and the staging of history in American higher education', *American Historical Review*, 105(3): 770–805.

Sherratt, A.G. (1995) 'Reviving the grand narrative: archaeology and long-term change', *Journal of European Archaeology*, 3(1): 1–32.

Stocking, G.W. (1987) *Victorian Anthropology*, New York and London: The Free Press, Collier Macmillan.

Trautman, T.R. (1992) 'The revolution in ethnological time', *Man* (New Series) 27(2): 379–397.

Ucko, P.J. (1968) *Anthropomorphic Figurines of Predynastic Egypt and Neolithic Crete with Comparative Material from the Prehistoric Near East and Mainland Greece*, London: Andrew Szmidla.

Volney, C.F. (1991) [1890; 1791] *The Ruins, or, Meditation on the Revolutions of Empires*, Baltimore: Black Classic Press.

Wengrow, D. (2003) 'Forgetting the *Ancien Régime*. Republican values and the study of the ancient Orient', in *Views of Ancient Egypt since Napoleon Bonaparte: Imperialism, Colonialism and Modern Appropriations*, D. Jeffreys (ed.), London: UCL Press, pp. 179–193.

CHAPTER 18

FIGURINES IN ACTION
Methods and Theories in Figurine Research

Peter F. Biehl

INTRODUCTION

Peter Ucko taught me two basic things about figurines: first, to study the evidence of their use before deposition and second to scrutinize the context in which the figurines were found. His thorough analyses showed me that in order to understand the creation, use and functions of figurines we have to make explicit use of social anthropology, ethnography and history in our archaeological analyses. It was due to his work that I began testing my method of contextual attribute analysis on figurines from ethnographic sources (Biehl 1999) in order to better understand their meaningfulness as symbolic material culture. In my study, I discovered patterns in the ethnographic record and began to look for similar patterns in the archaeological record. One such pattern is fragmentation. In this chapter, I will use fragmentation as a means of putting 'figurines in action' – that is, explaining how they may have functioned as communication conduits. I will also demonstrate how Ucko's major thesis, that 'Old World prehistoric figurines may not be homogeneous' (Ucko 1968: 443) and may have functioned in many ways, is still modern.

But before I do this, I will discuss how Peter Ucko's work swayed research on figurines of the European Neolithic. To start with, his groundbreaking work shifted analysis away from an almost exclusive preoccupation with fertility goddesses and magic. It is baffling that even today most archaeologists continue to automatically associate anthropomorphic figurines with cult and religious practices (Biehl 1997b, 2003). But what do we really know about cult and religion in prehistoric societies (Bertemes and Biehl 2001)? Can we still interpret anthropomorphic figurines as 'mother goddesses' (e.g. Gimbutas 1991) only because they depict female attributes and because we know of historically attested female goddesses?

What do we really know about figurines from ethnographic and historical sources (Ucko 1968: 420; Biehl 1999)?[1] Can we speak about dolls or toys only because we find ethnographic evidence of such use among the Lunda in Zambia (Cameron 1996: 18–42)? Can we identify ancestor cults because we have reports of figurines functioning as such among the Asante in Ghana (McLeod 1981)? Likewise, can we call every figurine an initiation device because informants tell us figurines were used in initiation rituals by the Turkana peoples in Kenya or the Tsongo in South Africa (Roumeguere and Roumeguere-Eberhardt 1960; Best 1993; Cameron 1996: 86–87, 95)?

If these sorts of analyses and interpretations form the basis of our research, then we have a problem. The vast majority of the figurines from Africa were collected as art objects (Biehl 1999) and – like most prehistoric European figurines – were found isolated (Ucko 1968: 66; Biehl 1996: 153–154; Biehl 2003: 341–344) and devoid of any context in which we can neatly insert them.

In their article, 'Rethinking Figurines', Conkey and Tringham highlight the importance of context. 'The lack of context for figurines in traditional analyses of later periods has been discussed by a number of recent studies', they write. But, they add, ' "context" in the case of these and other authors refers primarily to spatial context: the fact is that, as with the Upper Paleolithic figurines, the figurines are from the surface or have no exact provenance, or it is not known with what other kinds of materials they were associated' (Conkey and Tringham 1998: 28). Tringham was able to associate figurines with houses and pits in her research on Opovo and to show that 'these contextual and descriptive data provide crucial clues to the meanings and meaningfulness of material culture' (Conkey and Tringham 1998: 35). Marcus too has pointed out that 'to interpret figurines, archaeological context is crucial' (Marcus 1996: 291). But even with sound contextual information such as we have, for example, for the Oaxaca figurines in Mexico, Marcus stresses that

> without the sixteenth-century documents for the region, we might never have realized that their [the figurines] disappearance from the archaeological record probably had to do not simply with stylistic change or artifact popularity, but with the rise of a stratified society in which full-time priests monopolized the most important rituals involving ancestors. (Marcus 1996: 291)

The rise of the priests altered the household rituals women used to invoke the spirits of their ancestors using the figurines.

The best way to understand the meaning of figurines from archaeological, historical and ethnographic records is, as Peter Ucko suggested almost 40 years ago, to start with an interpretation of the figurines themselves (Ucko 1968: xvi). Given the astounding results of Ucko's work, it seems stunning that archaeologists who have studied figurines in the past have, for the most part, used two different approaches. The first was purely typological analysis – looking at one or several subjectively selected attributes of figurines through time and space (Neustupný 1956; Höckmann 1968; Kalicz 1970; Radunčeva 1977; Todorova 1980; Bartel 1981; Podborský 1983; Pogoševa 1985; Pokorna 1983; Vajsov 1984, 1990; Bánffy 1986; Konceva 1989; Milojković 1990; Rutkowski 1990; Konova 2004). The problem with this approach has been that it has not examined the figurines as a whole – a combination of all their different attributes. It has also not incorporated the functional meaning of the artifacts nor succeeded in setting them in an understandable context (Biehl 1996, 2003).

The second approach has tried to view the artifacts as representations of goddesses, dolls, toys and tokens of identification.[2] It has also interpreted them as forms of primitive contracts, part of birthing rituals, sexual imagery, ancestor cults, teaching devices, sorcery tools, magic, healing or initiation (Talalay 1983; Gimbutas 1991; Cauvin 1994). Most of these interpretations followed Ucko's suggestion for including ethnographical and historical analogies but have lacked grounding in typological and empirical–statistical analysis of the figurines themselves (Ucko 1968: 172–173; Biehl 1996b).

In addition to these two approaches, there are some new methods which might be called 'interpretative' (Biehl 2003: 44–50). Bailey in particular has studied figurines extensively and has come up with thought-provoking interpretations (Bailey 1991, 1994a, 1994b, 1996, in press; see also Conkey and Tringham 1998: 38–39). On the basis of his studies of figurines from northeast Bulgaria, he emphasised the idea of competition between households and the role figurines might have played. His early interpretations viewed the figurines as a simple expression of individual identity or 'individualisation'. Now, he has begun to analyse the way people use representations of human bodies to make socio-political statements and to understand their own identities and to negotiate their relationships to 'others' via figurines (Bailey in press).

Goodison and Morris point out that 'for the presentation of findings, the empirical method of the discipline has required that archaeologists proceed *from* the material evidence *to* their conclusions' (Goodison and Morris 1998: 9) and not the other way around, reminding us of a basic principle when dealing with symbolic material culture. In contrast, Marija Gimbutas' approach – 'argument by assertion' – is very problematical and, for this reason, has received much criticism (Conkey and Tringham 1995: 216, 1998; Meskell 1995; Biehl 1997a).

This chapter is about the possibility of analysing, reconstructing and 'reading' the symbolic meaning of anthropomorphic figurines within the theoretical and methodological framework Peter Ucko formulated and exemplified with his study of figurines. One way to do that is to study the decoration on the figurines, an approach I have published elsewhere (Biehl 1996). Another example is the fragmentation of figurines, a feature already noted by Ucko (1968: 68). Does fragmentation only represent accidental breakage or does it have a symbolic meaning and message? The basic question is what is the meaning of the fragmentation of anthropomorphic figurines and how can archaeologists analyse it? In addition, can we find evidence about the nature of belief systems and the relationship of people to the natural and supernatural world in prehistoric cognitive systems? And finally, can archaeologists apply analogy to overcome the fragmented evidence and information of the function and use of figurines inherent in the archaeological record by studying similar patterns within the ethnographic records?

In order to better understand these issues I will use an example which will exemplify the methodological groundwork of the study of anthropomorphic figurines from archaeological records.

FRAGMENTATION IN ARCHAEOLOGY

Breaking, bending, rendering useless or destroying artifacts is an important and well-documented phenomenon in European prehistory and protohistory. An enormous body of work from a wide range of topics, regions and time periods has been collected on the subject and numerous theories have attempted to explain why it occurred.[3] Clearly, the pattern was widespread and we see it appear and then disappear on an irregular basis until medieval times. Unfortunately, we still have no explanation for what it means. Part of the problem, I believe, is our way of interpreting the breakage and our obsession with identifying what both the fragmented parts and the fragmentation represented. Were they evidence of contracts, signs of initiation or fertility? Indications of death?

I believe we could greatly benefit by taming our passion for clear-cut answers and taking one step back. In other words, instead of looking at the end result, I suggest we look at the process of breakage and the transformation that occurred as a figurine changed from a whole to a collection of incomplete fragments. If we believe the breakage was intentional, then we must accept that the act of breakage involved communication. But of what sort?

I would like to begin by addressing the issue of communication in prehistory – or more precisely how prehistoric people used artifacts to communicate. I shall then discuss the mode of transmission of their knowledge and communicative skills and what we can do to understand these systems today. Finally, I shall present a theoretical and practical framework that will help us recognise, analyse and interpret such communicative acts.

In written publications, I have already clarified my belief that the high percentage of broken anthropomorphic figurines in the Southeast European Neolithic and Copper Age indicates that the figurines did not simply break, but were broken (Biehl 1996, 1997a, 1997b, 1999, 2000, 2003). Like creation, I believe destruction is a communicative act. And it must be added that these figurines were not simply broken and left as a fragmented whole. They were left incomplete, that is their fragmented parts were separated. Obviously, this creates a difficult problem for archaeologists, who are people who like to put broken pieces together to form a whole. From the moment these pieces were broken, I seek to demonstrate in this chapter, it became impossible to reunite them. Not only were the parts separated but the fragments took on new meaning: they could no longer be part of the same object. I shall contend that this was done as a deliberate and symbolic act known, understood and undertaken over a large area of Southeastern Europe and passed down from generation to generation.

The key element on which my thesis is based is the concept of 'context'. We are all aware of the difficult issues surrounding contexts and that easy-to-read contexts are more of a rarity than a norm (Conkey and Tringham 1998: 28). Fragments pose an especially difficult problem as their contexts are even more puzzling. Generally, there is little or no diagnostic information about their spatial provenance, chronological assignment or meaningful association with other artifacts or features. Sometimes, sadly, even when there is some existing context, archaeologists make the mistake of only studying portions of it. Usually, this is the portion that suits their narrow research interest or that helps prove their individual thesis. Again, in most cases, there is almost no context in which we can neatly insert the fragments and no diagnostic information to guide us. Our standard tools are virtually useless. And yet we have the fragments. The question is: what are we to do with them? I hope that we all agree that we cannot simply disregard them and label them unapproachable and incomprehensible. In order to include artifacts with little to no context in our study, I suggest the following (Figure 18.1).

We should begin to view each artifact as a context in itself. In other words, an artifact should be studied as a so-called 'closed find',[4] that is as a contextual structure of meaningful

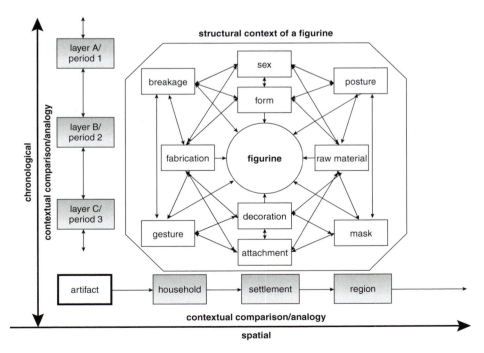

Figure 18.1   Schematic diagram of the attributes of a structural context of a complete figurine.

attributes, or a 'structural context'. With this as our theoretical framework, we can begin to recognise the system under which an artifact was created by conceptualising and then contextualising all discernible attributes of its structure. This procedure allows us to view the artifact as the physical end-product and the material reflection – or the 'coming into form/being' – of a vast variety of individual and collective decisions that were both practical and ideological. These decisions underscore and may help us read and reconstruct the cultural rules to which the individual maker of an artifact had to conform. In order to study these attributes and begin to see patterns in them, we must first separate all discernible attributes into the smallest of categories. That means chronological and geographical, material and ideological and even functional. This is what the method of contextual attribute analysis[5] does. It is based on the idea that each artifact should be viewed as its own structural context and that each artifact was made according to a code system. When all of the attributes have been analysed and compared, we can begin to understand the significance of an artifact and eventually of its fragments and gain insight into its hidden, symbolic 'language' and the communication system embedded in it. Once we accept the idea that such a code system may have existed within a prehistoric community, we must then decipher what roles the individual played, how the code was transmitted and what meaning(s) the breaking of an artifact carried.

Unfortunately, scientific works devoted solely to communication systems in prehistoric societies are quite rare. 'The lack of theories of social action and the lack of explicit use of social anthropology and history sources for thinking about the context of figurines has severely limited many of the interpretations of figurines' (Conkey and Tringham 1998: 40). Archaeologists have, therefore, had to rely on work generated by other social scientists, such as Habermas' communication theory, which has greatly influenced my research (Habermas 1983). Habermas' theory of communicative acts highlights the role of the individual in a society, stating that individual behaviour is often a reflection of social mores and patterns, or what he called the communication community. I have incorporated his ideas and used them as a starting point for my own research and writing on the role of the individual in prehistoric communication systems. Using information on the individual, I have then identified patterns in which groups of individuals behaved in a similar – or collective – manner (Biehl 2000). This, I believe, is a reliable method for conceptualising cultural patterns and communication systems.

I shall explain this new approach to interpreting fragments and provide some examples. I will begin with what I call 'fragmentation rules', that is, patterns I have found that help decode the symbolic meaning in the prehistoric communication system of the Southeast European Copper Age.

BREAKING ARTIFACTS: A CASE STUDY

My examples come from my studies of the Gradešnica–Krivodol culture complex in Western Bulgaria. The data I shall present here is based on the systematic coding of 381 clay figurines from 33 settlements. I used contextual attribute analysis on the basis of the structural context of an artifact in order to do the coding. The first step in analysing figurines was to separate the broken from the whole. Then, every gesture, gender characteristic or mask or decoration must be studied and seen in relation to each other. Breaks are as important as the state of preservation of the figurine. Complete figurines should be analysed first.

One of the biggest problems of working with fragments is sex.[6] One would think this would be obvious and that is precisely the problem. Too often, our certainty leads to errors. Generally, we assume a figurine with breasts or a pubic triangle/vagina or both is female and that a figurine with a penis is a male. Sometimes, a female is also identified by a swollen/pregnant abdomen and a male by a beard. When a figurine does not possess any of these discernible sex characteristics, it is called asexual. During the Neolithic and Copper Age periods in Southeastern Europe however, figurines with both breasts and penises have been found.[7] Such figurines create grave problems for archaeologists who work with fragments of figurines – normally the upper or lower portions. Generally, they base the sex of the figurine on what they have. But what about what they don't have? What if the missing portion of a figurine with breasts had a penis? Or what if a figurine with a penis also had breasts? Since so much about incomplete figurines is speculative, it seems logical to conclude that analysis must begin with complete figurines. Once the attributes of complete figurines known to be male, female, androgynous or asexual have been studied and classified through attribute analysis, then the more complicated study of incomplete figurines can be attempted in the same manner. This procedure is a crucial part and, for that reason, a new methodology for the analysis of figurines is indispensable and can best be seen by a brief look at the state of preservation of the figurines (Figure 18.2).

Next to the complete figurines,[8] I have differentiated the broken sections between a so-called potential breakage/point of fracture and non-potential breakage/point of fracture. The first notion includes breakage at physically weak parts of the figurine such as the extremities, neck etc. As a rule, a large percentage of the breakages – whether they were at these parts or others – has been attributed to the method of fabrication. But oddly, there are an equal number of fragments that have been broken at 'non-potential breakage points' as there are figurines with breakage in understandable, or potential, breakage points. By non-potential breakage point I mean a break at a strong part of a figurine's body, such as the hips (Figure 18.3).

In the Gradešnica–Krivodol culture complex, many figurines are broken in such a manner.[9] Another strong indication of intentional breakage is vertical breakage occurring at the mid-section of the body. We have several completely excavated settlements in Southeastern Europe of that period and it can be stated that missing or broken-off parts of the figurines were not found in the settlements.[10] This is a strong indication that at one point, the figurines were deliberately broken. It also indicates that the act of breaking held some significance and that, once they were broken, the fragments took on new significance. In other words, in terms of meaning, the fragments became and continue to be 'whole objects'.

But why were the figurines broken as they were? I believe the best way to answer this question is through contextual attribute analysis. I have attempted this on the figurines from the Gradešnica–Krivodol culture complex and have come up with the following results (Figure 18.4): Only the figurines with female attributes – breasts or vaginas – were deliberately broken. Non-potential breakages never occur on figurines with all male attributes. Moreover, we can only find it on figurines that are decorated and are standing with outstretched or downward directed arms.[11]

To me, this is a clear indication that breakage was not random. Guidelines existed and were followed. Only certain figurines were broken and, when they were, it was only at a certain place on the figurine's body. In the Gradešnica–Krivodol culture complex, the body parts that were found in most cases were the chest and stomach. In other words, the figurines were mainly broken – or at least the user tried to break them – at the genitals. At first glance, this would back up traditional interpretations that link figurines to fertility. But this is too facile and is undoubtedly only one facet of their meaning and function. To highlight this point, I would like to look at the body part most often found in settlements – the chest and stomach (Figure 18.5).

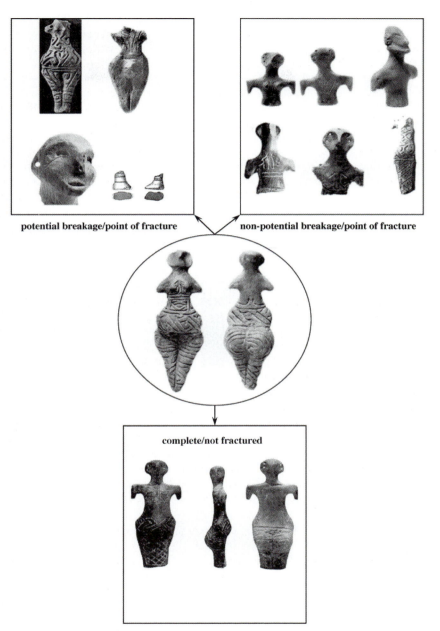

Figure 18.2   Schematic diagram of the three states of preservation of figurines from the Early Copper Age Culture Complex Gradešnica–Krivodol in Western Bulgaria.

Elsewhere, I have shown that fully decorated figurines – with elements of 'clothing', aesthetic ornamentation and symbols – are almost uniformly broken at the hips or genital zone (Biehl 1996, 2003).[12] I have also demonstrated that the chest and stomach sections of the Copper Age seem to have been the most important regions in terms of symbolic meaning (Figure 18.6). These areas are the most decorated and show a startling similarity

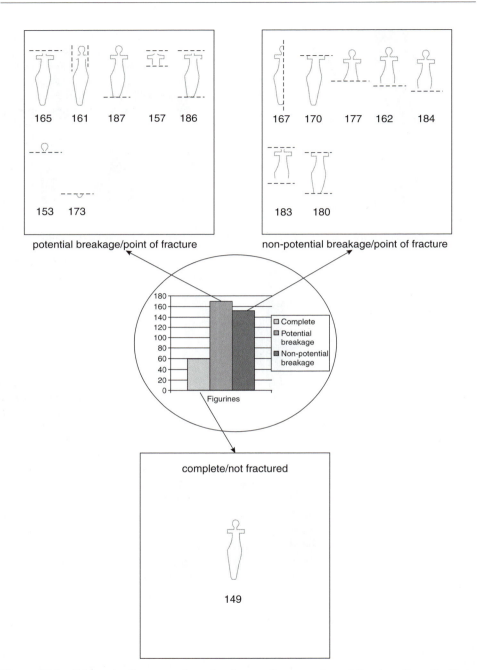

Figure 18.3   Schematic diagram and graph of state of preservation of figurines from the Early Copper Age Culture Complex Gradešnica–Krivodol in Western Bulgaria.

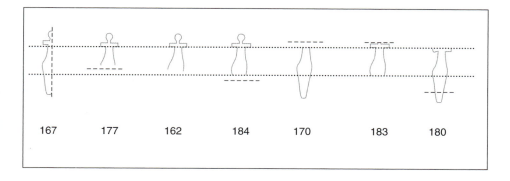

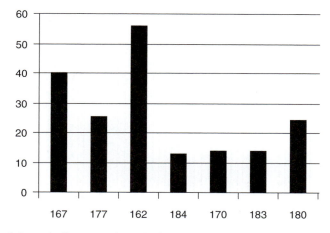

Figure 18.4 Schematic diagram and graph of state of preservation of deliberately broken figurines from the Early Copper Age Culture Complex Gradešnica–Krivodol in Western Bulgaria.

in the sort of symbols that could be placed on them. The torso was also the portion of the figurine that was kept in the domestic context after breakage. I believe that the symbolism on the figurines meant something to those who kept, saw and used them. Therefore, the figurines had more than just one ritual use. They maintained a value even after they were broken.[13] The value may have shifted, but clearly, they were kept in homes and brought something other than aesthetic pleasure to users. And whatever they meant, clearly, the figurines were used to establish some sort of exchange between individuals and the supernatural and individuals and their community.

We are just beginning to ask important questions like 'why some societies did manufacture figurines, whereas others did not'? (Ucko 1996: 304). It is clear now that 'the figurines do not occur in equal quantities (or forms) everywhere in Europe and the Near East from the Upper Palaeolithic to the Neolithic' (Conkey and Tringham 1998: 27). Hansen (2001) shows the importance of studying such a spatio-temporal distribution of figurines in the European Neolithic. He also points out 'the possible filiation between Palaeolithic and Neolithic figurines in Europe' (Demoule 2001: 281). On the basis of Hansen's article, Demoule highlights that 'the presence of figurines in certain regions (Balkans and Central Europe) and their absence from others (west Mediterranean Cardial Neolithic) suggests that there were differences in ideological and religious organization' (Demoule 2001: 281).

Figurine #	State of Preservation								Sex	Figurine Attribute Type																	Decoration			Decoration Area			Piercing			Standing Posture		"Leaning"		Location	
										"divided" standing									"divided" sitting				"undivided"																		
	162	161	184	183	157	186	180	167	B V/P 0/?	C	D	N	?	R	W	AL	Y	AQ	H	AJ	AR	AH	K	A	P	B	VS	v■0	?	1245	1247	?			?	1756	1772	1766	1793	FL	?
351	x								B	x																	1					?	A								?
355	x								B	x																	1					?		x						87	
367	x								B	x																	1					?		x							?
690	x								B	x																	1					?		x							?
352	x								?	x																			?			?		x							?
397	x								B	x																			?			?		x							?
629	x								?	x																			?				B						x		?
688	x								B	x																			?					x							?
313	x								B		x																2					?		x							?
344	x								B		x																1					?		x							?
316	x								B			x															2					?		x							?
317	x								B			x															1				x			x				x		87	
321	x								B			x															1					?		x							?
822	x								B			x															1					?	A							87	
656	x								B			x															1					?		x							?
423	x								B			x															1					?	A							59	
324	x								B			x															2					?	A								?
325	x								B			x															1					?	A								?
332	x								B			x																	?			?		x							?
335	x								B			x																	?			?		x							?
338	x								B			x																	?			?		x							?
661	x								?				?														6					?		x							?
474	x								B						x													x						x					x		?
379	x	x							?	x																	2					?	A								?
689	x	x							B	x																	1					?	A								?
384	x	x							B		x																	x					A							87	
326	x	x							B			x															1					?			?						?
327	x	x							B			x															1					?	A								?
328	x	x							B			x															1					?	A								?
330	x	x							B			x															2					?			?						?
331	x	x							B			x															1					?	A								?
336	x	x							B			x															1					?	A								?
354	x	x							B			x															2					?			?						?
413	x	x							B			x																	?			?			?						?
652	x	x							?			x															2					?		x							?
667	x	x							B			x															1					?	A								?
350	x	x							B				?														6					?			?						?
649	x	x							?									x										x						x				x			?
378		x	x						B	x																	14					?		x						99	
383		x	x						B	x																		x				?	A							59	
487		x	x						?		x																6					?			?					59+87	
353		x	x						B			x															1					?			?						?
366		x	x						B			x															1					?	A								?
365			x						B	x																	1					?		x							?
318			x						B			x															1				x		A					x		59	
333			x						B			x															1					?		x							?
349			x						B			x															2					?		x							?
655			x						B			x															1					?	A								?

Figure 18.5 Correlation diagram of state of preservation, sex, figurine type, decoration, piercing, posture and stability of clay figurines of the Gradešnica–Krivodol culture complex.

We are also just at the beginning of scrutinising 'why some societies appear to have many more figurines than others, and why the proportions of figurine sexes vary' (Ucko 1996: 304). The 'socio-cultural context' of the figurines in the European Neolithic and Copper Age has been described in many different ways. I think most archaeologists agree that the fifth millennium BC in Southeast Europe is characterised by production and population growth, an increasing degree of permanence in settlements and a social system of increasing complexity.[14] I believe that these processes were accompanied by and somehow expressed through the quantitative and qualitative climax in figurine production and use. This served to connect large areas with a symbolic communication system in which the figurines played a central role (Biehl 2003).

But we have not yet started to approach the fascinating question of gender or the fact that 'there is no evidence about sex/gender of the makers or of the audience for whom the

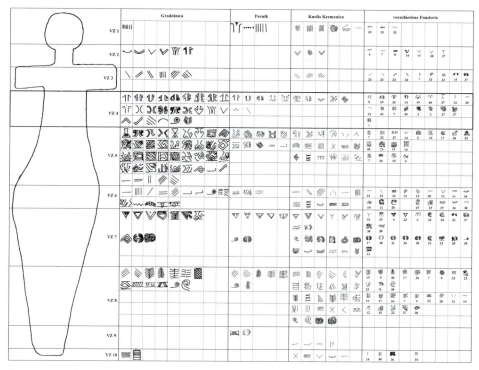

Figure 18.6   Correlation diagram highlighting the unbroken portion of figurines and the placement of design motifs of clay figurines of the Gradešnica-Krivodol culture complex.

images were intended, although this could also be investigated' (Ucko 1996: 303; Conkey and Tringham 1998: 36). In reviewing methods and theories in figurine research, I am convinced that

> the more we read about the meaning and role of visual imagery in anthropology and history, the more it becomes clear that archaeologists need to take into account the fact that there are certain to have been multiple perceptions and interpretations of the figurines by the prehistoric social actors themselves. (Conkey and Tringham 1998: 42; see also Haaland and Haaland 1996: 298; Ucko 1996: 301).

CONCLUSIONS

In summary, I believe the creation, transformation and destruction of figurines was a socio-ritual practice that was performed for specific reasons and according to known rules. The fate of a figurine, that is how it was made and what it was used for, is directly related to how it was decorated. Many of the figurines – both broken and whole, decorated and undecorated – have been found within the same archaeological context. Being deposited together indicates that they may have been used together and that their differences played a role in a complex belief system. Again, a whole figurine held one symbolic meaning, a broken one another. I would argue that the 'change' in the figurines – that is the existence of similar, yet not altogether the same forms – underscores this 'transformation'. In this case, the addition of the masks would also be included in the transformation – just another step as the figurine metamorphosed from one form of life/state of being to another. At first, such an interpretation may seem far-fetched. Luckily, it can be grounded in fact and in the contextual attribute analysis of the figurines and the results can also be proven through an empirical–statistical classification system.

But it seems clear to me that these representations and the variety in which they are found both broken and unbroken provide evidence of a complex thought system in which firmly encoded symbolism existed. In forming a figurine, someone took an abstract idea and transformed it into a representative object. They then used the figurines, or at least some of them, to express, capture and better understand life's most pivotal moments – birth, the importance of social relations, the need for food and, finally, death. Often the last stage in the creation of a figurine was its destruction. But before and even while a figurine was broken or destroyed, the symbolism of the whole and the fragment spoke to the people using it. The fragmentation of the figurine was just another communicative act that was embedded in a complex symbolic communication system in the Southeast European Neolithic and Copper Age. Studying these communicative acts can provide important and potentially fascinating insights into the belief systems of prehistoric societies.

ACKNOWLEDGEMENTS

I would like to thank Bob Layton for reading this text and for giving me insightful comments. Thanks are also owed to Eszter Bánffy and John Chapman who read and commented on parts of this chapter. Finally, I want to express my gratitude to Peter Ucko for the long discussion we had during the Euro-TAG meeting in Southampton in 1992. His enthusiasm for figurine research and his method of study influenced both my PhD dissertation and my further research greatly.

NOTES

1 Herein lies the only shortcoming of Peter Ucko's work. I absolutely agree with his statement that 'although in no case can exact equation be presumed, analogies between the contexts and features of the prehistoric figurines [...] and those of historic and ethnographic figurine complements do show the variety of possible reasons behind the manufacture of anthropomorphic figurines' (Ucko 1968: 443); and consequently that 'on the basis of more detailed and specific analogies with historic and ethnographic figurines it has been possible to suggest [...] some could well have been children's dolls, others initiation figures, other vehicles for sympathetic magic etc., etc.' (Ucko 1968: 444). But I think that although the main part of this work was 'entirely devoted to a study of the figurines themselves' (Ucko 1968: 16), the same groundbreaking and thorough attribute analysis Ucko did on prehistoric figurines could have been applied to the source of his analogies (Biehl 1999). But it is not. The work of collecting and reviewing the rich ethnographic and historic material can't be praised enough – it was this work that shifted analysis away from an almost exclusive preoccupation with fertility goddesses and magic. But methodologically it falls short by putting two seemingly inconvertible categories of structural entities of material culture side by side. If we don't work with the same empirical-statistically based methods such as attribute analysis – including all discernable attributes such as 'state of preservation, provenience, present whereabouts, material used for manufacture/techniques, arm-positions, position and shape of head, descriptions of breasts or penis, posture, buttock-protrusion, ornamentation, techniques for ornamentation and anatomical details' (Ucko 1968: 67) – on the subject *and* source of the analogies, it remains a disjoint approach (Biehl 1999).
2 For a detailed discussion and bibliography see Ucko 1968.

3 See Chapman 2000 for an extended bibliography.

4 The notion of the 'closed find' has been developed from Oscar Montelius' notion and definition of a 'secure find' as 'the sum of objects which has been found under such conditions that it can be assumed that they were deposited at the same time' (Montelius 1903; see also Eggers 1986: 91, 91–105; Trigger 1989: 157). Although Montelius focused on chronological questions, the epistemological potential of his conception of material context provides the groundwork to make inferences between material culture and the socio-economic and ideological-religious contexts of the societies that left it behind.

5 The notion 'contextual' used in this chapter has no connection to the so-called contextual archaeology (Hodder 1987). Its conception and meaning is clearly different from Hodder's definition of the context of an archaeological attribute as 'the totality of the relevant environment, where "relevant" refers to a significant relationship to the object – that is, a relationship necessary for discerning the object's meaning' (Hodder 1982a: 23, 27, 211; 1982b; 1985: 14; 1987: 4; 1991: 121–155; 1999). Although Hodder insists that a context is always 'situation specific', his conclusions are rather frustrating. His relativistic statement that context also depends on and varies with the dimensions of variation in similarities and differences being considered and with the questions being asked consequently leads to the conclusion that 'in many areas contextual archaeology can hardly begin until more data have been collected' (Hodder 1991: 146). Most important, the notion of context/contextual which I am applying in this chapter refutes Hodder's assertions that, first, 'an object out of context is not readable', and second, that 'in prehistoric archaeology, the further one goes back in time, so that the survival rates diminish, the more difficult it becomes to ground hypotheses in data' (Hodder 1991: 146). I present a new conception of context which includes 'artifacts out of context' which overwhelmingly form the archaeological record. For a detailed definition of this new conception of *context* and its application in the *contextual attribute analysis*, see Biehl 2003.

6 'Quantitative analyses of Upper Palaeolithic imagery make it clear that there are also images of males and that, by and large, most of the imagery of humans-humanoids cannot readily be identified as male or female' (see also Ucko 1968: 173–176; Ucko and Rosenfeld 1972; Biehl 1996: 162–163; 2003: 264–272; Conkey and Tringham 1998: 27).

7 A few examples of figurines with both breast and penis include Krivodol (Radunčeva n.d.: 68, figure 81), Kurilo Kremenica (Vajsov 1984: figure 20,7), Guinova Mogila (Petkov 1934: figure 244) and Antre Corycien (Marangou 1992: 364, figure 15); see also the figurines from Szegvár-Tüköves (Korek 1990, figurines IV and V).

8 In this diagram complete figurines are indicated with the attribute number 149.

9 See in figure 2 the attribute numbers: 177, 162, 184, 183; for vertical breakages that occur at the mid-section of the body, see attribute number 167.

10 In Bulgaria, see Drama (Lichardus 2000), Ovčarovo and Goljamo Delčevo etc. (Todorova 1982, 1986; Todorova and Vajsov 1993).

11 See figure 4, attribute types M, D and C.

12 Here I want to stress the importance of studying the different materials the figurines were made of (Biehl 2003: 256–275). In my work I have distinguished between the uses of clay and bone figurines, and the bone figurines seem to have had an entirely different use and function than the clay figurines. Their abstract and schematically represented expressions likely referred to the communicative actions practiced with the clay figurines. They do not appear to have been 'actively' used in these practices: they have never been broken. The bone figurines were lighter and seem to have had a more mobile use, meaning they were probably worn around the neck or sewn onto clothes (Biehl 2003: 376).

13 Conkey and Tringham make an interesting inference between the destruction of a house and other material culture: they write 'the destruction of a house was a deliberate and symbolic destruction of the house, perhaps at the end of a household cycle, at the same time as ensuring its continuity of visibility and presence through its mass of indestructible material. There are other aspects of the Eneolithic material record of south-east Europe in which the idea of "killing" but ensuring continuity could resonate, as seen from our material in Opovo: topping

up the pits with burned rubble, filling a well with burned rubble, breaking grindstones and placing them in the houses to be burned, breaking stone axes and placing them with figurines in pits – and the act itself of breaking figurines and depositing them in the fill of garbage pits and in the foundations of a house' (Conkey and Tringham 1998: 38). Another theory is John Chapman's theory of 'enchainment' and 'accumulation' (Chapman 2000). In a recent article he 'examined the possible explanations for fragmentation of artifacts and concluded that there is strong empirical evidence for deliberate fragmentation as a major means of affecting the social practice of enchainment' (Chapman 2001: 102).

14 Conkey and Tringham point out that 'archaeologists envision villages in which social differentiation and inequality, due to the differing demographic cycles of households rather than a permanent social ranking, were essential elements of social and economic action. Such differences among interpretations of the social-cultural context of the figurines obviously leads to very different interpretations of their meaningfulness' (Conkey and Tringham 1998: 37–38).

REFERENCES

Bailey, D.W. (1991) *The Social Reality of Figurines from the Chalcolithic of Northeastern Bulgaria*, unpublished PhD dissertation, Cambridge.

Bailey, D.W. (1994a) 'Reading prehistoric figurines as individuals', *World Archaeology*, 25: 204–222.

Bailey, D.W. (1994b) 'The representation of gender: homology or propaganda', *Journal of European Archaeology*, 2.2: 215–228.

Bailey, D.W. (1996) 'The interpretation of figurines: the emergence of illusion and new ways of seeing', *Cambridge Archaeological Journal*, 6: 291–295.

Bailey, D.W. (2005) *Prehistoric Figurines. Representation and Corporeality in the Neolithic*, London: Routledge.

Bánffy, E. (1986) 'Bemerkungen zur Methodologie der Erforschung vorgeschichtlicher figuraler Plastik', *Prähistorische Zeitschrift*, 61/2: 152–157.

Bartel, B. (1981) 'Cultural associations and mechanisms of change in anthropomorphic figurines during the Neolithic in the Eastern Mediterranean basin', *World Archaeology*, 13: 73–86.

Best, G. (1993) *Marakwet and Turkana: New Perspectives on the Material Culture of East African Societies*, Frankfurt am Main: Museum für Völkerkunde.

Biehl, P.F. (1996) 'Symbolic communication systems. Symbols on anthropomorphic figurines in Neolithic and Chalcolithic southeast Europe', *Journal of European Archaeology*, 4: 153–176.

Biehl, P.F. (1997a) 'Overcoming the "Mother-Goddess-Movement": a new approach to the study of human representations', in A. Vasks (ed.), Selected Papers of the Second Annual Meeting European Association of Archaeologists in Riga/Latvia (1996), *Proceedings of the Latvian Academy of Science*, Section A, No. 5/6, 59–67.

Biehl, P.F. (1997b) 'Buchbesprechung: Christina Marangou, Figurines et Miniatures du Néolithique Récent et du Bronze Ancien en Grèce', BAR International Series 576, Oxford 1992. *Saarbrücker Studien und Materialien zur Altertumskunde*, Bd. 4/5, 1995–1996: 273–292.

Biehl, P.F. (1999) 'Analogy and context: a re-construction of the missing link', in *Ethno-Analogy and the Reconstruction of Prehistoric Artefact Use and Production*, L. R. Owen and M. Porr (eds), Urgeschichtliche Materialhefte 14, Tübingen: MoVince Verlag, pp. 13–26.

Biehl, P.F. (2000) 'Das Individuum und die Kommunikationsgemeinschaft in der Vorgeschichte. Zum erkenntnistheoretischen Potential der kontextuellen Merkmalanalyse am Beispiel der frühkupferzeitlichen Menschenstatuetten Bulgariens', in *Monumentum Jan Rulf*, I. Pavlu and P. Sommer (eds), Památky Archeologické Supplementum, Praha: Academy of Science and Archaeological Institute, pp. 32–52.

Biehl, P.F. (2003) *Studien zum Symbolgut der Kupferzeit und des Neolithikums in Südosteuropa*, Saarbrücker Beiträge zur Altertumskunde, Bd. 64 (mit CD-ROM), Bonn: Dr Rudolf Habelt Verlag.

Bertemes, F. and P.F. Biehl (2001) 'The archaeology of cult and religion: an introduction', in *The Archaeology of Cult and Religion*, P.F. Biehl, F. Bertemes and H. Meller (eds), Budapest: Archaeolingua, pp. 1–11.

Biehl, P.F., F. Bertemes and H. Meller (eds) (2001) *The Archaeology of Cult and Religion*, Budapest: Archaeolingua.

Cauvin, J. (1994) *Naissance des divinités, Naissance de l'agriculture: La Révolution des Symboles au Néolithique*, Paris: CNRS Éditions.

Cameron, E.L. (1996) *Isn't s/he a doll? Play and Ritual in African Sculpture*, Los Angeles: UCLA Fowler Museum of Cultural History.

Chapman, J.C. (2000) *Fragmentation in Archaeology. People, Places and Broken Objects in the Prehistory of South Eastern Europe*, London and New York: Routledge.

Chapman, J.C. (2001) 'Object fragmentation in the Neolithic and Copper Age of Southeast Europe', in *The Archaeology of Cult and Religion*, P.F. Biehl, F. Bertemes and H. Meller (eds), Budapest: Archaeolingua, pp. 89–105.

Conkey, M.W. and R.E. Tringham (1995) 'Archaeology and the goddess: exploring the contours of feminist archaeology', in *Feminism in the Academy. Rethinking the Disciplines*, D.C. Stanton and A.J. Stewart (eds), Ann Arbor: University of Michigan Press, pp. 199–247.

Conkey, M.W. and R.E. Tringham (1998) 'Rethinking figurines: a critical view from archaeology of Gimbutas, the "Goddess" and popular culture', in *Ancient Goddesses. The Myths and the Evidence*, L. Goodison and C. Morris (eds), London: British Museum Press, pp. 22–45.

Demoule, J.-P. (2001) 'Archaeology of cult and religion. A comment, or how to study irrationality rationally', in *The Archaeology of Cult and Religion*, P.F. Biehl, F. Bertemes and H. Meller (eds), Budapest: Archaeolingua, pp. 279–284.

Eggers, H.J. (1986) *Einführung in die Vorgeschichte* (überarbeitete Neuausgabe), München and Zürich: Piper.

Gimbutas, M. (1991) *The Civilization of the Goddess*, San Francisco: Harper and Row.

Goodison, L. and C. Morris (1998) 'Introduction: exploring female divinity: from modern myths to ancient evidence', in *Ancient Goddesses. The Myths and the Evidence*, L. Goodison and C. Morris (eds), London: British Museum Press, pp. 6–21.

Habermas, J. (1983) *Moralbewußtsein und kommunikatives Handeln*, Frankfurt: Suhrkamp.

Haaland, G. and R. Haaland (1996). 'Levels of meaning in symbolic objects', *Cambridge Archaeological Journal* 6: 295–300.

Hansen, S. (2001) 'Neolithic sculpture. Some remarks on an old problem' in *The Archaeology of Cult and Religion*, P.F. Biehl, F. Bertemes and H. Meller (eds), Budapest: Archaeolingua, pp. 37–52.

Höckmann, O. (1968) *Die menschengestaltige Figuralplastik der südosteuropäischen Jungsteinzeit und Steinkupferzeit*, Hildesheim: Lax.

Hodder, I. (1982a) *The Present Past: An Introduction to Anthropology for Archaeologists*, London: Batsford.

Hodder, I. (1982b) *Symbols in Action. Ethnoarchaeological Studies of Material Culture*, Cambridge: Cambridge University Press.

Hodder, I. (1985) 'Postprocessual archaeology', in *Advances in Archaeological Method and Theory*, Vol. 8, M.B. Schiffer (ed.), New York: Academic Press, pp. 1–26.

Hodder, I. (1987) 'The contextual analysis of symbolic meanings', in *The Archaeology of Contextual Meanings*, I. Hodder (ed.), Cambridge: Cambridge University Press, pp. 1–10.

Hodder, I. (1991) *Reading the Past. Current Approaches to Interpretation in Archaeology*, 2nd edn, Cambridge: Cambridge University Press.

Hodder, I. (1999) *The Archaeological Process. An Introduction*, Oxford: Blackwell.

Kalicz, N. (1970) *Götter aus Ton, das Neolithikum und die Kupferzeit in Ungarn*, Budapest: Corvina.

Konceva, T. (1989) 'Kultplastik und Schmuck aus der spätneolithischen Siedlung bei Nova Zagora', in *Tell Karanovo und das Balkan Neolithikum*, Institut für Klassische Archäologie der Universität Salzburg (ed.), Salzburg: Institut für Klassische Archäologie (Schriftenreihe des Instituts für Alte Geschichte und Altertumskunde, Reihe 1, 7), pp. 43–63.

Konova, L. (2004) 'Kultfigurinen aus Ton aus dem Gebiet von Konevo, Kreis Elhovo', in *Von Domica bis Drama. Gedenkschrift für Jan Lichardus*, V. Nikolov and K. Bacvarov (eds), Sofia: Archäologisches Institut mit Museum der Bulgarischen Akademie der Wissenschaften, pp. 205–212.

Korek, J. (1990) 'Szegvár-Tüzköves. Eine Siedlung der Theiß-Kultur', in *Alltag und Religion. Jungsteinzeit in Ost-Ungarn*, W. Meier-Arendt and P. Raczky (eds), Frankfurt: Museum für Vor-und Frühgeschichte, pp. 53–66.

Lichardus, J. (2000) *Forschungen in der Mikroregion Drama 1983–1999*, Bonn: Dr Rudolf Habelt GmbH.

Marangou, C. (1992) *Figurines et miniatures du Néolithique Récent et du Bronze Ancien en Grèce*, Oxford: British Archaeological Reports (International Series 576).

Marcus, J. (1996) 'The importance of context in interpreting figurines', *Cambridge Archaeological Journal*, 6: 285–291.

McLeod, M.D. (1981) *The Asante*, London: British Museum Publications.

Meskell, L. (1995) 'Goddesses, Gimbutas and "New Age" archaeology', *Antiquity* 69: 74–86.

Milojković, J. (1990) 'The anthropomorphic and zoomorphic figurines', in *Selevac, a Neolithic Village in Yugoslavia*, R. Tringham and D. Krstic (eds), Los Angeles: Institute of Archaeology UCLA, pp. 397–436.

Montelius, O. (1903) 'Die Methode' in *Die älteren Kulturperioden im Orient und in Europa* I, Stockholm: Selbstverlag; Berlin: Asher in Kommission.

Neustupný, J. (1956) 'Studie o eneolitickén plastice' *Sbornik Národ. Muz. Praha*, 10.

Podborský, V. (1983) 'K Metodice a možnostem studia plastika lidu s moravskou Malovanou Keramikou', *Sbornik Praci Filozoficka fakulty Brnenske University*, 28: 7–93.

Pogoševa, A.P. (1985) 'Die Statuetten der Tripolje-Kultur', *Beiträge zur Allgemeinen und Vergleichenden Archäologie*, 7: 95–242.

Pokorna, Z. (1983) 'K interpretaci zenske neoliticke plastiky', *Sbornik Praci Filozoficka fakulty Brnenske University*, 28: 104–111.

Petkov, N. (1934) 'Materiali za prouchvane na predistoricheskata epokha v Balgariya', *Bulgarska Akademiya na Naukite, Izvestiya na Arkheologicheskiya Institut*, 8: 429–434.

Radunčeva, A. (1977) *Prehistoric Art in Bulgaria from the 5th to the 2nd millennium B.C.*, Oxford: British Archaeological Reports, B.A.R. Intern. Series 13.

Radunčeva, A. (n.d.) *Die prähistorische Kunst in Bulgarien, Fünftes bis zweites Jahrtausend v.u.Z*, Sofia: Sofia Press.

Roumeguere, P. and J. Roumeguere-Eberhardt (1960) Poupées de fertilité et figurines d'argile: leurs lois initiatiques', *Journal de la Société des Africanistes*, 30: 205–223.

Rutkowski, B. (1990) 'Prayer (adoration) gestures in prehistoric Greece', *Archeologia*, 41: 9–20.

Talalay, L.E. (1983) *Neolithic Figurines of Southern Greece, Their Form and Their Function*, PhD dissertation, Indiana University.

Talalay, L.E. (1993) *Dolls, Deities and Devices. Neolithic Figurines from Franchi Cave, Greece*, (Excavations at Franchi Cave, Greece 9), Bloomington: Indiana University Press.

Todorova, H. (1980) 'Klassifikacija i cislovoj kod plastiki neolita, eneolita i rannej bronzovoj epocha Bolgarii', *Studia Praehistorica*, 3: 43–64.

Todorova, H. (1982) *Kupferzeitliche Siedlungen in Nordostbulgarien*, Materialien Allgemeiner und Vergleichender Archäologie 13, München: Beck.

Todorova, H. (1986) *Kamenno-mednata epocha v Balgarija*, Sofija: Izdat. Nauka i Izkustvo.

Todorova, H. and I. Vaisov (1993) *Novo-kamennata epocha v Balgarija*, Sofija: Izdat. Nauka i Izkustvo.

Trigger, B.G. (1989) *A History of Archaeological Thought*, Cambridge: Cambridge University Press.

Ucko, P.J. (1968) *Anthropomorphic Figurines of Predynastic Egypt and Neolithic Crete, with Comparative Material from the Prehistoric Near East and Mainland Greece*, London: Andrew Szmilda (Royal Anthropological Institute Occasional Papers No. 24).

Ucko, P.J. (1996) 'Mother, Are You There?', *Cambridge Archaeological Journal*, 6: 300–304.

Ucko, P.J. and A. Rosenfeld (1972) 'Anthropomorphic representations in Palaeolithic art', *Santander Symposium*. Actes del Symposium Internacional del Arte Prehistorico: Santander: 149–211.

Vajsov, I. (1984) 'Antropomorfnaya plastika iz praistoriceskogo poseleniya Kurilo-Kremenitsa Sofijskogo okruga' *Studia Praehistorica*, 7: 33–64.

Vajsov, I. (1990) 'La sculpture anthropomorphe du site néolithique d'Oussoe près du village d'Asparoukhovo, dep. de Varna', *Studia Praehistorica*, 10: 103–141.

CHAPTER 19

OBJECTS OF THE PAST
Refocusing Archaeology

Fekri A. Hassan

A FOREWORD

It is only fitting that I dedicate this chapter to Peter Ucko, with whom I discussed the content when I was offered a position at the Institute of Archaeology at University College London (UCL). At that time, Peter was a dean at Southampton. Since then I have had many occasions to share my ideas with him whenever his overtaxing schedule allowed. The gist of this chapter is I hope in the spirit of Peter's quest in archaeology – to place archaeology well within the domain of contemporary society. His commitment to a comparative approach, to an inclusive world archaeology and to the political and social issues of managing archaeological heritage are worthwhile goals in a world upset by divisive national and sectarian pursuits, dehumanising inequities and the plunder and misuse of the archaeological past.

PREAMBLE

Archaeology today is a contested field. Its mission, goals and methods are in flux, and it is likely that a new generation of archaeologists will lead archaeology to a fresh horizon. However, no matter where archaeology goes it will be fed by subterranean currents that extend back in history to the dawn of humankind. It will also have to contend with its own past and its own archaeology.

In this chapter I hope to place contemporary archaeology within the stream of the history of knowledge to contrast contemporary archaeology with other domains of knowledge that dealt with ancient objects. I also hope to show that a primary focus on artifacts (and artifact-centred constructs) is too restrictive and that it is closely linked with a Euro-American industrial worldview. A revision of what we consider as the primary object of our study, and how we consider it, will, I contend, provide archaeologists today with a deeper understanding of the role objects of the Past play in shaping our world today and how they serve as an integral component of ideological beliefs and self-identity.

Today, with the end of modernity, objects of the past are pawns in various ideological/political campaigns. Archaeologists, situated within the domain of cross-cultural and transhistorical investigation, and, I hope, with the ability to reflect upon the human condition throughout time in various places, should be able to contribute to the making of the emerging global society. At the least, they should be able to confront and discredit claims by those who wish to distort, falsify or misinform others about our human past.

Archaeology, as history, can be a source of insights into what happened and why it happened. Both may alert us to the follies or shortsightedness of our present actions (Gilbert 1972). Not that we will find particular cases identical with our present situation, or that we can identify simple causal laws, but we can certainly infer common schemata and basic structural dynamics. More importantly, I think, archaeology provides us with a basis for examining the deeper layers of our cultural genesis and the evolutionary depth of our psyche and sociality. It can enable us to understand the power of objects, and the fundamental metaphors, tropes and genres that make us human.

OBJECTS OF THE PAST

In this chapter, I hope to elucidate the idea that '*Objects of the Past*' is the most fundamental concept in archaeology. I use Objects of the Past here to refer to artifacts, monuments, relics, antiques and antiquities. The specific terms used to refer to Objects of the Past are closely linked with the shifting focus of archaeological interests. I also use the word 'archaeology' as the study of the human past from material traces and their context.

My point of departure here is that Objects of the Past have been given different labels in the past (well before archaeology as a discipline began to appropriate such objects for its academic domain), and that archaeology today must begin to re-examine its own language, beginning with the commonly accepted term 'artifact' as a fundamental term in referring to the subject matter of archaeology. I argue that our starting point should be to regard the so called 'artifacts' and other material remains of the past (Objects of the Past) as a materialisation of human cognition within a social matrix. Objects of the Past have been from the beginning a material projection and actualisation of ideas that were socially communicated, debated, validated or refuted. A so-called 'Oldowan' chopping tool was not simply an artifact for some functional purpose, it was much more than that – a concrete thing in the world, subject to social transactions, although it originated in the mind of a maker. It is the dynamic interplay between the ideas of an individual, the created object and the ideas generated by social others concerning such an object that makes 'Objects of the Past' a keyhole for entering the social world of the human past.

A power of some sort was probably attached to such objects that contributed to killing animals, setting fire to forests and transforming food, stones and habitats. Objects, as such, are magical and powerful. Later in the human trajectory, objects could be deliberately made to influence the 'metaphysical' world, a dimension of the human mind, created in symmetry with the 'physical' world. Certain objects became the conduit of interactions between the two worlds. As objects pass from the present to the past, they undergo a change in their social significance. Some objects, by virtue of their affiliation with powerful persons or issues, become more powerful and potent as they make their way into the realm of the 'dead'. They become magical by virtue of transcending death and surviving loss, decay and degeneration. Not unlike nature, another main source of legitimisation, objects of the past are sources of empowerment. They establish order and direction and set boundaries and limits. It is not surprising in this context that the earliest monuments in Egypt and elsewhere welded temples, nature and cosmos in a single formulation.

With the emergence of state societies, it became possible to create monumental objects that were used to legitimise and give meaning to the lives of people in the world's earliest power blocs. Today, objects from forks and knives to skyscrapers still legitimate and give meaning to the present – they influence our perceptions of ourselves and others and shape our vision of the future. Objects of the past in our societies today also serve as a cultural armature of the present. They are sacred icons of culture, and the manifest testimony of our destiny. They are often embedded and signified within a matrix of discourse and ritual practices. Objects of the Past, however, are contested and created constantly to reconfigure the shape of our thoughts and the course of our actions. Each generation, with all its varied social groups, uses the past to position or reposition itself in the social arena. Through discourse and actions, the objects of the past lose or gain meanings. Certain objects, however, remain prominent as carriers of social messages, even though the content and intent of the message may radically change.

THE OBJECTIFICATION OF SELF

The self is the object first learned in the mirror.
(Paraphrasing Jacques Lacan, 1968)

Culture is a product not of coping with the environment, but of coping with the human mind in the presence of others. Our cognitive and psychological formulations are the outcome of an equilibration between an inner domain of mental operations and the perceptions of others and nature. We recognise an inner self as an anchor, a datum point and as a firm (malleable but not fluid) construct for organisation and action. The coherency and durability of the self is grounded in our biological heritage, a heritage acquired in turn from an evolutionary process of eliminating traits that hinder adequate perception, organisation and action.

The Self as a mental construct is apparently not restricted to any single group of people or a certain historical epoch (see discussions of Marcel Mauss's notion of self in Carrithers, Collins and Lukes 1985). It also appears that the Self is no more than a window to the deeper compartments of the mind, but it is a flexible aperture with many filters and special lenses. Access to the deeper mind is restricted and regulated in order to guarantee the internal integrity of the organism and maintain its operational adequacy.

Objects serve as props and landmarks of the Self. They are durable mnemonic devices that sustain a sense of stability and permanence necessary for action in a changeable and evanescent world of appearances, utterances and acts. Certain objects, especially those linked to the core cognitive formulations are likely to be singled out. Their survival is ensured in order to reinforce the fundamental mental structures. In as much as ritual serves to reiterate and strengthen mental structures and organisational categories, certain objects are also curated for the same purpose.

The conservation of the past, in objects, is essential for the persistence and stability of human coping strategies, but the creativity of the mind bars rigidity and ossification. Objects of the Past linked to the schemata of timeless nature, historical continuity, historical causality, and maternal [or generically paternal] belonging, and imbued with the comfort of familiarity, and the mystery of survival amid decay and death, are powerful icons in the dynamics of self. The creativity of the mind is necessary in dealing with perceptions that jar with its organisational and operative capabilities. It is also necessary in managing its own storehouse of information and organisational architecture to minimise chaos, disarray, heterogeneity, memory load and inefficiency. Accordingly, the Mind and its Self actively reconfigure their contents and structure continuously at the surficial level, and occasionally at a deeper level. The latter is likely to be marked by discontinuity and a change in image projected and perceived by others (personality). The Mind and Self engage in innovative and transformative processes by reference and through objects that serve as the currency for social selection (acceptance, rejection, modification). Certain objects are devalued and others perhaps brought into the social limelight. The course of human cultural evolution was shaped by the ancestral objects that informed and legitimised change.

Ervin Goffman (1956) sees the Self as a sacred object, treated with ritual and presented with care to others. The presentation of Self (deliberately or unintentionally) is achieved through speech and actions, using clothing, material acquisitions and settings to mark boundaries and set a stage for actions, and to convey status, social position, age, occupation and gender. The setting also serves to communicate schemata and social formulations in an act of personifying the Self (an embodiment of the Self as persona). The objects, the visible and declarative extensions of the Self, are the currency of human negotiations and interactions – the phenotypic manifestation of invisible processes. From this point of view they serve as the medium for acceptability or rejection. The rejection of persona (*persona non grata*) can lead either to a representation of persona for acceptability, a reorganisation of Self to conform to an acceptable persona or an elimination of the offender socially or physically, thus providing the operational basis for sociocultural evolution.

IMMORTAL OBJECTS: THE ENDURING SYMBOLS

Because they are durable, material items are the most stable kinds of symbols.
William D. Lipe (1984)

The human mind is capable of thinking of timelessness, but it also must situate itself in a world of movement and change marking the passage of time. There is a basic contradiction in the human psyche. The need exists to arrest time to prevent anxiety and cognitive processing and reprocessing, but the emergence of our species has been predicated upon our ability to cope rapidly with sensory data and even to alter the perceived sources of unpleasant or harmful inputs.

Death and bodily decay are potent markers of time and change. Death disrupts not only social relations and roles, but also undermines a pattern of belonging and the need for mental durability and persistence. Bodily decay alerts us to the passing of time, enhances our awareness of the termination of our allotted span and may interfere with our ability to continue to think or act as we used to. The death and decay of others, especially those close to us, are also 'ours' through a process of identification. By transforming the dead into a material proxy – a stelae or a stone, a statue, a wax mask (imago, the wax mask moulded upon the face of the dead ancestor kept in the wings of the *aula* of the family house) or a photograph, we hope to hold on to the deceased. To that object we can turn for an affirmation of who we are, as moulded by our relationship with the person, who has now vanished.

Perhaps our invention of the soul is no more than another attempt to conserve the Self, to *exist* beyond material existence. But even the soul may be given form and matter engaging in various deeds and activities. Our attitudes to death may vary historically and they do vary among cultures (Stone 1987: 393–410), but in death as manifest in its objects (orientation, superstructure, goods etc.) we affirm and sustain our visions of self and society. In New England, tombstones became more iconographically elaborate with the rise of individualism, and with confidence in social prosperity by the mid-eighteenth century; grinning skulls gave way to winged cherub's heads (Stone 1987: 408). Death may also be an occasion to mark norms and ideals through objects and rituals. We may also resurrect the dead on stamps, public statuary, renovated buildings, or reviving crafts to bolster a new sense of self and to remake society.

Death and decay manifest in ruins and age-worn objects (preferably set within an aesthetic setting of gardens and flowers or next to the sea), and if they are not smelly or messy, can heighten our feelings of the dramatic evanescence of moments of love, glory or happiness. They can mark moments of existential reflection, recharging the self or prompting a change of course. We may also attempt to conceal death and decay by insisting on newness, remodeling, adaptive use and renovation. The use of cosmetics to impersonate a desired self, to conceal blemishes and marks of age is congruent with attempts to banish decay and dilapidation from our objective surroundings. In the same manner order, beauty and harmony of our material environment is reflexive with the self.

ANCESTRAL OBJECT AND THE VALIDATION OF THE PRESENT

Its [Archaeology] subject is modern man ..., and its material is the work of man's hands.
Sir Leonard Woolley (1967)

Objects of the Past are ancestral. They are the roots of being and the basis for a kinship with parental sources of power that legislate what is right and what is wrong. These parental (ancestral) forces also punish and reward. The objects are the intermediaries between ancestors and their descendants. Visits to the shrines of long-vanished ancestors, saints or leaders reaffirm their power and our allegiance. The first official archaeological projects are evidently those undertaken in Mesopotamia and Ancient Egypt to restore and repair the shrines of gods and previous kings. A text from Mesopotamia gives the names of kings who had piously repaired the structure of a shrine called 'Tummal' (Lloyd 1987: 92).

The transition in certain human societies from certain modes of subsistence to others, often associated with political transformations, has been accompanied by a change in the nature of Objects of the Past. The rise of divine states, beginning with Ancient Egypt and Mesopotamia, was marked by the emergence of objects of power that gained their potency from supernatural sources, namely, stone monuments – stelae, pyramids, obelisks, temples, churches and mosques. The overlap between royalty, nobility and divinity in these states (regardless of their chronology) was the medium for the selection, development, preservation and conservation of icons of kingship and nobility that eventually assimilated the supernatural powers and later made it possible for these icons to represent kingship as an autonomous symbol of power.

Coming closer to the present, the search for England's antiquities in the sixteenth century is rather informative. Rejecting the papal claim to imperial authority in the West, Henry VIII asserted a regal power as legitimate as that of Constantine. The king's royal subjects were no longer permitted to regard the papacy as the source from which the English church was derived and sustained. One of the pioneers in the antiquarian search for a non-Roman church was John Bale, a passionate Protestant bishop and reformer. Rebelling against his monastic past, Bale repudiated everything Roman. John Leland, Bale's friend and collaborator, was commissioned in 1533 to search after 'England's antiquities' as royal chaplain and 'king's antiquary'.

The transformation from a state predominantly conceived in terms of religion to a state overwhelmingly centred on the person of king (initially still with religion and its objects as legitimising foundation) was associated with a change in the objects of state power. The beginnings may be traced back to the Renaissance when Greek and Roman sculptures of gods and goddesses in human bodies created a world that made palpable the break from the medieval, Christian world. Objects of worldly pleasure and beauty became the icons of the newly established power and social order (Kristeller 1961).

The culmination of this trajectory is evident in the rise of absolutist monarchy in later seventeenth century. Louis XIV (reign 1643–1715) artfully created a theatre of power and magnificence both in his own person, the performance of his court and the grandiose palace at Versailles. The statues of Apollo, god of the sun, legitimised Louis's claim not as the Sun King, but in reality as the Sun God – a reincarnation of Apollonian splendour and magnificence. Beauty, inspired by classical prototypes coupled with the sensual pleasures enjoyed by the leisured (secularised) classes, created an art in which classical themes and figures were transformed to convey sensuality and eroticism, as in the paintings of Boucher (1703–1770). This marks the emergence of a paradigm of objects of the past as objects of beauty and art, with the bodies of women (reflecting a masculine perspective and power) as one of its key elements. This marks the birth of Art History as a fundamental domain of Classical Archaeology.

In 1860, Heinrich Schliemann, whose father read him Homer on the Trojan War, began to look for Troy. In 1875, he declared that he found it at the ruins of Hissarlik in Turkey. Thomas (1979) presents Schliemann's work as that of a scientist, the first to establish scientific standards of archaeological excavations. If this is true, we may glimpse here the transition from the paradigmatic concept of objects as objects of art and beauty to objects of science and technology. It also marks a change in the nature of state power with significant implications for how Objects of the Past are deployed in the social arena.

ARTIFACTS AND THE INDUSTRIALISATION OF CULTURE

Modern archaeology defines itself in terms of the *arti-fact* – of that which is manufactured by man. Assemblages of artifacts exhibiting similarities in form and manufacture are *industries*. The term *culture*, that once referred to refined, *cultivated* manners characteristic and worthy of the city-dweller (f.L. *civitas* (*civis* citizen)) became now conflated with industry. Objects of ancient technology entered and dominated the Objects of the Past. Objects of the Past also celebrated *progress* (technological turned moral). They legitimise the man-made society – the fulfilment of historical destiny, marking a transition from following the will of God to working within the laws of human historical change. This outlook runs through the doctrines of Vico, St Simon, Comte and Karl Marx. In addition, the progress of society was legitimised in the context of 'evolutionary' progress in nature, well articulated by Charles Darwin (1859). In parallel to the emergence of an archaeological schema grounded in *Objects of the Technological Past* (superimposed on *objets d'art*), the skulls of human ancestors were ranked along a progressive trajectory ending with the intelligent, wise, knowing man (*Homo sapiens*).

Museums and exhibits emerged within this context to celebrate science and technology, the new god of the Industrial civilisations. The museum became the temple where objects of science and technology were icons of a new era. In archaeology, science became the prevailing paradigm in prehistory during the 1960s, although it has subsequently been rejected in some quarters, under the heading of 'post-processualism'.

KITSCH AND CULTURE

One can say, indeed, without serious fear of contradiction that archaeology – and more particularly prehistoric archaeology, which makes no demands on literary scholarship – has established itself as one of the few forms of entertainment at once harmless and equally acceptable to all grades of society.

Grahame Clark (1973: 252)

Today, archaeology as an academic discipline receives a marginal support from governments, foundations and public agencies. Gifts and donations from corporations and patrons are limited but are especially important for museums. The change in patronage and the prevalence of an academic/scientific ethos has allowed many archaeologists to tackle issues that are not directly related to the acquisition of beautiful objects for private or museum collections – a practice, however, that has not altogether disappeared. Fancy museum exhibits catering to the enchanting qualities of treasures, gold, power and mystery still draw millions of visitors to museums and exhibits and can be successful commercial enterprises (The Treasures of Tut-Ankh-Amun, Ramsess II and the Gold of the Pharaohs exhibitions, just to mention a few capitalising on Egyptian heritage).

The support for archaeology today is also not separable from tourist visits to archaeological sites at home and abroad. Travel has become one of the major industries creating a legitimate channel within modernity for the romantic impulse. Regulated tours provide a safe encounter with Objects of the Past in an exotic setting briefly arranged between air-conditioned bus stops and luxurious hotels. Travel also provides a taste of being 'rich and famous', and, through an encounter with 'backward' nations, offers a sense of superiority and legitimisation of the European style. Objects of the Past are extricated from the people that created them, and definitely from their descendants, and are used to glorify a past associated with mighty kings, great lords and superb artists. The tourist industry also fosters the manufacture of replica and reproductions of Objects of the Past. Reproductions are often selected and modified to appeal to the taste of foreign tourists. In the process, the past acquires a new identity. Acquisition of Objects of the Past for their artistic and antique value (and industrial acquisitive sentiment feeding on ancestral aristocratic proclivities) also provides a basis for looting, smuggling and illicit trade in antiquities.

The neo-romantic fascination with Objects of the Past engenders a genre of media reporting, journalism and travel books. Short of visiting sites abroad, one watches or reads with consuming interest, accounts of adventure, exotic objects and strange places intermixed with fanciful and fantastic stories of spells, occult forces and mysterious powers. Objects of the Past have also become a source of rich iconography of a 'New Age' cult that reaches to a new habitat for the Self – nature and antiquity.

On the other hand, the regimentation, conformity and discipline of modern technological society, apparently a necessity in meeting the needs of millions of people crowded in urban islands, as well as the lack of faith in the governments, seems also to have fostered cynicism and detachment. With no sacred bonds to the ancestors, the state, God or country and not even a strong attachment to family, anomic responses include whimsy and a lack of reverence to cultural patrimony. The Sphinx in Las Vegas captures the iconography of this attitude, so does the Mona Lisa with a moustache.

The end of modernity coincides with the transformation of industry, the hegemony of information technology and a shake-up of the eighteenth-century nationalism. The challenge to traditional nationalism comes both from the emergence of ethnic identities on the one hand and the call for globalisation on the other. Ethnic movements provide minorities in nation-states with a legitimacy grounded in the category of 'people' and 'ancestry'. It invokes the sentiments of the 'tribe' and is not without the production of Objects of the Past [and native languages] as flags of ethnic identity and legitimacy. Folk crafts are also revived or invented to link the present with the past.

Liberation movements, such as those behind the emergence of nation-states in Afrolasia, have adopted non-Western ideologies and have also looked to Objects of the Past to flag and authenticate their actions. Struggles by Egyptian nationalists to ban the treasuries of Tut-Ankh-Amun from being exported to England (a struggle they won) marked the beginning of the road to independence from the British occupation. The mausoleum of the leader of the Egyptian nationalists, Saad Zaghloul, and his statues in Cairo and Alexandria are an adaptation of the Pharaonic style. The statue of the Renaissance of Egypt, in Pharaonic style, represents Egypt as a woman next to a sphinx. The memorial for Egyptian soldiers killed in the October War is modelled after a pyramid (Hassan 1998). In Africa, a state was named after its major ruin – Zimbabwe. In China, the significance of archaeological discoveries to political ideology is clearly evident. In addition, the tension in Afrolasian countries between native scholars and foreign archaeologists concerning access to sites and archaeological materials continues and is not likely to diminish in the near future. (For a brief, cogent review see Clark 1973: 257 ff.)

The emergence of new identities may at times also be linked with the destruction or removal of objects that legitimise or proclaim an objectionable past. In countries with a rich history or multi-ethnic or diverse religions or sects, politicians and power-brokers manipulate a variety of objects of the past to further their goals. The destruction of a mosque in India (Hassan 1995), the debate over the archaeological excavations in Jerusalem and the conflicting attitudes toward Pharaonic monuments among Islamic fundamentalists are important issues in the archaeological arena (Hassan 1998).

THE GLOBAL IMPERATIVE

If prehistory may be said to serve its highest social purpose in helping to promote human solidarity, one should never forget that societies are composed of individuals.

Grahame Clark (1973: 264)

The emergence of the idea of 'people' must now take its place in the evolutionary trajectory of the group that individuals identify with. The family and the community are the real units where we engage in face-to-face interactions. Beyond that level, associations are consolidated by imaginary bonds through ancestral descent, a common history, a common language, a shared religion or a specific geographic setting: the supra-local group as an idea (an abstraction) that assumes validity, authenticity and legitimacy through a communality of speech, rituals and objects. Common ancestry, a transmutation of the blood parents backwards to a common parent, is one of the most central notions in the making of group identity – the ancestor may be an actual great-grandparent or grandparent, a fictive human ancestor, a naturalistic ancestor or a supernatural ancestor. A god is conceived as a parent (in Heaven). All the believers are accordingly brothers and sisters. In Christianity and Islam, the first great religions to proclaim the universal brotherhood of humankind, all human beings are descended from Adam and Eve. A country is also conceived within the same metaphorical schema as the motherland or fatherland. The language of a nation is the mother tongue. The destruction of the idols that belonged to various tribes by the Prophet Mohammed was not just a proclamation of monotheism, but it was also an obliteration of ethnic schism. The obliteration of the religious Objects of the past of specific tribes and its replacement by a single object of pilgrimage – the Qaba – reinforced the unity of humankind in Islam. The differences between people in Islam were not predicated upon racial origin or language, but on piety and devotion to the principles of Islam – equality, compassion and social justice.

The rise of European nationalism was closely linked with military conflicts between European nations and military occupation of countries in Africa, Asia and the Americas. Patriotism and chauvinism led millions of young draftees to slaughter on the battlefield. Political propaganda dehumanised the enemy and promoted stereotypes that justified brutality and murder. The peoples outside Europe were generically considered barbarous, cruel, stupid, lazy, illiterate, filthy, undisciplined, godless and lustful. These were the generous descriptions. Edward Spitzka in an article in *American Anthropologist* published in 1903 suggested that the brain weight of a Zulu was between that of a gorilla and the European scientist Cuvier (Pandian 1985: 82).

Architecture, art and archaeology promoted nationalism and Western supremacy, and ignored or denigrated the achievements of ethnic minorities or the poor working classes who belonged to people from Black Africa, Eastern or Southern Europe, or even from the poor enclaves in Western Europe.

The erosion of the legitimacy of the nationalist state is now rivalled by a return to ethnicity and religion. The two provide an answer to the deep need for belonging and are rooted in the fundamental affiliation to an ancestral group (ethnicity) and to a religion (Christianity or Islam) that bonds people together in a new pact against the tyrannies and injustice of modern states. The resurgence of ethnicity and religionism are potentially divisive. The idea of a common humanity has never been more appropriate or practical than at present. Philosophers have occasionally conceived this 'outlandish' notion, especially when commerce brought peoples from different tribes, clans or nations together. It was conceived of by some Roman philosophers. Marcus Aurelius viewed himself as a citizen of the world. It was conceived and articulated as the central vision and mission of Christianity and Islam, and, before the emergence of nationalist states in Europe, it was eloquently expressed by philosophers and historians. Globalisation and a common humanity again became a viable notion in the aftermath of the European nationalist wars and as a result of the benefits of global trade (see Earley 1997 for an overview of social evolution and the current planetary crisis).

Michael Ignatieff (1986: 139) makes a plea for a global society united in belonging to a fragile green and blue earth – a new object of belonging that can save us from a century of total war when the object of our belonging was the nation. Ignatieff calls for a 'language adequate to the time we live in'. 'We need words to keep us human', he reiterates (Ignatieff 1986: 141–142). From the vantage point of this chapter, we need objects to keep us human, to make us one and to legitimise and authenticate our common humanity. Archaeologists have a lot of work ahead of them. The critique of capitalism, the debates concerning explanatory devices and stances, the agonizing self-criticism largely confined to professional journals, books from prestigious university presses and meetings held in luxurious hotels, should give way to a common vision of the ultimate mission of archaeology as a social activity engaged in the making of the future from the relics of the past. It is remarkable that anthropology and archaeology working within nationalist and even racist paradigms have produced evidence for a common biological ancestry and a common human cultural heritage. The diversity of human cultures represents but variations on a common theme, a common experience and a common fate. The flame of civilisation has been passed from place to place; the ideals of justice, peace and love have been repeatedly spoken by visionaries, prophets and common folk.

Eric R. Wolf in his masterful book *Anthropology* concluded, 'We have asserted and demonstrated the unity of man in the articulation of the cultural process; to deny these links with our past and present is to put blinders on our vision, to retreat to a narrower adaptation, to turn our backs to what we may yet become' (Wolf 1974: 96).

SUMMARY AND FINAL REMARKS

In this chapter, my primary objective was to redefine the subject matter and scope of archaeology by drawing attention to the recent historical construction of the notion of 'artifacts' which became, along with its (industrial) semantic and semiotic fields, the domain of archaeological investigations. Earlier concepts of what I call here 'Objects of the Past' as 'sacred' objects and 'artworks' persist and are confined primarily to religion and art history.

The fundamental notions implied in the concept 'Objects of the Past' are based on the premise that objects of the past are integral to the making of Self and society by virtue of their durability, functionality, transformative potential and presence in the world 'independent' of transient human bodies and events. Invested with ancestral human signatures, Objects of the Past are a magical link between the past and the present. They serve as an armature of the present and launching pads of the future.

By recognising the inclusive concepts of 'Objects of the Past' archaeology is liberated from its industrial straightjacket and enabled to take its place as a social inquiry into the role of Objects of the Past in human affairs. Refocussing archaeological investigations in this way dissolves the contrived attempts to repair the apparent rift between so called 'tangible' and 'intangible' heritage and provides a unified intellectual paradigm for mobilising archaeological knowledge in resolving contemporary social issues. The change in focus comes also with a new horizon of engagement with the present and future. The Feminist movement and globalisation have forced archaeologists to engage in debates on gender, ethnicity and identity. This welcome change in topics of interest has to be buttressed by a paradigmatic shift in the core concept of archaeological materials. This will enable archaeology to take the lead in opening domains that address other pressing issues of grave consequences for human welfare and survival, such as depletion and pollution of resources, water scarcity, civic rights and governance, spirituality and religion, and ethics.

REFERENCES

Carrithers, M., S. Collins and S. Lukes (eds) (1985) *The Category of the Person*, Cambridge: Cambridge University Press.

Clark, G. (1973) *Archaeology and Society: Reconstructing the Prehistoric Past*, New York: Barnes & Noble.

Darwin, C. (1859) *On the Origin of Species by Means of Natural Selection, or, The Preservation of Favoured Races in the Struggle for Life*, 1st edn, 1st issue, London: J. Murray.

Earley, J. (1997) *Transforming Human Culture: Social Evolution and the Planetary Crisis*, Albany: SUNY Press.

Gilbert, A.N. (ed.) (1972) *In Search of a Meaningful Past*, Boston: Houghton-Mifflin.

Goffman, E. (1956) 'The nature of deference and demeanor', *American Anthropologist*, 58: 475–499.

Hassan, F.A. (1995) 'The World Archaeological Congress in India: politicizing the past', *Antiquity*, 69: 874–877.

Hassan, F.A. (1998) 'Memorabilia: archaeological materiality and national identity in Egypt', in *Archaeology Under Fire: Nationalism, Politics and Heritage in the Eastern Mediterranean and Middle East*, L. Meskell (ed.), London: Routledge, pp. 200–216.

Ignatieff, M. (1986) *The Needs of Strangers*, New York: Penguin.

Kristeller, P.O. (1961) *Renaissance Thought: The Classic, Scholastic and Humanist Strains*, New York: Harper and Row.

Lacan, J. (1968) *The Language of the Self*, Baltimore: Johns Hopkins.

Lipe, W.D. (1984) 'Value and meaning in cultural resources', in *Approaches to the Archaeological Heritage*, H. Cleere (ed.), Cambridge: Cambridge University Press, pp. 1–11.

Lloyd, S. (1987) *The Archaeology of Mesopotamia: From the Old Stone Age to the Persian Conquest*, London: Thames and Hudson.

Pandian, J. (1985) *Anthropology and the Western Tradition: Towards an Authentic Anthropology*, Prospect Heights: Waveland Press.

Stone, L. (1987) *The Past and the Present Revisited*, London: Routledge and Kegan Paul.

Thomas, D.H. (1979) *Archaeology*, New York: Holt, Rinehart and Winston.

Wolf, E.R. (1974) *Anthropology*, New York: Norton.

Woolley, L. (1967) *Digging Up the Past*, London: Pelican Books.

CHAPTER 20

THE MULTIDISCIPLINARY STUDY OF AGRICULTURAL ORIGINS
'One World Archaeology' in Practice?

David Harris

A PERSONAL PRELUDE

In celebrating Peter Ucko's manifold contributions to archaeology in its widest sense, it is perhaps appropriate for me to offer some thoughts on a topic that is not one of his 'own' but through which I encountered first his name, and then himself: the origins of agriculture. I had joined the staff of the Department of Geography at University College London (UCL) in 1964, having already, under Carl Sauer's influence at Berkeley in the late 1950s, responded enthusiastically to his 'invitation to study the various lines of evidence as to the growth of the agricultural arts' (Sauer 1952: 103–104). In the middle 1960s, I was assessing current literature on plant domestication and the origins of agriculture and among the many papers I then read for the first time was one entitled 'Predynastic developments in the Nile Valley' by Arkell and Ucko (1965). Arkell's name I already knew, but 'Ucko' was unfamiliar. It sounded intriguing, even mysterious. Was this author an Egyptian, perhaps a Nubian, colleague of Arkell's? Enquiry soon revealed that, far from being a denizen of a distant land, 'P. J. Ucko' was a very near neighbour indeed – lecturer in the UCL Department of Anthropology, a modest stone's throw from my own office in the Foster Court building. I sought him out, and thus made an academic acquaintance who was to become a close friend of (thus far) four decades.

The seminal event that revealed, at least to me, that in many ways Peter and I were on the same academic 'wavelength' was the first international meeting of the 'Research Seminar in Archaeology and Related Subjects' which he had founded. The theme of the meeting was 'The Domestication and Exploitation of Plants and Animals' and it took place at the Institute of Archaeology (adjacent to UCL) in May 1968. It brought together a galaxy of scholars from many disciplines and led to the impressively prompt publication of a 581-page volume that was to exert an enduring influence on its subject (Ucko and Dimbleby 1969). During the memorable two days of the meeting I came to appreciate how completely committed Peter was to a worldwide and multidisciplinary vision of archaeology and anthropology. This chimed with my own academic outlook, which was born of a geographer's sense of the unity of the Earth and nourished by opportunities, while an undergraduate at Oxford and a graduate student at Berkeley, to take courses in geology, world ethnography, anthropology/archaeology and botany, as well as geography.

The resounding success of the 1968 meeting was followed, in December 1970, by an even more ambitious international meeting of the Research Seminar, also held at the Institute of Archaeology, on the theme of 'Settlement Patterns and Urbanization', which in turn gave birth to a 979-page volume with 91 contributors (Ucko et al. 1972). The scale, intellectual quality and success of these two seminar meetings flowed from the breadth of Peter's academic vision, his energy, his powers of persuasion and his organisational and editorial skills. He continued to display these qualities throughout his subsequent career in Canberra, Southampton and back at UCL, most particularly in the *One World Archaeology* (*OWA*) series of thematic volumes that he launched after the first World Archaeology Congress (WAC) at Southampton in 1986.

ONE WORLD ARCHAEOLOGY

OWA is the now familiar acronym for the series of books that Peter launched and sustained, and which, under his guidance, brought within its scope a uniquely broad range of themes that have profoundly changed how archaeology is perceived and practised. Above all, it has helped transform archaeology into a genuinely worldwide subject – a point emphasised by Nicholas Saunders (2004) when, in reviewing the recently launched magazine *Current World Archaeology*, he stated 'The rise of world archaeology has been one of the great advances over the past 20 years, ever since Peter Ucko's ground breaking conference in Southampton in 1986'.

The phrase 'One World Archaeology' (OWA) epitomises Peter's vision of the scope and role of archaeology in the modern world, but its meaning is not self-evident. Rather, it can be said to have multiple meanings; indeed, one of the virtues of the phrase is that it is creatively ambiguous. It certainly conveys a sense of unity and comprehensiveness, but what, more precisely, does it mean? When I try to unravel the ambiguity, three distinctive but not mutually exclusive connotations suggest themselves. First, and perhaps closest to Peter's own conception, is the idea of encompassing all the world's peoples and their cultures and involving them both in their 'own' archaeology and in the broad enterprise of 'archaeology and related subjects' that he first put into practice in an international context in the 1968 seminar. Second, and intimately linked to the first meaning, is the connotation that archaeology is actively part of our world, not an arcane pursuit of obscure evidence of the dead, of little relevance to the interests and concerns of the living. This means that archaeology cannot, and should not try to, avoid involvement in present-day ethical and political issues, especially those on which the activities of archaeologists impinge directly, such as the question of whether human remains and items of material culture should be 'repatriated' from museums and other collections to the nations, areas or people from which they came, or the wider-related question of 'who owns the past?'. And uniting the first and second meanings of OWA is the aspiration that, if archaeology is practised according to them, it will foster greater cross-cultural understanding in the world as a whole.

The third connotation of OWA that seems to me to be distinctive is perhaps more literal than the other two, but is likewise comprehensive. It proceeds from a vision of our planet as a physical whole that has witnessed humanity's emergence, worldwide dispersal and creation of kaleidoscopic cultural diversity. It invites archaeologists to approach the evidence of past human behaviour comparatively and thematically, and, while not underestimating the importance of culture- and site-specific research, attaches great significance to the search for higher-level explanations of major cultural changes, such as the emergence of modern humans and the development of sedentary life, agriculture and urban civilisation. And it works towards a unified history of humanity. It is this third manifestation of what is conveyed by OWA that I find most compelling, and that I propose to explore more fully in the rest of this chapter, by examining the familiar, much debated but still poorly understood theme of 'agricultural origins'.

Like research on early human evolution, study of the origins and early development of agriculture has been, from its beginnings in the nineteenth century, a multidisciplinary endeavour. Cynics might say that both fields of study try to compensate for inadequate direct evidence by building untestable hypotheses on meagre data, but that would be to underrate the power of the multidisciplinary and comparative methods they employ to investigate specific questions. This can be illustrated by examining some aspects of the history and present state of research on agricultural origins.

EARLY RESEARCH ON THE HOMELANDS OF CULTIVATED PLANTS AND DOMESTIC ANIMALS

The earliest enquries focused not on agriculture itself but on the questions of where, and to a lesser extent when, plants and animals were domesticated. As early as 1805 the great German geographer and polymath Alexander von Humboldt remarked, in his *Essai sur la Géographie des Plantes* (1807: 28 [my translation]) that 'The origin, the first homeland, of the plants most useful to man and which have accompanied him from the remotest epochs, is a secret as impenetrable as the first dwelling place of all domestic animals'. This state of general ignorance persisted for another 50 years, until the Swiss botanist Alphonse de Candolle published the first account of the origin of cultivated plants in his *Géographie botanique raisonnée ou Exposition des Faits principaux et des Lois concernant la Distribution géographique des Plantes de l'Epoque actuelle* (de Candolle 1855: 809–993). In 1882 he produced what he described as 'an entirely new and more extended work' entitled simply *Origine des Plantes cultivées*, which appeared in an English translation two years later (de Candolle 1882, 1884; quotation on page v of the English version). De Candolle's treatment of the subject was comprehensive and explicitly multidisciplinary; he even listed and evaluated in an introductory chapter his 'Methods for discovering or proving the origin of [cultivated] species' as those of 'Botany', 'Archaeology and Palaeontology', 'History' and 'Philology' and argued that they should be 'combined and estimated according to their relative value' (1884: 8). Thus he established the conceptual framework and working methods of a new branch of science that was worldwide in scope, comparative in its approach, and committed to the critical use of diverse sources of evidence. The *Origin of Cultivated Plants* was to have a profound influence on later students of plant domestication, notably the Russian botanist and plant breeder Nikolai Vavilov who transformed the field of study – by studying it in the field – in the first half of the twentieth century (see Vavilov 1997 and later in this chapter).

The significance of de Candolle's contribution is even more apparent when it is measured against the only (remotely) comparable work of the late nineteenth century: Victor Hehn's *Kulturpflanzen und Haustiere in ihrem übergang aus Asien nach Griechenland und Italien sowie in das übrige Europa – historisch-linguistische Skizzen* (1870), translated into English and published in 1885 as *The Wanderings of Plants and Animals from their First Home*. Hehn was a German classicist and philologist, and although he described his book as an 'historico-linguistic sketch' it was in fact a substantial pioneering study of the origins and dispersals of (some) cultivated plants and domestic animals species by species. It is not as analytical, critical of its sources, or, being concerned mainly with introductions into the Mediterranean world, as geographically comprehensive as de Candolle's great work, but it is nonetheless a remarkable achievement. However, judging by the barbed comments made by both authors they had little respect for each other's efforts: de Candolle remarks (1884: 28) that 'I cannot help smiling when, at the present day, savants [Hehn?] repeat well-known Greek and Latin phrases, and draw from them what they call conclusions. It is trying to extract juice from a lemon which has already been repeatedly squeezed', and according to Hehn's translator, J.S. Stallybrass, 'Professor

Hehn thinks that of late years the Scientist has had too much his own way, that it is time for the Historic and Philologic methods to come into play, and have their say' (1885: ix). So much for interdisciplinary collaboration – despite the fact that both authors acknowledged that their 'conclusions' were based on multiple lines of evidence!

By the beginning of the twentieth century, areas of origin of many cultivated plants and rather fewer domestic animals had been broadly defined and some evidence assembled of when and by what means they were dispersed, but the questions of just *how* domestication occurred and agriculture began had attracted very little attention. Charles Darwin had published in 1868 his seminal study of *The Variation of Animals and Plants under Domestication*, and in it had speculated briefly but presciently about how 'The savage inhabitants of each land … would … take the first step in cultivation by planting … near their abodes … useful plants … improved varieties [of which] would sooner or later arise. Or a wild and unusually good variety of a native plant might attract the attention of some wise old savage, and he would transplant it, or sow its seed' (Darwin 1868: Vol. I, 309–310). Darwin's interest in domestication focused, however, on changes induced by artificial selection rather than on where, when and how plants and animals had been domesticated in the past.

It was practical interest in plant breeding and crop improvement that fostered, in the early twentieth century, a new approach to the origins of cultivated plants. It was then that Vavilov defined the 'where' question in terms of 'centres of origin', and brought to bear on it the knowledge he had acquired by first-hand observation during his many plant-collecting expeditions in Asia, Africa, Europe and the Americas for the Soviet All-Union Institute of Plant Industry (and its predecessors) in Leningrad (Hawkes 1990: 4; Dorofeyev and Filatenko 1992: xix–xx).

CENTRES OF ORIGIN

Although de Candolle does refer to 'centres' of agriculture 'whence the most useful species were diffused' (1884: 3), it was Vavilov who fully formulated the concept (Harris 1990: 8–11). He first defined a series of centres in 1926 in his *Studies on the Origin of Cultivated Plants* (published in the same volume in both Russian and English), and although he dedicated it to the memory of de Candolle he criticised the latter's assumption that the area in which the wild relatives of a cultivated plant occur is its 'native country'. He did so on two grounds: one, the wild relatives were not necessarily the progenitors of the cultivated forms and two, many species were not known outside cultivation. He regarded varietal diversity in cultivated plants as the best guide to their likely areas of origin and defined his centres according to where such diversity was greatest. In his first map he delineated five such centres: Southwestern Asia (including northern India), Southeastern Asia (essentially eastern China, Korea and part of Japan), the Mediterranean basin, Abyssinia and the mountains of Mexico and South America, but in later publications he increased the total. He also distinguished between primary and secondary centres of diversity and pointed out that because evolution continued in time and space the diversity of a crop plant was sometimes greater in its secondary centre, distant from the primary centre in which it had originated. Secondary centres commonly occur in continents or smaller regions to which the crops concerned were introduced long after they were domesticated. The diversity found in the secondary centres often relates to factors other than the antiquity of their cultivation, whereas in a primary centre it is interpreted as the consequence of domestication and prolonged human selection within the centre (for a recent analysis of the factors responsible for secondary areas of crop diversity, with examples drawn from Africa, see Pickersgill 1998).

Vavilov did not only distinguish between primary and secondary centres of varietal diversity. He also inferred that the primary centres were the homelands or centres of origin of most cultivated plants, and, by extension, of 'primeval agriculture' (1926: 218–220). De Candolle had also made this latter assumption – it is implicit in the 'General Remarks' with which he introduces the *Origin of Cultivated Plants* where he briefly describes 'Primitive Agriculture' (1884: 1–7) – but Vavilov's exposition is much more detailed and explicit. He argues that 'mountainous districts, being the centres of varietal diversity, were also the home of primeval agriculture', that 'in locating the centres where the cultivated plants have originated we come near to establishing the principal homesteads of human culture', and, in a final bold statement which shows how his thinking was far ahead of his time, he refers 'the origin of the cultivated plants to the remotest past for which the usual archaeological periods of five or ten thousand years are but a short term' (1926: 219, 244).

By explicitly linking the three concepts of centres of varietal diversity, centres of origin of cultivated plants and primeval agriculture and by portraying the centres as spatially discrete areas in the first version and subsequent revisions of his world map, Vavilov exerted a profound and enduring, but ultimately negative, influence on the thinking of later scholars concerned with agricultural origins. I have discussed this influence in some detail elsewhere (Harris 1990: 11–15), particularly its impact on Western scholars after the Second World War, notably Portères (1950, 1962), Sauer (1952), Burkill (1953), Harlan (1971) and Hawkes (1983), and will not follow that intellectual trail again here. It is sufficient to emphasise how strongly the Vavilovian concept, and geographical pattern, of centres of origin constrained research on the beginnings of agriculture in the second half of the twentieth century. This is particularly true of its reinterpretation by Harlan (1971), which gave primacy to just three 'nuclear' centres (Southwest Asia, North China and Mexico) and consigned much of the rest of the world to the status of 'non-centres'. This reinforced the already widespread assumption that agriculture had begun earlier in the nuclear centres than elsewhere – with the result that research in other regions of the world was discouraged.

In 1990 I suggested that 'the mental template of the Vavilovian concept of centres of origin' had distorted research on agricultural origins and that we needed to focus 'on the evolutionary history of individual crops and regional crop associations' in order to 'gain a better understanding of how and when agriculture emerged and developed in different regions of the world' (Harris 1990: 15). Since 1990 there has been a welcome move in that direction, as research in regions outside the Vavilovian centres has increased and begun to generate evidence of independent trajectories of plant domestication and early agriculture, for example in tropical West Africa (Neumann 1999; D'Andrea *et al.* 2001) and eastern North America (Smith 1992, 2001a). Likewise, new research within some of the Vavilovian centres (but outside Harlan's three nuclear ones) has produced comparable evidence, for example in southern India (Fuller *et al.* 2004) and highland Papua New Guinea (Golson 1997; Denham *et al.* 2003, 2004). Thus, some 50 years after Western scholars began to be influenced by Vavilov's concept of centres of crop diversity, transmuted by him and others into centres of origin of crops and thence of agriculture, it is at last being replaced by one of multiple areas of local domestication and agricultural beginnings.

It is clear that the studies by Vavilov and other twentieth-century scholars of the distribution and evolution of cultivated plants strongly influenced the way in which agricultural origins were conceptualised. In contrast, early studies of the ancestry of domestic animals, which were undertaken by such German scholars as Keller (1909, 1913), Antonius (1922), Hilzheimer (1926) and Klatt (1927), were much less influential. They were less concerned with the concept of centres of origin and the results of their investigations were not integrated with the studies of cultivated plants (although Sauer did offer an integrated interpretation in his 1952 synthesis). The lack of integration of the two fields of study was no doubt partly due to the fact that none of these early German publications was translated into English, unlike the works of Hehn, De Candolle and Vavilov. It was not until 1963 that a general study of the history of domestic animals was published in English, by Frederick Zeuner, who was well aware of the need to bring zoological and archaeological evidence more closely together and 'to present it as a whole' (Zeuner 1963: 10). His example was followed by later students of animal domestication, for example Herre and Röhrs (1973), Clutton-Brock (1981) and Helmer (1992), and zooarchaeology (of which the study of animal domestication is only one part) is now firmly established as a sub-discipline in its own right. However, the tradition of treating it and its sister sub-discipline of archaeobotany (or palaeoethnobotany) as separate realms of knowledge remains strong, partly because each sub-discipline quite properly requires specialised expertise and training. Nevertheless, it is regrettable that the synthesis of archaeobotanical and zooarchaeological data is not routinely attempted in local- and regional-scale studies of the beginnings of agriculture. At global and continental scales there is a greater readiness to try to integrate the plant and animal data, as is evident in several of the numerous, mainly edited volumes on the origins and spread of agriculture that have been published since 1990, for example Cowan and Watson (1992), Gebauer and Price (1992), Price and Gebauer (1995), Smith (1995), Harris (1996a), Piperno and Pearsall (1998) and Price (2000).

NEW DIRECTIONS IN INTERDISCIPLINARY RESEARCH: THE IMPACT OF NOVEL TECHNIQUES

The foregoing commentary on early studies of the origins of cultivated plants and domestic animals shows that investigation of the subject has from the start been a multidisciplinary undertaking. It is also apparent that there is a need for closer integration of the evidence derived from the disparate fields on which the subject draws. In recent years this need has become more imperative as new sources of evidence derived from the application of novel techniques have become available. Most obviously relevant is the application of such techniques to the identification and dating of plant and animal remains from archaeological sites, for example by means of parenchyma, phytolith, and starch-grain analysis, and the direct radiocarbon dating of very small organic samples by the AMS (accelerator mass spectrometric) technique. But other new methods of investigation, notably DNA analysis of living populations of domestic animals, crops and their wild relatives, are also yielding results of great significance for the study of agricultural origins.

AMS radiocarbon dating

Since its inception in the 1980s (Gowlett and Hedges 1986; Harris 1987), AMS dating has increasingly replaced the conventional radiocarbon method as the standard technique for dating archaeologically recovered plant and animal remains. Because it can be applied to extremely small (< 0.3 g) samples it has greatly expanded the range of organic materials that can be dated, which now extends to such microscopic structures as phytoliths, pollen and starch grains. Increased use of the AMS technique has been accompanied by more widespread citation of dates calibrated in calendar years before present, thus facilitating the chronological correlation between sites and between regions that is a prerequisite for worldwide comparative investigation of the beginnings of agriculture.

Parenchyma, phytolith and starch-grain analysis

The micromorphological techniques of parenchyma, phytolith, and starch-grain analysis are also playing an increasingly important role in agricultural-origins research by providing evidence of types of previously disregarded organic material that are both relevant in themselves and capable of generating illuminating comparisons with data derived from more conventional analyses of such macroscopic remains as seeds and bones.

The technique of *parenchyma analysis* was developed by Hather (1988, 1991, 1994, 2000), who showed that plant parenchyma and vascular tissues preserved by charring could be identified, sometimes to species level. The soft-tissue remains of vegetatively reproduced root and tuber crops survive less well in archaeological contexts than the seeds of cereals and of fruit- and nut-bearing trees, and parenchyma analysis has provided a new means of investigating the role of root and tuber cultivation, principally in the tropics where such crops are staples in many traditional agricultural systems. Using this technique, Hather and Hammond (1994) were for example able to identify manioc (*Manihot esculenta*) at the Preclassic Maya site of Cuello in Belize, and Hather and Kirch (1991) demonstrated the pre-Columbian presence of sweet potato (*Ipomoea batatas*) in central Polynesia, and the technique is beginning to be more widely applied, for example in India (Fuller *et al.* 2004: 126).

Since the 1980s, *phytolith analysis* has been transformed from an experimental technique pioneered by a few enthusiasts, notably Piperno (1988) and Pearsall (Pearsall and Piperno 1993), into a mainstream specialism that is now being applied in many different archaeological and environmental contexts. Phytoliths are silicified particles of plant tissue that retain the shape of individual cells and can be identified to the level of family, genus and sometimes species. They are resistant to decay and occur widely in soils and sediments in tropical and temperate environments. Phytolith analysis is particularly valuable in research on the origins and early development of agriculture in humid tropical environments where plant macro-remains tend to survive archaeologically less well than in drier tropical and temperate environments.

The technique has so far contributed most to knowledge of early cultivation in the American tropics, much of which has been brought together by Piperno and Pearsall in their book on the origins of agriculture in the lowland Neotropics (1998). Since then, Piperno and Stothert (2003) have published evidence for domesticated squash (*Cucurbita* sp.) at two Early Holocene archaeological sites in southwestern Ecuador, using phytolith size as the criterion of domestication (based on data they acquired by measuring a large collection of wild and domesticated species). Also, Piperno has shown that phytolith analysis can yield new insights into the prehistory of root and tuber cultivation by identifying phytoliths diagnostic of two tuber crops of the lowland root-crop complex – arrowroot (*Maranta arundinacea*) and leren (*Calathea allouia*) – recovered from rockshelter sites in central Panama, which suggests that they were probably being cultivated in the early Holocene, prior to *c.* 7000 BP (Piperno and Pearsall 1998: 213–217). Farther south, in temperate South America, phytoliths of maize and domesticated squash have been identified at a mid-Holocene site (Los Ajos) in the wetlands of southeastern Uruguay (Iriarte *et al.* 2004). These finds, together with starch-grain evidence for the presence of maize and other crops (see later in the text), suggest that cultivation began much earlier than previously thought in this part of South America, which has long been designated a non-agricultural region of 'hunter–gatherers'.

Phytolith analysis has not yet been widely applied in research on agricultural origins in the Asian and African tropics, but some investigations have been undertaken. In central China for example, Zhao (1998) has recovered rice phytoliths from successive levels in a cave site

(Diaotonghuan) south of the middle Yangzi which, he argues, provide evidence of wild-rice exploitation in the Late Palaeolithic (*c*. 12,000–11,000 BP) and the cultivation of domesticated rice by the beginning of the Neolithic, but both the dating of the site and determining whether the phytoliths are from wild or domestic rice remains problematic. Farther north in China, Rosen and her Chinese colleague Zhao Zhijun are using phytolith analysis to investigate early agriculture in the Yiluo basin south of the Huanghe (Yellow) River, where their preliminary results indicate that although foxtail millet (*Setaria italica*) was the main Neolithic crop, rice was also cultivated this far north before the end of the period (Rosen 2001/2002). In Southeast Asia and tropical Africa the potential of phytolith research is also beginning to be explored. For example, at the Kuk swamp site in highland Papua New Guinea analysis of changes in the types and abundance of banana (*Musa* and *Ensete* spp.) phytoliths suggests that Eumusa bananas, formerly thought to have originated in mainland Southeast Asia, were domesticated in New Guinea and subsequently dispersed to Southeast Asia, a conclusion independently supported by genetic research (Lebot 1999: 621–622; Denham *et al*. 2003). In addition, in West Africa *Musa* (not *Ensete*) phytoliths recovered at the site of Nkang in Cameroon have provided evidence (disputed by Vansina 2004) that bananas were being cultivated as early as *c*. 2500 BP (Mbida *et al*. 2000, 2001, 2004).

Starch-grain analysis is a potentially valuable technique because starch grains occur in plants in a wide variety of forms, can be diagnostic to genus and sometimes species level, and survive in a variety of depositional environments (Cortella and Pochettino 1994). It is developing into a useful method for investigating past plant use, particularly through the recognition that starch grains are commonly preserved in residues on stone tools and other implements (Hall *et al*. 1989; Loy 1994), but more study is needed of the decomposition of starch grains in soils (Haslam 2004).

Pioneering research in the field has been carried out in Australia and Melanesia (Fullagar *et al*. 1992; Barton *et al*. 1998; Therin *et al*. 1999), where, for example, starch grains from the taro genus *Colocasia* have been identified in residues on stone tools of early Holocene age in highland Papua New Guinea and of late Pleistocene age in the northern Solomon Islands (Loy *et al*. 1992; Denham *et al*. 2003). Starch-grain analysis is also beginning to generate evidence relating to early agriculture in the American tropics. For example, at the rockshelters in central Panama already mentioned, where phytolith evidence was found of the root crops arrowroot and leren, Piperno and her colleagues have studied starch grains from grinding stones excavated at one of the sites (Aguadulce) and identified them as from maize and three members of the root-crop complex: arrowroot, manioc and yam (*Dioscorea* spp.) (Piperno and Holst 1998; Piperno *et al*. 2000). The grinding stones came from preceramic horizons at the site dated to between 7000 and 5000 BP and thus provide early direct evidence of root-crop cultivation in the American tropics. Also, in the Orinoco valley, Venezuela, Perry (2004) has used starch-grain analysis to examine the relationship between stone-tool type and function. And in temperate South America analysis of starch grains identified as from maize kernels, fruit rinds of *Cucurbita* squash, *Phaseolus* sp. beans and *Canna* sp. rhizomes have been recovered at three mid-Holocene mound sites (Los Ajos, Isla Larga and Los Indios) in the wetlands of southeastern Uruguay, indicating early cultivation of introduced crops in a region previously considered to have been non-agricultural in pre-Hispanic times (Iriarte *et al*. 2004).

Analysis of phytoliths and starch grains is becoming increasingly important in research on agricultural origins because they extend the range of potentially identifiable organic materials below the macroscopic level (as does the much longer-established technique of pollen analysis) and because they survive in a wide variety of depositional contexts including soils, sediments and stone tools. But because they are so small it is generally more difficult to determine whether they represent wild or (morphogenetically) domesticated plants than it is when identifying macro-remains such as seeds. Nevertheless, attempts to establish criteria for discriminating between wild and domesticated forms, mainly on the basis that larger cell and grain size is diagnostic of domestication, are showing promise, for example with rice (Zhao 1998), squash (Piperno and Stothert 2003) and manioc and sweet potato (Perry 2002).

DNA analysis of domestic animals and plants

Beyond these micromorphological techniques that increase our capacity to identify and interpret remains of domestic and other plants exploited in the past, there is a realm of novel, biomolecular research that is also beginning to have a major impact on the study of agricultural origins: analysis of the DNA of present-day domestic animals and crop plants to determine their ancestry and probable areas of origin (Jones and Brown 2000).

Most of the investigations of *domestic animals* have been of major agriculturally important livestock groups – cattle, sheep, goats, pigs and water buffalo – but some other socially and economically valued domesticates less directly involved in agriculture, such as dogs, horses and camelids, have also been studied. The DNA-based molecular markers most commonly analysed are mitochondrial (mt) DNA, microsatellite, and, less frequently, Y-chromosome sequences, and the most striking overall result so far is that the data point strongly to many animals having been domesticated more than once, in different regions (Bruford *et al.* 2003). For example, analysis of mtDNA and microsatellite sequences of modern cattle breeds point to two, possibly three, areas of cattle domestication: taurine (humpless) cattle in the Levant and perhaps also independently in North Africa, and zebu (humped) cattle in the northwest of the Indian subcontinent (Loftus *et al.* 1994; Bradley *et al.* 1996; MacHugh *et al.* 1997; Troy *et al.* 2001; Hanotte *et al.* 2002; Kumar *et al.* 2003). Likewise, mtDNA data imply at least two centres of goat domestication, in Southwestern and Eastern Asia (Luikart *et al.* 2001; Joshi *et al.* 2004), and sheep (Hiendleder *et al.* 1998, 2002), pigs (Giuffra *et al.* 2000; Kijas and Andersson 2001, *Larson et al.* 2005) and water buffalo (Lau *et al.* 1998) also apppear to have two or more centres of domestication in Eurasia.

Analyses of DNA of domesticated horses, dogs and the South American llama and alpaca have also revealed that their origins were more complex than was previously believed. Studies of the mtDNA of domestic horses suggest that they were repeatedly domesticated across a broad swathe of inner Asia from many different groups of wild horses that were captured, tamed and bred (Lister *et al.* 1999; Vilà *et al.* 2001; Jansen *et al.* 2002). In contrast to horses, analysis of the mtDNA of domestic dogs indicates a common origin from a single gene pool and points to Eastern Asia as the probable area of domestication (Leonard *et al.* 2002; Savolainen *et al.* 2002), and mtDNA and microsatellite analysis of the South American camelids confirms that both the wild guanaco and the wild vicuña of the central Andes contributed to the ancestry of the llama and alpaca, although precisely how they did so is not yet resolved (Stanley *et al.* 1994; Kadwell *et al.* 2001).

Genetic studies of present-day domestic animals and their probable wild progenitors are transforming our ability to determine where the former originated and whether they were domesticated once only or several times in different areas. But the genetic data from living animals only provide very broad estimates of when and where domestication events occurred. For a more detailed chronological and geographical understanding of animal domestication we must turn to zooarchaeological evidence, especially direct evidence from ancient DNA extracted from archaeologically preserved bones and teeth (and in exceptional circumstances of preservation of hair, skin and other soft tissues).

When the feasibility of extracting and amplifying fragments of DNA from such sources was first demonstrated, great expectations were raised that it would make possible more precise determination of where and when animal (and plant) domestications had taken place. But it has proved more difficult than anticipated to obtain informative sequences of ancient DNA, even from apparently well preserved samples – a problem that is especially acute with samples taken at sites in hot and humid environments. However, there have been some successes, for example with Pleistocene wild cattle (*Bos primigenius*) from Britain (MacHugh *et al.* 1997) and with ancient (pre-European contact) dogs from North and South America (Leonard *et al.* 2002), and it is likely that as techniques improve ancient DNA will make a greater contribution to studies of domestication.

In recent years research on the origins and spread of domesticated *crop plants* by analysing DNA sequences has also advanced, although not so comprehensively as for the animals. Major cereal crops, notably maize, wheat and rice, have been the target of most investigations, which have revealed greater evolutionary complexity than previous genetic analyses, for example of proteins, indicated. This is evident in studies of maize, in which protein variation suggested a single origin of domestic maize from a particular sub-species of wild maize (*Zea mays* ssp. *parviglumis*) in southwestern Mexico (Doebley 1990), whereas investigation of ancient DNA from archaeological specimens has suggested that multiple genetic lineages from populations of wild maize have contributed to domestic maize (Goloubinoff *et al.* 1993). One interpretation of this evidence is that maize was domesticated several times in different areas within its range as a wild plant, but, as maize is an outbreeder, the multiple lineages could alternatively be attributed to introgression from wild plants following an initial domestication event.

It has long been known that wheat (*Triticum* spp.) was domesticated in Southwest Asia early in the Holocene, and archaeobotanists have recovered ancient remains of the principal domesticated species cultivated in the region in the Neolithic: diploid einkorn wheat, tetraploid emmer wheat and hexaploid bread wheat. DNA analysis of both modern and ancient wheat is now helping to unravel the complex evolutionary history of the genus and is suggesting that some of the cultivated species may have been domesticated once only in a single locality whereas others appear to have been domesticated more than once in several different areas. Thus Heun *et al.* (1997) analysed samples from populations of wild einkorn in Southwest Asia and concluded that einkorn was probably domesticated in the Karacadağ mountains in southeastern Turkey because it is most closely related to a wild population confined to that region. Brown and his colleagues (Brown *et al.* 1993; Jones *et al.* 1998; Brown 1999) have argued that domestic emmer comprises multiple genetic lineages in Southwest Asia and was probably domesticated at least twice, whereas Salamini *et al.* (2002) suggest that emmer, as well as einkorn, was domesticated in southeastern Turkey. Recent studies of modern and ancient DNA in rice (Chen *et al.* 2003) indicate that it was probably domesticated twice, the japonica races in China and the indica races in India.

Fewer DNA studies of vegetatively reproduced tuber and fruit crops have been carried out, but Lebot (1999) has summarised biomolecular evidence for a group of Melanesian crops in a review that relates directly to debates about the origins of agriculture in Southeast Asia and Melanesia. He concludes, for example, that *Musa* bananas were first domesticated in New Guinea and that cultivars of them were transported to Southeast Asia where they hybridized with local wild species, and that both taro (*Colocasia esculenta*) and the greater yam (*Dioscorea alata*) are likely to have been independently domesticated in New Guinea and Southeast Asia. Also, Yoshino (2002: 103–112) has presented DNA and isozyme evidence for multiple genetic and geographical origins of wild and domesticated forms of taro in South and Southeast Asia, Melanesia and northern Australia.

TOWARDS A ONE-WORLD UNDERSTANDING OF THE BEGINNINGS OF AGRICULTURE

As new analytical techniques come to play a larger role, old 'certainties', such as the concept of three primary centres of origin and the presumption that single rather than multiple domestication of a plant or animal species was the norm, are giving way to more complex and tentative hypotheses. The question of just what we mean when we speak of agriculture and domestication is being debated afresh (Denham *et al.* in press), and there is a growing recognition that ancestral peoples all over the world managed 'wild' plants and animals in ways that defy the dichotomy between agriculture and hunting–gathering that is deeply embedded in Western thought (Harris 1996b; Smith 2001b). In his paper Smith conceptualises the middle ground between farming and foraging as 'low-level food production' and elegantly articulates its complexity and antiquity. This trend marks an important shift in our world view of past human subsistence, and adds another dimension to the concept of One World Archaeology. It replaces a simplistic vision of a universal hunter–gatherer past followed by transitions to agriculture in a few primary centres with a realisation that many, perhaps most, of the world's peoples have contributed to the process by which the 'wild' has been gradually transformed into the 'domestic' domain that we inhabit today. This view does not privilege the 'primary' centres which Western scholars have tended to associate with early manifestations of urban civilisation, such as the Levant, north China and Mexico. It replaces that world view with one that regards the investigation of past subsistence practices of – and by – people of all regions and cultures as equally legitimate and capable of contributing to our understanding of how agriculture arose and spread. And in so doing it encompasses all three connotations of Peter's OWA identified at the beginning of this chapter.

At the same time, geographically comprehensive, comparative investigation of agricultural origins is becoming a more realistic prospect. The electronic availability of a vast amount of newly published data now allows much easier access to a wide range of evidence from archaeological, biological, ethnographic and historical sources. It greatly facilitates the 'one-world' study of the beginnings of agriculture that depends on maintaining and enhancing the multidisciplinary and interdisciplinary tradition that has been an integral part of the subject since the time of Hehn and de Candolle. The discipline of archaeology occupies a central position in this enterprise through the data it generates and the questions it asks about how people lived in the past. But archaeology alone is not enough. It is Peter Ucko's 'archaeology and related subjects' that provides the framework needed to advance our understanding of how, where, when and why agriculture arose and became the mainstay of human existence. The comparative worldwide study of agricultural origins can indeed contribute to a unified history of humanity that encompasses all the world's peoples and cultures.

REFERENCES

Antonius, O. (1922) Grundzuege einer, *Stammesgeschichte der Haustiere*. Jena G. Fischer.

Arkell, A.J. and P.J. Ucko (1965) 'Review of predynastic developments in the Nile valley', *Current Anthropology*, 6: 145–166.

Barton, H., R. Torrence and R. Fullagar (1998) 'Clues to stone tool function re-examined: comparing starch grain frequencies on used and unused obsidian artifacts', *Journal of Archaeological Science*, 25: 1231–1238.

Bradley, D.G., D.E. MacHugh, P. Cunningham and R.T. Loftus (1996) 'Mitochondrial diversity and the origins of African and European cattle', *Proceedings of the National Academy of Sciences USA*, 93: 5131–5135.

Brown, T.A. (1999) 'How ancient DNA may help in understanding the origin and spread of agriculture' *Transactions of the Royal Society London B*, 354: 89–98.

Brown, T.A., R. G. Allaby, K.A. Brown and M.K. Jones (1993) 'Biomolecular archaeology of wheat: past, present and future,' *World Archaeology*, 25: 64–73.

Bruford, M.W., D.G. Bradley and G. Luikart (2003) 'DNA markers reveal the complexity of livestock domestication' *Nature Reviews Genetics*, 4: 900–910.

Burkill, I.H. (1953) 'Habits of man and the origins of the cultivated plants of the Old World', *Proceedings of the Linnean Society of London*, 64: 12–42.

Chen, W.B., I. Nakamura, Y.I. Sato and H. Nakai (2003) 'Distribution of deletion type in CpDNA of cultivated and wild rice', *Japanese Journal of Genetics*, 68: 597–603.

Clutton-Brock, J. (1981) *Domesticated Animals from Early Times*, London: Heinemann, British Museum (Natural History).

Cortella, A.R. and M.L. Pochettino (2004) 'Starch grain analysis as a microscopic diagnostic feature in the identification of plant material' *Economic Botany*, 48: 171–181.

Cowan, C.W. and P.J. Watson (eds) (1992) *The Origins of Agriculture: An International Perspective*, Washington: Smithsonian Institution Press.

D'Andrea, A.C., M. Klee and J. Casey (2001) 'Archaeobotanical evidence for pearl millet (*Pennisetum glaucum*) in sub-Saharan West Africa', *Antiquity*, 75: 341–348.

De Candolle, A. (1855) *Géographie botanique raisonnée ou exposition des Faits principaux et des Lois concernant la Distribution géographique des Plantes de l'Epoque actuelle*, 2 vols, Paris: Victor Masson.

De Candolle, A. (1882) *Origine des Plantes cultivées*, Paris: Germer Baillière.

De Candolle, A. (1884) *Origin of Cultivated Plants*, London: Kegan Paul, Trench.

Denham, T.P., J. Golson and P.J. Hughes (2004) 'Reading early agriculture, at Kuk Swamp, Waghi Valey, Papua New Guinea: the archaeological features (Phases 1–3), *Proceedings of the Prehistoric Society*, 70: 259–297.

Denham, T.P., J. Iriarte and L. Vrydaghs (eds) (in press), *Rethinking Agriculture: Archaeological and Ethnoarchaeological Perspectives*, London: UCL Press.

Denham, T.P., S.G. Haberle, C. Lentfer, R. Fullagar, J. Field, M. Therin, N. Porch and B. Winsborough (2003) 'Origins of agriculture at Kuk Swamp in the highlands of New Guinea', *Science*, 301: 189–193.

Doebley, J. (1990) 'Molecular evidence and the evolution of maize', in *New Perspectives on the Origin and Evolution of New World Domesticated Plants*, P.K. Bretting (ed.), Supplement *Economic Botany* 44(3), pp. 6–27.

Dorofeyev, V.F. and A.A. Filatenko (1992) 'Preface', in *N. I. Vavilov Origin and Geography of Cultivated Plants*, V.F. Dorofeyev (ed.), Cambridge: Cambridge University Press (first published in Russian in 1987, Leningrad: Nauka), pp. xix–xxxi.

Fullagar, R., B. Meehan and R. Jones (1992) 'Residue analysis of ethnographic plant-working and other tools from northern Australia', in *Préhistoire de l'Agriculture: Nouvelles Approches Expérimentales et Ethnographiques*, P. Anderson-Gerfaud (ed.), Paris: CNRS, Monographie du CRS 6, pp. 39–53.

Fuller, D.Q., R. Korisettar, P.C. Venkatasubbaiah and M.K. Jones (2004) 'Early plant domestications in southern India: some preliminary archaeobotanical results', *Vegetation History and Archaeobotany*, 13: 115–129.

Gebauer, A.B. and T.D. Price (eds) (1992) *Transitions to Agriculture in Prehistory*, Madison: Prehistory Press, Monographs in World Archaeology 4.

Giuffra, E., J.M.H. Kijas, V. Amarger, Ö. Carlborg, J.-T. Jeon and L. Andersson (2000), 'The origin of the domestic pig: independent domestication and subsequent introgression', *Genetics*, 154: 1785–1791.

Goloubinoff, P., S. Paabo and A.C. Wilson (1993) 'Evolution of maize inferred from sequence diversity of an *Adh2* gene segment from archaeological specimens', *Proceedings of the National Academy of Sciences USA*, 90: 1997–2001.

Golson, J. (1997) 'From horticulture to agriculture in the New Guinea highlands', in *Historical Ecology in the Pacific Islands: Prehistoric Environmental and Landscape Change*, P.V. Kirch and T.L. Hunt (eds), New Haven: Yale University Press, pp. 39–50.

Gowlett, J.A.J. and R.E.M. Hedges (eds) (1986) *Archaeological Results from Accelerator Dating*, Oxford: Oxford University Committee for Archaeology', Monograph 11.

Hall, J., S. Higgins and R. Fullagar (1989) 'Plant residues on stone tools', in *Plants in Australian Archaeology*, W. Beck, A. Clarke and L. Head (eds), Brisbane: University of Queensland, pp. 136–60.

Hanotte, O., D.G. Bradley, J.W. Ochieng, Y. Verjee, E.W. Hill and J.E.O. Rege (2002) 'African pastoralism: genetic imprints of origins and migrations', *Science*, 296: 336–339.

Harlan, J.R. (1971) 'Agricultural origins: centers and noncenters', *Science*, 174: 468–474.

Harris, D.R. (1987) 'The impact on archaeology of radiocarbon dating by accelerator mass spectrometry', *Philosophical Transactions of the Royal Society London A*, 323: 23–43.

Harris, D.R. (1990) 'Vavilov's concept of centres of origin of cultivated plants: its genesis and its influence on the study of agricultural origins', *Biological Journal of the Linnean Society*, 39: 7–16.

Harris, D.R. (ed.) (1996a) *The Origins and Spread of Agriculture and Pastoralism in Eurasia*, London: UCL Press and Washington: Smithsonian Institution Press.

Harris, D.R. (1996b) 'Domesticatory relationships of people, plants and animals', in *Redefining Nature: Ecology, Culture and Domestication*, R. Ellen and K. Fukui (eds), Oxford: Berg, pp. 437–63.

Haslam, M. (2004) 'The decomposition of starch grains in soils: implications for archaeological residue analysis', *Journal of Archaeological Science*, 31: 1715–1734.

Hather, J.G. (1988) 'The anatomical and morphological interpretation of charred parenchymatous plant tissues, unpublished PhD thesis, University of London.

Hather, J.G. (1991) 'The identification of charred archaeological remains of vegetative parenchymatous tissues, *Journal of Archaeological Science*, 18: 661–675.

Hather, J.G. (1994) 'The identification of charred root and tuber crops from archaeological sites in the Pacific', in *Tropical Archaeobotany: Applications and New Developments*, J.G. Hather (ed.), London: Routledge, pp. 51–64.

Hather, J.G. (2000) *Archaeological Parenchyma*, London: Archetype.

Hather, J.G. and N. Hammond (1994) 'Ancient Maya subsistence diversity: root and tuber remains from Cuello, Belize', *Antiquity*, 68: 330–335.

Hather, J.G and P.V. Kirch (1991) 'Prehistoric sweet potato (*Ipomoea batatas*) from Mangaia Island, central Polynesia', *Antiquity*, 65: 887–893.

Hawkes, J.G. (1983) *The Diversity of Crop Plants*, Cambridge, MA: Harvard University Press.

Hawkes, J.G. (1990) 'N. I. Vavilov – the man and his work', *Biological Journal of the Linnean Society*, 39: 3–6.

Hehn, V. (1870) *Kulturpflanzen und Haustiere in ihrem Übergang aus Asien nach Griechenland und Italien sowie in das übrige Europa – historisch-linguistische Skizzen*, Berlin: Gebrüder Borntraeger.

Hehn, V. (1885) *The Wanderings of Plants and Animals from their First Home*, trans. J. S. Stallybrass, London: Swan Sonnenschein.

Helmer, D. (1992) *La Domestication des Animaux par les Hommes préhistoriques*, Paris: Masson.

Herre, W. and M. Röhrs (1973) *Haustiere – zoologisch gesehen*, Stuttgart: Gustav Fischer.

Heun, M., R. Schäfer-Pregl D. Klawan R. Castagna. M. Accerbi B. Borghi and F. Salamini (1997) 'Site of einkorn wheat domestication identified by DNA fingerprinting', *Science*, 278: 1312–1314.

Hiendleder, S., H. Lewalski, R. Wassmuth and A. Janke (1998) 'The complete mitochondrial sequence of the domestic sheep (*Ovis aries*) and comparison with the other major ovine haplotype', *Journal of Molecular Evolution*, 47: 441–448.

Hiendleder, S., B. Kaupe, R. Wassmuth and A. Janke (2002) 'Molecular analysis of wild and domestic sheep questions current nomenclature and provides evidence for domestication from two different subspecies', *Proceedings of the Royal Society London B*, 269: 893–904.

Hilzheimer, M. (1926) *Natürliche Rassengeschichte der Haussäugetiere*, Berlin and Leipzig: de Gruyter.

Humboldt, A. von (1807) [1959] *Essai sur la Géographie des Plantes*, London: Society for the Bibliography of Natural History facsimile.

Iriarte, J., I. Holst, O. Marozzi, C. Listopad, E. Alonso, A. Rinderknecht and J. Montanña (2004) 'Evidence for cultivar adoption and emerging complexity during the mid-Holocene in the La Plata basin', *Nature*, 432: 614–617.

Jansen, T., P. Forster, M.A. Levine, H. Oelke, M. Hurles, C. Renfrew and J. Weber (2002) 'Mitochondrial DNA and the origins of the domestic horse', *Proceedings of the National Academy of Sciences USA*, 99: 10905–10910.

Jones, M. and T. Brown (2000) 'Agricultural origins: the evidence of modern and ancient DNA', *The Holocene*, 10: 769–776.

Jones, M.K., R.G. Allaby and T.A. Brown (1998) 'Wheat domestication', *Science*, 279: 302–303.

Joshi, M.B., P.K. Rout, A.K. Mandal, C. Tyler-Smith, L. Singh and K. Thangaraj (2004) 'Phylogeography and origin of Indian domestic goats', *Molecular Biology and Evolution*, 21: 454–462.

Kadwell, M., M. Fernandez, H.F. Stanley, R. Baldi, J.C. Wheeler, R. Rosadio and M.W. Bruford (2001) 'Genetic analysis reveals the wild ancestors of the llama and alpaca', *Proceedings of the Royal Society London B*, 268: 2575–2584.

Keller, O. (1909, 1913) *Die Antiker Tierwelt*, Vol. 1 (1909), Vol. 2 (1913), Leipzig: Wilhelm Engelmann.

Kijas, J.M.H. and L. Andersson (2001) 'A phylogenetic study of the origin of the domestic pig estimated from the near-complete mtDNA genome', *Journal of Molecular Evolution*, 52: 302–308.

Klatt, B. (1927) *Enstehung der Haustiere (Handbuch der Vererbungswissenschaft, Bd 3)*, Berlin: Gebrueder Borntraeger.

Kumar, P., A.R. Freeman, R.T. Loftus, C. Gaillard, D.Q. Fuller and D.G. Bradley (2003) 'Admixture analysis of South Asian cattle', *Heredity*, 91: 43–50.

Larson, G., K. Dobney, U. Albarella, M. Fang, E. Matisoo-Smith, J. Robins, S. Lowden, H. Finlayson, T. Brand, E. Willerslev, P. Rowley-Conwy, L. Andersson and A. Cooper (2005) 'Worldwide phylogeography of wild boar reveals multiple centers of pig domestication', *Science*, 307: 1618–1621.

Lau, C.H., R.D. Drinkwater, K. Yusof, S.G. Tan, D.J.S. Hetzel and J.S.F. Barker (1998) 'Genetic diversity of Asian water buffalo (*Bubalus bubalis*): mitochondrial D-loop and cytochrome *b* sequence variation', *Animal Genetics*, 29:253–264.

Lebot, V. (1999) 'Biomolecular evidence for plant domestication in Sahul', *Genetic Resources and Crop Evolution*, 46: 619–628.

Leonard, J.A., R.K. Wayne, J. Wheeler, R. Valadez, S. Guillén and C. Vilà (2002) 'Ancient DNA evidence for Old World origin of New World dogs' *Science*, 298: 1613–1616.

Lister, A.M., M. Kaldwell, L.M. Kaagan, W.C. Jordan, M.B. Richards and H.F. Stanley (1999) 'Ancient and modern DNA from a variety of sources in a study of horse domestication', *Ancient Biomolecules*, 2: 267–280.

Loftus, R.T., D.E. MacHugh, D.G. Bradley, P.M. Sharp and P. Cunningham (1994) 'Evidence for two independent domestications of cattle', *Proceedings of the National Academy of Sciences USA*, 91: 2757–2761.

Loy, T.H. (1994) 'Methods in the analysis of starch residues on prehistoric stone tools', in *Tropical Archaeobotany: Applications and New Developments*, J.G. Hather (ed.), London: Routledge, pp. 86–114.

Loy, T.H., M. Spriggs and S. Wickler (1992) 'Direct evidence for human use of plants 28,000 years ago: starch residues on prehistoric stone artifacts from the northern Solomon Islands', *Antiquity*, 66: 898–912.

Luikart, G., L. Gielly, L. Excoffier, J.-D. Vigne, J. Bouvet and P. Taberlet (2001) 'Multiple maternal origins and weak phylogeographic structure in domestic goats', *Proceedings of the National Academy of Sciences USA*, 98: 5927–5932.

MacHugh, D.E., M.D. Shriver, R.T. Loftus, P. Cunningham and D.G. Bradley (1997) 'Microsatellite DNA variation and the evolution, domestication and phylogeography of taurine and zebu cattle (*Bos taurus* and *Bos indicus*)', *Genetics*, 146: 1071–1086.

Mbida, C.M., W. van Neer and L.Vrydaghs (2000) 'Evidence for banana cultivation and animal husbandry during the first millennium BC in the forest of southern Cameroon', *Journal of Archaeological Science*, 27: 151–162.

Mbida, C.M., H. Doutrelepont, L. Vrydaghs, R.L. Swennan, R.J. Swennan, H. Beeckman, E. de Langhe and P. de Maret (2001) 'First archaeological evidence of banana cultivation in central Africa during the third millennium before present', *Vegetation History and Archaeobotany*, 10: 1–6.

Mbida, C.M., H. Doutrelepont, L. Vrydaghs, R.L. Swennan, R.J. Swennan, H. Beeckman, E. de Langhe and P. de Maret (2004) 'Yes there were bananas in Cameroon more than 2000 years ago', *InfoMusa*, 13: 40–42.

Neumann, K. (1999) 'Early plant food production in the West African Sahel: new evidence', in *The Exploitation of Plant Resources in Ancient Africa*, M. van der Veen (ed.), New York: Kluwer Academic, pp. 73–81.

Pearsall, D.M. and D.R. Piperno (eds) (1993) *Current Research in Phytolith Analysis: Applications in Archaeology and Paleoecology*, Philadelphia: University Museum of Archaeology and Anthropology, MASCA Research Papers in Science and Archaeology 10.

Perry, L. (2002) 'Starch granule size and the domestication of manioc (*Manihot esculenta*) and sweet potato (*Ipomoea batatas*)', *Economic Botany*, 56: 335–349.

Perry, L. (2004) 'Starch analyses reveal the relationship between tool type and function: an example from the Orinoco valley of Venezuela', *Journal of Archaeological Science*, 31: 1069–1081.

Pickersgill, B. (1998) 'Crop introductions and the development of secondary areas of diversity', in *Plants for Food and Medicine*, H.D.V. Prendergast, N.L. Etkin, D.R. Harris and P.J. Houghton (eds), Kew: The Royal Botanic Gardens, pp. 93–105.

Piperno, D.R. (1988) *Phytolith Analysis: An Archaeological and Geological Perspective*, San Diego: Academic Press.

Piperno, D.R. and I. Holst (1998) 'The presence of starch grains on prehistoric tools from the humid neotropics: indications of early tuber use and agriculture in Panama', *Journal of Archaeological Science*, 25: 765–776.

Piperno, D.R. and D.M. Pearsall (1998) *The Origins of Agriculture in the Lowland Neotropics*, San Diego: Academic Press.

Piperno, D.R. and K.E. Stothert (2003) 'Phytolith evidence for early Holocene *Cucurbita* domestication in southwest Ecuador', *Science*, 299: 1054–1057.

Piperno, D.R., A.J. Ranere, I. Holst and P. Hansell (2000) 'Starch grains reveal early root crop horticulture in the Panamanian tropical forest', *Nature*, 407: 894–897.

Portères, R. (1950) 'Vielles agricultures africaines avant le XVIème siècle. Berceaux d'agriculture et centres de variation', *L'Agronomie Tropicale*, 5: 489–507.

Portères, R. (1962) 'Berceaux agricoles primaries sur le continent africain' *Journal of African History*, 3: 195–210.

Price, T.D. (ed) (2000) *Europe's First Farmers*, Cambridge: Cambridge University Press.

Price, T.D. and A.B. Gebauer (eds) (1995) *Last Hunters–First Farmers: New Perspectives on the Prehistoric Transition to Agriculture*, Santa Fe: School of American Research Press.

Rosen, A. (2001/2002) 'Environmental and cultural change in the Yiluo basin, east-central China', *Archaeology International 2001/2002*: 51–53.

Salamini, F., H. Ozkan, A, Brandolini, R. Schaefer-Pregl and W. Martin (2002) 'Genetics and geography of wild cereal domestication in the Near East', *Nature Reviews Genetics*, 3: 429–441.

Sauer, C.O. (1952) *Agricultural Origins and Dispersals*, New York: American Geographical Society.

Saunders, N. (2004) 'Windows on new digs worldwide', *The Times Higher Educational Supplement 22 October 2004*: 30.

Savolainen, P., Y.-p. Zhang, J. Luo, J. Lundeberg and T. Leitner (2002) 'Genetic evidence for an east Asian origin of domestic dogs', *Science*, 298: 1610–1613.

Smith, B.D. (ed.) (1992) *Rivers of Change: Essays on Early Agriculture in Eastern North America*, Washington: Smithsonian Institution Press.

Smith, B.D. (1995) *The Emergence of Agriculture*, New York: Scientific American Library.

Smith, B.D. (2001a) 'Documenting plant domestication: the consilience of biological and archaeological approaches', *Proceedings of the National Academy of Sciences USA*, 98: 1324–1326.

Smith, B.D. (2001b) 'Low-level food production', *Journal of Archaeological Research*, 9: 1–43.

Stanley, H.F., M. Kadwell and J.C. Wheeler (1994) 'Molecular evolution of the family Camelidae: a mitochondrial study', *Proceedings of the Royal Society London B*, 256: 1–6.

Therin, M., R. Fullagar and R. Torrence (1999) 'Starch in sediments: a new approach to the study of subsistence and land use in Papua New Guinea', in *The Prehistory of Food: Appetites for Change*, C. Gosden and J. Hather (eds), London: Routledge, pp. 438–462.

Troy, C.S., D.E. MacHugh, J.F. Bailey, D.A. Magee R.T. Loftus, P. Cunningham, A.T. Chamberlain, B.C. Sykes and D.G. Bradley (2001) 'Genetic evidence for Near-Eastern origins of European cattle', *Nature*, 410: 1088–1091.

Ucko, P.J. and G.W. Dimbleby (eds) (1969) *The Domestication and Exploitation of Plants and Animals*, London: Duckworth.

Ucko, P.J., R. Tringham and G.W. Dimbleby (eds) (1972) *Man, Settlement and Urbanism*, London: Duckworth.

Vansina, J. (2004) 'Banana in Cameroon *c.* 500 BCE? Not proven', *Azania: Journal of the British Institute in Eastern Africa*, 38: 174–176.

Vavilov, N.I. (1926) *Studies on the Origins of Cultivated Plants*, Leningrad: Institut Botanique Appliqué et d'Amélioration des Plantes.

Vavilov, N.I. (1997) *Five Continents*, Rome: International Plant Genetic Resources Institute (this is an English version of a book originally planned and partly completed by Vavilov which was finally published on the 110th anniversary of his birth).

Vilà, C, J.A. Leonard, A. Götherström, S. Marklund, K. Sandberg, K. Lidén, R.K. Wayne and H. Ellegren (2001) 'Widespread origins of domestic horse lineages', *Science*, 291: 474–477.

Yoshino, H. (2002) 'Morphological and genetic variation in cultivated and wild taro', in *Vegeculture in Eastern Asia and Oceania*, S. Yoshida and P.J. Matthews (eds), Osaka: National Museum of Ethnology, Japan Center for Area Studies Symposium Series 16, pp. 95–116.

Zeuner, F.E. (1963) *A History of Domesticated Animals*, London: Hutchinson.

Zhao, Z. (1998) 'The middle Yangtze region in China is one place where rice was domesticated: phytolith evidence from the Diaotonghuan Cave, northern Jiangxi', *Antiquity*, 72: 885–897.

INDEX